2nd EDITION

RECORDED VERSIONS GUITAR

AUTHENTIC TRANSCRIPTIONS WITH NOTES AND TABLATURE

THE BEST OF OPETH

Photo by Stuart Wood

Music transcriptions by Chris Ackerman, Pete Billmann, Adonai Booth and Mike Butzen

ISBN 978-1-5400-0116-0

7777 W. Bluemound Rd. P.O. Box 13819 Milwaukee, WI 53213

In Australia Contact:
Hal Leonard Australia Pty. Ltd.
4 Lentara Court
Cheltenham, Victoria, 3192 Australia
Email: ausadmin@halleonard.com.au

Visit Hal Leonard Online at
www.halleonard.com

from *Still Life*

Benighted

Words and Music by Mikael Akerfeldt

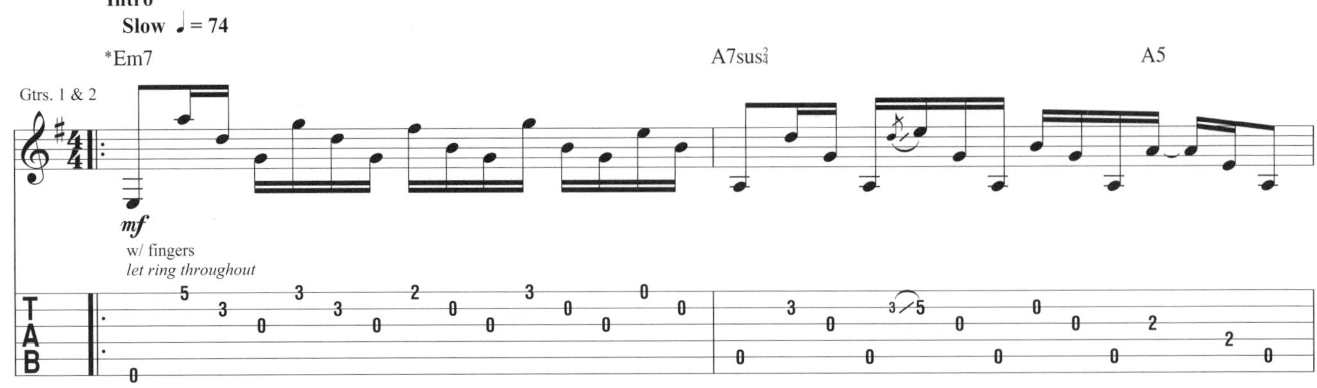

*Chord symbols reflect implied harmony.

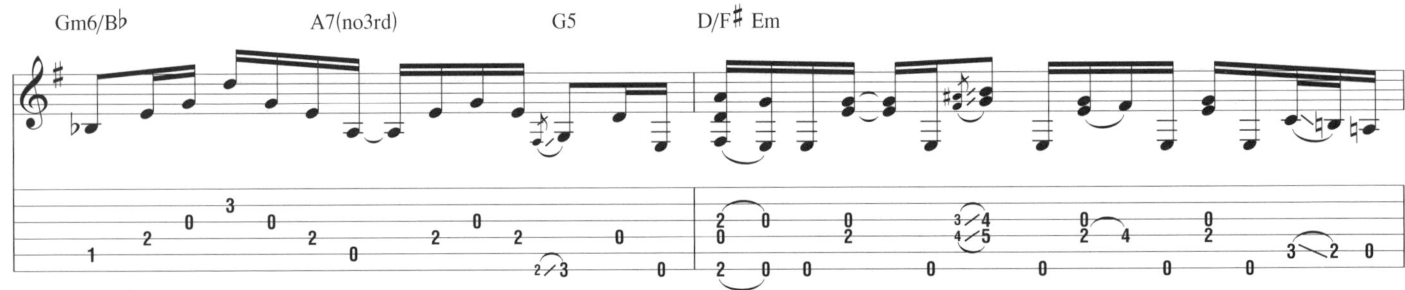

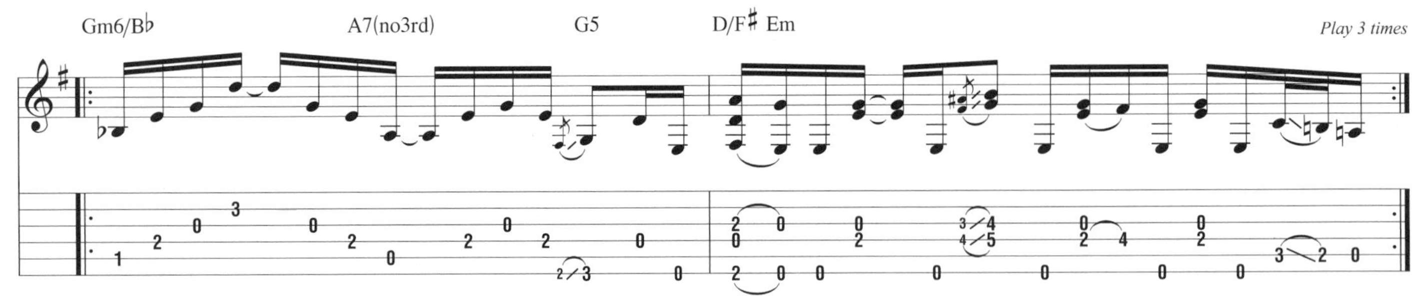

Verse
Em(add9)
Dadd4/F♯
Csus2
G/B
1. Come to this night. Here we'll be gone.
Riff A
So far a - way from our weak and crum - bling lives.
A5
Dsus4
E5
End Riff A
Gtrs. 1 & 2: w/ Riff A
Come to this night when days are done,
lost and a - stray in what's van - ished from your eyes.
Chorus
A13sus4
Esus2
Gmaj7
A13(no3rd)
C5add♯4
B5
What came and dis - tort - ed your sight
Riff B
Gtrs. 1 & 2
End Riff B

Gtrs. 1 & 2: w/ Riff B
A13sus4
Esus2 Gmaj7 A13(no3rd) C5add♯4 B5
saw you be - night - ed by your fright.
Verse
Gtrs. 1 & 2: w/ Riff A (2 times)
Em(add9) Dadd4/F♯ Csus2 G/B Em(add9) Dadd4/F♯ Csus2 G/B Em(add9) Dadd4/F♯ Csus2 G/B
2. Come to this night, your plight a - lone. Car-ry your weight. You are
A5 G/B Csus2 Dsus4 E5 Em(add9) Dadd4/F♯ Csus2 G/B Em(add9) Dadd4/F♯ Csus2 G/B
flawed as all of us. Come to this night, your on - ly home.
Em(add9) Dadd4/F♯ Csus2 G/B A5 G/B Csus2 Dsus4 E5
It's nev - er too late to re - pent, suf - fer the loss.
Chorus
Gtrs. 1 & 2: w/ Riff B (1 1/2 times)
A13sus4 Esus2 Gmaj7 A13(no3rd) C5add♯4 B5 A13sus4
What came and dis-tort - ed your sight
Esus2 Gmaj7 A13(no3rd) C5add♯4 B5 Em(add9)
saw you be-night - ed by your fright.
Gtr. 1
Gtr. 2

Interlude

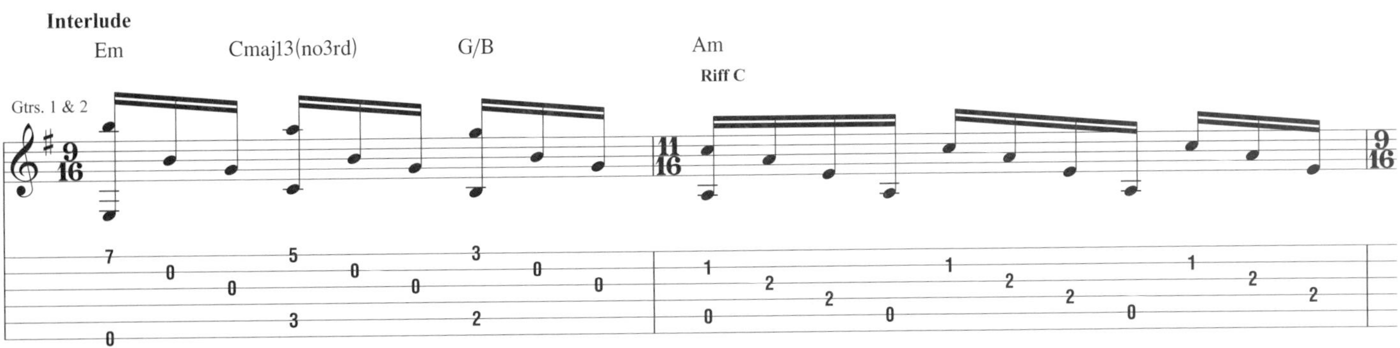

Em
Cmaj13(no3rd)
G/B
Am
Riff C
Gtrs. 1 & 2

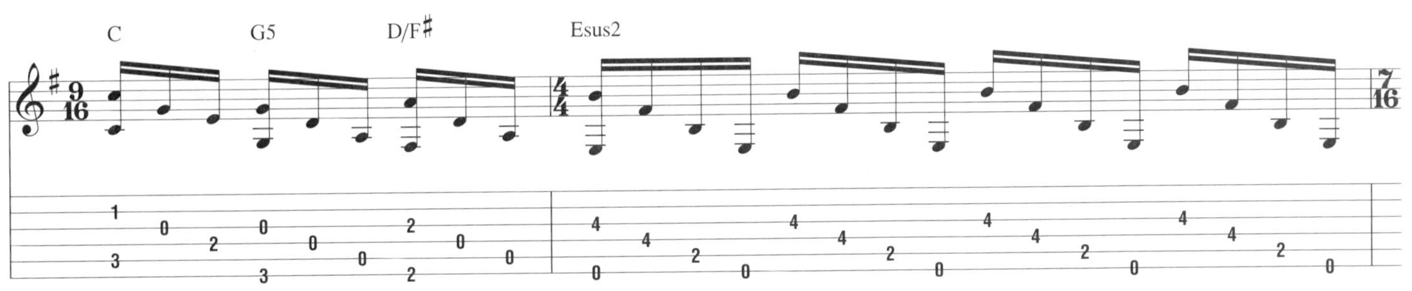

C
G5
D/F♯
Esus2

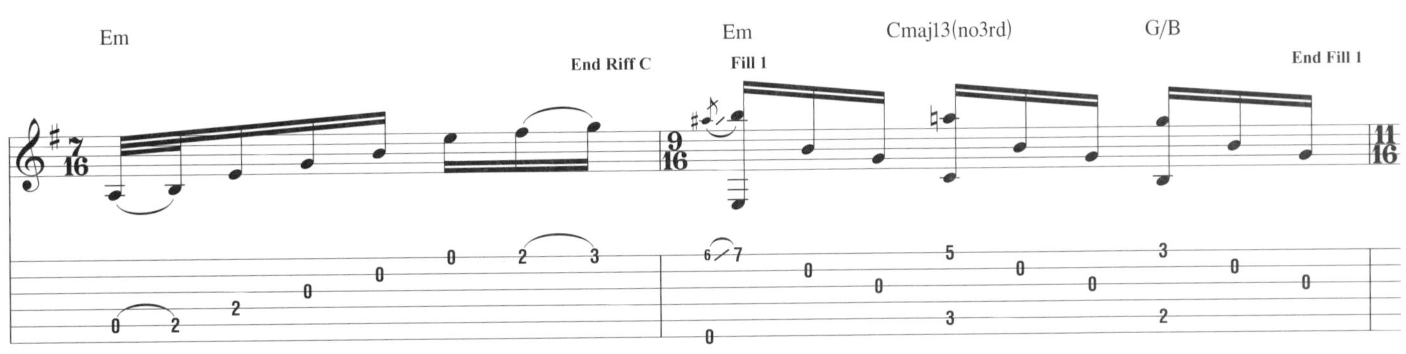

Em
End Riff C
Em
Fill 1
Cmaj13(no3rd)
G/B
End Fill 1

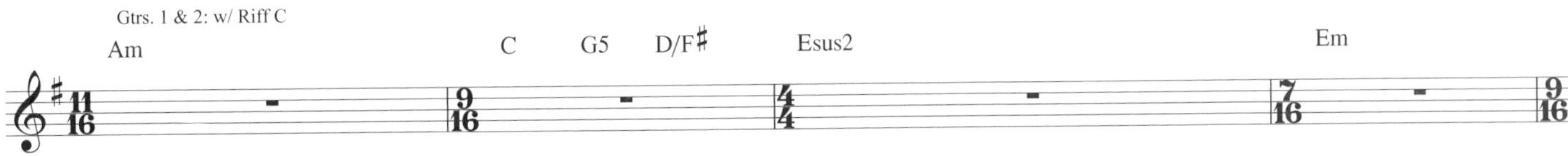

Gtrs. 1 & 2: w/ Riff C
Am
C
G5
D/F♯
Esus2
Em

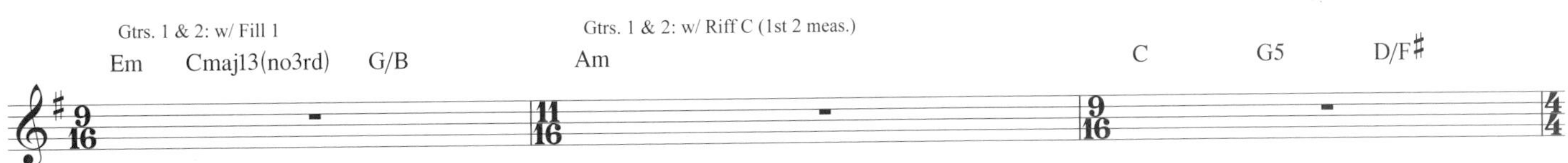

Gtrs. 1 & 2: w/ Fill 1
Em
Cmaj13(no3rd)
G/B
Gtrs. 1 & 2: w/ Riff C (1st 2 meas.)
Am
C
G5
D/F♯

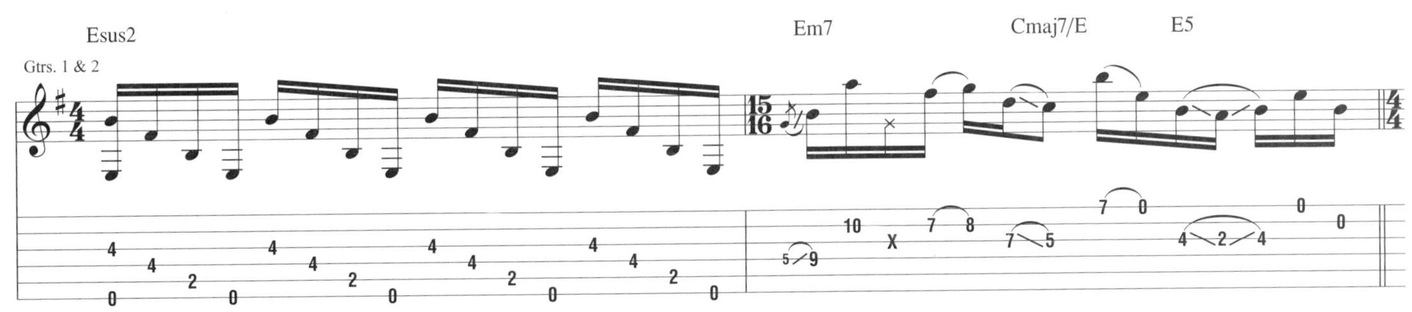

Esus2
Gtrs. 1 & 2
Em7
Cmaj7/E
E5

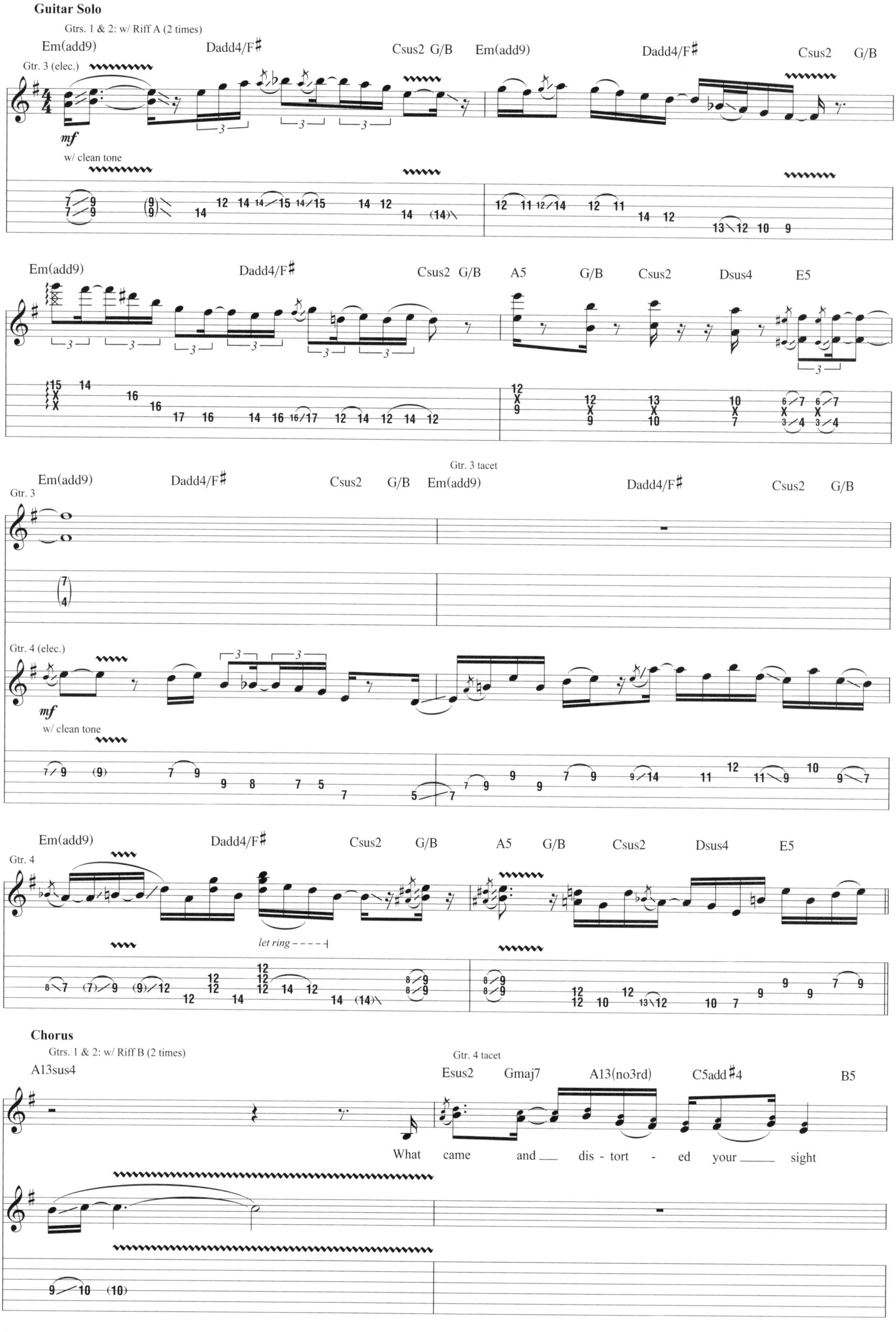
Guitar Solo
Gtrs. 1 & 2: w/ Riff A (2 times)
Em(add9) Dadd4/F♯ Csus2 G/B Em(add9) Dadd4/F♯ Csus2 G/B
Gtr. 3 (elec.)
mf
w/ clean tone
Em(add9) Dadd4/F♯ Csus2 G/B A5 G/B Csus2 Dsus4 E5
Gtr. 3 tacet
Em(add9) Dadd4/F♯ Csus2 G/B Em(add9) Dadd4/F♯ Csus2 G/B
Gtr. 3
Gtr. 4 (elec.)
mf
w/ clean tone
Em(add9) Dadd4/F♯ Csus2 G/B A5 G/B Csus2 Dsus4 E5
Gtr. 4
let ring
Chorus
Gtrs. 1 & 2: w/ Riff B (2 times)
A13sus4
Gtr. 4 tacet
Esus2 Gmaj7 A13(no3rd) C5add♯4 B5
What came and dis - tort - ed your sight

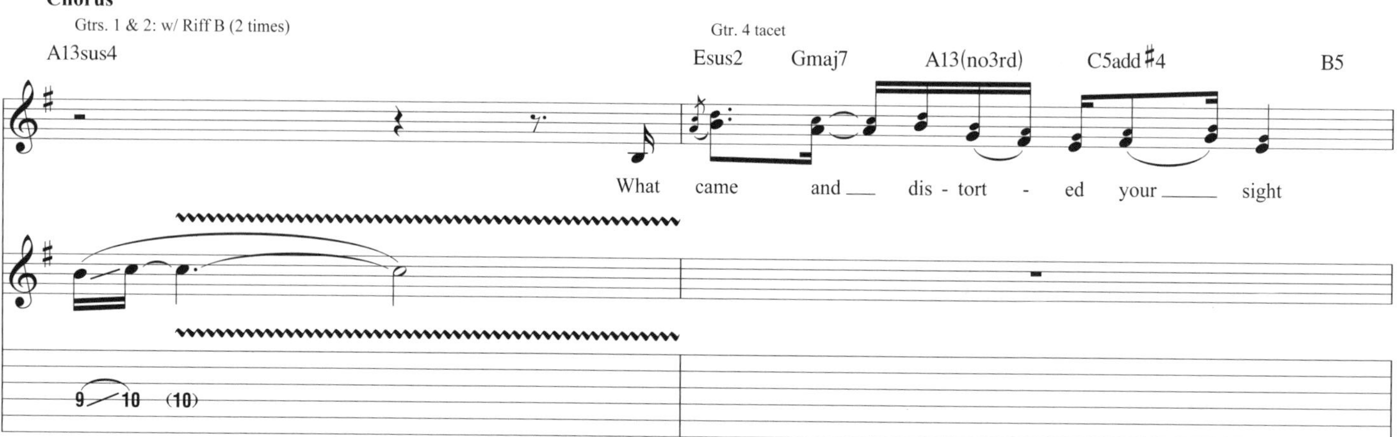

A13sus4
Esus2
Gmaj7
A13(no3rd)
C5add♯4
B5
saw you __ be - night - ed by your fright. ______
Verse
Gtrs. 1 & 2: w/ Riff A (2 times)
Em(add9)
Dadd4/F♯
Csus2
G/B
3. Come to this night, __ oh, when you're a - ble
to un-do your deeds __ and a-
A5
Dsus4
E5
tone with _ your lone - ly soul.
Once you're in - to this night, __ all minds are sta - ble.
For - get all your needs, _ lose the grip of ___ all ____ con - trol. _______
Outro
Am(add9)
D(add4)
Fmaj13♯11
Gtrs. 1 & 2
Riff D
End Riff D
Gtrs. 1 & 2: w/ Riff D (3 times)
Dadd4
Play 3 times
Em
Harm.

from *Damnation*

Closure

Words and Music by Mikael Akerfeldt

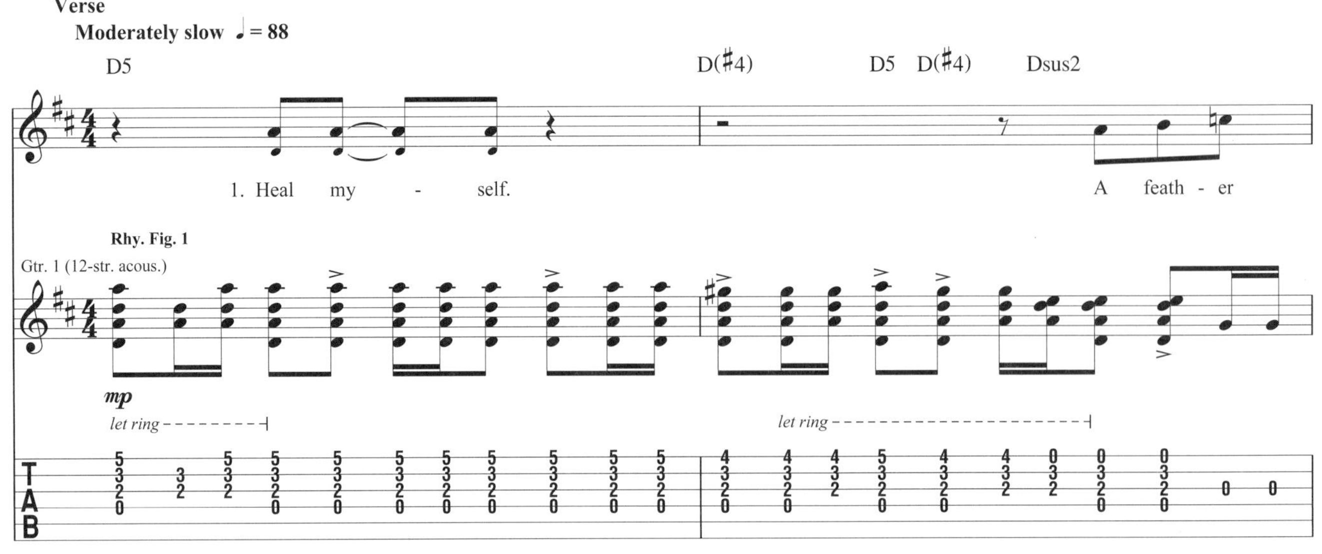

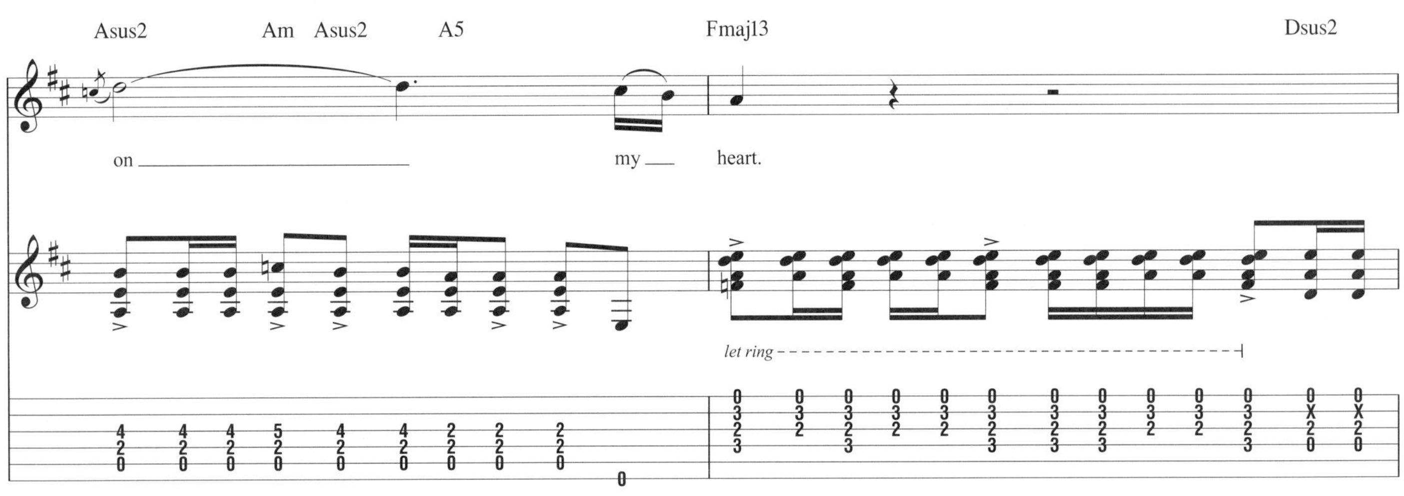

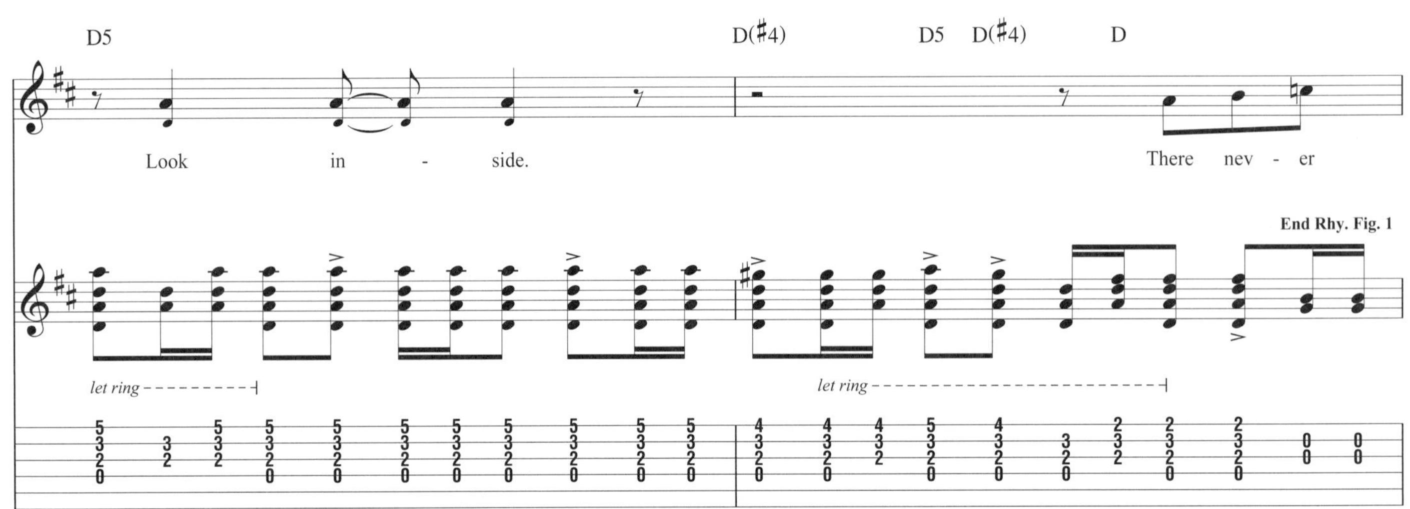

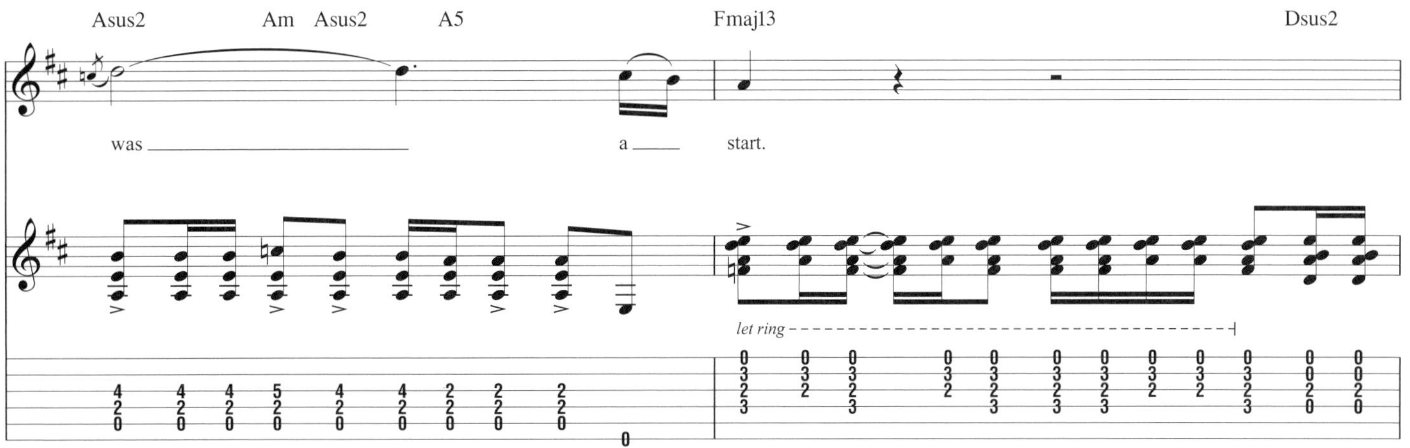

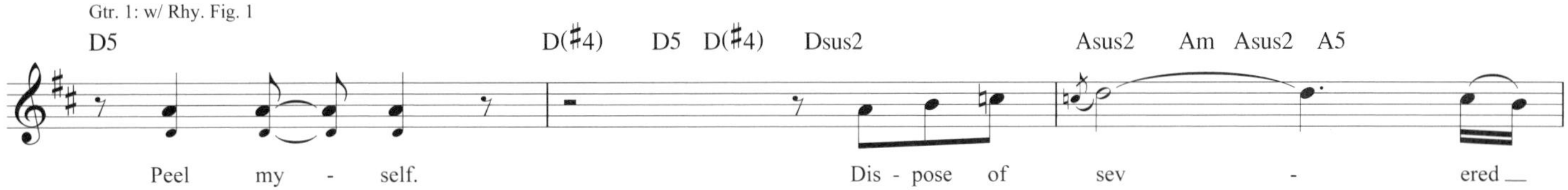

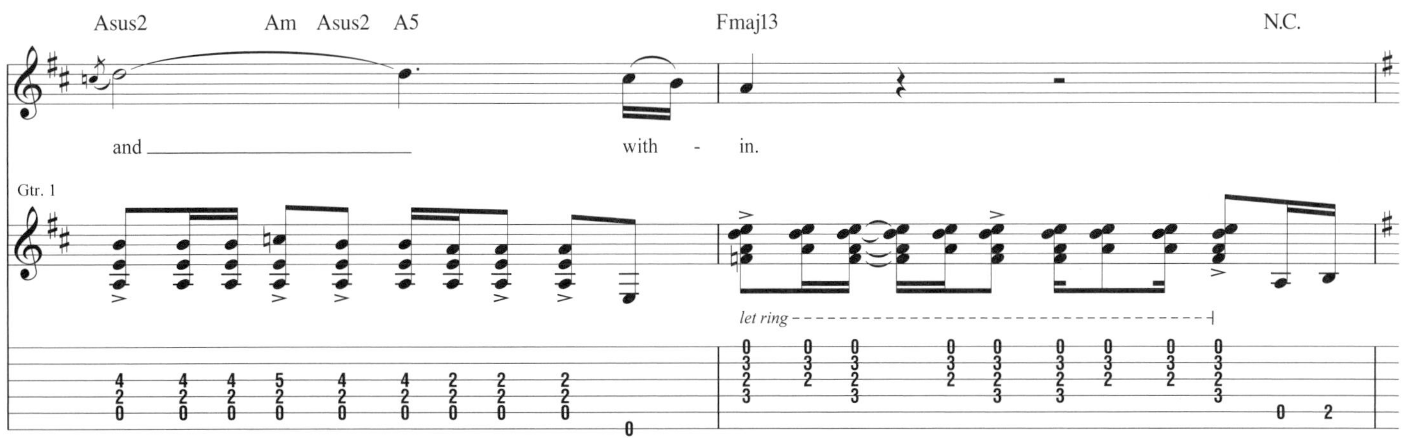

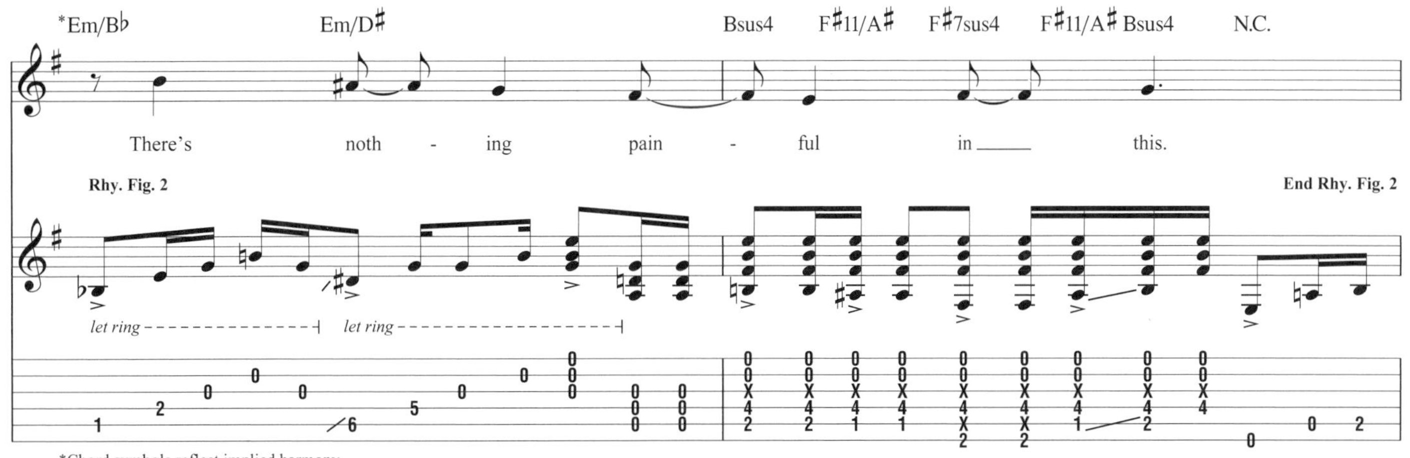

*Chord symbols reflect implied harmony.

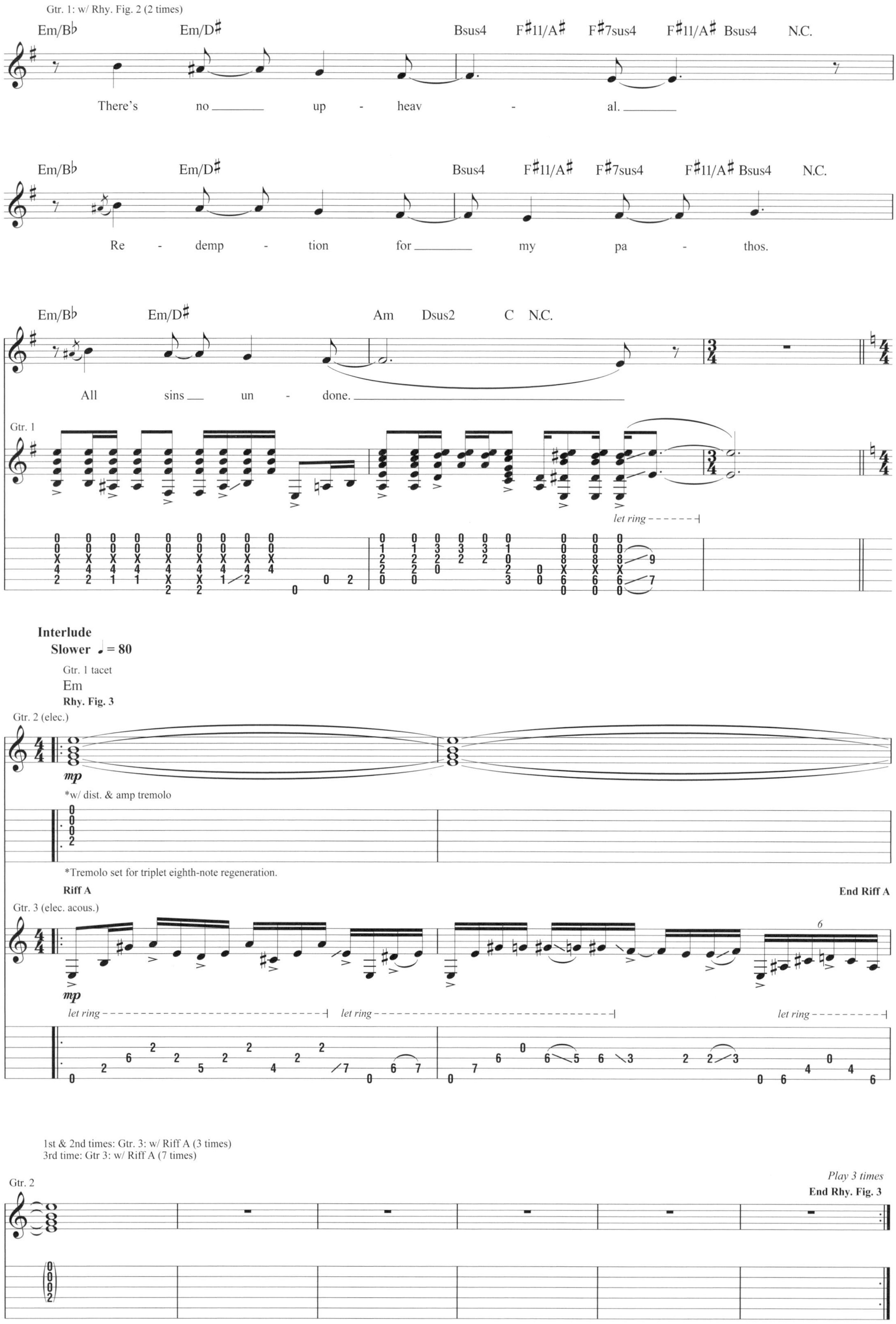

Gtr. 1: w/ Rhy. Fig. 2 (2 times)

Em/B♭ Em/D♯ Bsus4 F♯11/A♯ F♯7sus4 F♯11/A♯ Bsus4 N.C.

There's no up - heav - al.

Em/B♭ Em/D♯ Bsus4 F♯11/A♯ F♯7sus4 F♯11/A♯ Bsus4 N.C.

Re - demp - tion for my pa - thos.

Em/B♭ Em/D♯ Am Dsus2 C N.C.

All sins un - done.

Gtr. 1

let ring

Interlude

Slower ♩ = 80

Gtr. 1 tacet

Em

Rhy. Fig. 3

Gtr. 2 (elec.)

mp

*w/ dist. & amp tremolo

*Tremolo set for triplet eighth-note regeneration.

Riff A **End Riff A**

Gtr. 3 (elec. acous.)

mp

let ring let ring let ring

1st & 2nd times: Gtr. 3: w/ Riff A (3 times)
3rd time: Gtr 3: w/ Riff A (7 times)

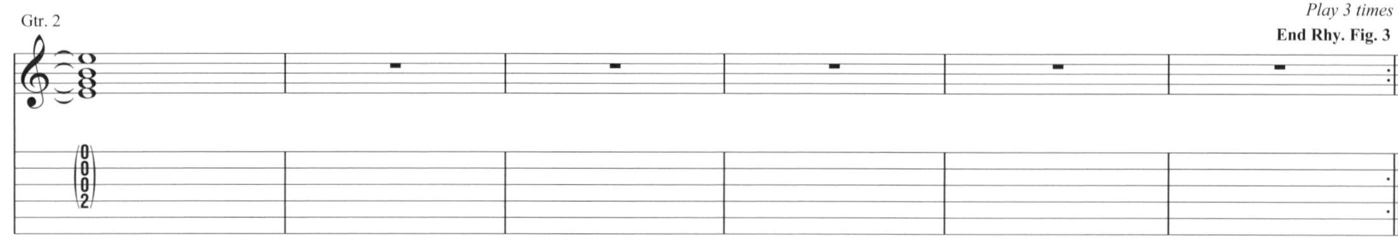

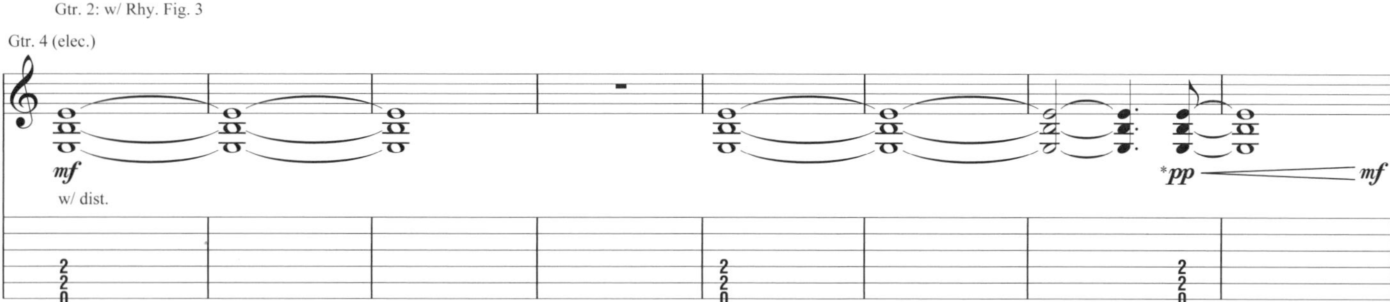
Gtr. 2: w/ Rhy. Fig. 3
Gtr. 4 (elec.)
mf
w/ dist.
*pp
mf
*Vol. swell

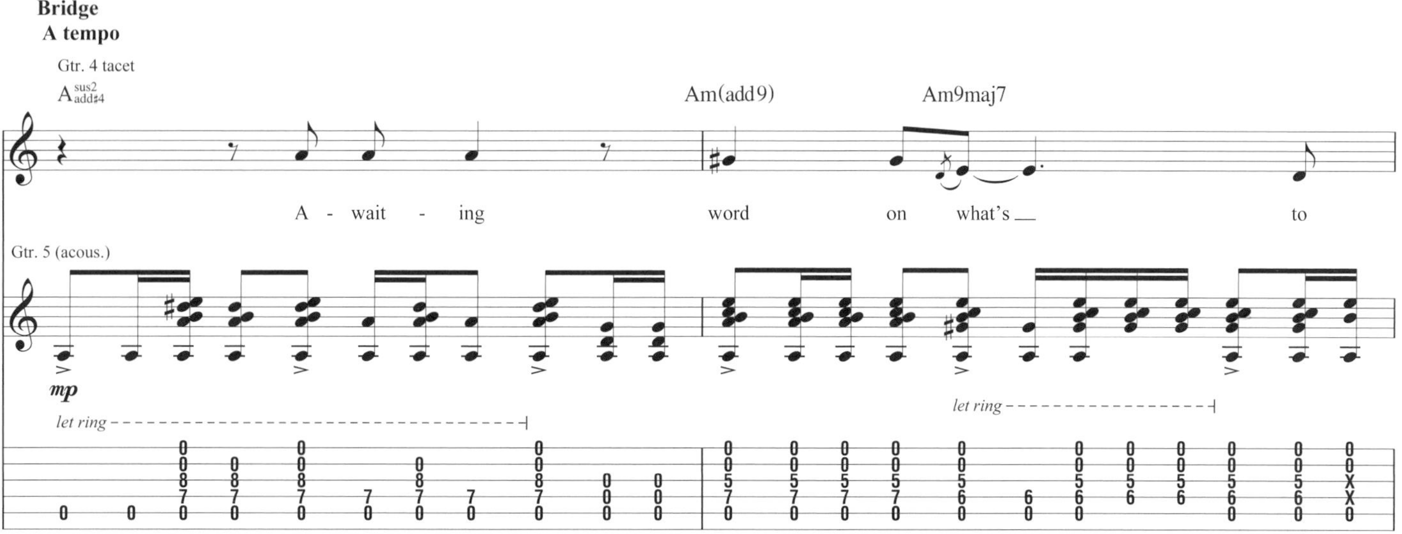
Bridge
A tempo
Gtr. 4 tacet
Asus2add#4
Am(add9)
Am9maj7
A - wait - ing word on what's to
Gtr. 5 (acous.)
mp
let ring
let ring

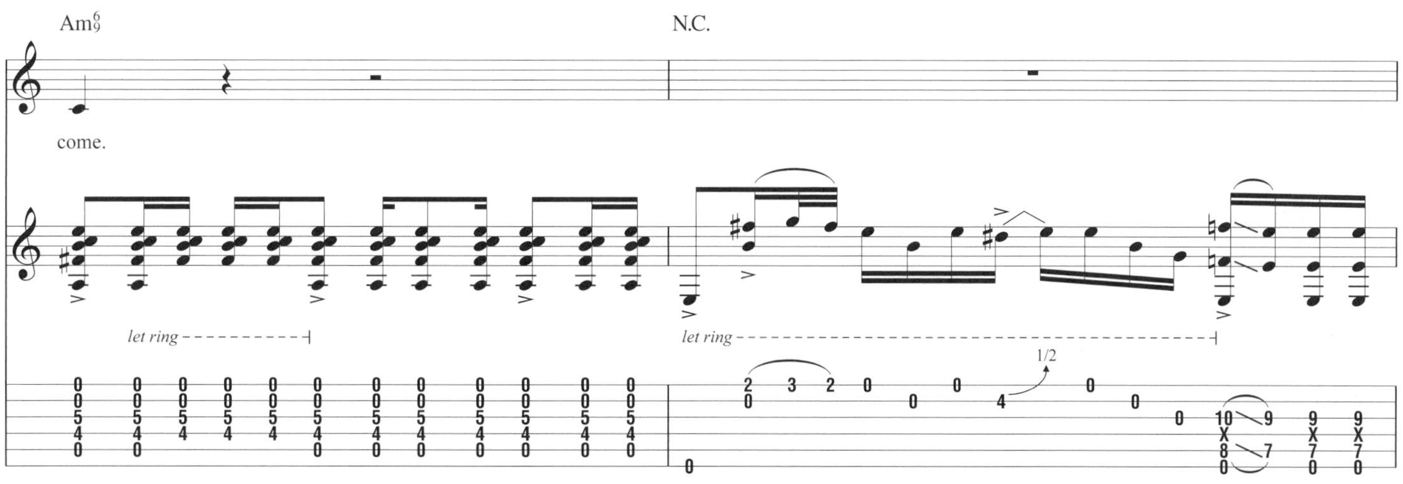
Am6/9
N.C.
come.
let ring
let ring
1/2

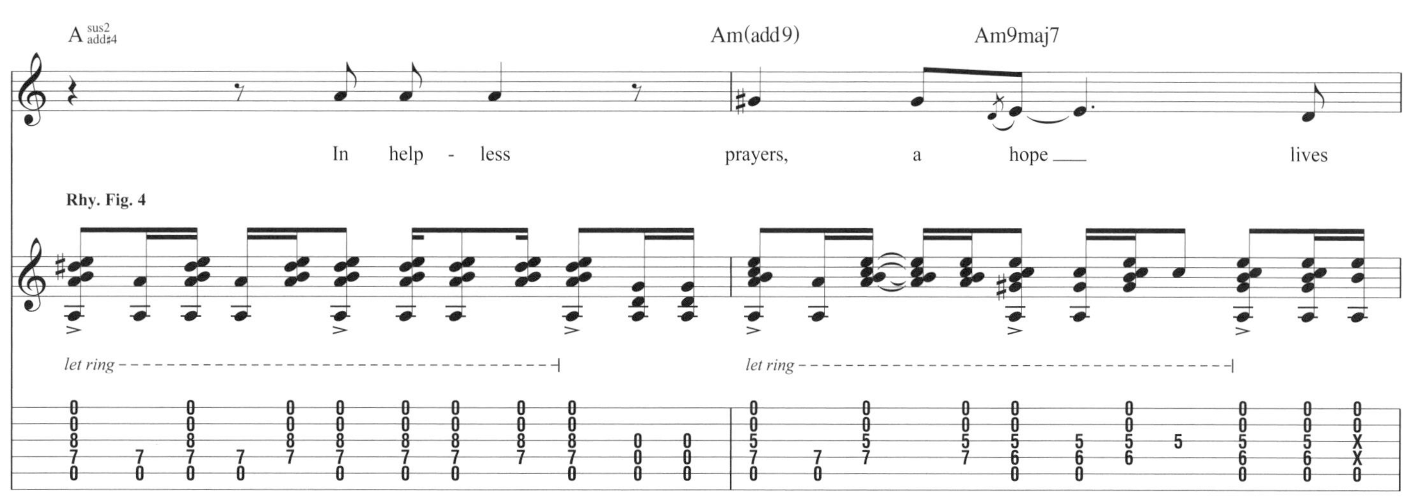
Asus2add#4
Am(add9)
Am9maj7
In help - less prayers, a hope lives
Rhy. Fig. 4
let ring
let ring

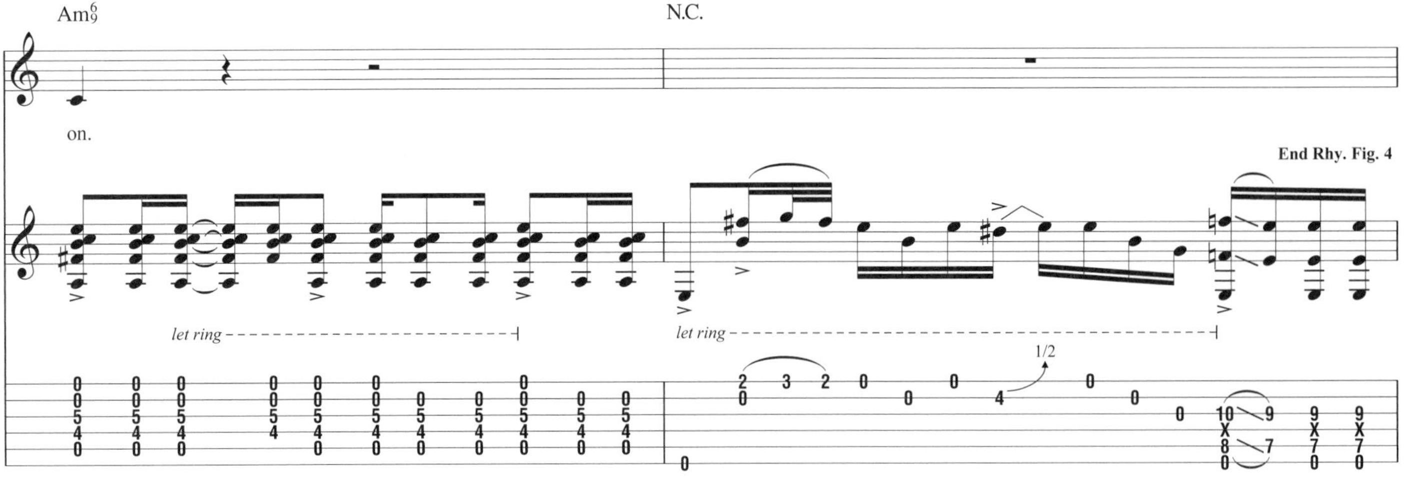
Am6/9
N.C.
on.
End Rhy. Fig. 4
let ring
let ring
1/2

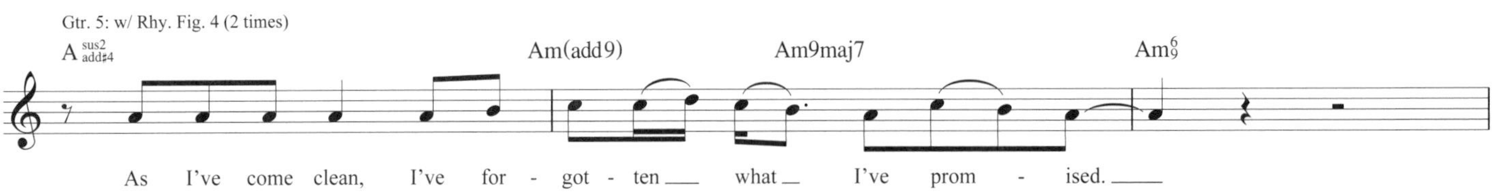
Gtr. 5: w/ Rhy. Fig. 4 (2 times)
Asus2 add♯4
Am(add9)
Am9maj7
Am6/9
As I've come clean, I've for - got - ten what I've prom - ised.

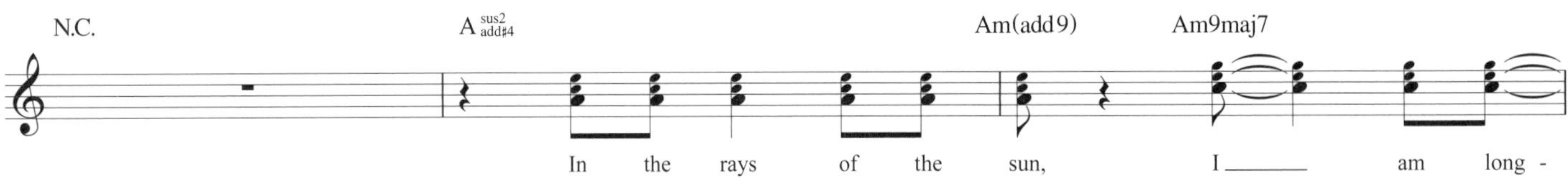
N.C.
Asus2 add♯4
Am(add9)
Am9maj7
In the rays of the sun, I am long -

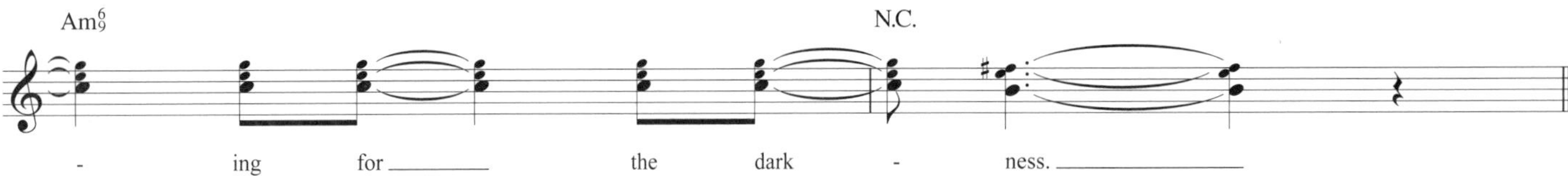
Am6/9
N.C.
- ing for the dark - ness.

Outro

Gtr. 5 tacet
Em
Riff B
Gtr. 6 (elec.)
mp
*w/ octaver, reverb & delay
*Octaver set for 1 octave above.
Rhy. Fig. 5
Gtr. 1

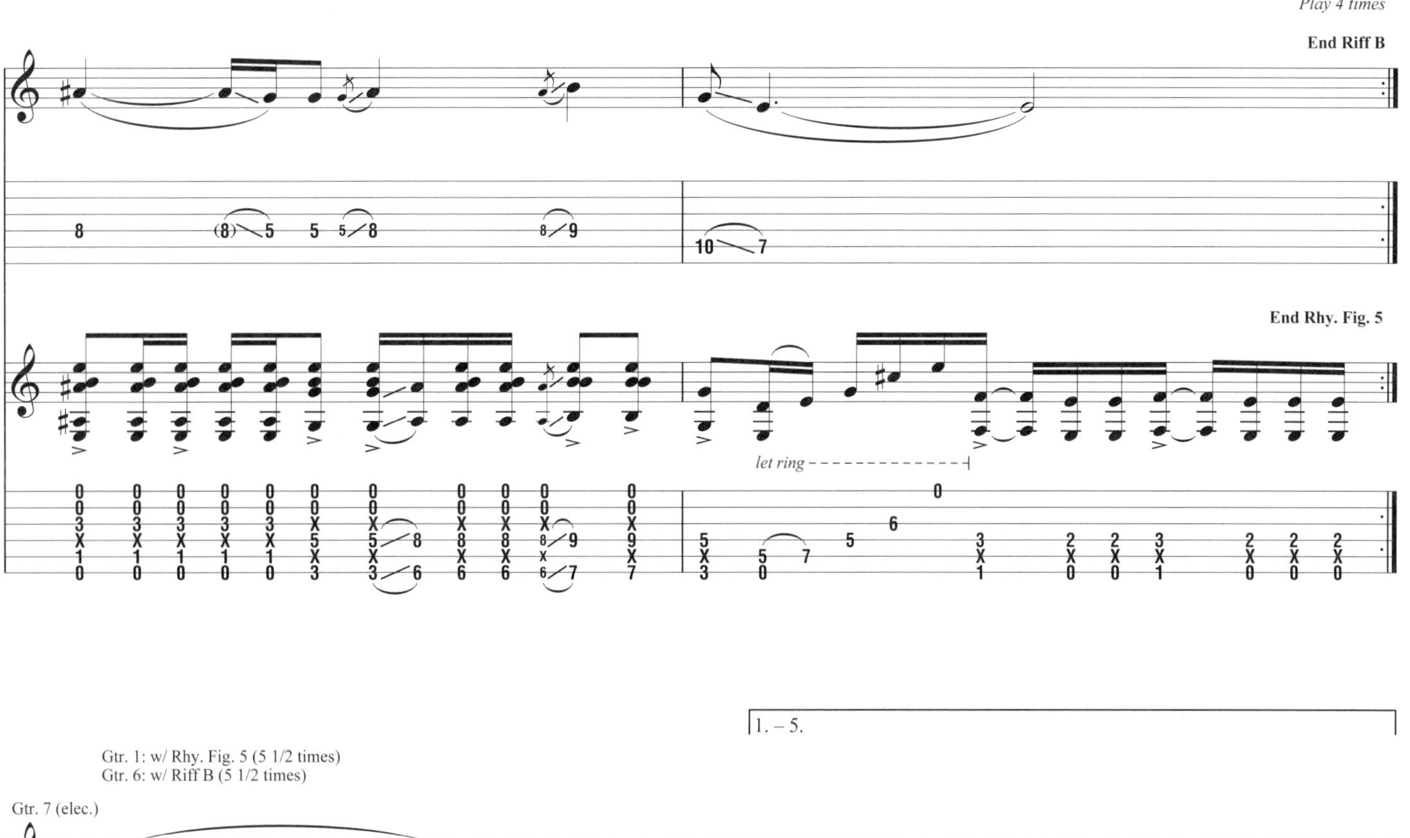
Play 4 times
End Riff B
End Rhy. Fig. 5
let ring

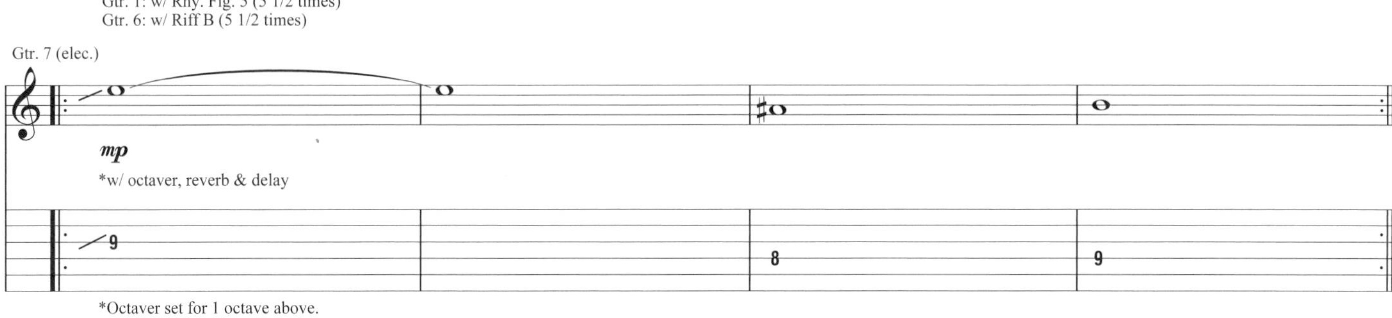
1. – 5.
Gtr. 1: w/ Rhy. Fig. 5 (5 1/2 times)
Gtr. 6: w/ Riff B (5 1/2 times)
Gtr. 7 (elec.)
mp
*w/ octaver, reverb & delay
*Octaver set for 1 octave above.

6.
N.C.
Gtr. 7
Gtr. 6
Gtr. 1
let ring

from *Watershed*

Coil

Words and Music by Mikael Akerfeldt

*Doubled throughout

**Chord symbols reflect implied harmony.

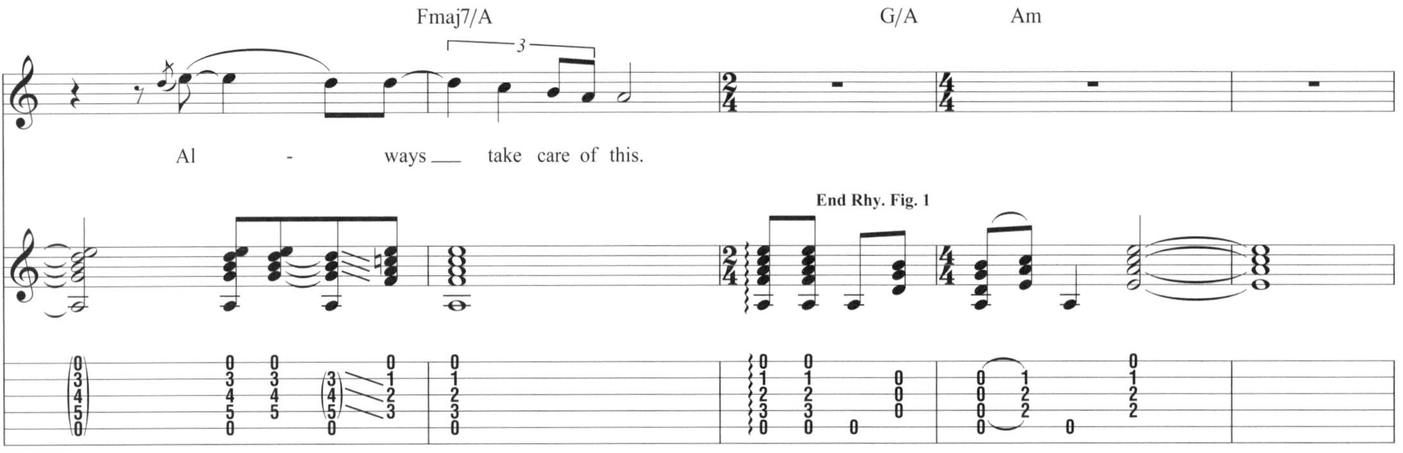

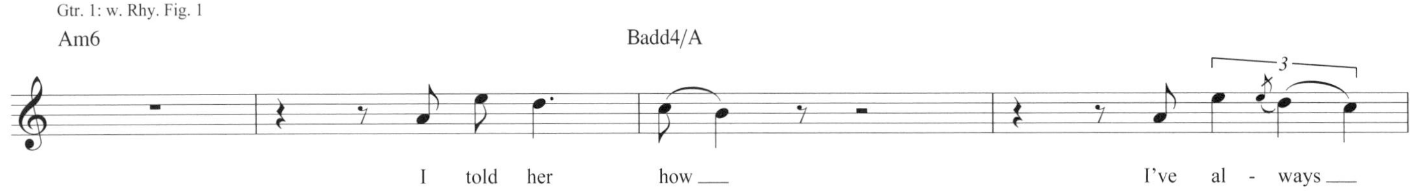

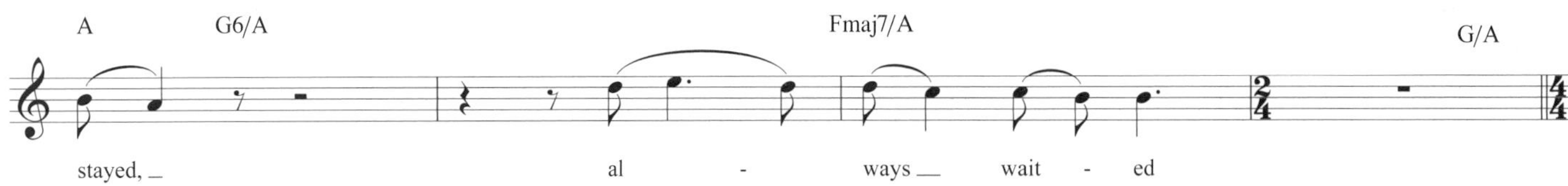

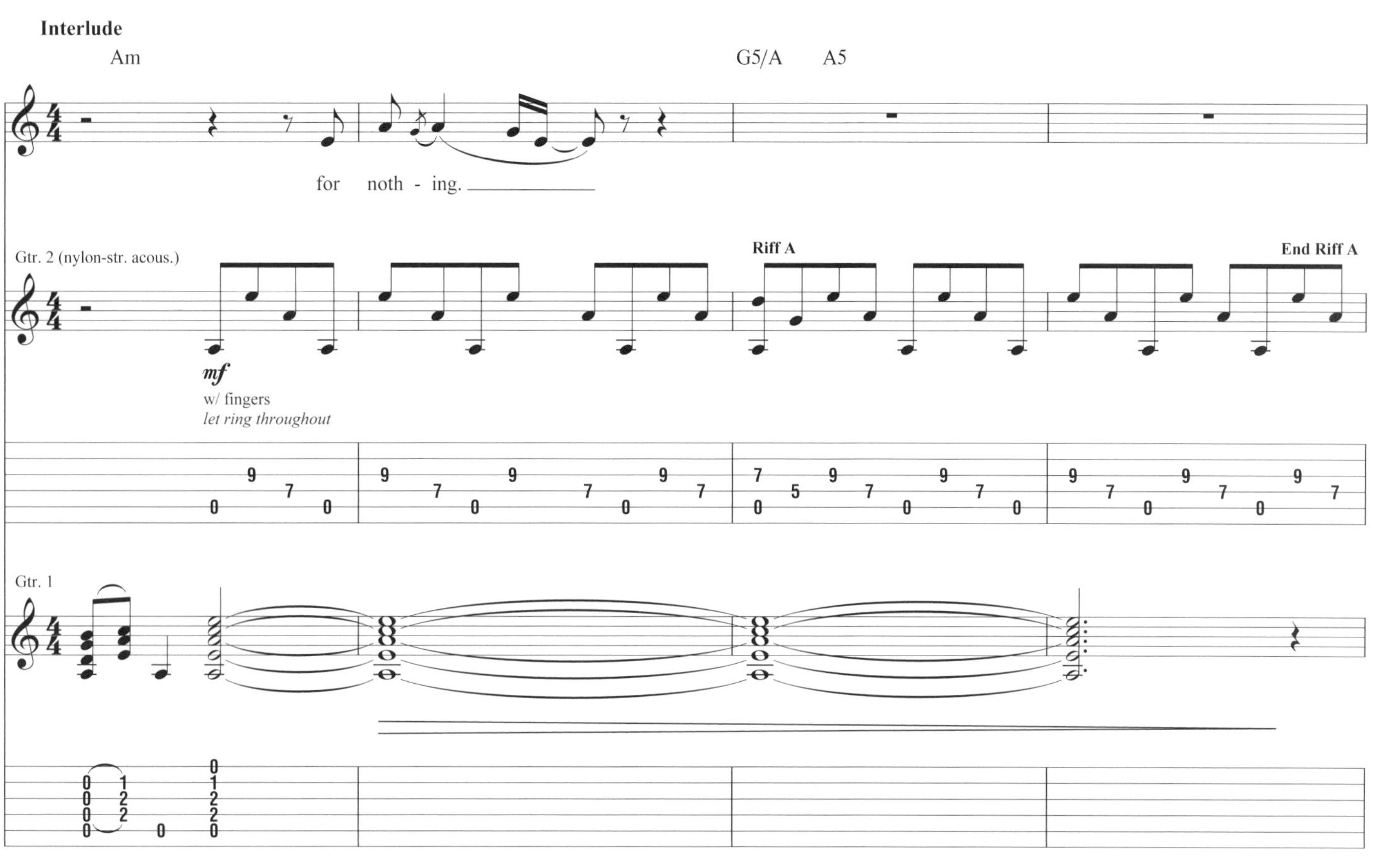
Interlude
Am
G5/A A5
for noth - ing.
Gr. 2 (nylon-str. acous.)
Riff A
End Riff A
mf
w/ fingers
let ring throughout
Gtr. 1

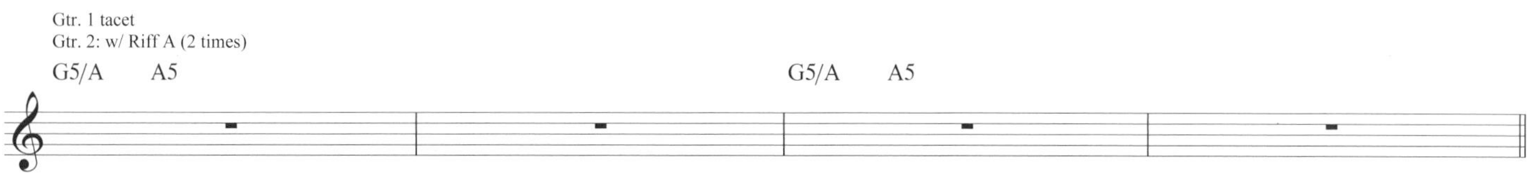
Gtr. 1 tacet
Gtr. 2: w/ Riff A (2 times)
G5/A A5
G5/A A5

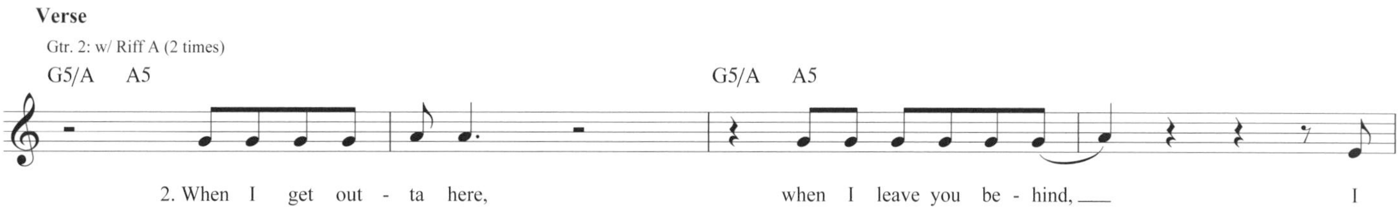
Verse
Gtr. 2: w/ Riff A (2 times)
G5/A A5
G5/A A5
2. When I get out - ta here,
when I leave you be - hind,
I

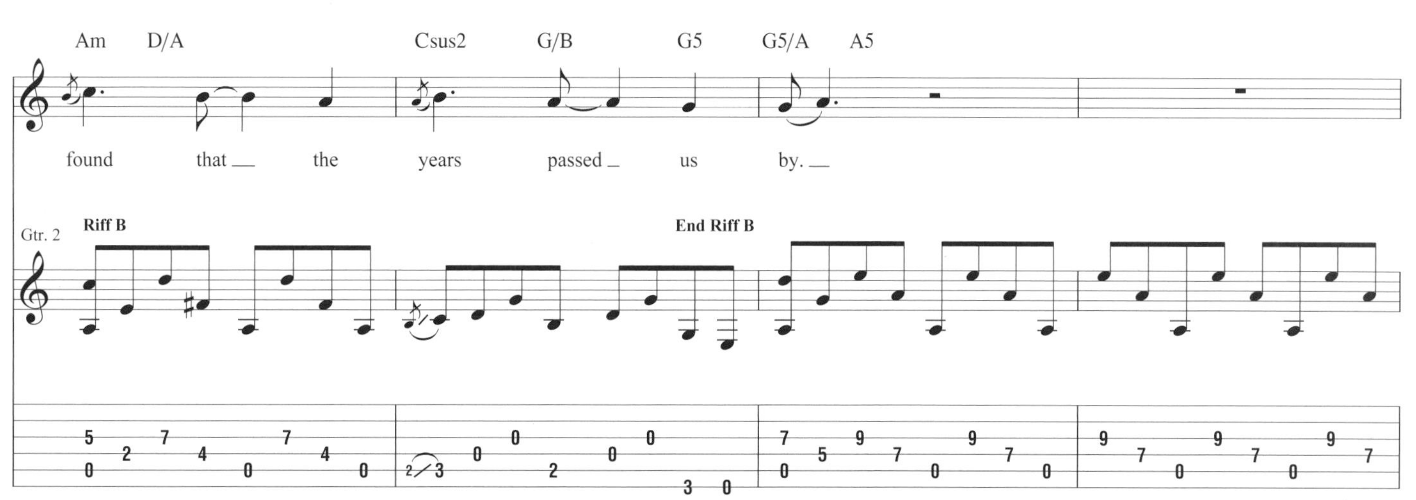
Am D/A
Csus2 G/B
G5
G5/A A5
found that the years passed us by.
Gtr. 2
Riff B
End Riff B

Gtr. 2: w/ Riff A (2 times)
G5/A A5
G5/A A5
Gtr. 2: w/ Riff B
Am D/A
When I get out - ta here,
when I leave you be - hind,
I found that the

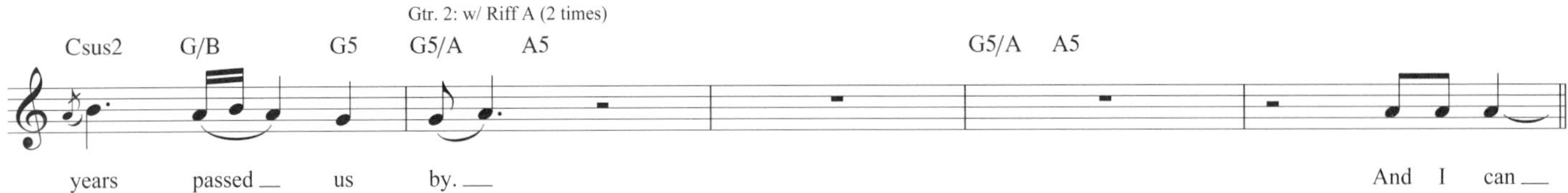
Gtr. 2: w/ Riff A (2 times)
Csus2 G/B G5 G5/A A5
G5/A A5
years passed us by.
And I can

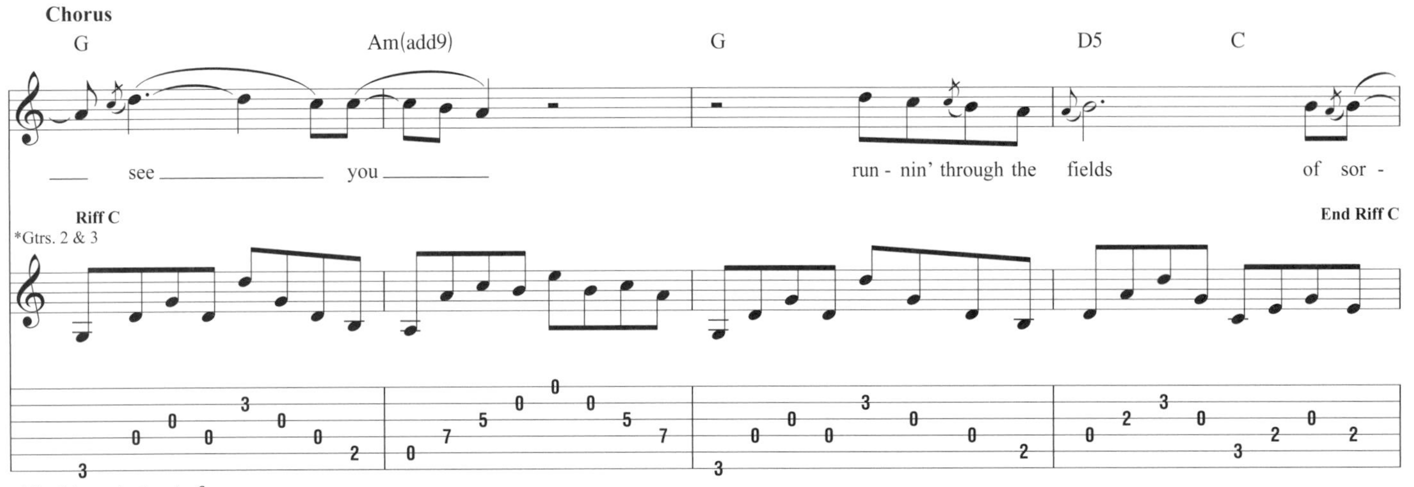
Chorus
G Am(add9) G D5 C
see you
run - nin' through the fields of sor -
Riff C
*Gtrs. 2 & 3
End Riff C

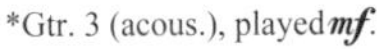
*Gtr. 3 (acous.), played mf.

Asus4 A A7
- row.
Yes, I can
Riff D
End Riff D

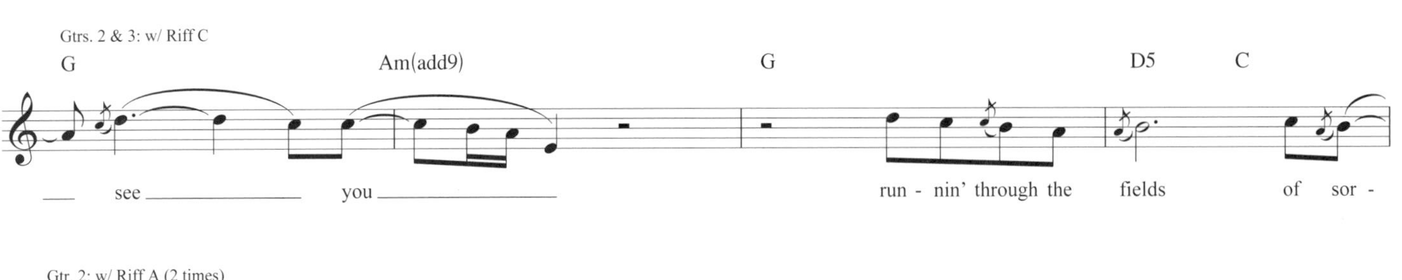
Gtrs. 2 & 3: w/ Riff C
G Am(add9) G D5 C
see you
run - nin' through the fields of sor -

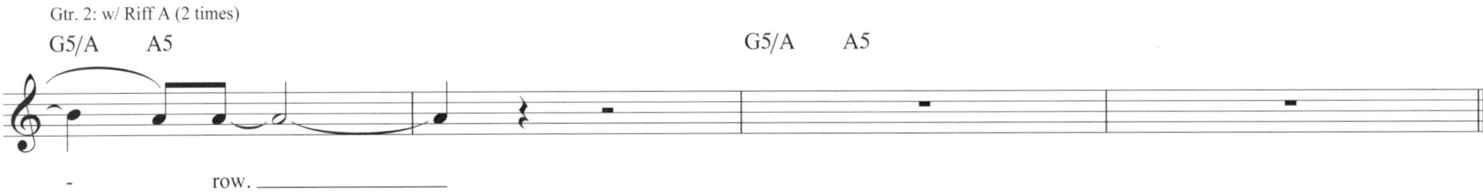
Gtr. 2: w/ Riff A (2 times)
G5/A A5
G5/A A5
- row.

Verse
Gtr. 2: w/ Riff A (2 times)
G5/A A5 G5/A A5
Female: 3. When you get out of here, when you leave me be - hind, you
Gtr. 2: w/ Riff B
Am D/A Csus2 G/B G5
Gtr. 2: w/ Riff A (3 times)
G5/A A5 G5/A A5
find that the years passed us by. When you get out
G5/A A5
Gtr. 2: w/ Riff B
Am D/A
of here, when you leave me be - hind, you find that those
Csus2 G/B G5
Gtr. 2: w/ Riff A (2 times)
G5/A A5 G5/A A5
years passed us by. And I can
Chorus
Gtrs. 2 & 3: w/ Riff C
G Am(add9) G D5 C
Gtrs. 2 & 3: w/ Riff D
Asus4 A
see you, run - ning through the fields of sor - row.
A7
Gtrs. 2 & 3: w/ Riff C
G Am(add9)
Yes, I can see you,
G D5 C
Gtr. 2: w/ Riff A (2 times)
G5/A A5 G5/A A5
run - ning through the fields of sor - row.
Outro
G5/A A5 G5/A A5 G5/A A5
Gtr. 2

from *Damnation*

Death Whispered a Lullaby

Words and Music by Mikael Akerfeldt and Steven Wilson

Gtr. 1: w/ Riff B
F#7sus4
G(#11)
Gtr. 2
Chorus
Gtr. 2 tacet
Asus2
Cm/E♭
Cmaj7(no3rd)
G/D
G/B
G5
Oh,
sleep my child.
Riff D
Gtr. 3 (elec.)
mf
w/ slight dist.
let ring
Riff C
Gtr. 1
End Riff C
Gtr. 1: w/ Riff C (3 times)
Gtr. 3
End Riff D
Gtr. 3: w/ Riff D

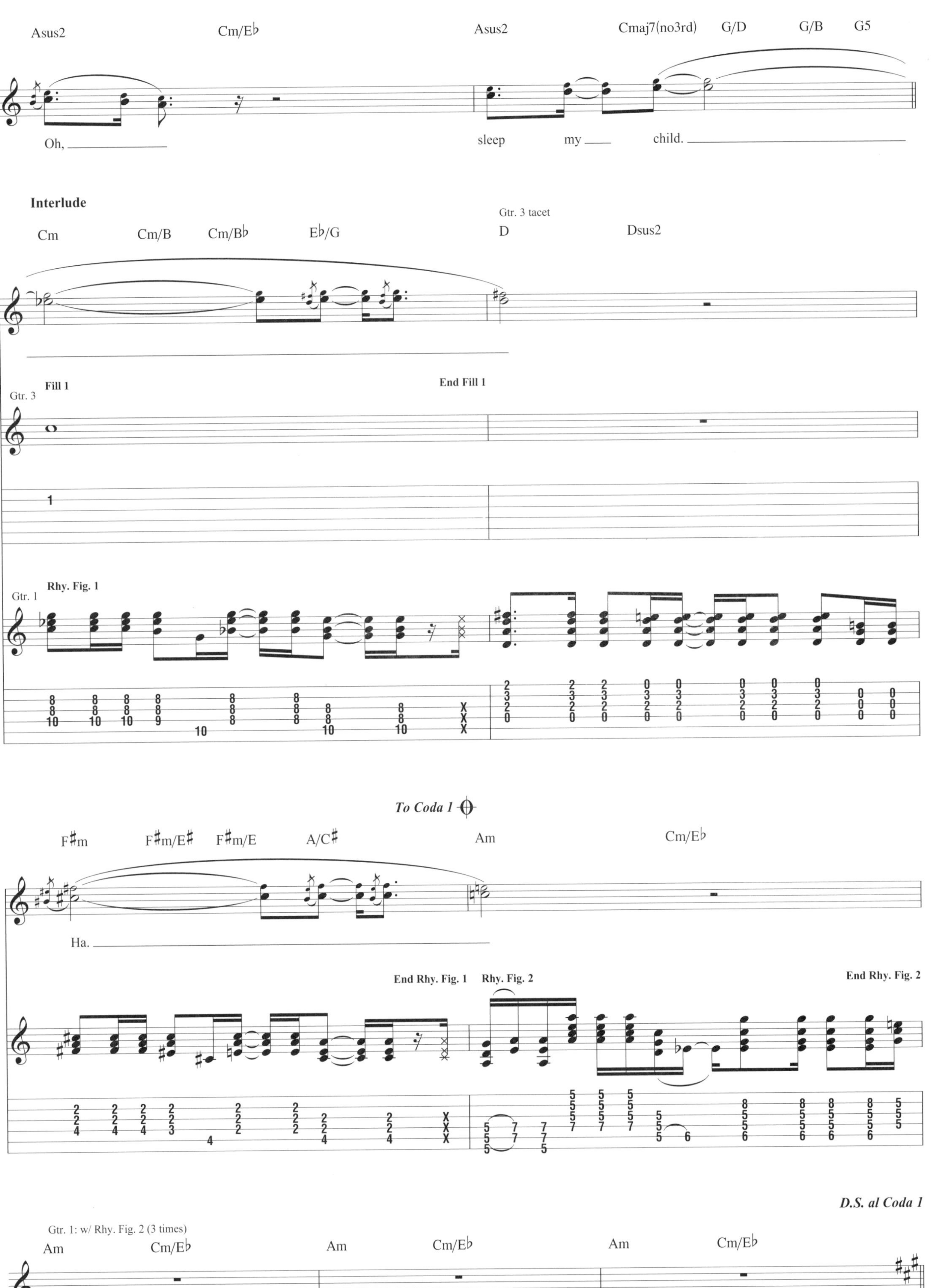
Asus2
Cm/E♭
Asus2
Cmaj7(no3rd)
G/D
G/B
G5
Oh,
sleep
my
child.
Interlude
Cm
Cm/B
Cm/B♭
E♭/G
Gtr. 3 tacet
D
Dsus2
Gtr. 3
Fill 1
End Fill 1
Gtr. 1
Rhy. Fig. 1
To Coda 1
F♯m
F♯m/E♯
F♯m/E
A/C♯
Am
Cm/E♭
Ha.
End Rhy. Fig. 1
Rhy. Fig. 2
End Rhy. Fig. 2
D.S. al Coda 1
Gtr. 1: w/ Rhy. Fig. 2 (3 times)
Am
Cm/E♭
Am
Cm/E♭
Am
Cm/E♭

Coda 1

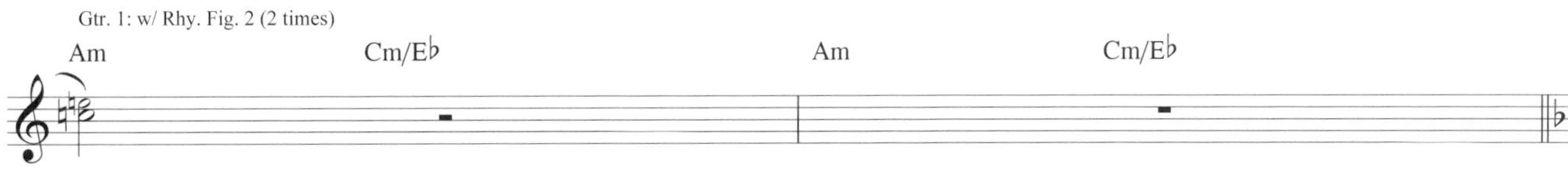
Gtr. 1: w/ Rhy. Fig. 2 (2 times)
Am
Cm/E♭
Am
Cm/E♭

Guitar Solo
Dsus2
Gtr. 4 (elec.)
mp
*< f
w/ dist. & heavy reverb
*Vol. swell
Rhy. Fig. 3
Gtr. 1

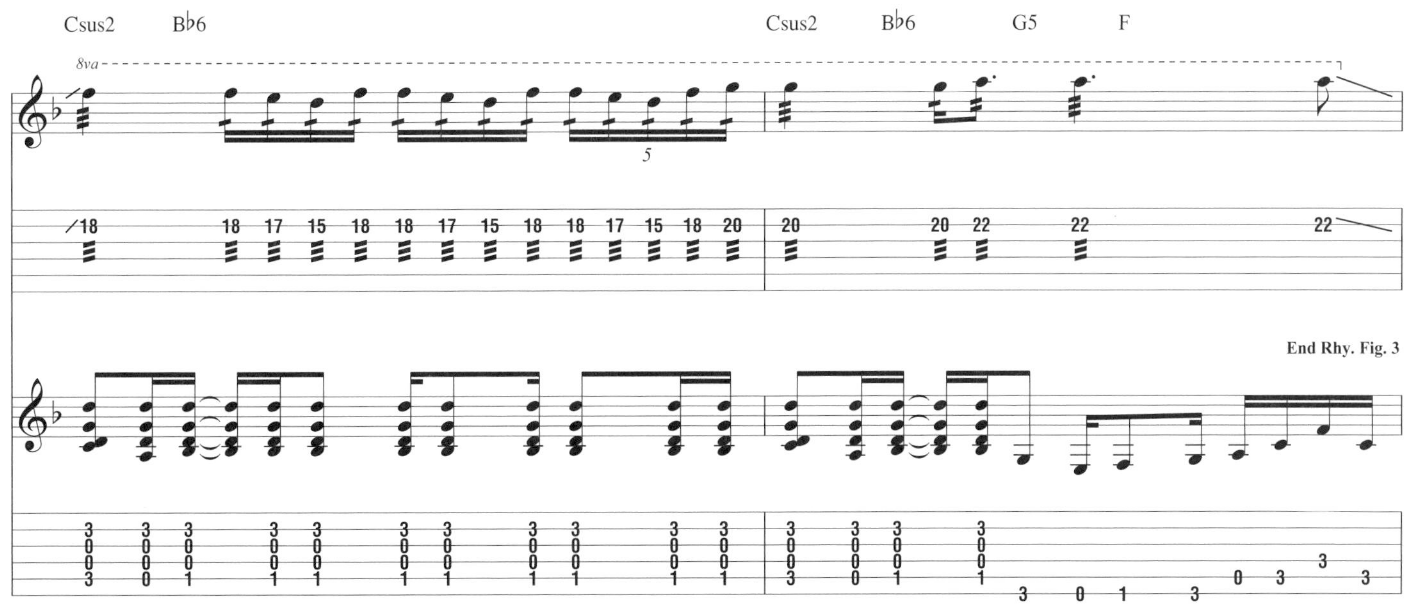
Csus2
B♭6
Csus2
B♭6
G5
F
8va
End Rhy. Fig. 3

Gtr. 1: w/ Rhy. Fig. 3 (1st 3 meas.)
Dsus2
Csus2
B♭6
Gtr. 4
loco
tr

Csus2
B♭6
G5
F
D5
Gtr. 4
w/ bar
grad. release
Gtr. 1
Interlude
Gtr. 1: w/ Riff A (2 times)
F♯5(♭9)
Gtr. 4 tacet
D.S. al Coda 2
Coda 2
Chorus
Gtr. 1: w/ Riff C (4 times)
Gtr. 3: w/ Riff D (2 times)
Asus2
Cm/E♭
Cmaj7(no3rd)
G/D
G/B
Oh,
sleep my child.
Interlude
Gtr. 1: w/ Rhy. Fig. 1
Gtr. 3: w/ Fill 1
Cm
Cm/B
Cm/B♭
E♭/G
D
Dsus2
F♯m
F♯m/E♯
F♯m/E
A/C♯
Ha.
Gtr. 1: w/ Rhy. Fig. 2 (2 times)
Am

Outro-Guitar Solo
Gtr. 1: w/ Rhy. Fig. 3 (3 3/4 times)
Dsus2
Csus2 B♭6
Csus2 B♭6 G5 F
Gtr. 4
8va
loco
*w/ delay
w/ bar
slack
*Set for eighth-note triplet regeneration w/ 4 repeats.
grad. dive
Harm.
Gtr. 1

from *My Arms, Your Hearse*

Demon of the Fall

Words and Music by Mikael Akerfeldt and Sven Peter Malcom Lindgren

Gtrs. 1, 4, 5 & 6: Drop D tuning:
(low to high) D-A-D-G-B-E

Gtrs. 2 & 3: Double Drop D tuning:
(low to high) D-A-D-G-B-D

Intro
Moderately ♩. = 68

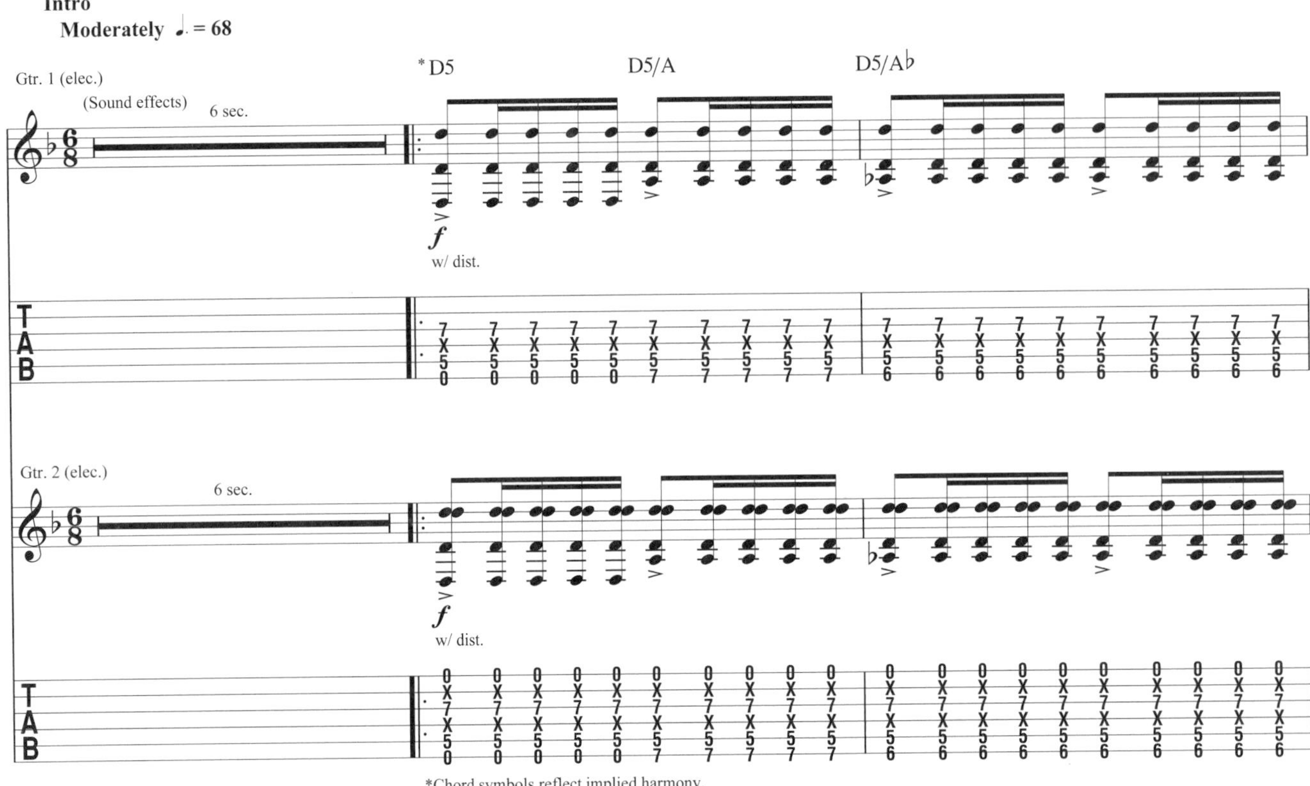

*Chord symbols reflect implied harmony.

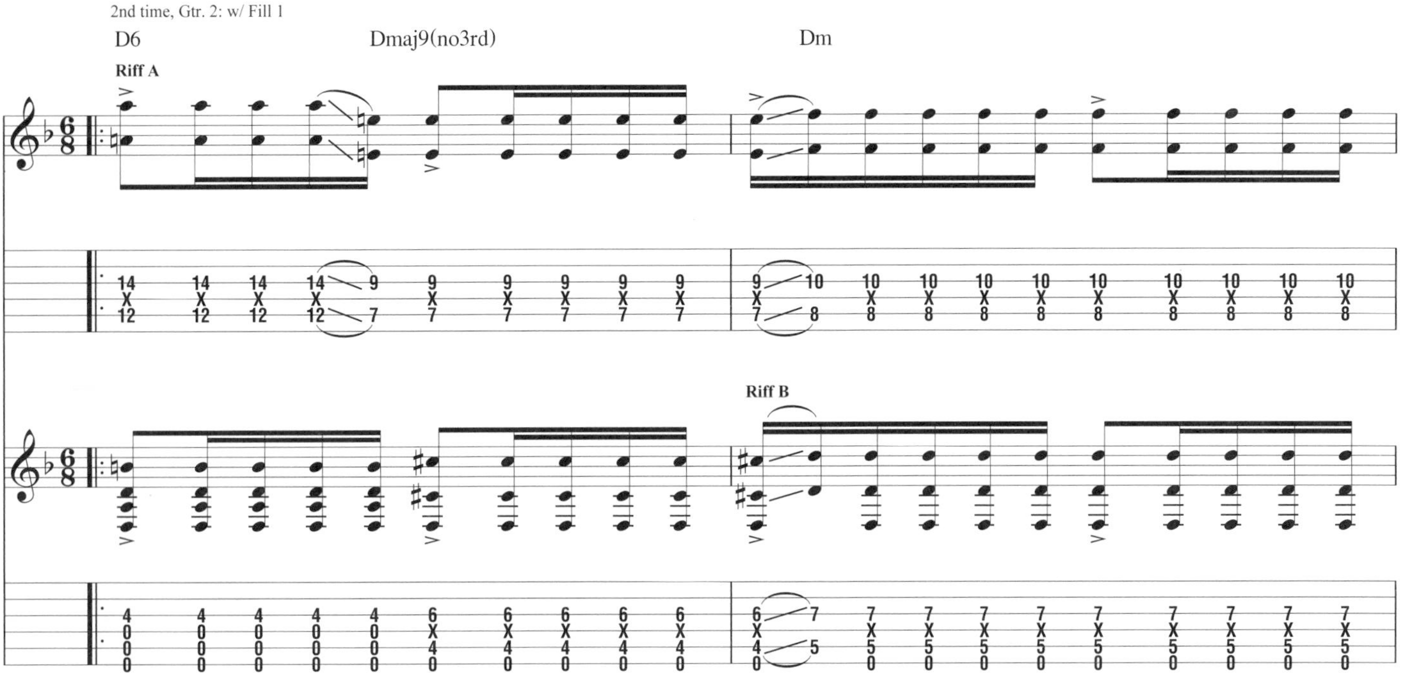
2nd time, Gtr. 2: w/ Fill 1
D6
Dmaj9(no3rd)
Dm
Riff A
Riff B

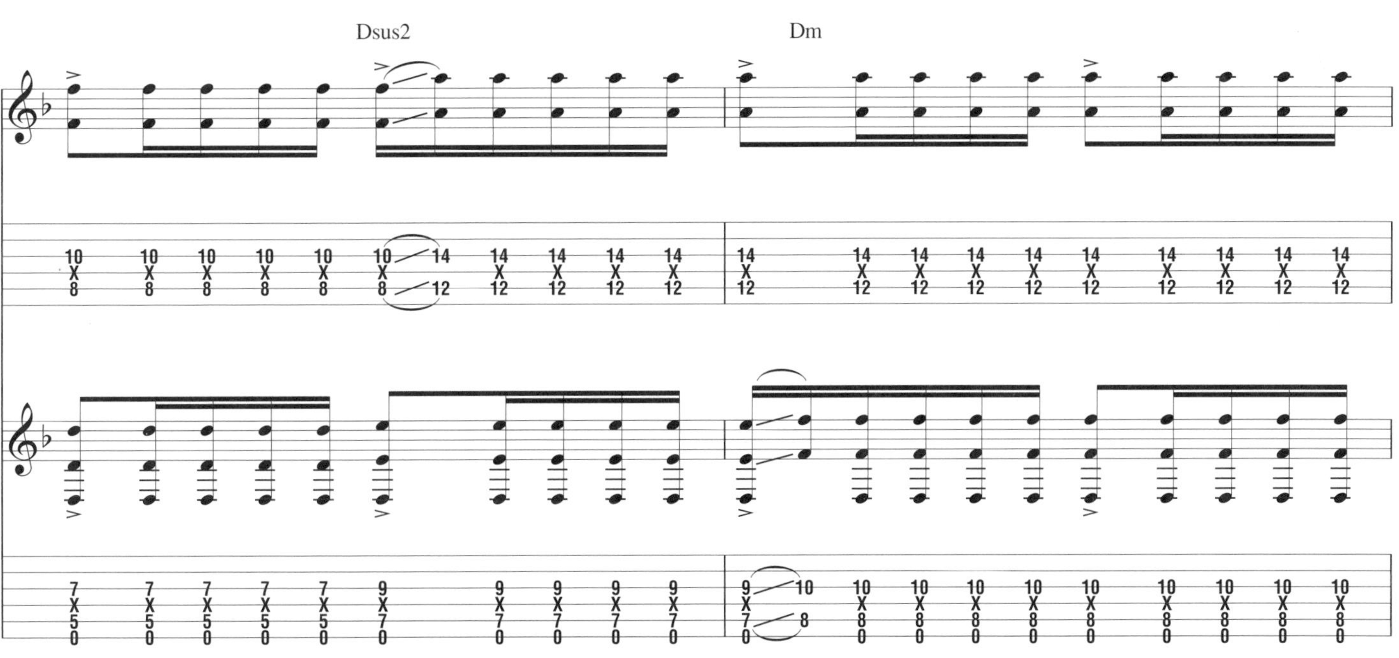
Dsus2
Dm

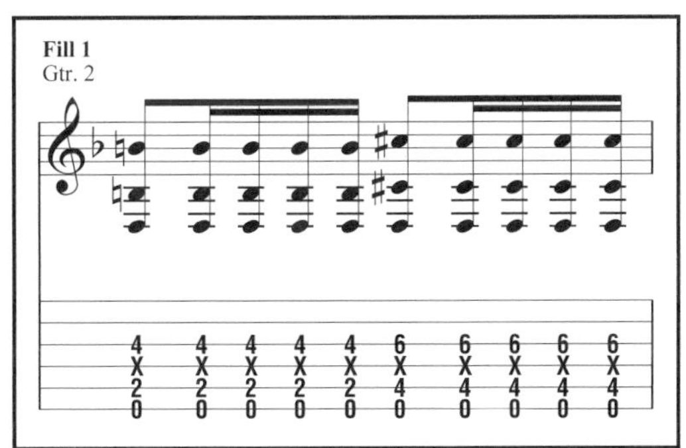
Fill 1
Gtr. 2

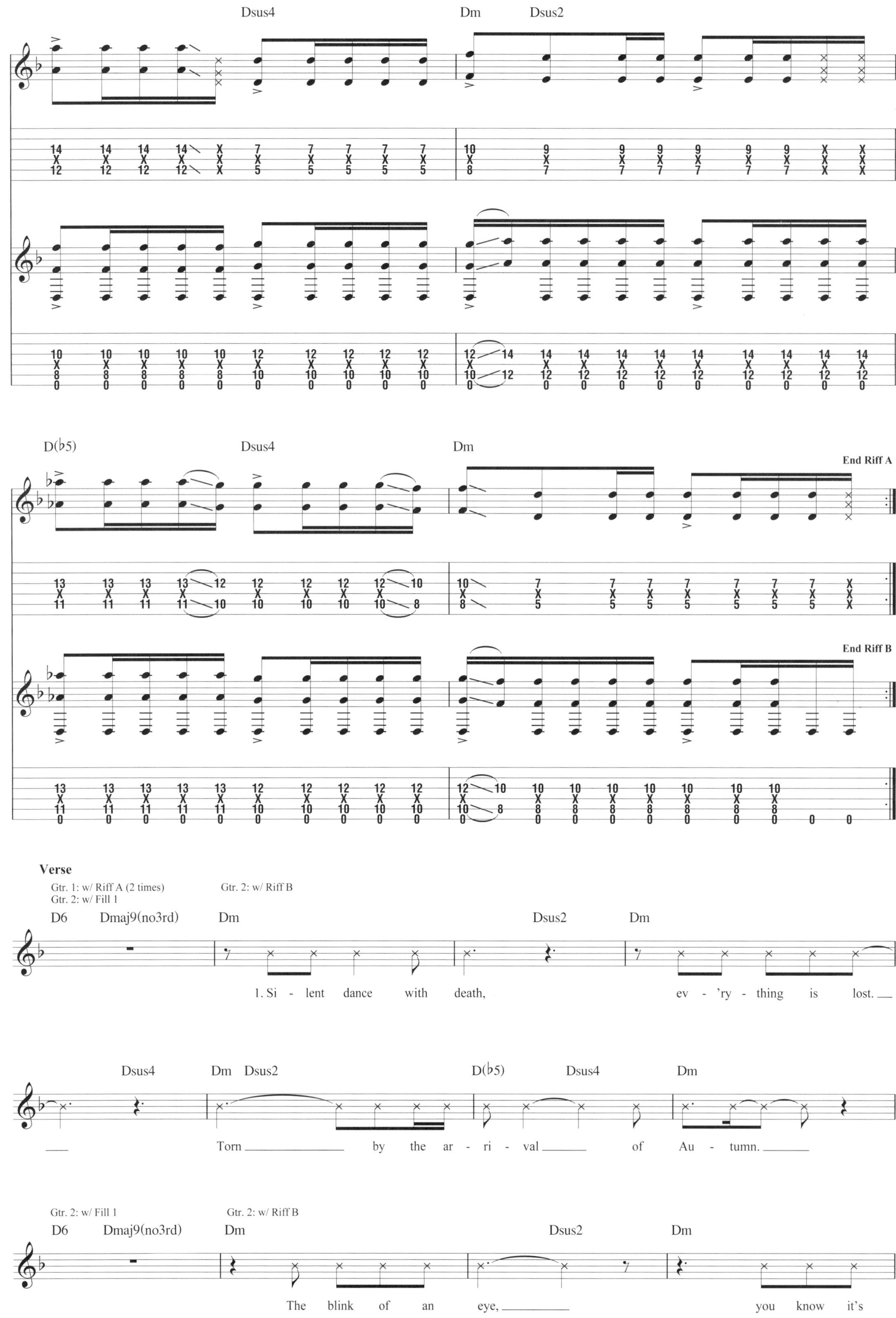
Dsus4
Dm
Dsus2
D(♭5)
Dsus4
Dm
End Riff A
End Riff B
Verse
Gtr. 1: w/ Riff A (2 times)
Gtr. 2: w/ Fill 1
Gtr. 2: w/ Riff B
D6
Dmaj9(no3rd)
Dm
Dsus2
Dm
1. Si - lent dance with death, ev - 'ry - thing is lost.
Dsus4
Dm
Dsus2
D(♭5)
Dsus4
Dm
Torn by the ar - ri - val of Au - tumn.
Gtr. 2: w/ Fill 1
Gtr. 2: w/ Riff B
D6
Dmaj9(no3rd)
Dm
Dsus2
Dm
The blink of an eye, you know it's

Dsus4
Dm Dsus2
D(♭5)
Dsus4
Dm
me.
You keep the dag - ger close at hand.
Chorus
E♭5
D5
E♭5
F5
A♭5
And you saw noth - ing.
Rhy. Fig. 1
*Gtrs. 1 & 2
P.M.
*Composite arrangement
Gsus2
Fsus2
End Rhy. Fig. 1
Gtrs. 1 & 2: w/ Rhy. Fig. 1 (2 3/4 times)
False love turned to pure hate. The wind cried a
lam - en - ta - tion be - fore merg - ing in with the grey.
Gtrs. 1 & 2
Gtr. 3 (12-str. acous.)
divisi
mf

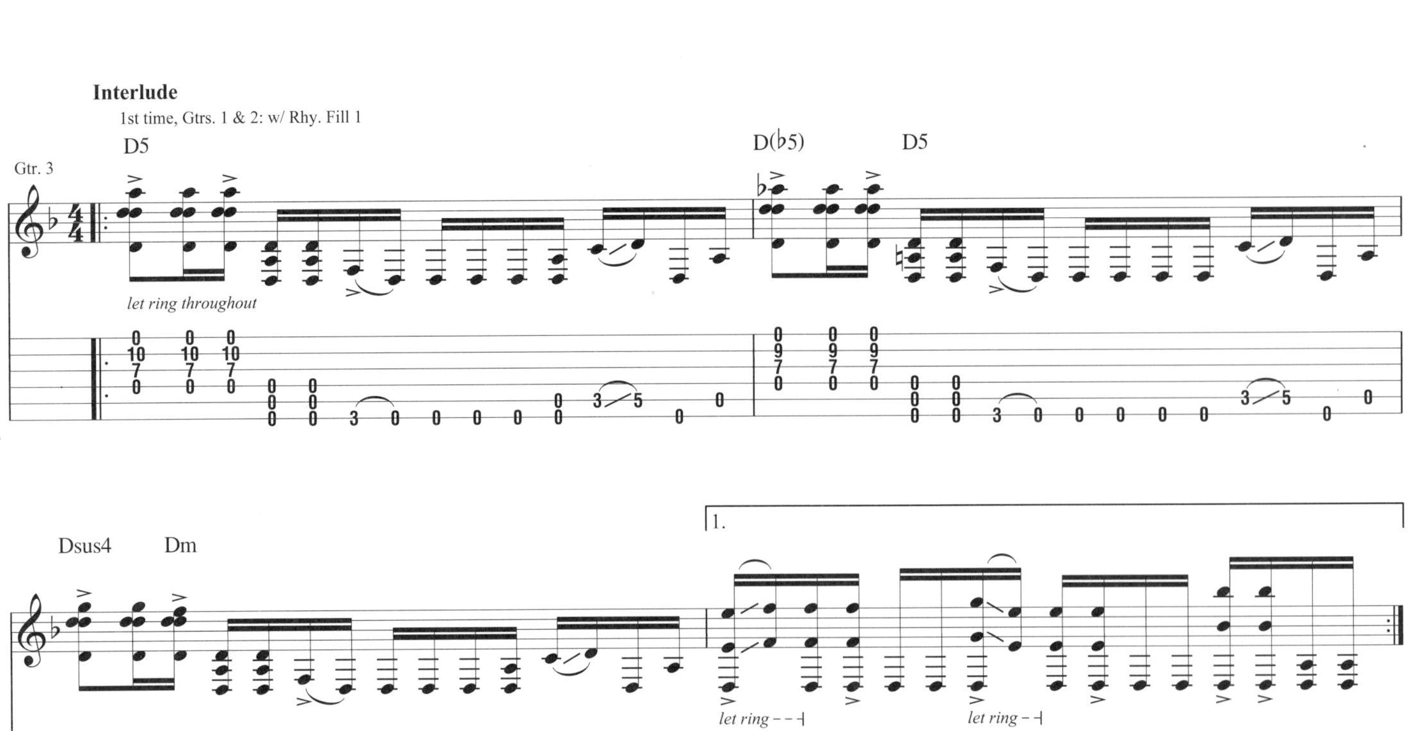
Interlude
1st time, Gtrs. 1 & 2: w/ Rhy. Fill 1
D5
D(♭5)
D5
Gtr. 3
let ring throughout
Dsus4
Dm
1.
let ring
let ring

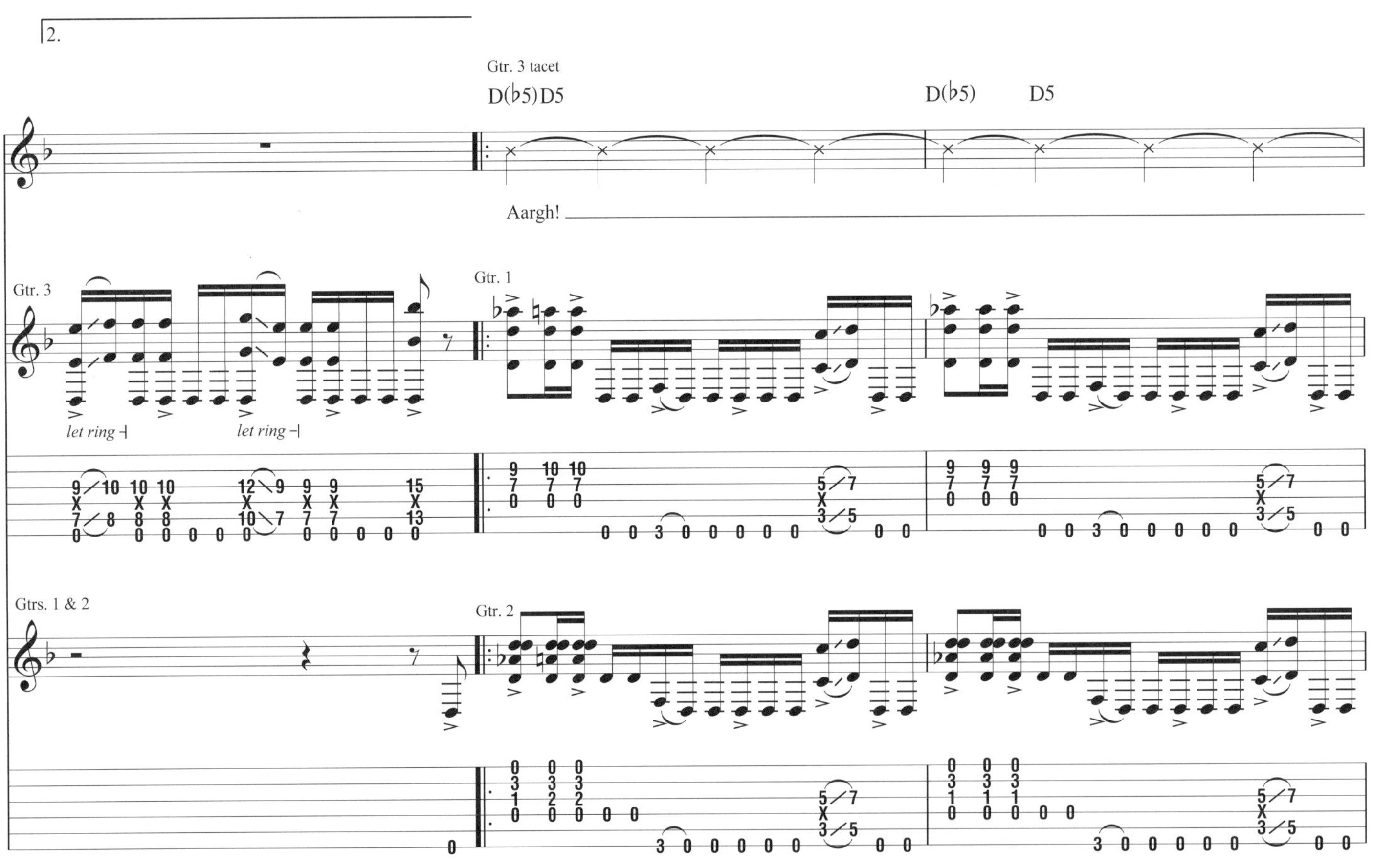
2.
Gtr. 3 tacet
D(♭5) D5
D(♭5)
D5
Aargh!
Gtr. 3
let ring
let ring
Gtr. 1
Gtrs. 1 & 2
Gtr. 2

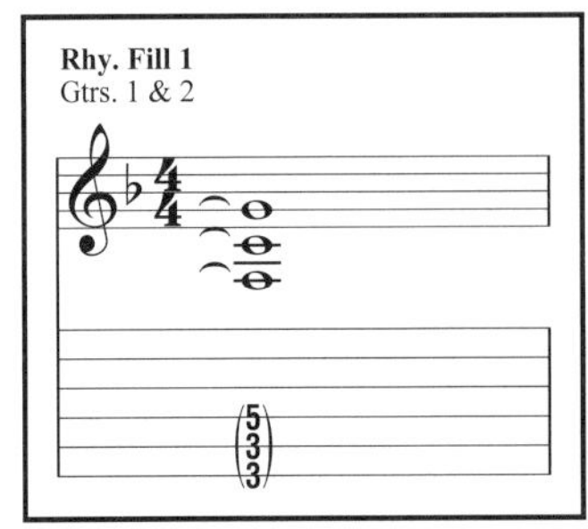
Rhy. Fill 1
Gtrs. 1 & 2

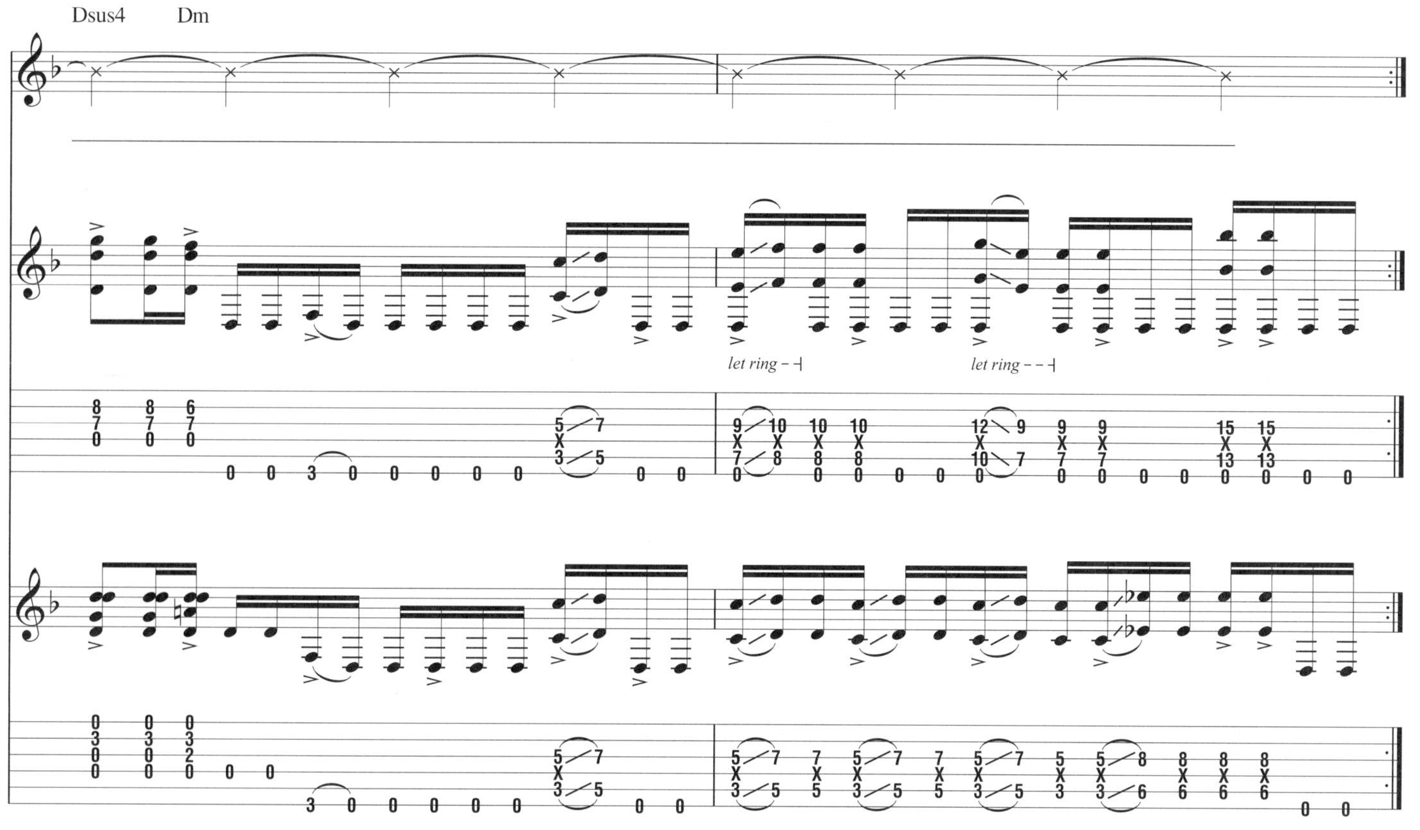

Chorus

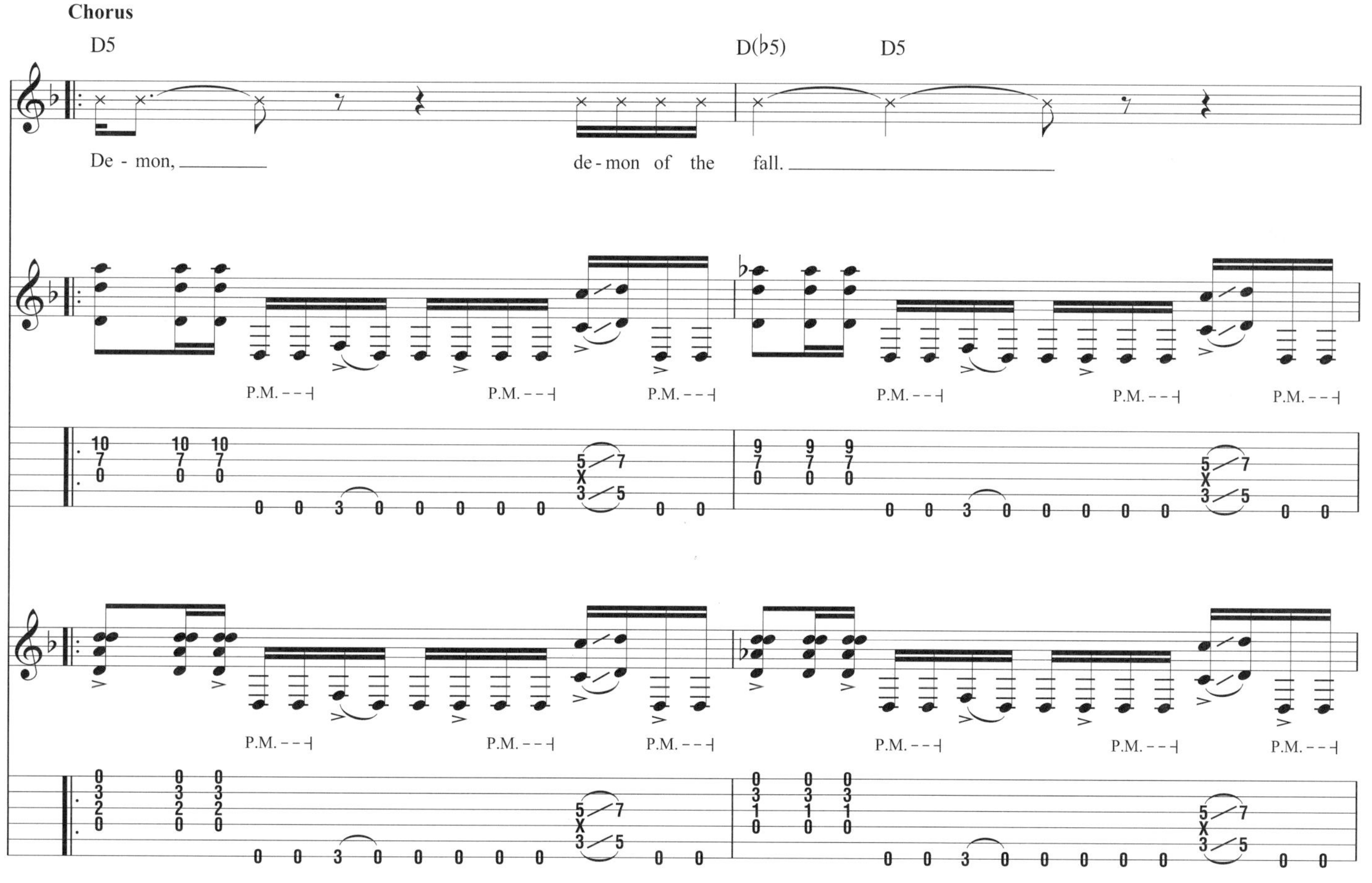

1.

Dsus4 Dm

De - mon, de-mon of the fall. Ah.

P.M. P.M. P.M. let ring P.M. let ring P.M. P.M.

P.M. P.M. P.M. P.M.

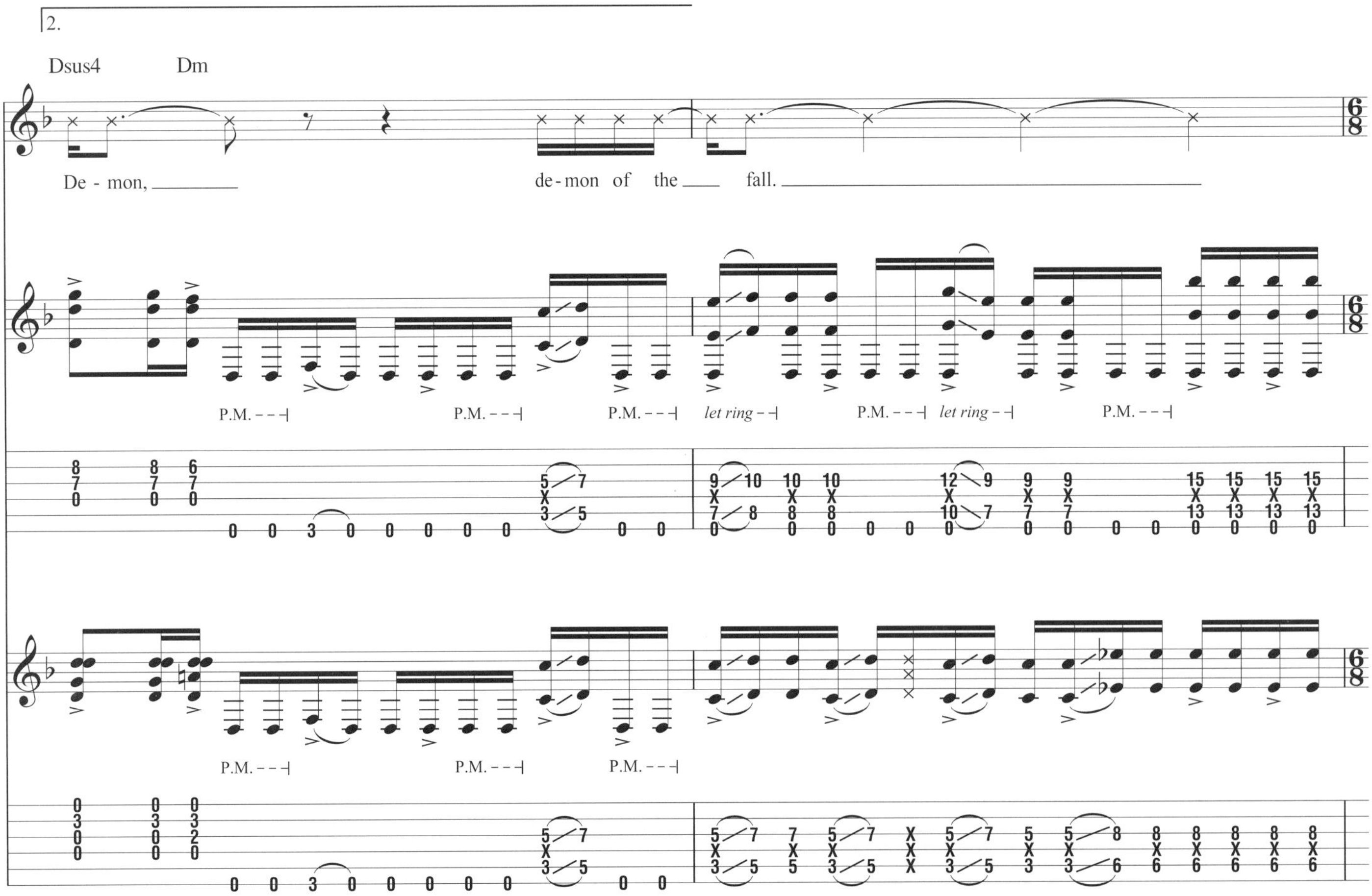

2.

Dsus4 Dm

De - mon, de-mon of the fall.

P.M. P.M. P.M. let ring P.M. let ring P.M.

P.M. P.M. P.M.

F♯m

N.C.

Gtr. 4 (acous.)

mf

let ring throughout

Gtr. 1

Gtr. 2

Bridge

Gtr. 4 tacet

D5

Dmaj7(no3rd)

Dm7

Gasp - ing for an - oth - er breath

Gtr. 1

let ring

Riff C

Gtr. 2

F E N.C.
she rose,
scream - ing at closed doors.
End Riff C

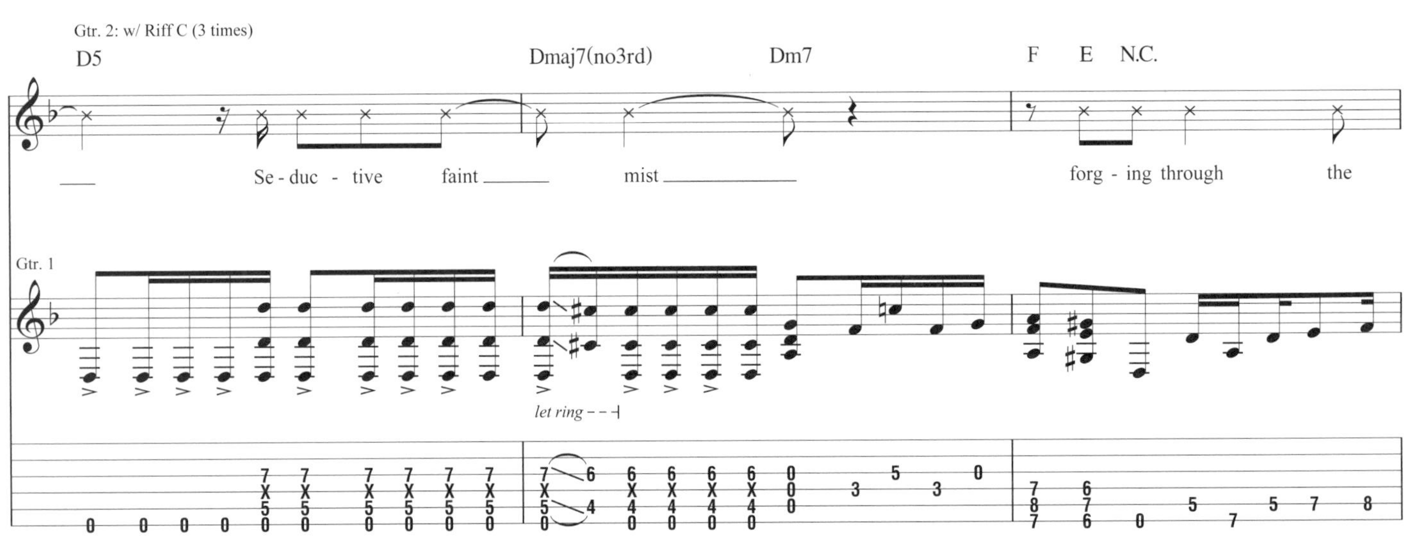
Gtr. 2: w/ Riff C (3 times)
D5
Dmaj7(no3rd)
Dm7
F E N.C.
Se - duc - tive faint mist
forg - ing through the
Gtr. 1
let ring

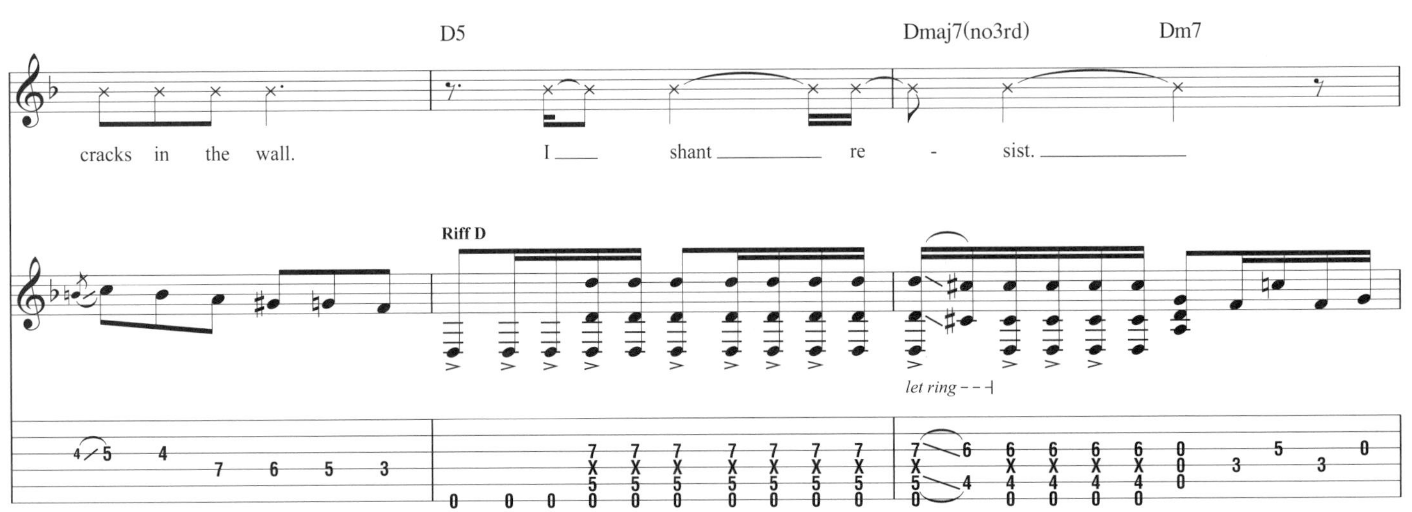
D5
Dmaj7(no3rd)
Dm7
cracks in the wall.
I shant re - sist.
Riff D
let ring

F E N.C.
In tears for all e - ter - ni - ty,
End Riff D
Gtr. 1: w/ Riff D
D5
Dmaj7(no3rd) Dm7
F E N.C.
she turned a - round and faced me for the first time.
Interlude
B♭m
A♭5
C
Gtr. 2
Gtr. 1
Riff E
End Riff E
Gtr. 1: w/ Riff E (2 1/2 times)
B♭m
A♭5
C
Gtr. 2

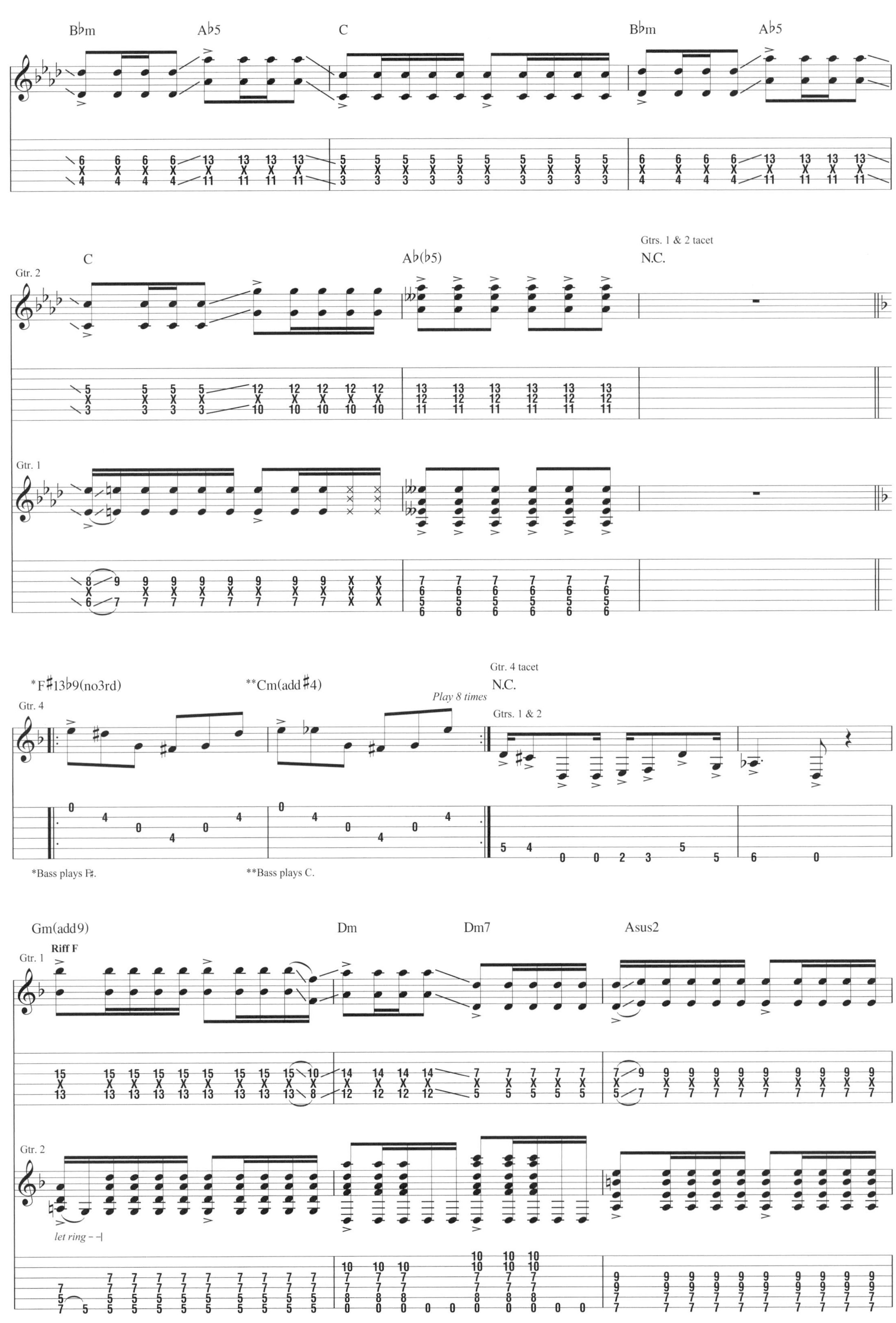
B♭m
A♭5
C
B♭m
A♭5
Gtr. 2
C
A♭(♭5)
Gtrs. 1 & 2 tacet
N.C.
Gtr. 1
let ring
*F♯13♭9(no3rd)
**Cm(add♯4)
Gtr. 4
Play 8 times
Gtr. 4 tacet
N.C.
Gtrs. 1 & 2
*Bass plays F♯.
**Bass plays C.
Gm(add9)
Riff F
Gtr. 1
Dm
Dm7
Asus2
Gtr. 2
let ring

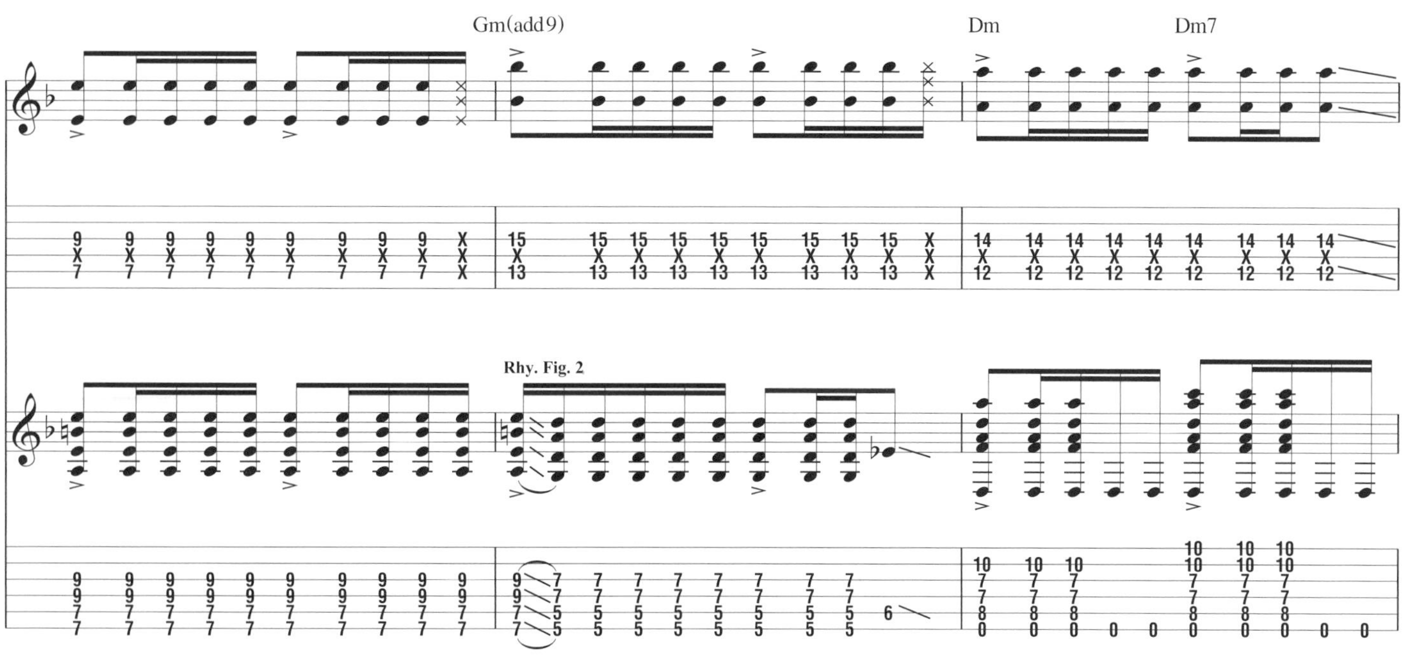

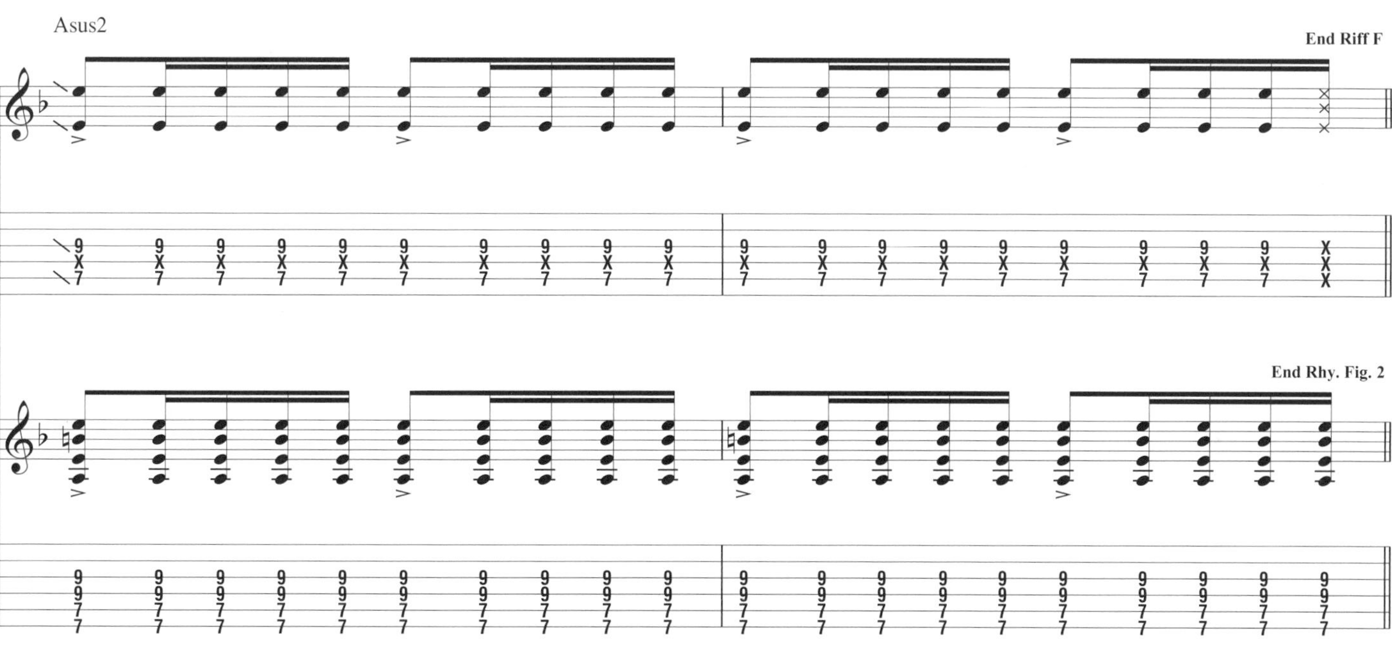

Bridge

Gtr. 1: w/ Riff F
Gtr. 2: w/ Rhy. Fig. 2 (2 times)

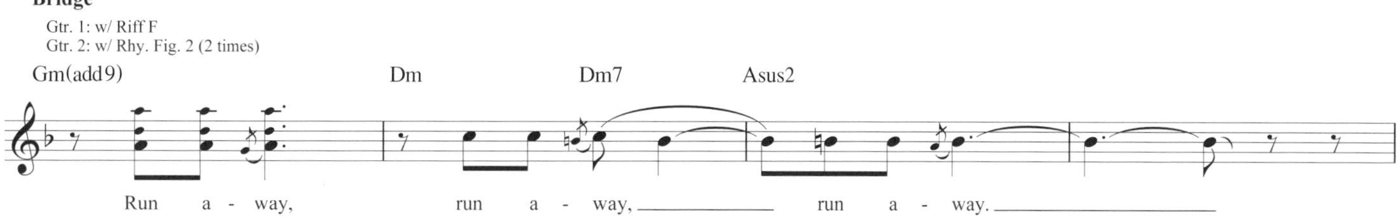

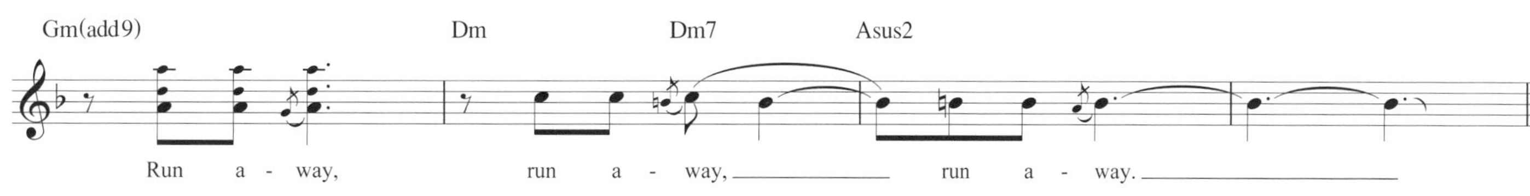

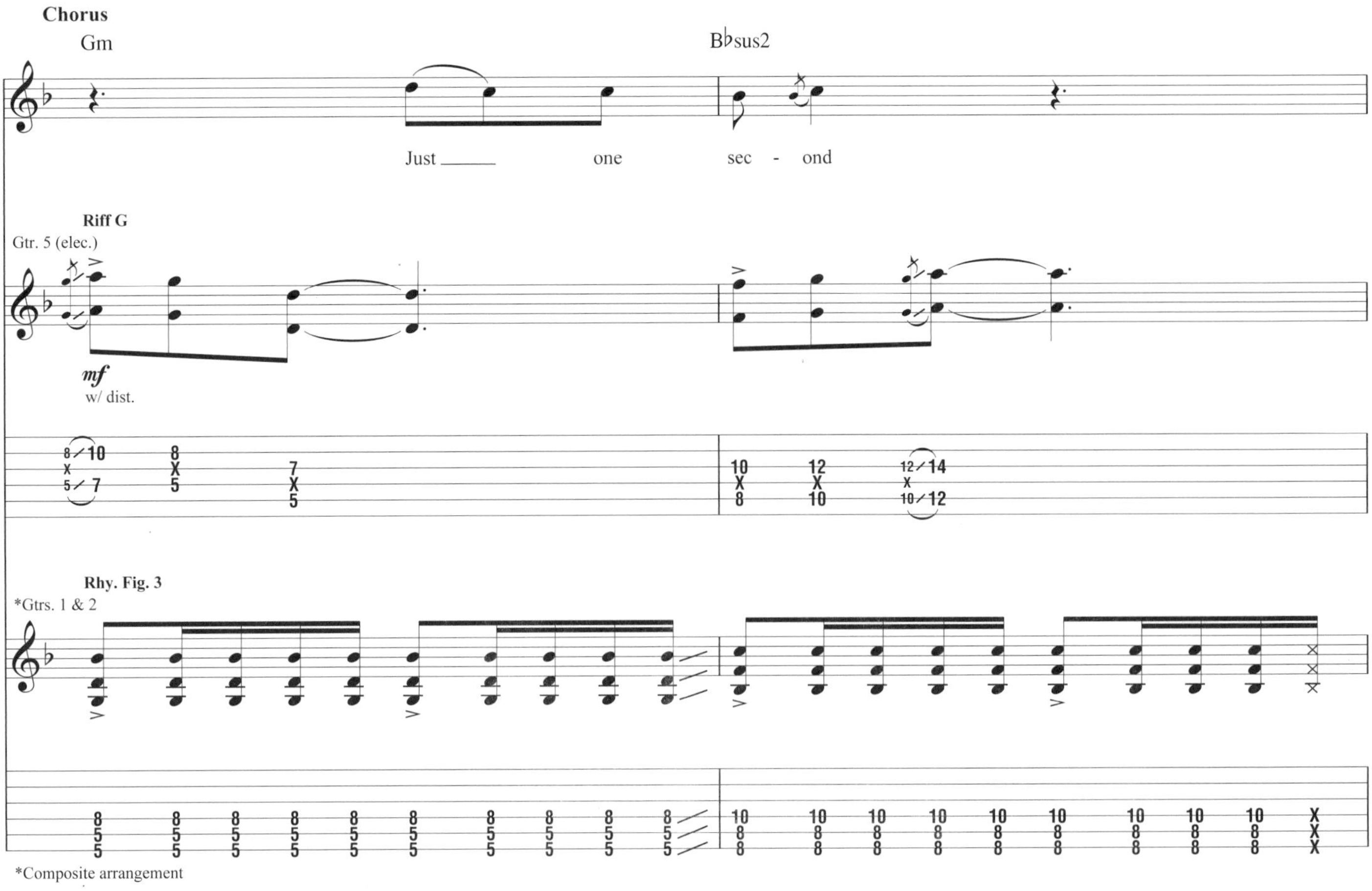
Chorus
Gm
B♭sus2
Just one sec - ond
Riff G
Gtr. 5 (elec.)
mf
w/ dist.
Rhy. Fig. 3
*Gtrs. 1 & 2
*Composite arrangement

Fsus2
Dsus4
and I was left with noth - ing.
End Riff G
End Rhy. Fig. 3

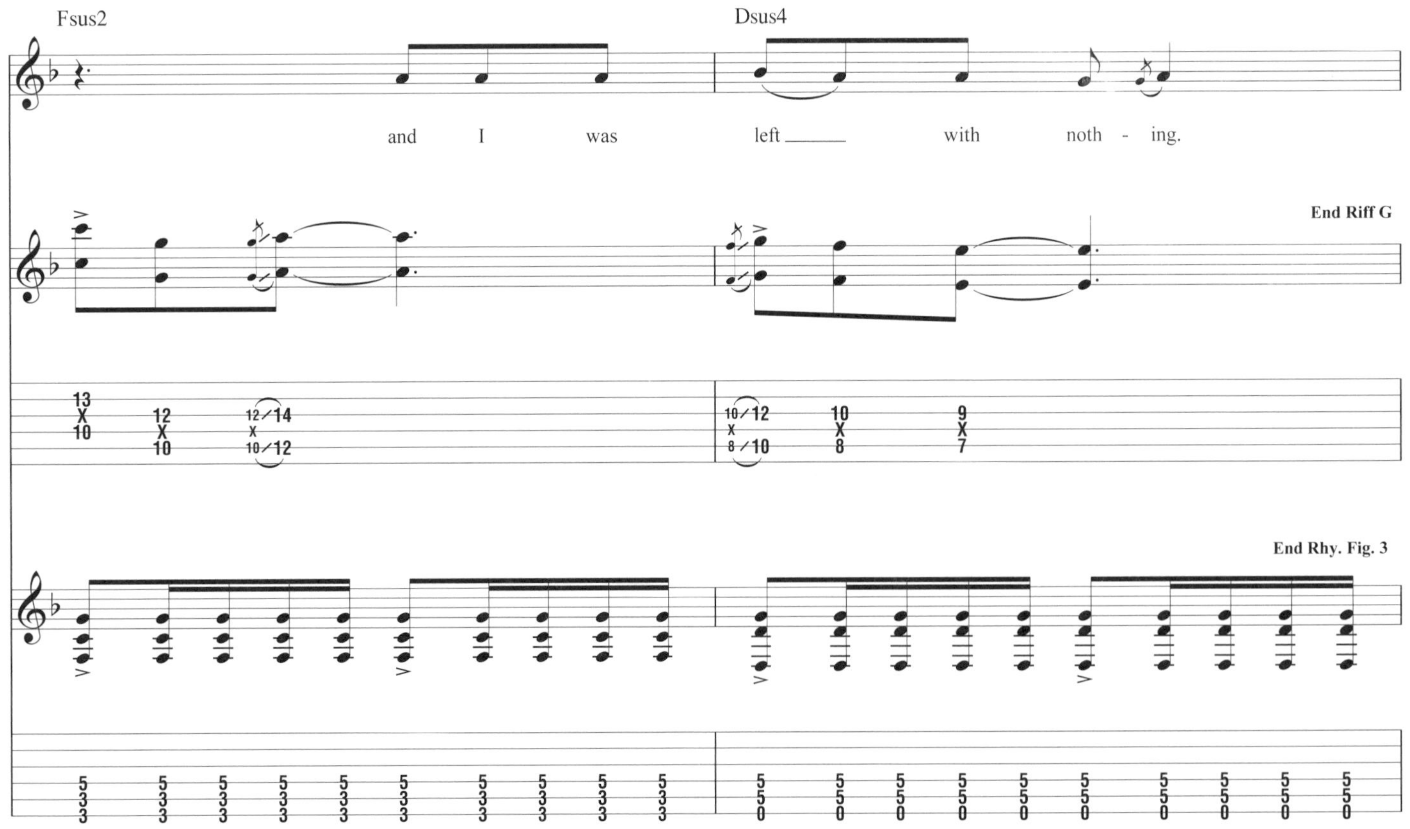

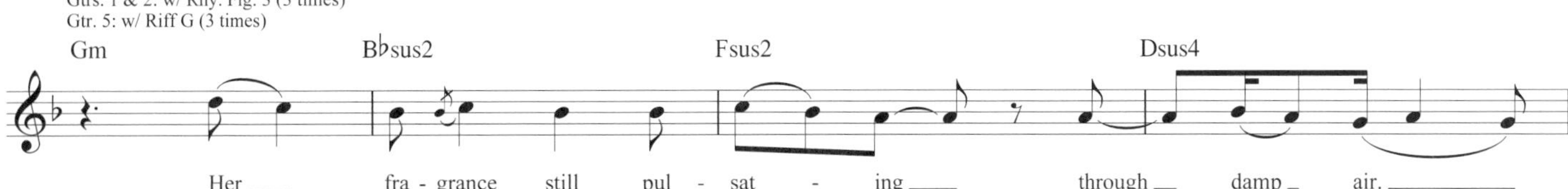

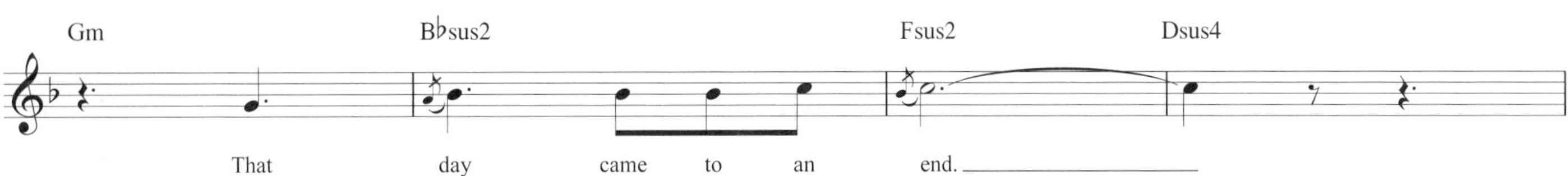

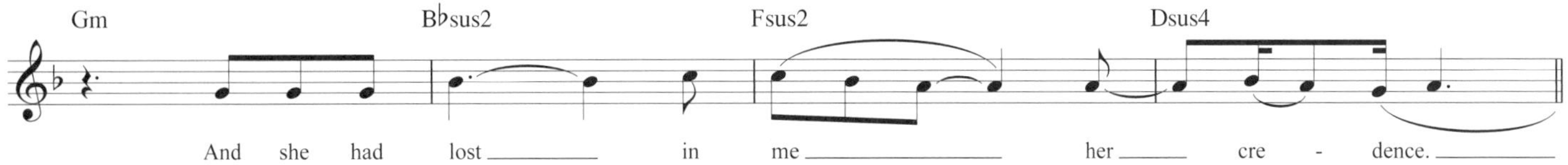

Guitar Solo

*Two gtrs. arr. for one.

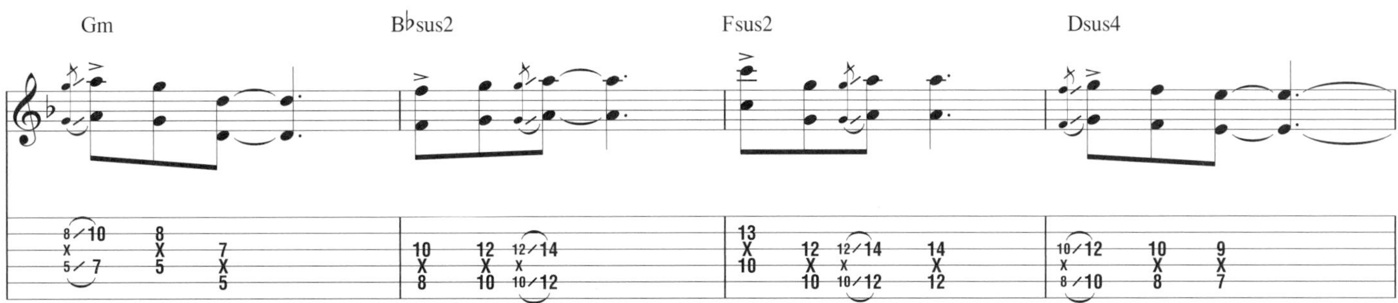

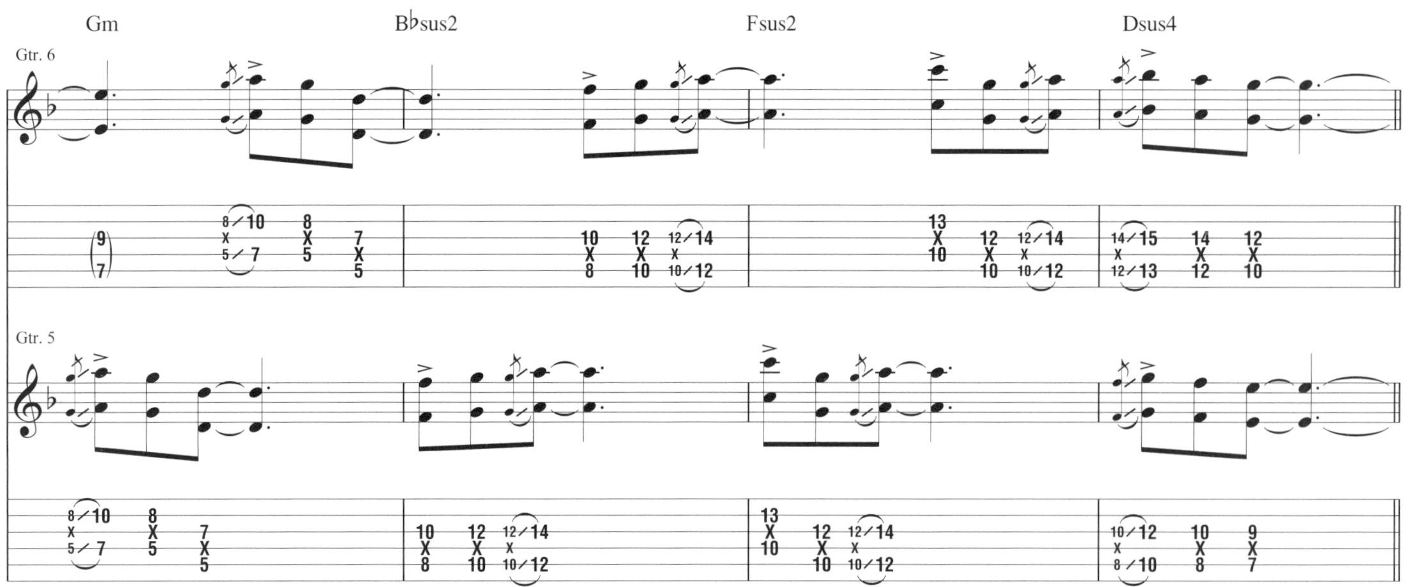

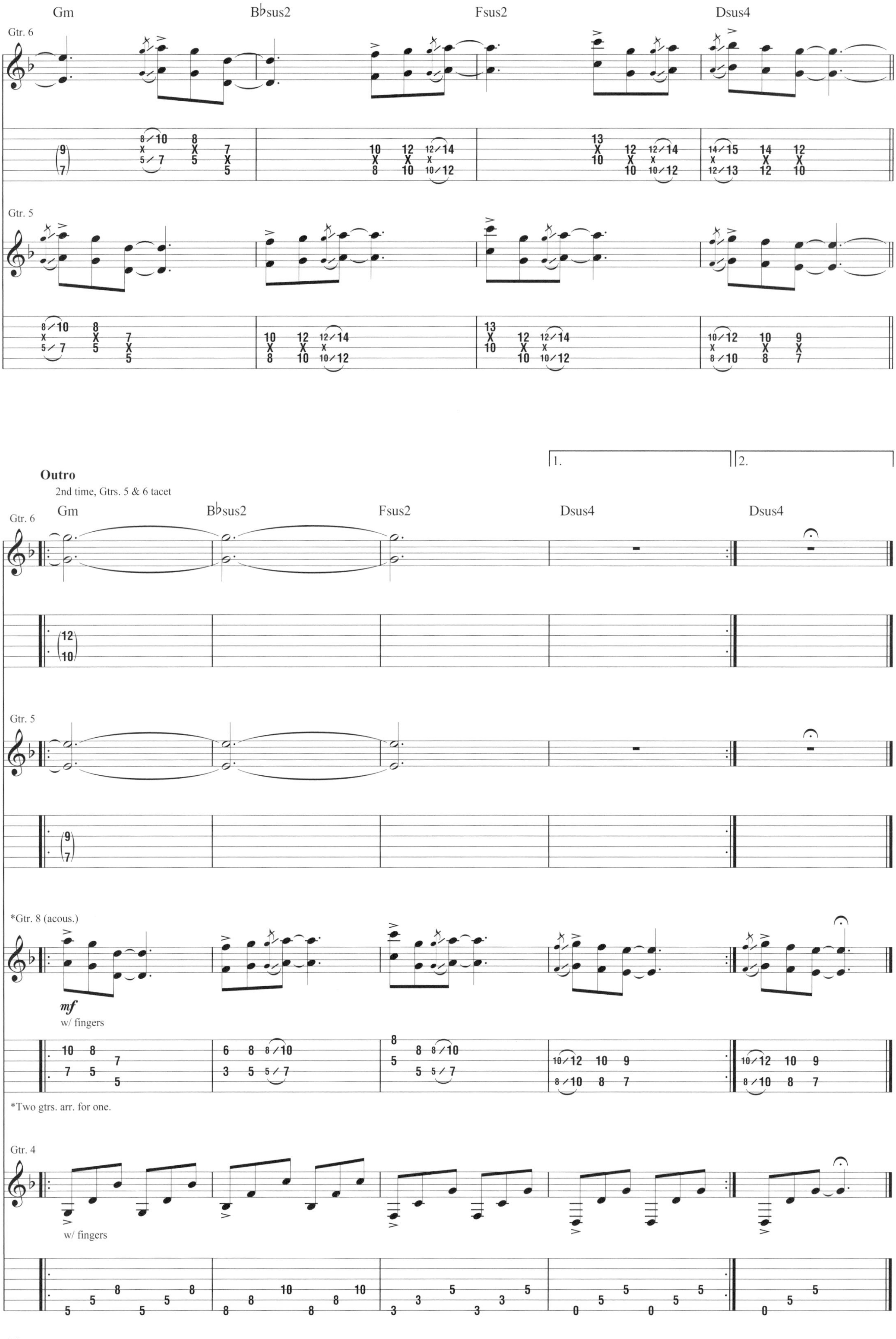

Outro

2nd time, Gtrs. 5 & 6 tacet

1.
2.

Gm
B♭sus2
Fsus2
Dsus4
Dsus4

Gtr. 6

Gtr. 5

*Gtr. 8 (acous.)

mf

w/ fingers

*Two gtrs. arr. for one.

Gtr. 4

w/ fingers

from *Sorceress*

Era

Words and Music by Mikael Akerfeldt

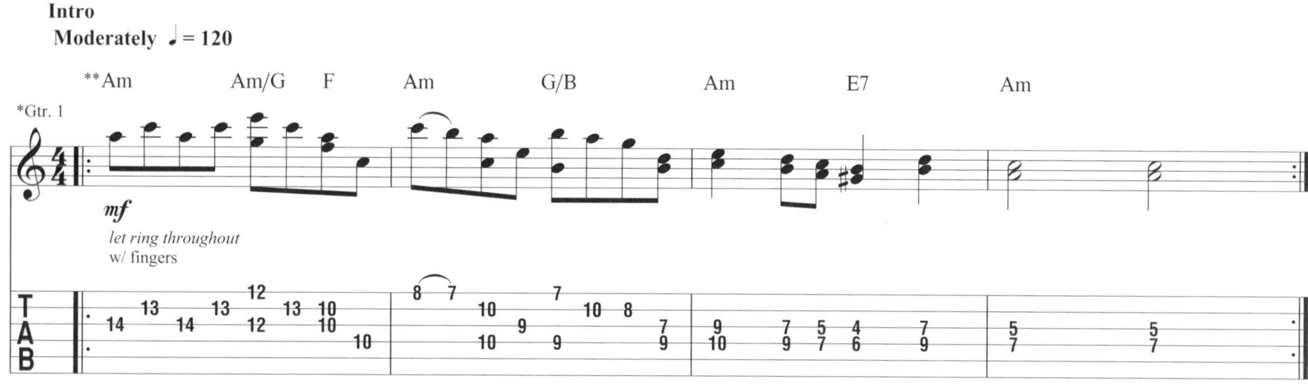

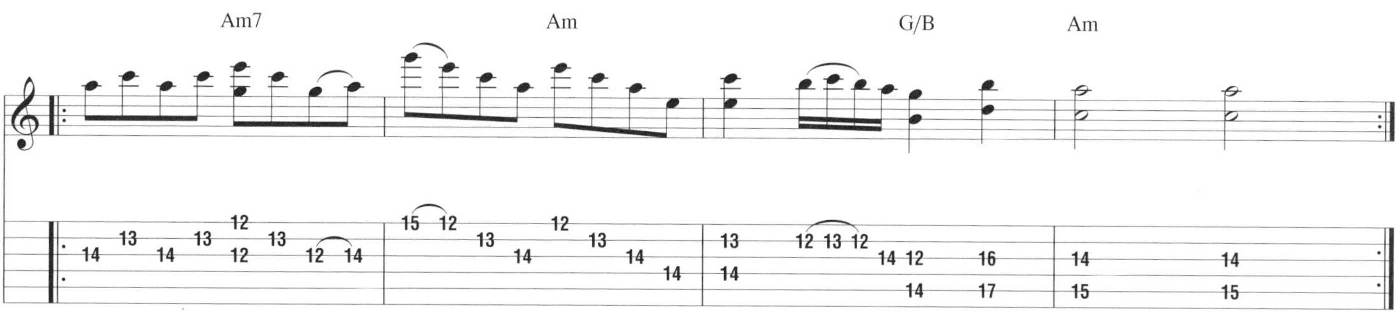

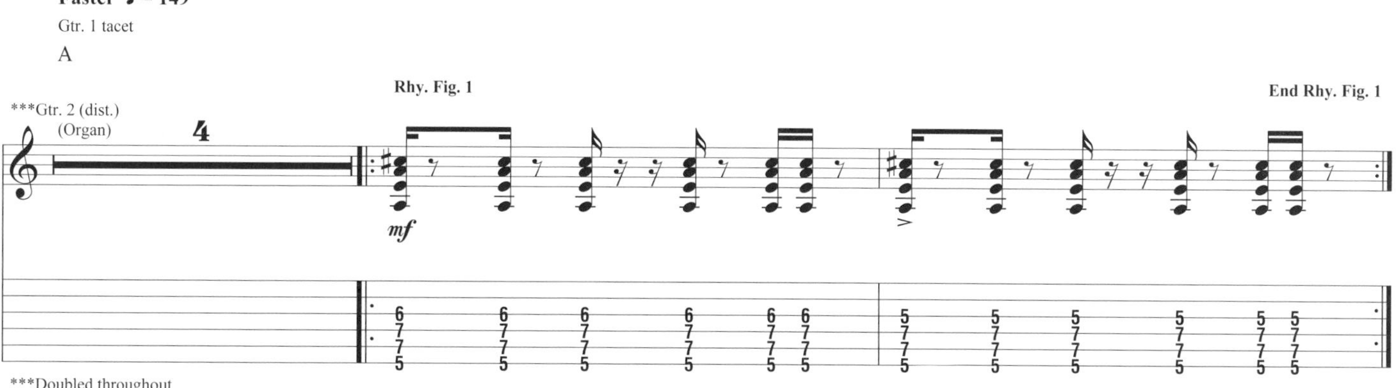

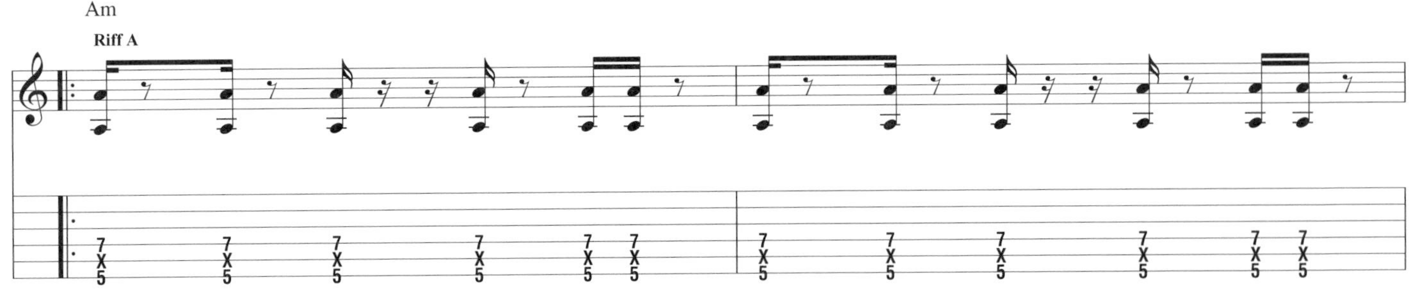
Am
Riff A
7 X 5

Dm/A
F/A
End Riff A

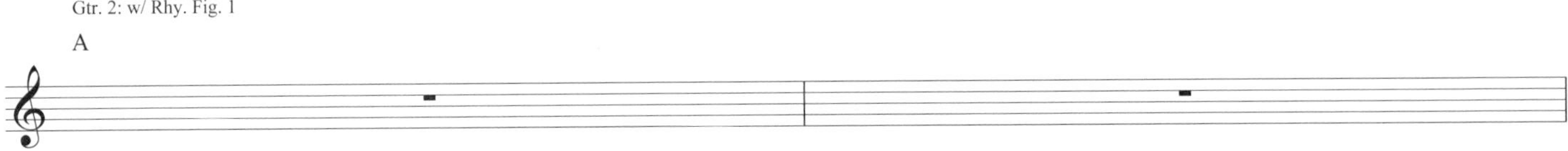
Gtr. 2: w/ Rhy. Fig. 1
A

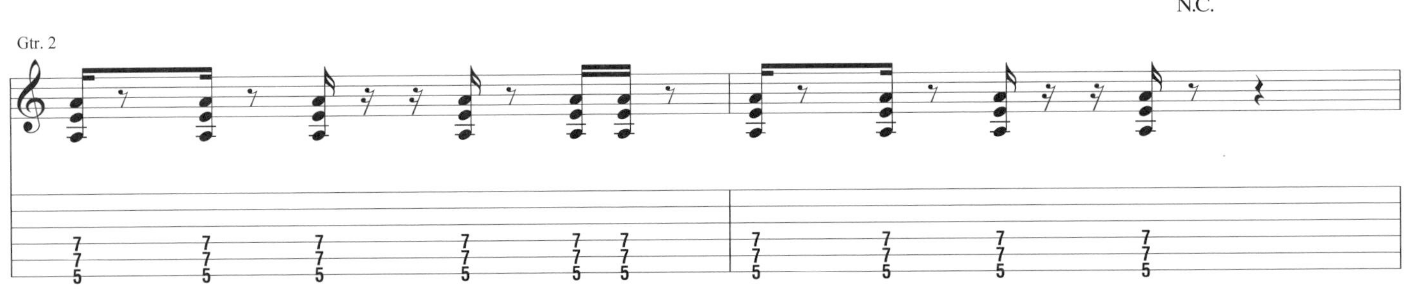
N.C.
Gtr. 2

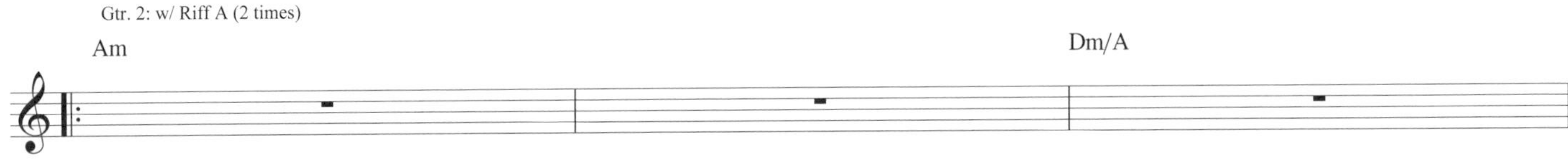
Gtr. 2: w/ Riff A (2 times)
Am
Dm/A

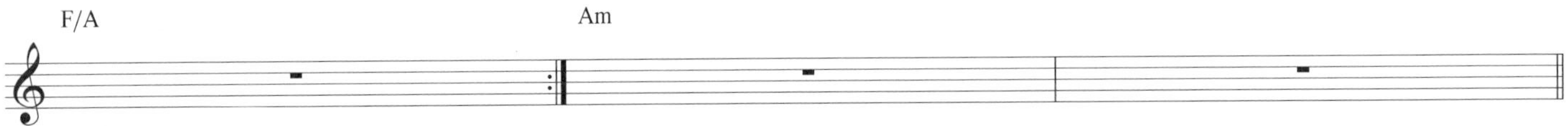
F/A
Am

Verse
A
Am
1. There's a sign in the rain
2. I hear a voice on the air.
Rhy. Fig. 2
Gtr. 2
D
Dm
End Rhy. Fig. 2
Am
ev - 'ry now and a - gain.
It has a warn - ing to share:
Rhy. Fig. 3
D
Dm
End Rhy. Fig. 3

Gtr. 2: w/ Rhy. Fig. 3 (2 times)
Am
D
Dm
It's a sym - bol of hope
"Don't be-lieve what you see.

Am
D
Dm
in the midst of a cat - a-stroph - ic ep - i - sode.
You can't per-ceive what you feel."

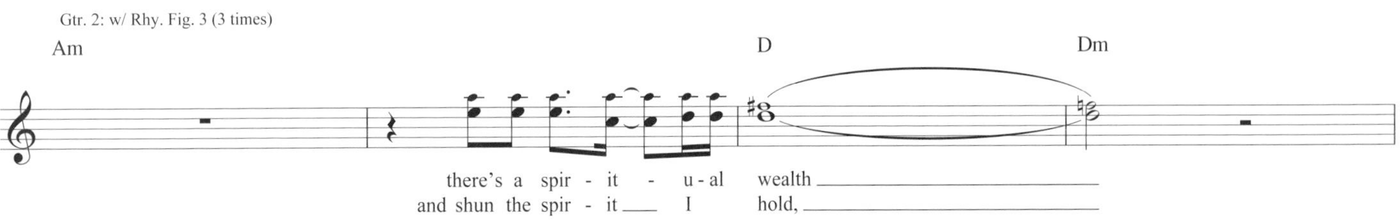
Gtr. 2: w/ Rhy. Fig. 2
A
Am
D
Dm
In the hour of death
But if I do what I'm told

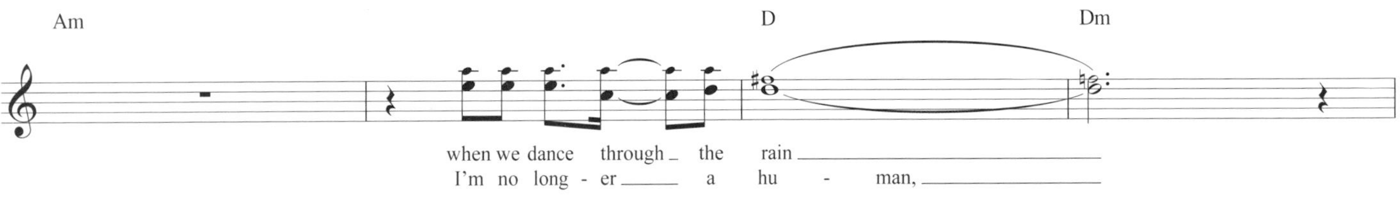
Gtr. 2: w/ Rhy. Fig. 3 (3 times)
Am
D
Dm
there's a spir - it - u - al wealth
and shun the spir - it I hold,

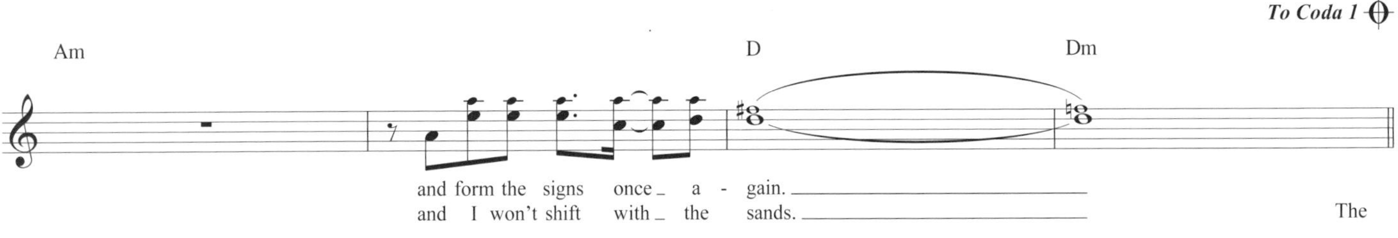
Am
D
Dm
when we dance through the rain
I'm no long - er a hu - man,

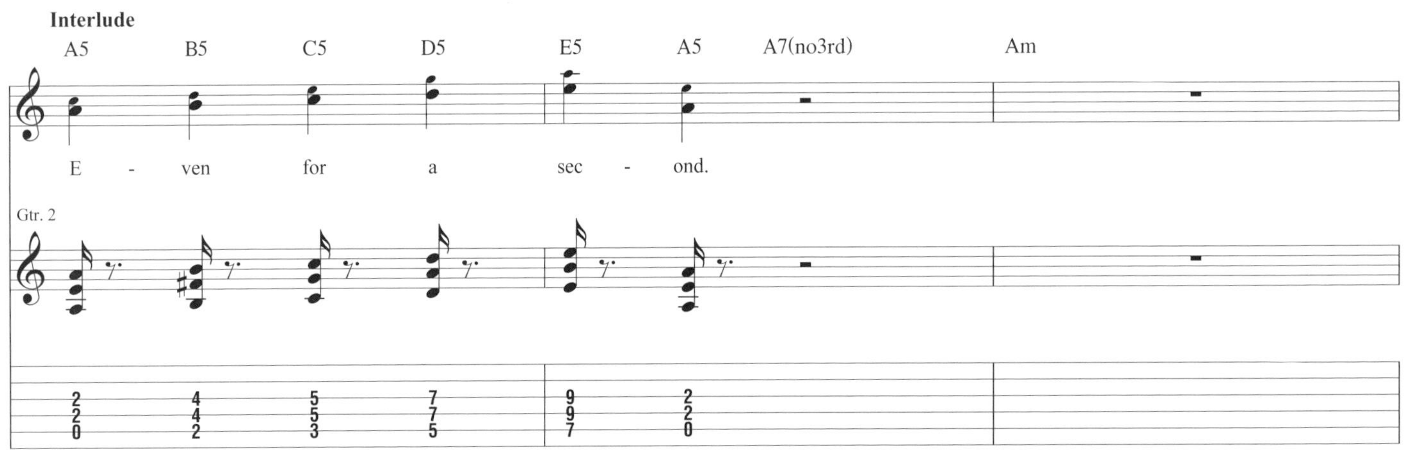
To Coda 1
Am
D
Dm
and form the signs once a - gain.
and I won't shift with the sands.
The
Interlude
A5 B5 C5 D5 E5 A5 A7(no3rd) Am
E - ven for a sec - ond.
Gtr. 2

D.S. al Coda 1

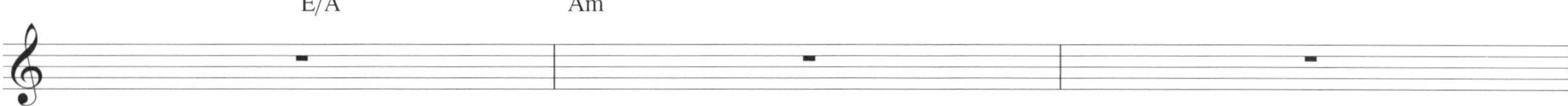

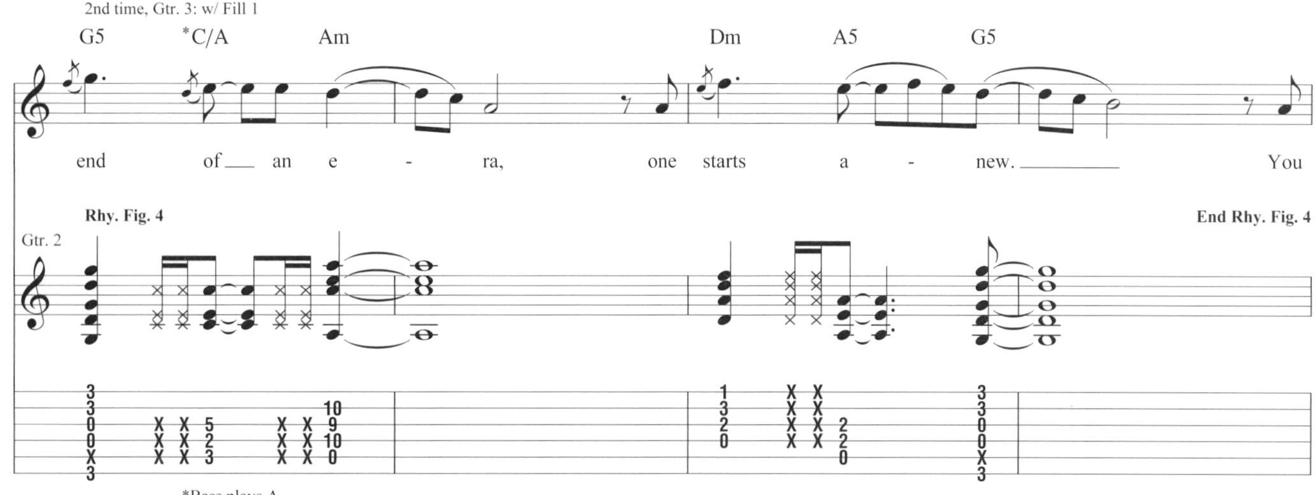

Gtr. 2: w/ Rhy. Fig. 4 (3 times)
2nd time, Gtr. 2: w/ Rhy. Fig. 4 (3 1/2 times)

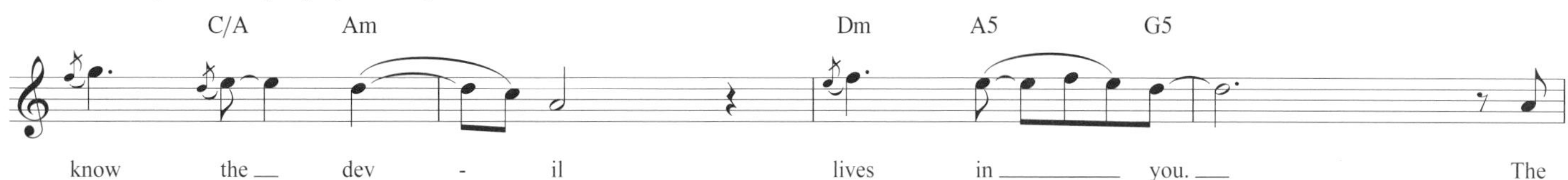

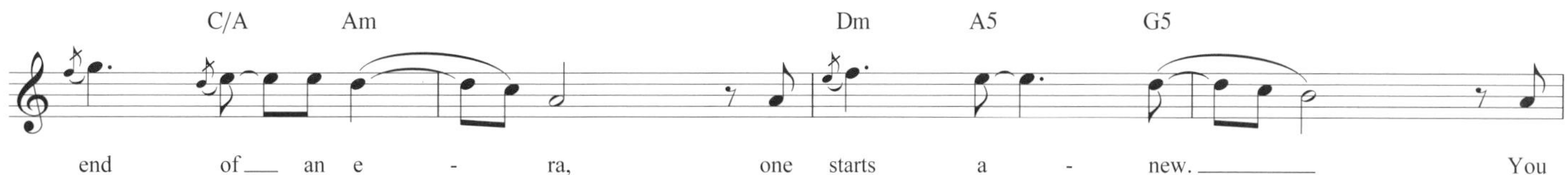

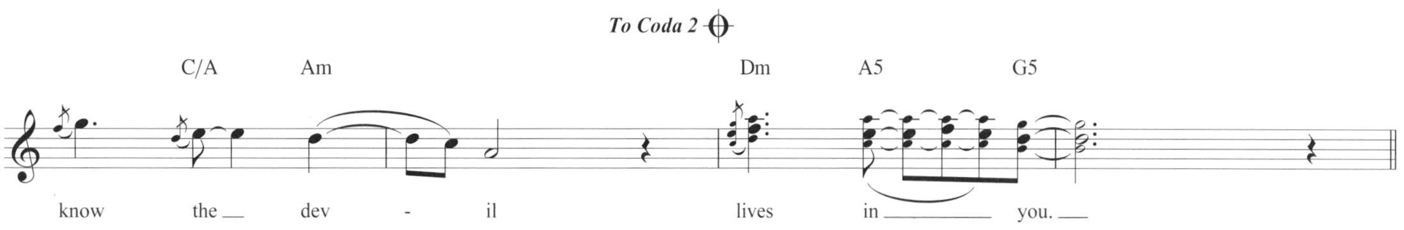

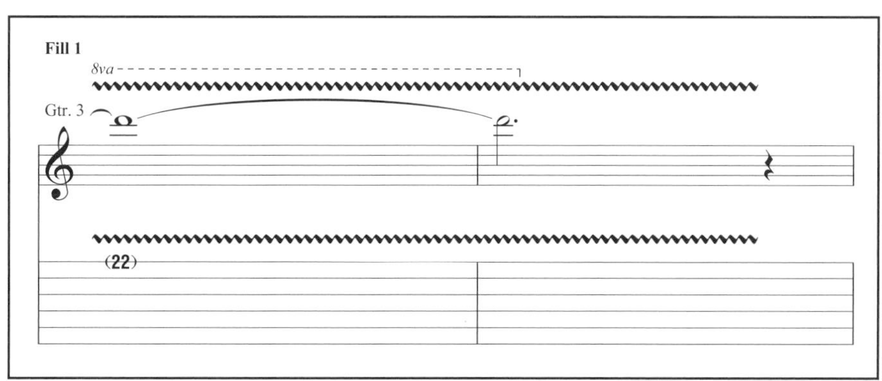

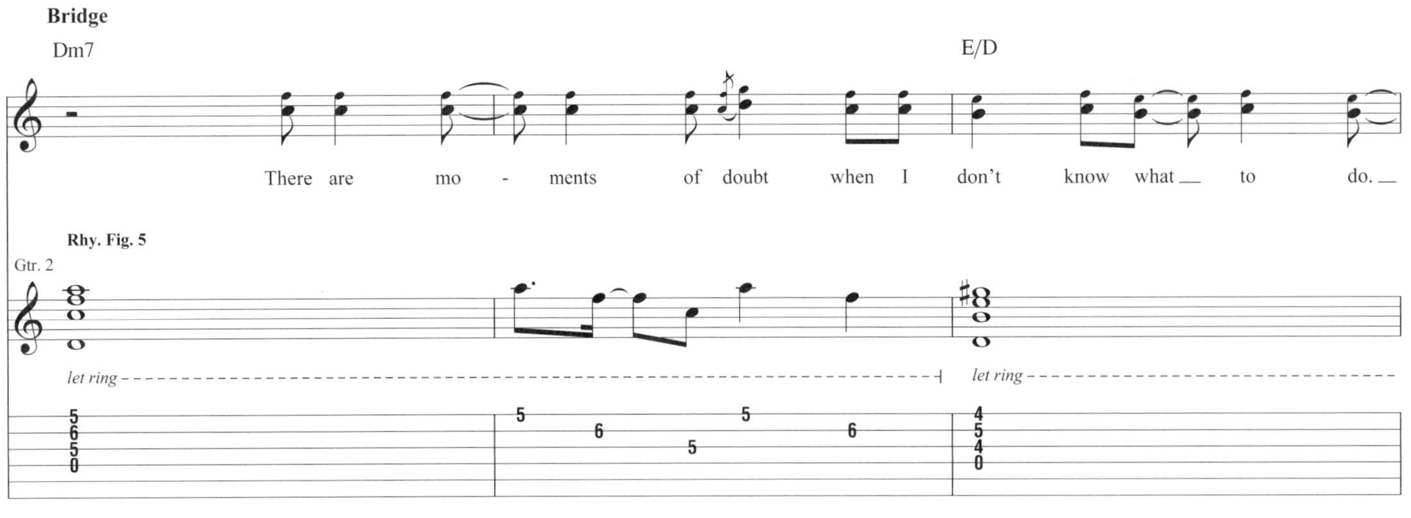
Bridge
Dm7
E/D
There are mo - ments of doubt when I don't know what to do.
Rhy. Fig. 5
Gtr. 2
let ring
let ring

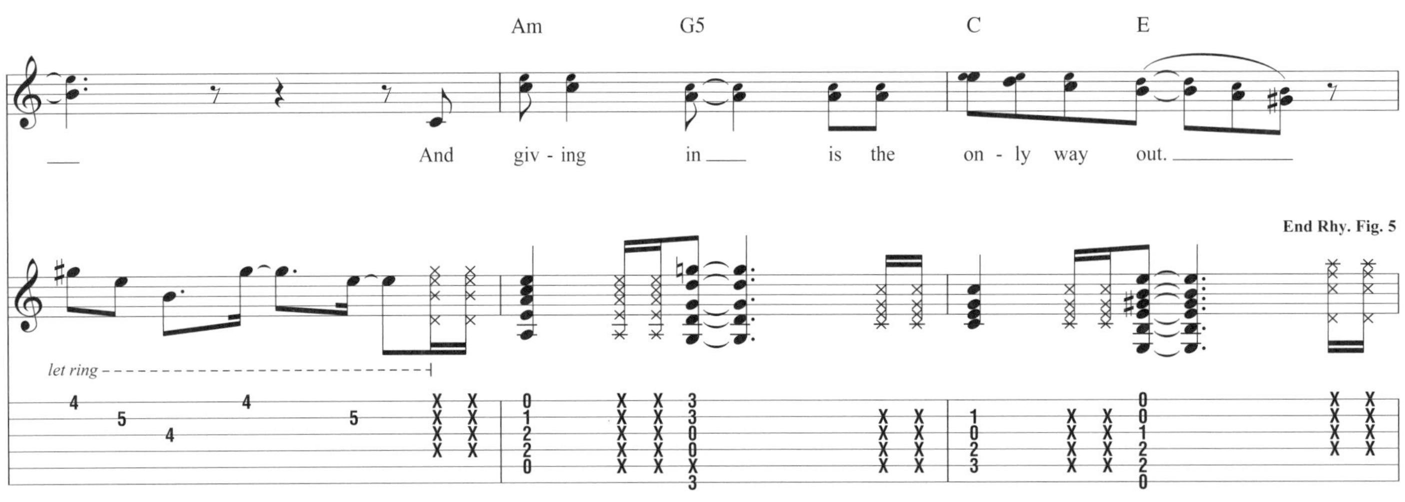
Am
G5
C
E
And giv - ing in is the on - ly way out.
End Rhy. Fig. 5
let ring

Gtr. 2: w/ Rhy. Fig. 5
Dm7
E/D
And when there's too much shout - ing a - bout how I should choose, in - ca -

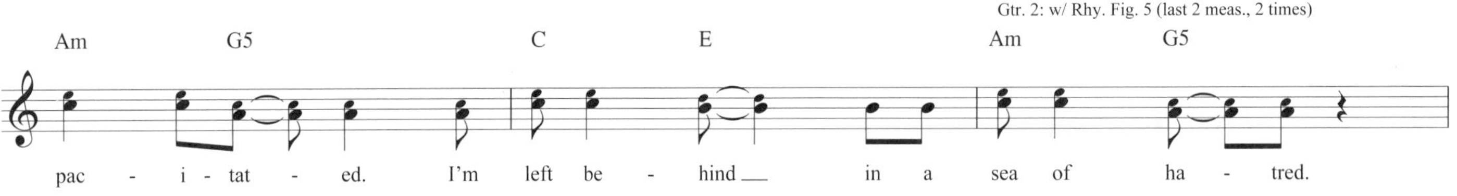
Gtr. 2: w/ Rhy. Fig. 5 (last 2 meas., 2 times)
Am
G5
C
E
Am
G5
pac - i - tat - ed. I'm left be - hind in a sea of ha - tred.

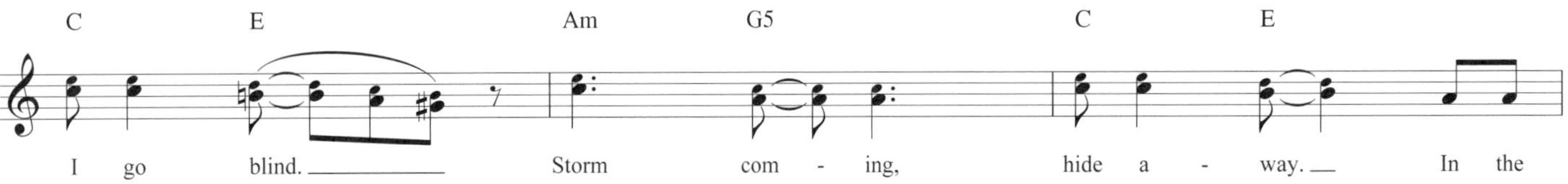
C
E
Am
G5
C
E
I go blind. Storm com - ing, hide a - way. In the

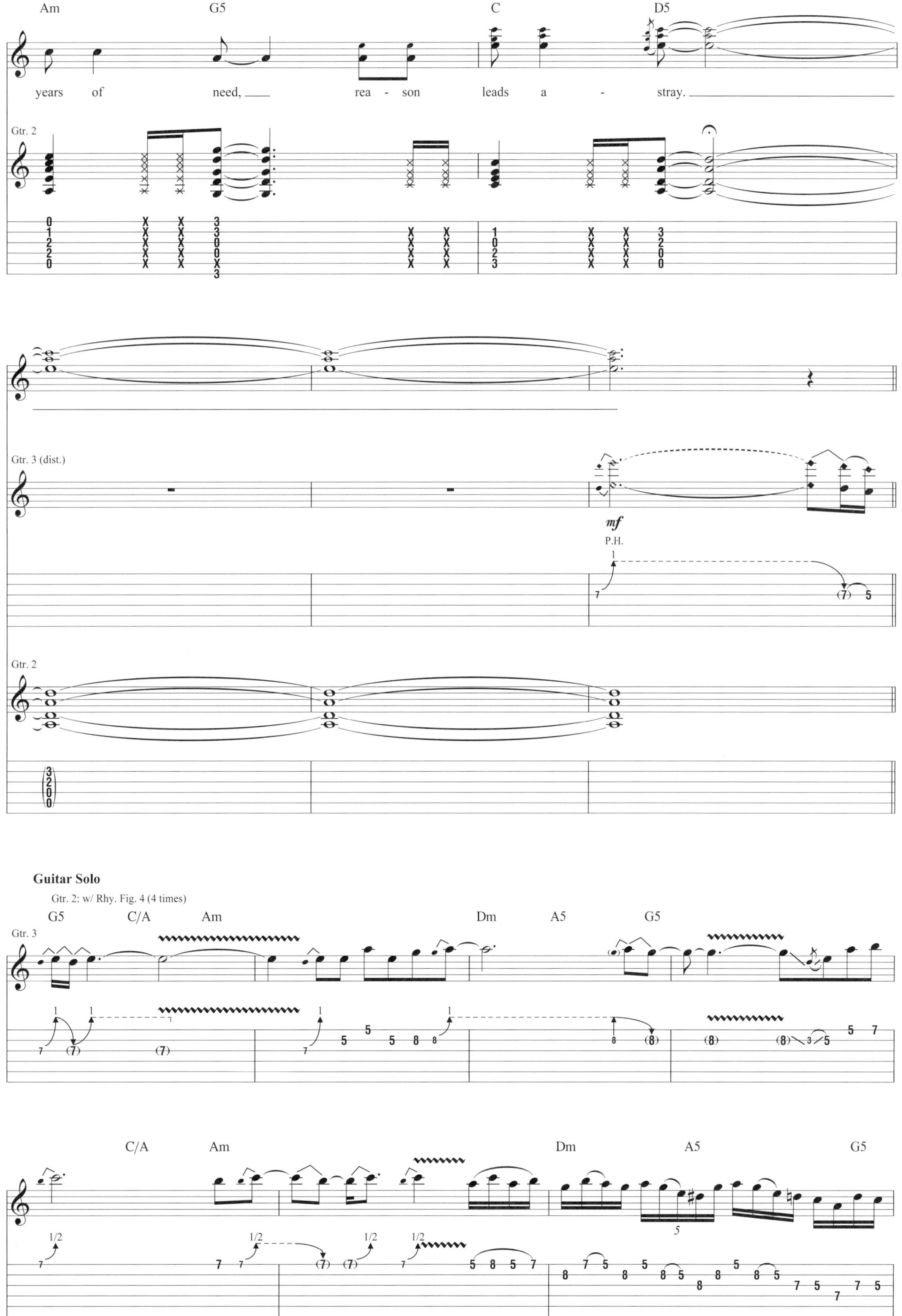
Am
G5
C
D5
years of need, rea - son leads a - stray.
Gtr. 2
Gtr. 3 (dist.)
mf
P.H.
Gtr. 2
Guitar Solo
Gtr. 2: w/ Rhy. Fig. 4 (4 times)
G5
C/A
Am
Dm
A5
G5
Gtr. 3
C/A
Am
Dm
A5
G5

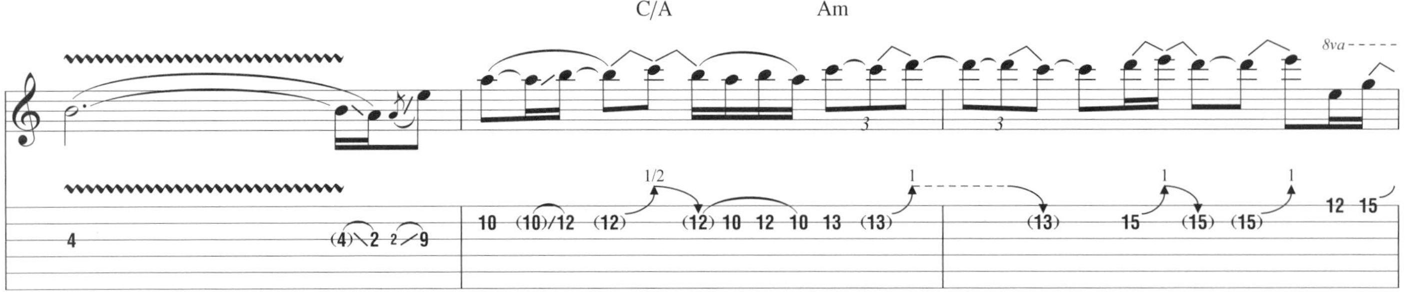
C/A
Am
8va

Dm
A5
G5
C/A
Am
8va
loco

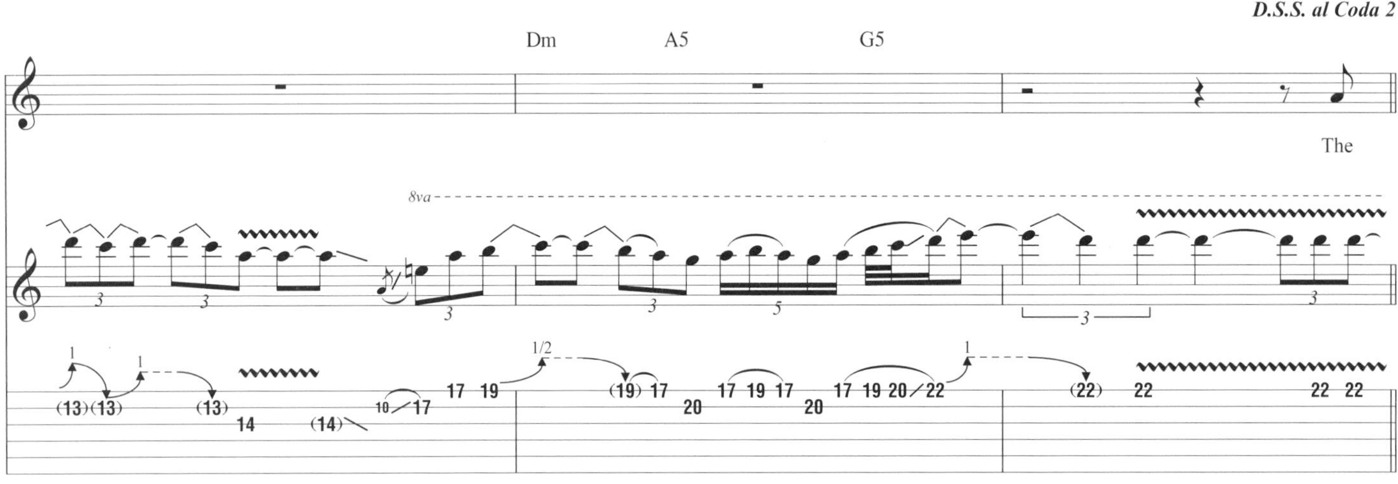
D.S.S. al Coda 2
Dm
A5
G5
The
8va

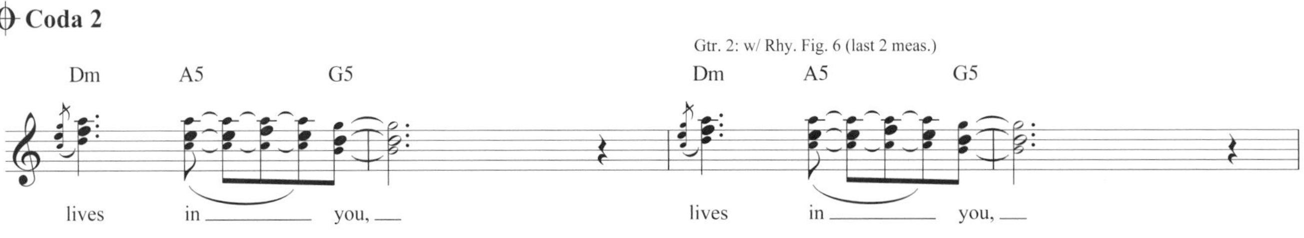
Coda 2
Gtr. 2: w/ Rhy. Fig. 6 (last 2 meas.)
Dm
A5
G5
lives
in
you,
Dm
A5
G5
lives
in
you,

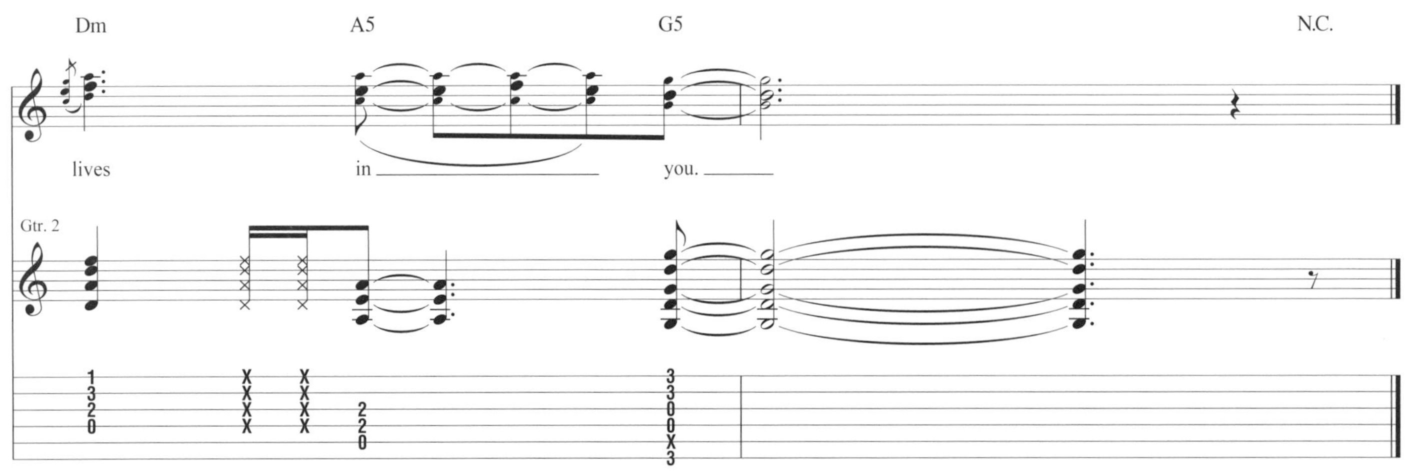
Dm
A5
G5
N.C.
lives
in
you.
Gtr. 2

from *Ghost Reveries*

Ghost of Perdition

Words and Music by Mikael Akerfeldt

Open Dm(add9) tuning:
(low to high) D-A-D-F-A-E

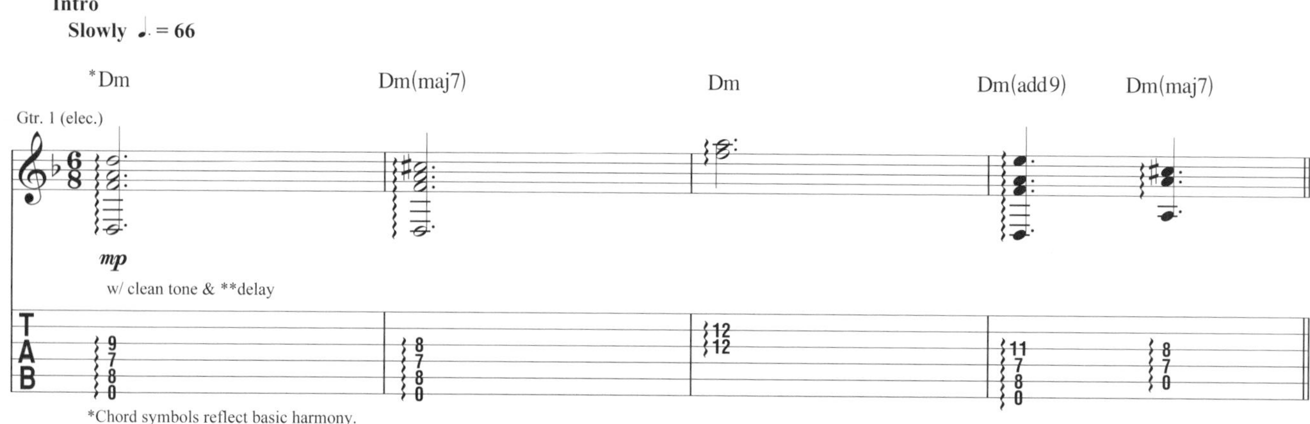

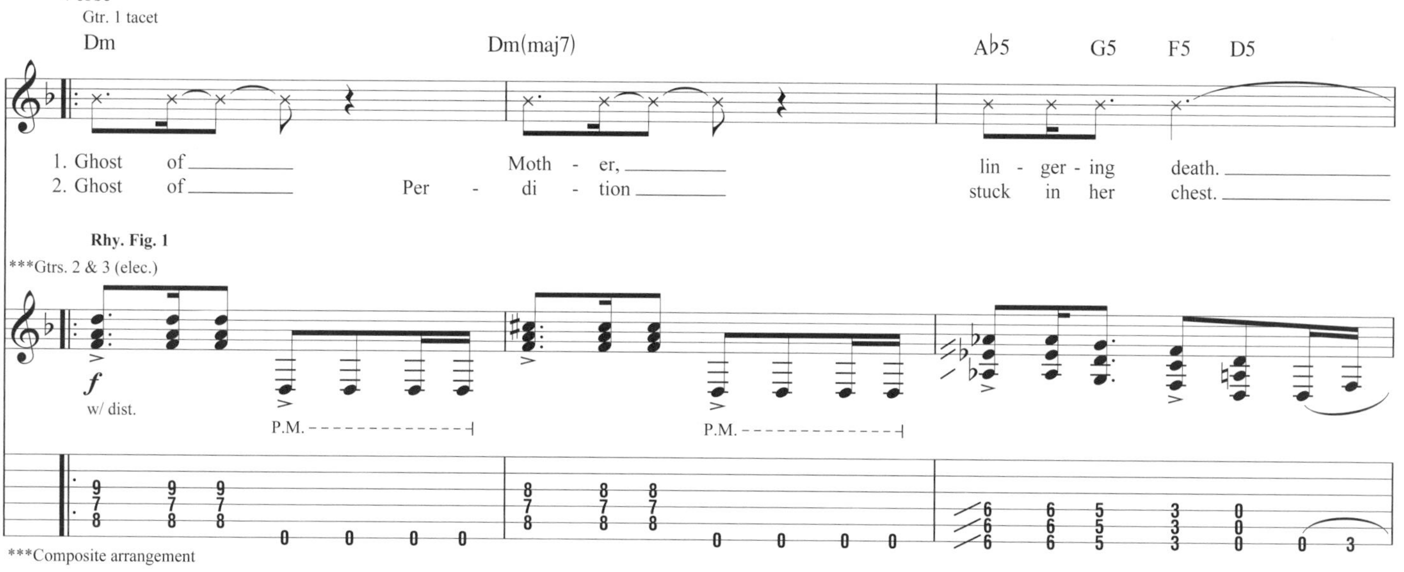

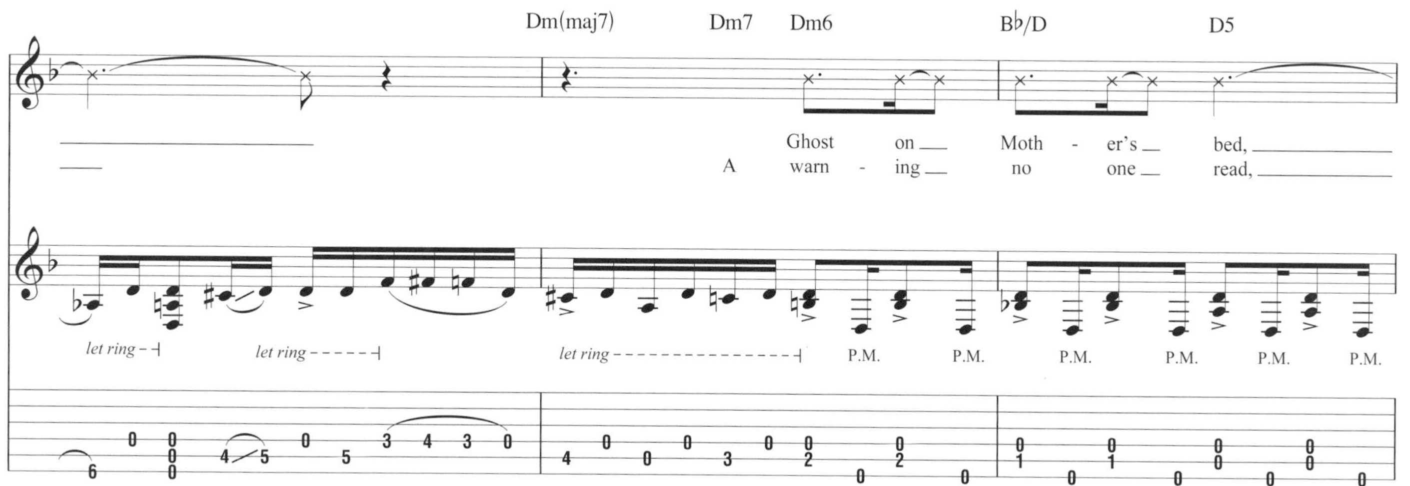

G5
D5
Dm
black strands on the
trag - ic
P.M.
P.M.
P.M.
P.M.

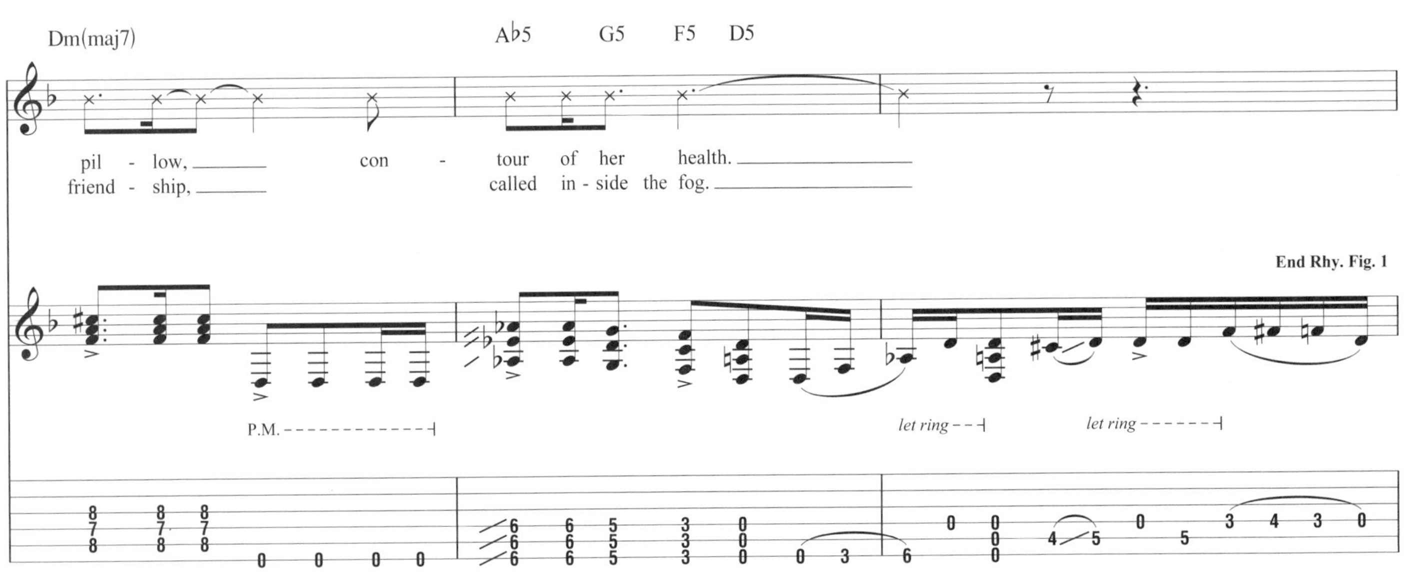
Dm(maj7)
A♭5 G5 F5 D5
pil - low, con - tour of her health.
friend - ship, called in - side the fog.
End Rhy. Fig. 1
P.M.
let ring
let ring

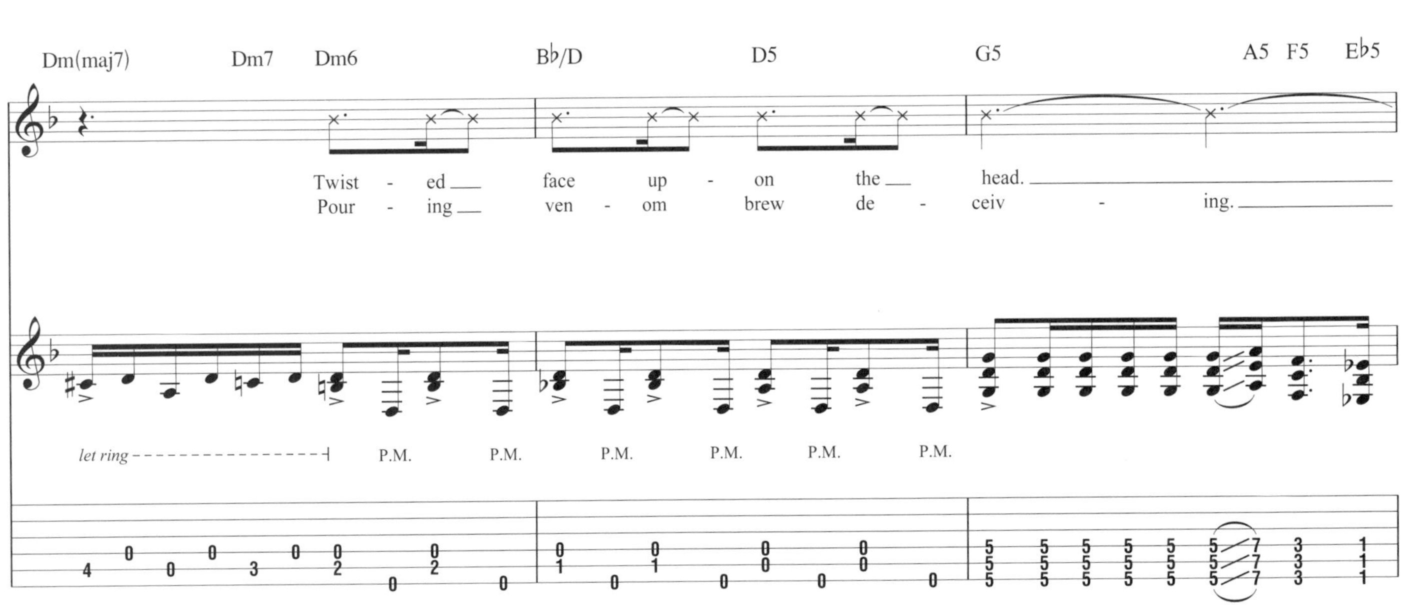
Dm(maj7) Dm7 Dm6
B♭/D
D5
G5
A5 F5 E♭5
Twist - ed face up - on the head.
Pour - ing ven - om brew de - ceiv - ing.
let ring
P.M. P.M. P.M. P.M. P.M. P.M.

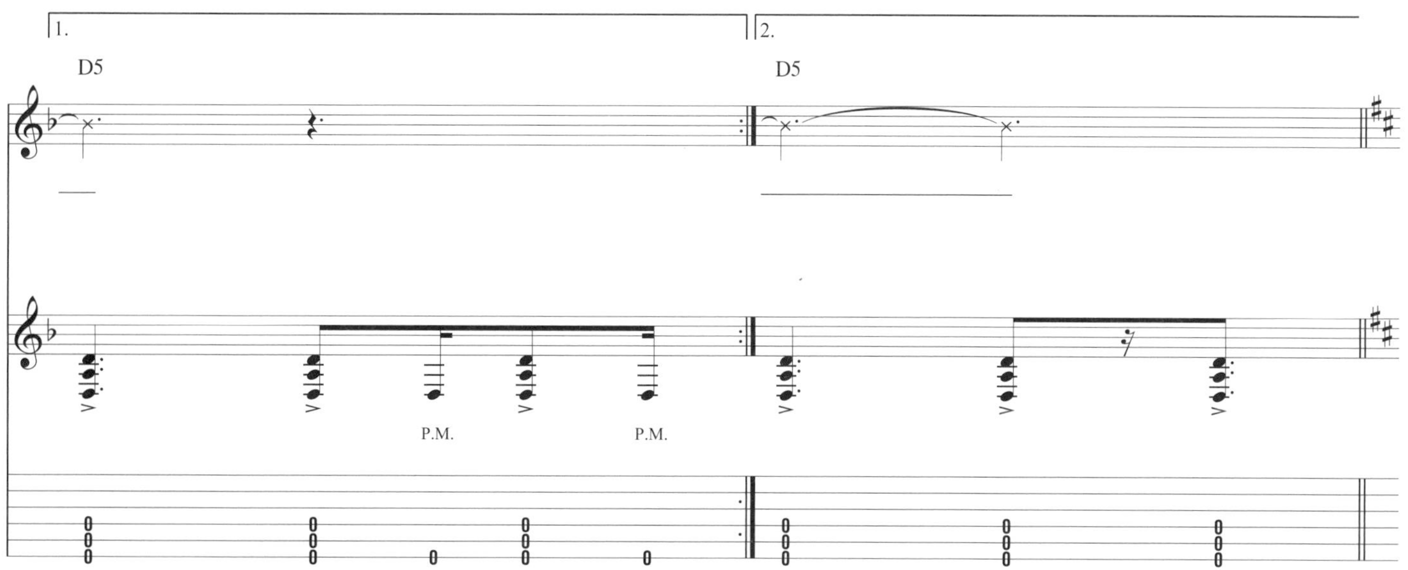

Interlude

Gtr. 2 tacet

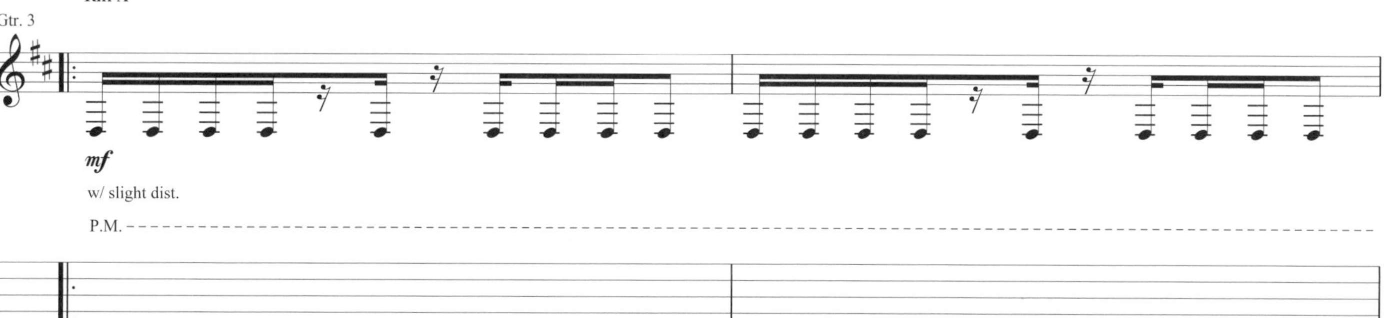

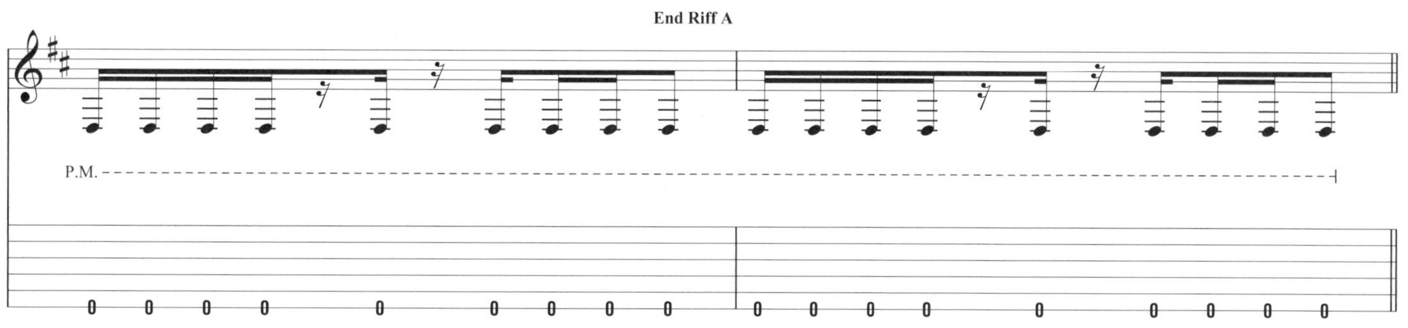

Bridge

Gtr. 3: w/ Riff A

*Bkgd. Vocs. sung 2nd time.

Interlude

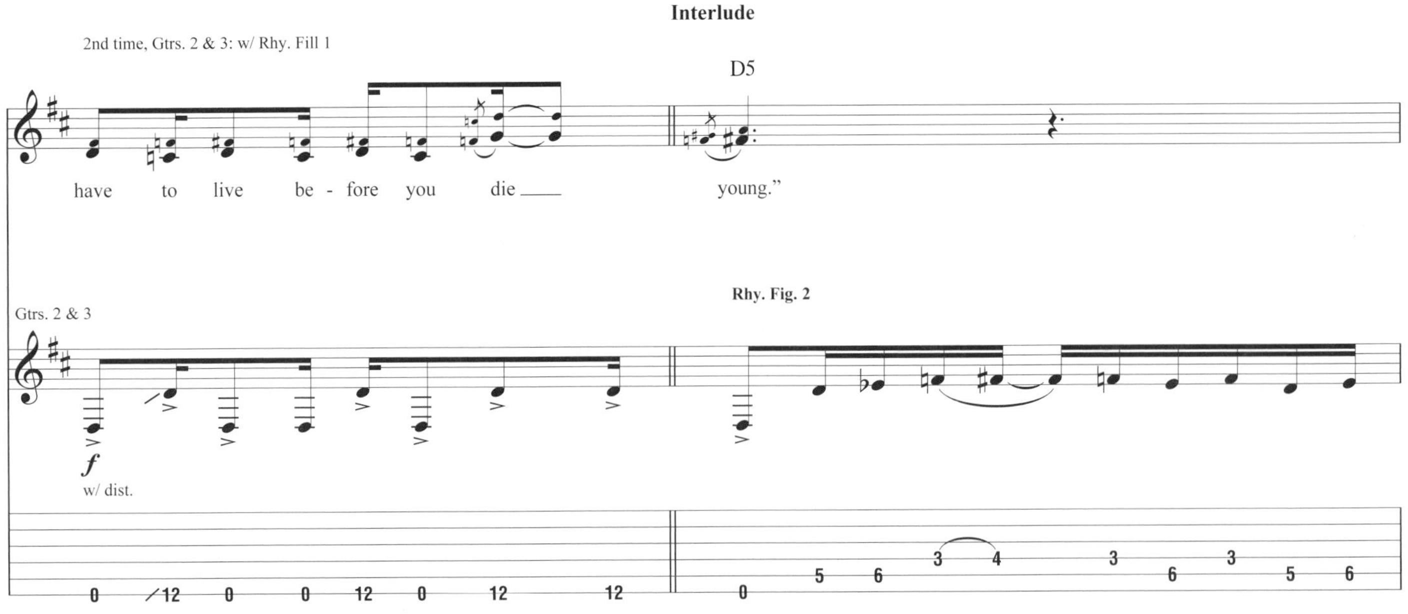
2nd time, Gtrs. 2 & 3: w/ Rhy. Fill 1
D5
have to live be - fore you die
young."
Rhy. Fig. 2
Gtrs. 2 & 3
w/ dist.

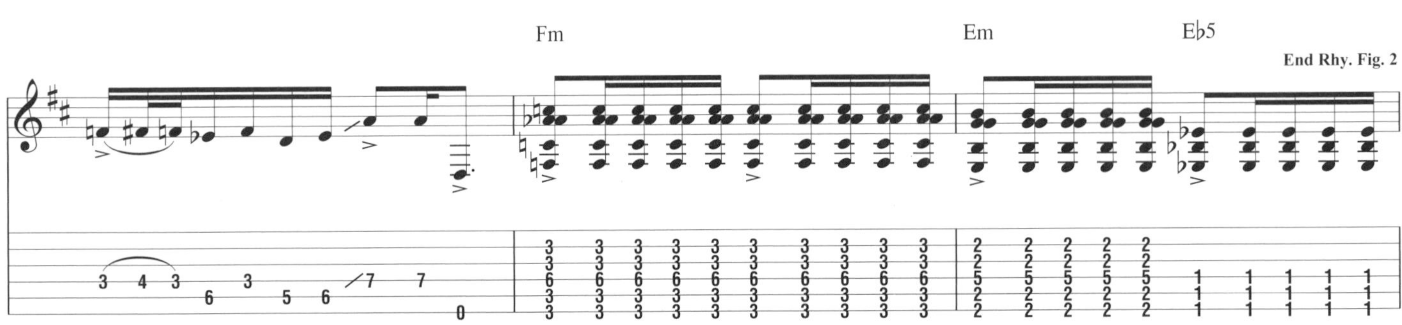
Fm
Em
E♭5
End Rhy. Fig. 2

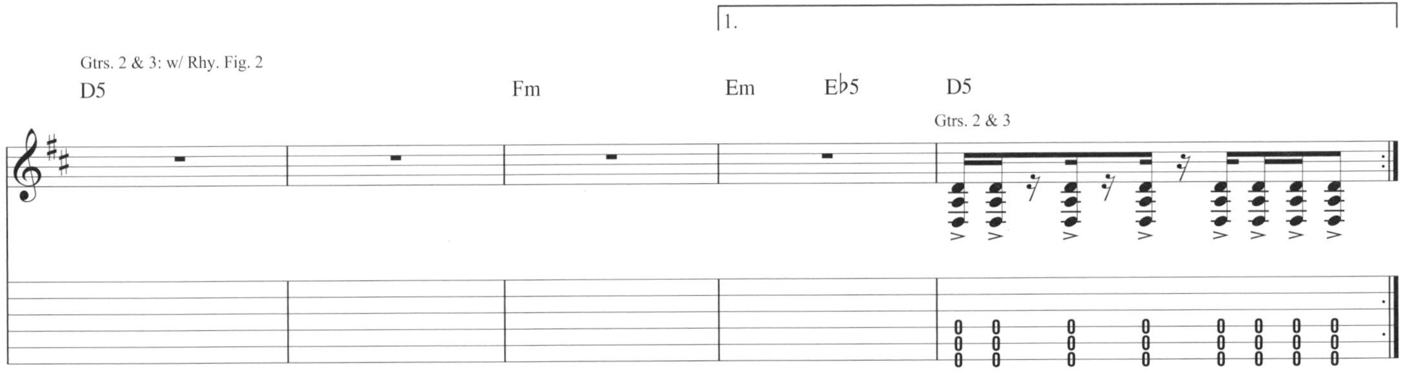
1.
Gtrs. 2 & 3: w/ Rhy. Fig. 2
D5
Fm
Em
E♭5
D5
Gtrs. 2 & 3

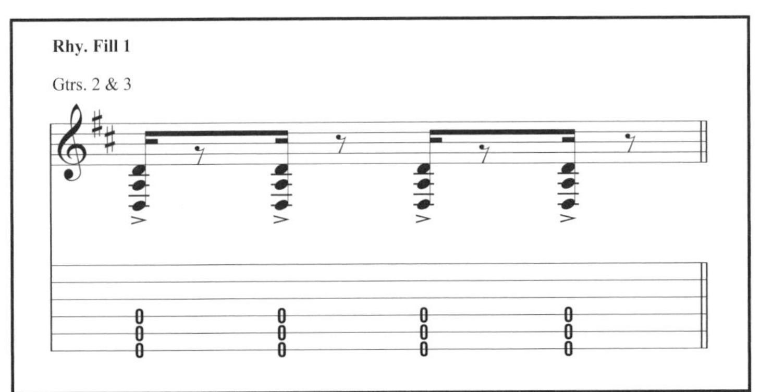
Rhy. Fill 1
Gtrs. 2 & 3

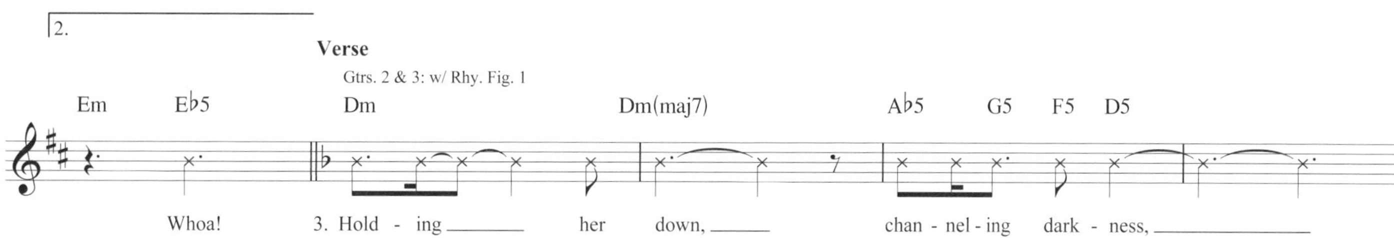
2.
Verse
Gtrs. 2 & 3: w/ Rhy. Fig. 1
Em Eb5 Dm Dm(maj7) Ab5 G5 F5 D5
Whoa! 3. Hold - ing her down, chan - nel - ing dark - ness,

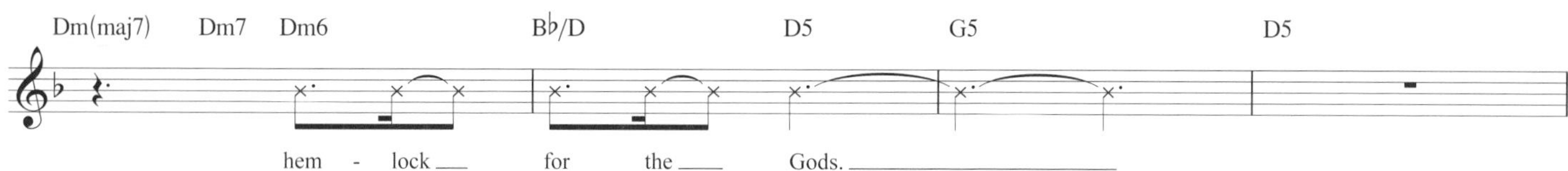
Dm(maj7) Dm7 Dm6 Bb/D D5 G5 D5
hem - lock for the Gods.

Dm Dm(maj7) Ab5 G5 F5 D5
Fad - ing re - sis - tance, drain - ing the weak - ness,

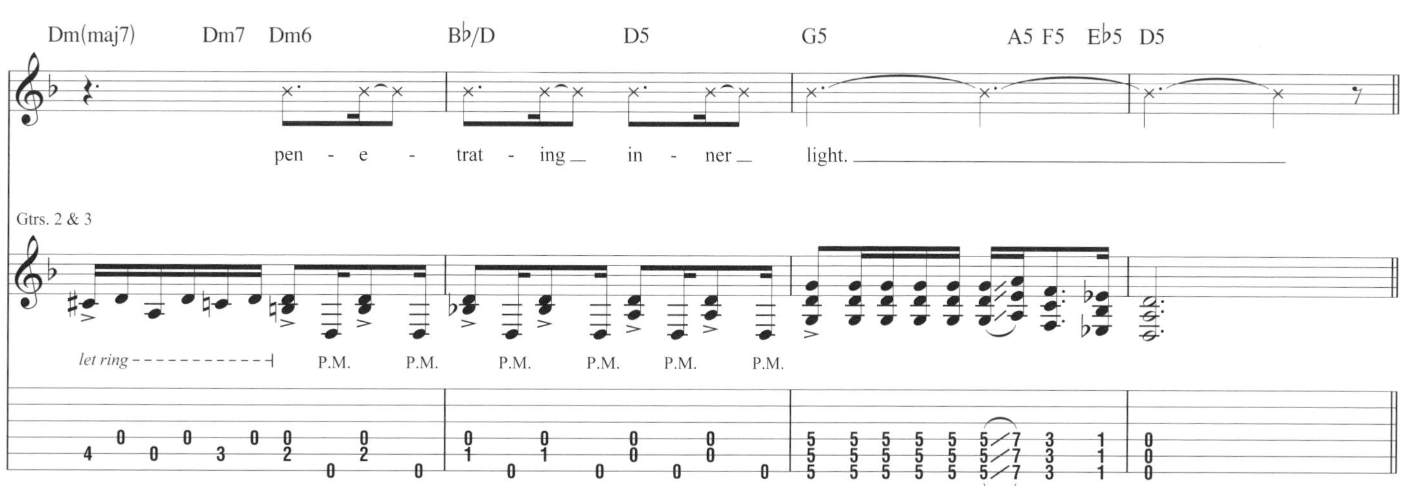
Dm(maj7) Dm7 Dm6 Bb/D D5 G5 A5 F5 Eb5 D5
pen - e - trat - ing in - ner light.
Gtrs. 2 & 3
let ring
P.M.

Bridge
Gtrs. 2 & 3 tacet
Dm(add9) F#m(add9) Dm6/9
Road in - to the dark, un - a - ware,
Gtr. 4 (acous.)
mp
Harm.
let ring throughout

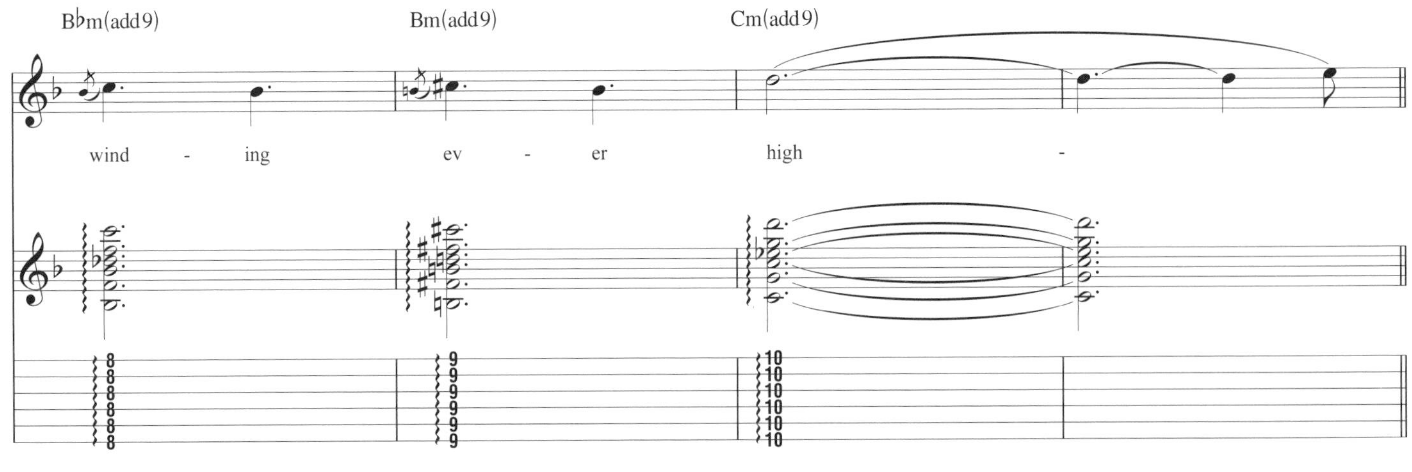
B♭m(add9)
Bm(add9)
Cm(add9)
wind - ing ev - er high -
8 8 8 8 8 8 8
9 9 9 9 9 9 9
10 10 10 10 10 10 10

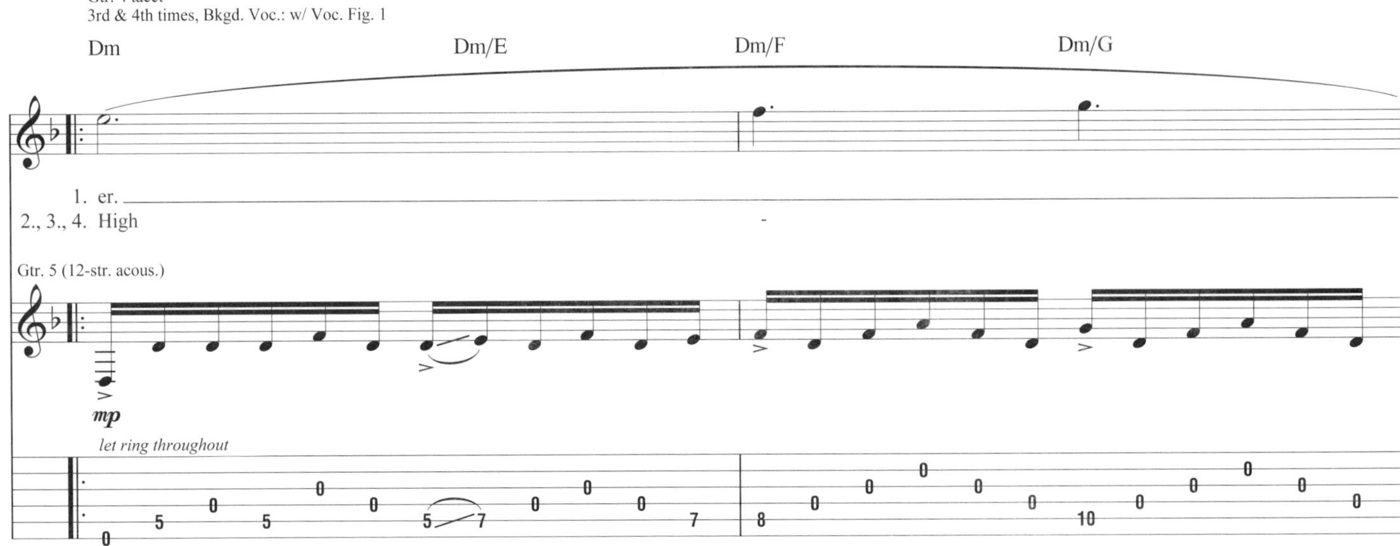
Gtr. 4 tacet
3rd & 4th times, Bkgd. Voc.: w/ Voc. Fig. 1
Dm
Dm/E
Dm/F
Dm/G
1. er.
2., 3., 4. High -
Gtr. 5 (12-str. acous.)
mp
let ring throughout

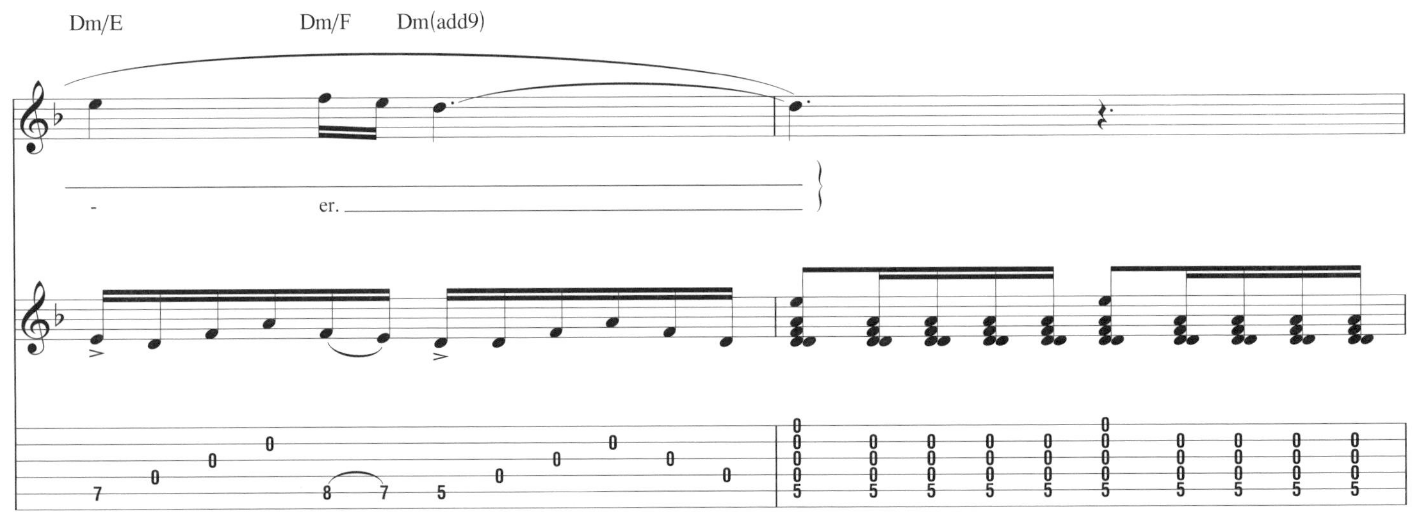
Dm/E
Dm/F
Dm(add9)
- er.

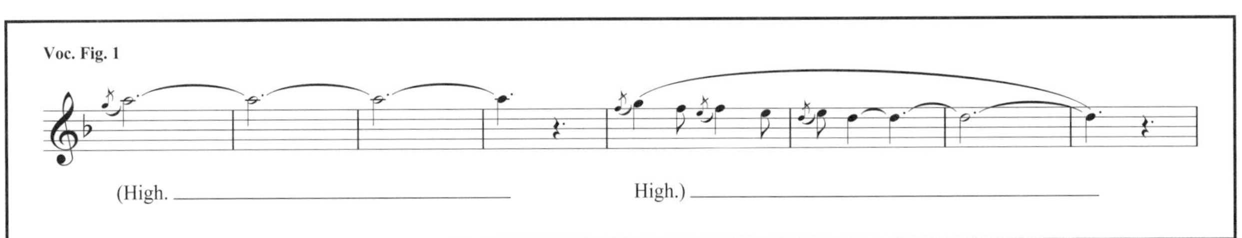
Voc. Fig. 1
(High.
High.)

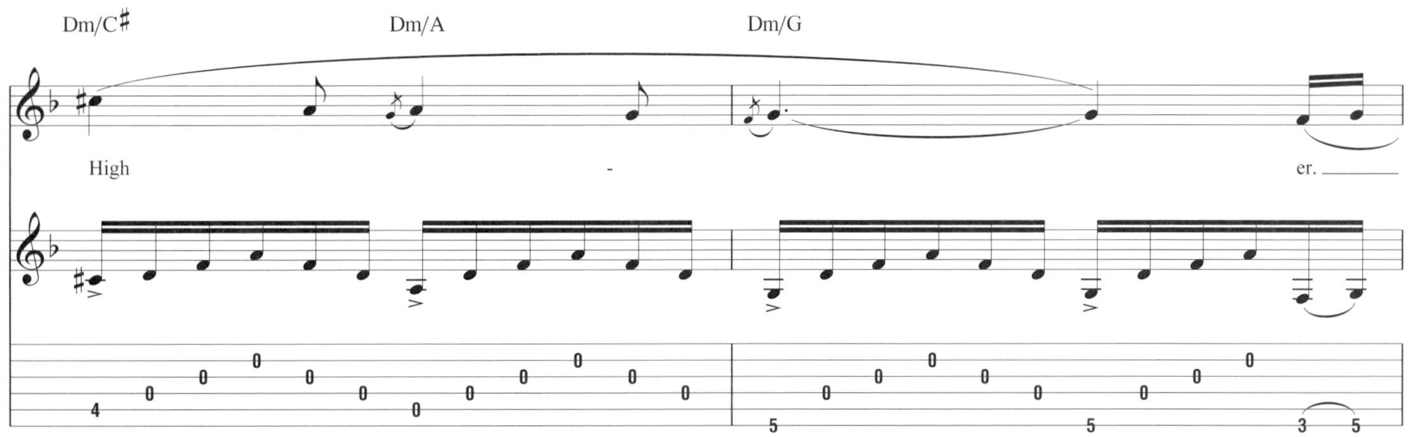

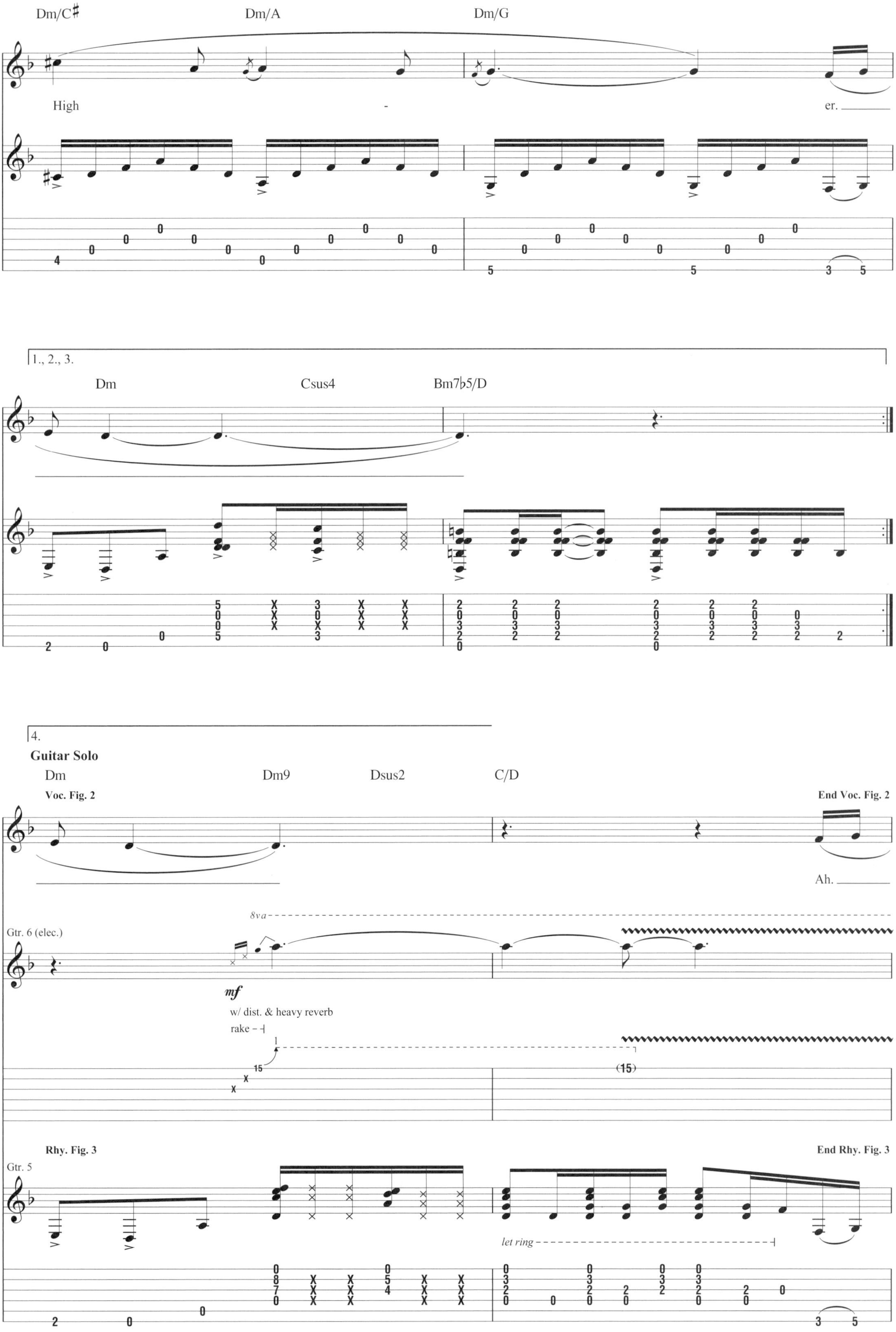

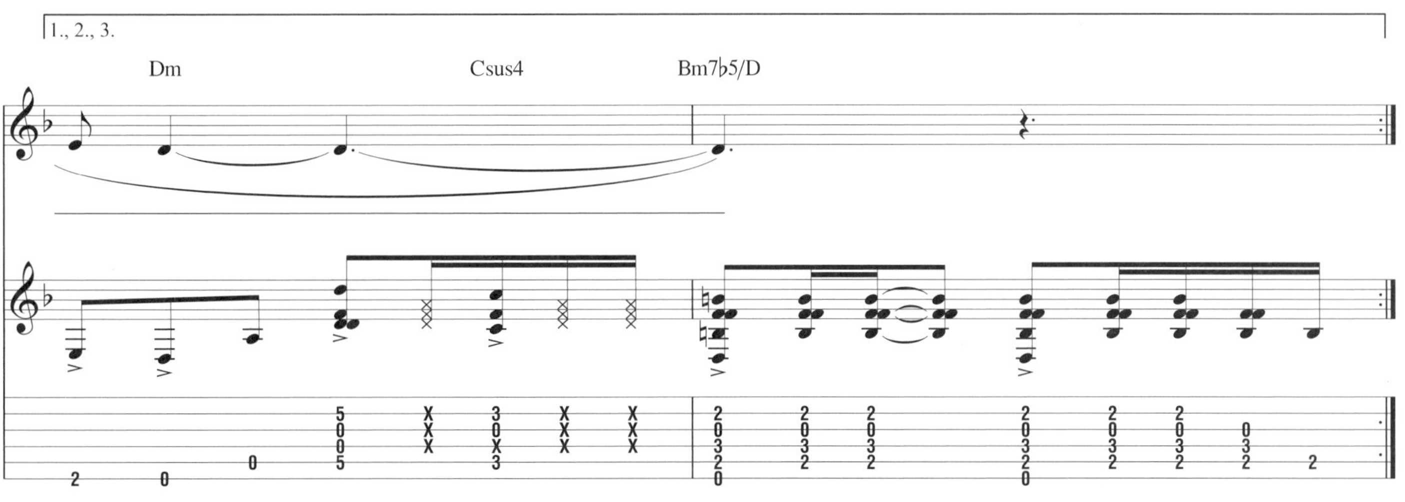

4.

Guitar Solo

Dm Dm9 Dsus2 C/D

Voc. Fig. 2

End Voc. Fig. 2

Ah.

Gtr. 6 (elec.)

8va

mf

w/ dist. & heavy reverb

rake

Rhy. Fig. 3

End Rhy. Fig. 3

Gtr. 5

let ring

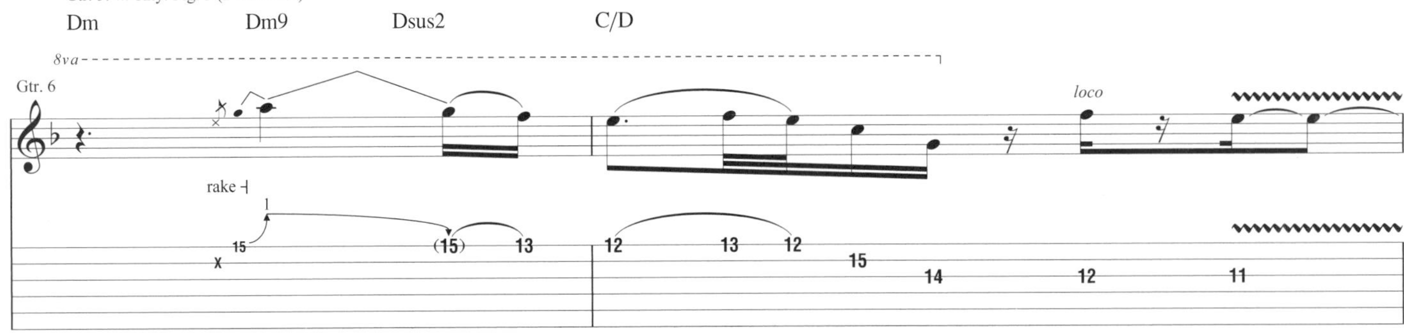

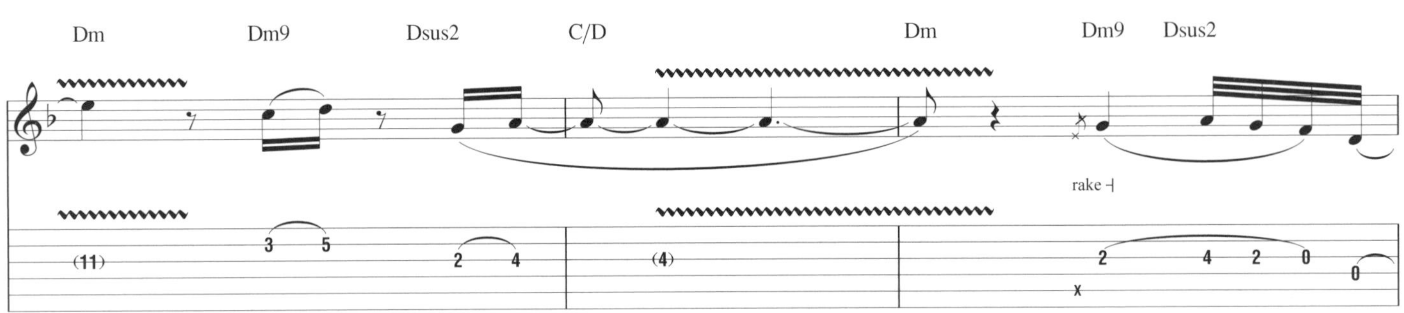

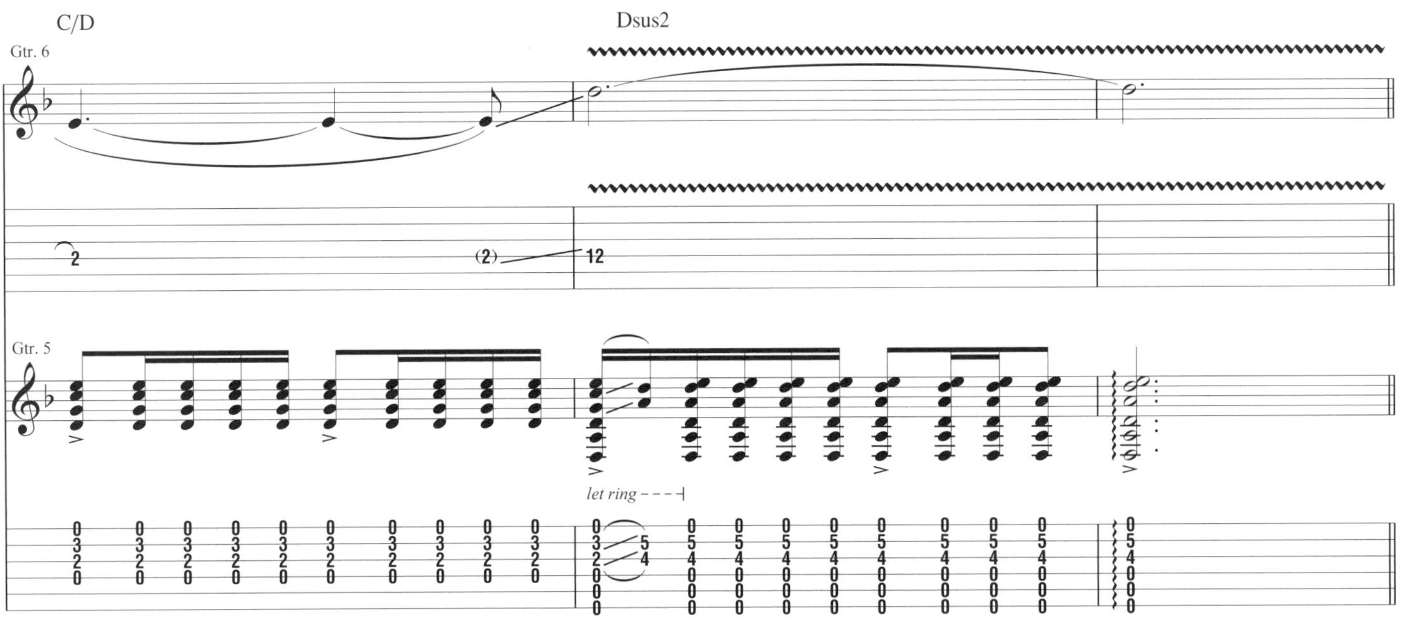

Interlude

Gtrs. 5 & 6 tacet

D5

Gtrs. 2 & 3

Play 7 times

P.M.

P.M.

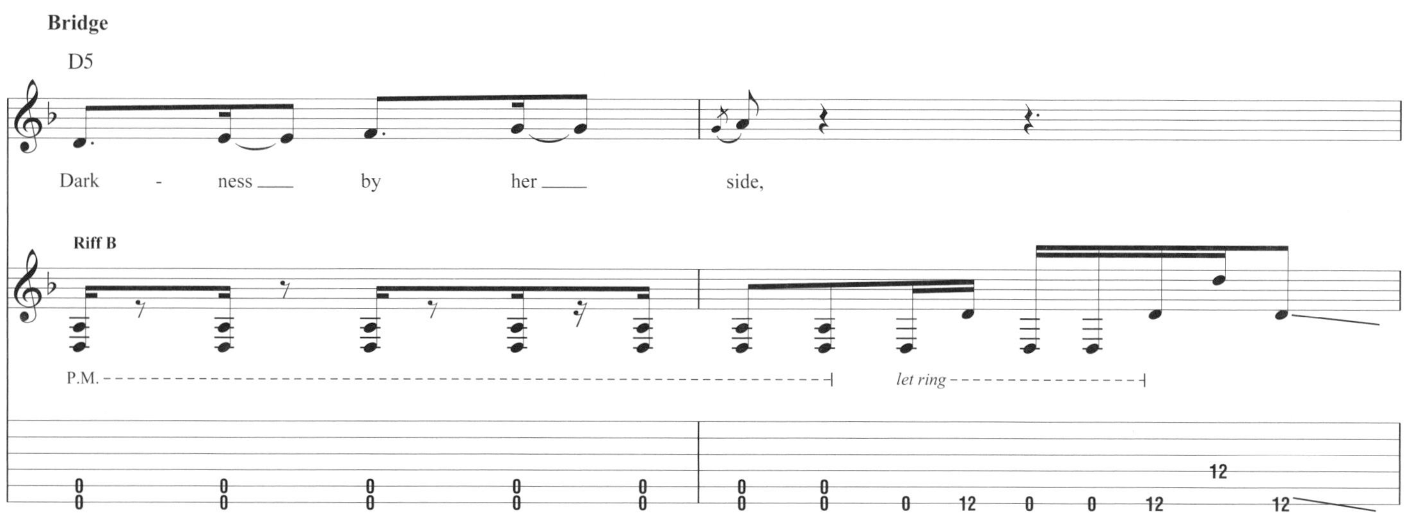
Bridge
D5
Dark - ness by her side,
Riff B
P.M.
let ring

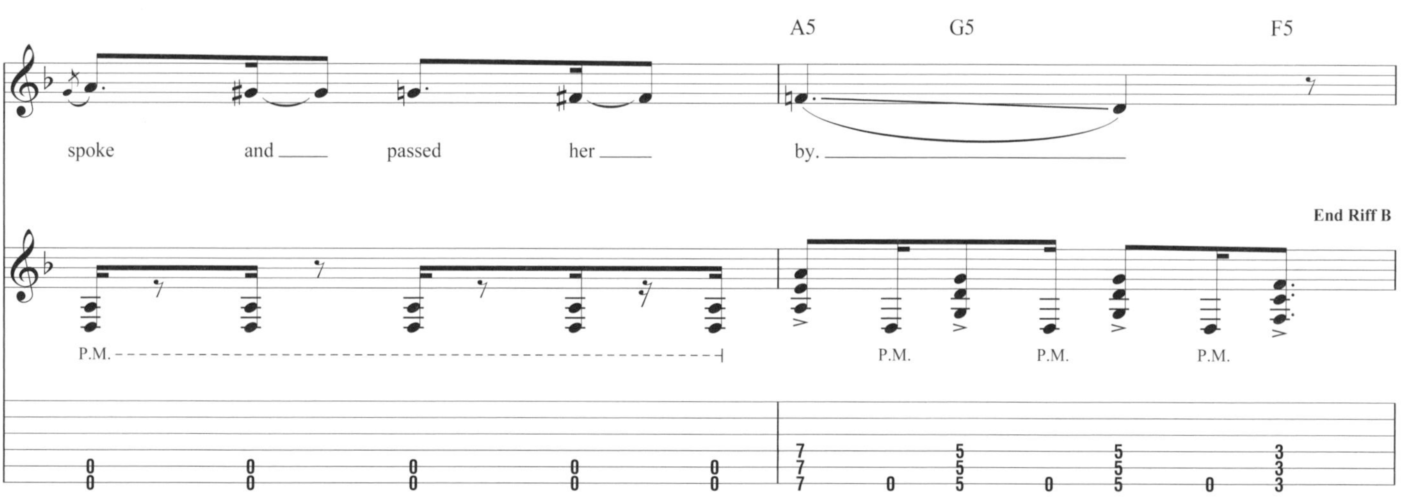
A5 G5 F5
spoke and passed her by.
End Riff B
P.M.
P.M. P.M. P.M.

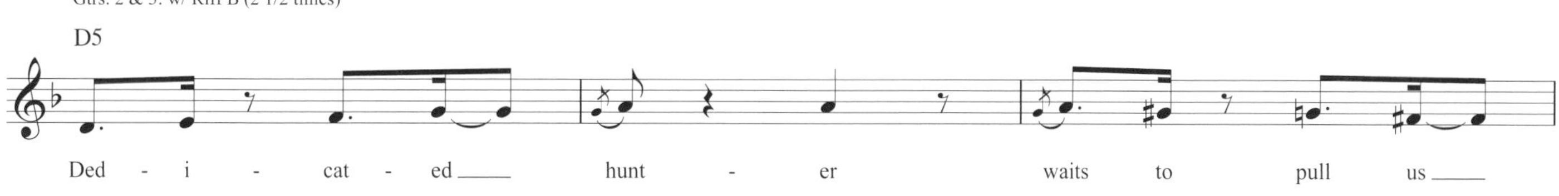
Gtrs. 2 & 3: w/ Riff B (2 1/2 times)
D5
Ded - i - cat - ed hunt - er waits to pull us

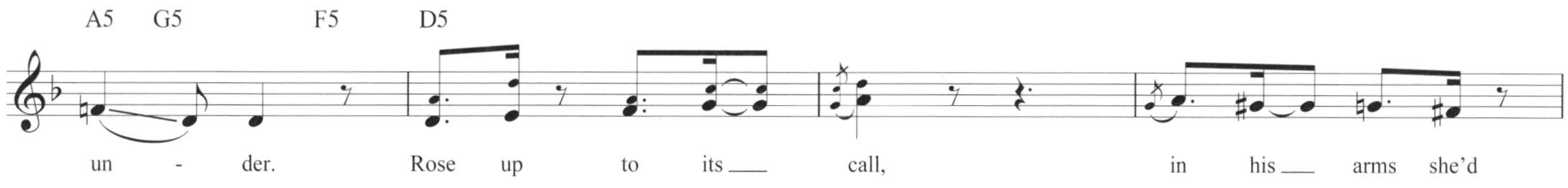
A5 G5 F5 D5
un - der. Rose up to its call, in his arms she'd

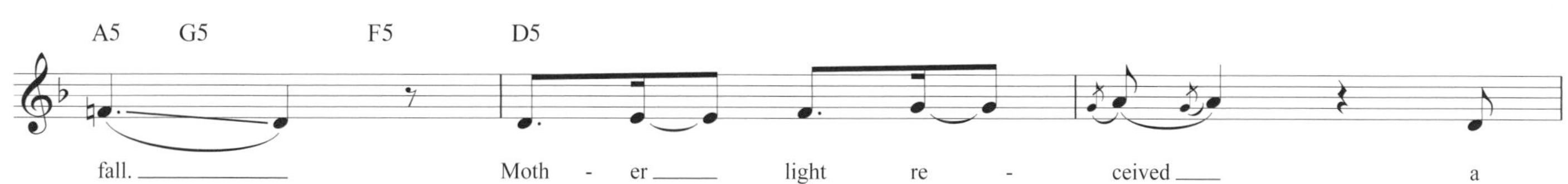
A5 G5 F5 D5
fall. Moth - er light re - ceived a

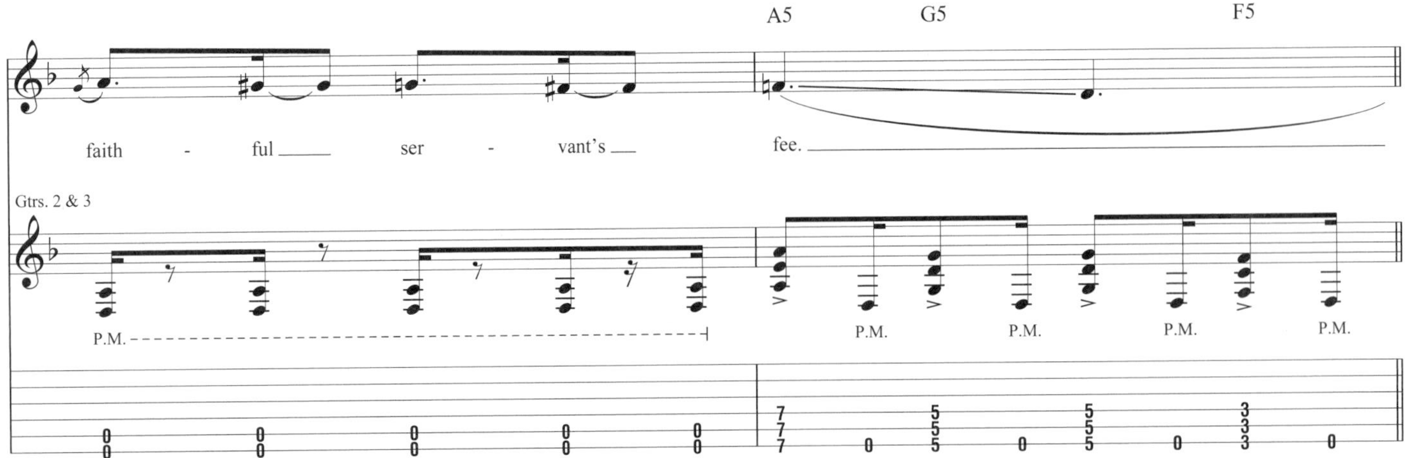
A5
G5
F5
faith - ful ser - vant's fee.
Gtrs. 2 & 3
P.M.

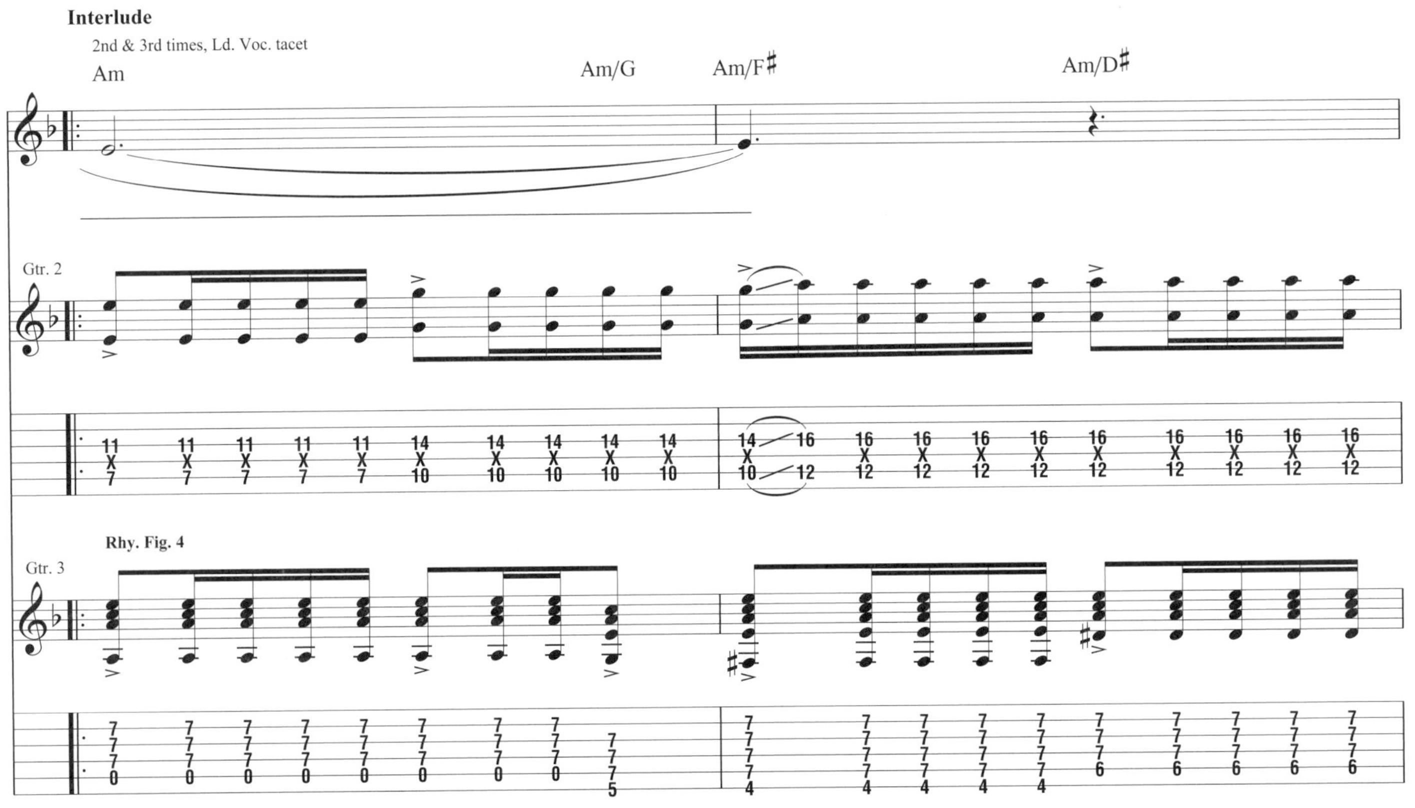
Interlude
2nd & 3rd times, Ld. Voc. tacet
Am
Am/G
Am/F♯
Am/D♯
Gtr. 2
Rhy. Fig. 4
Gtr. 3

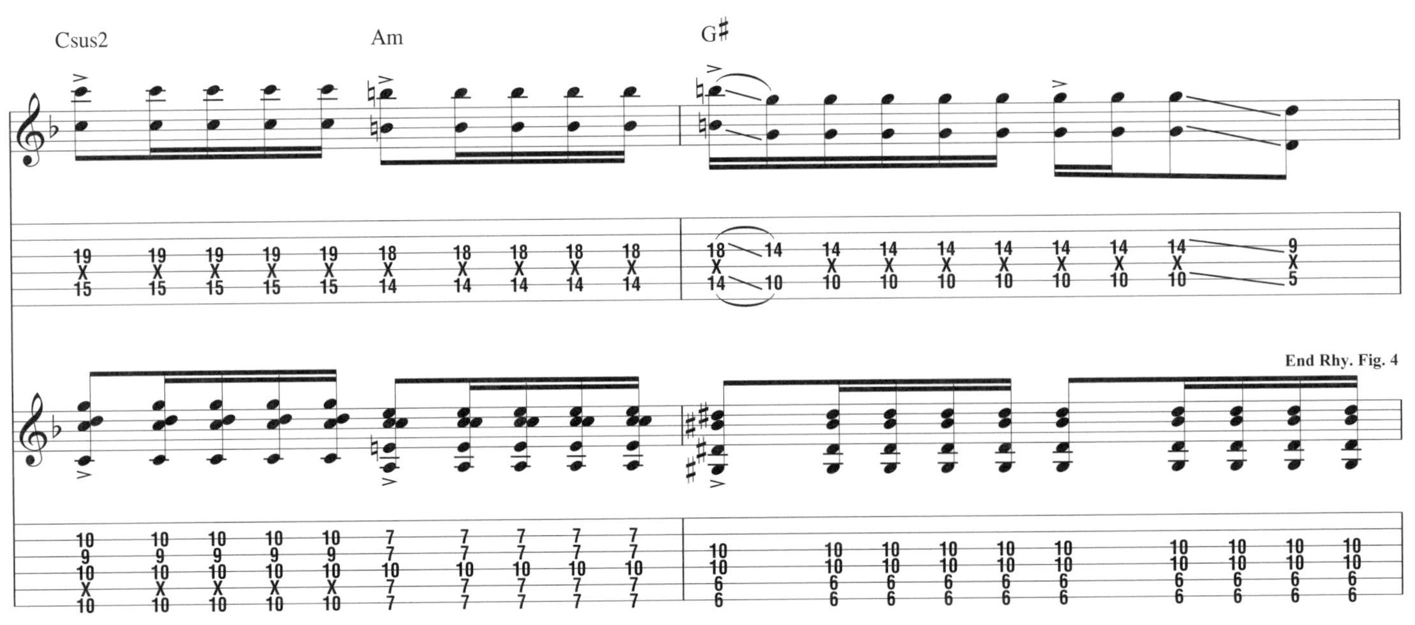
Csus2
Am
G♯
End Rhy. Fig. 4

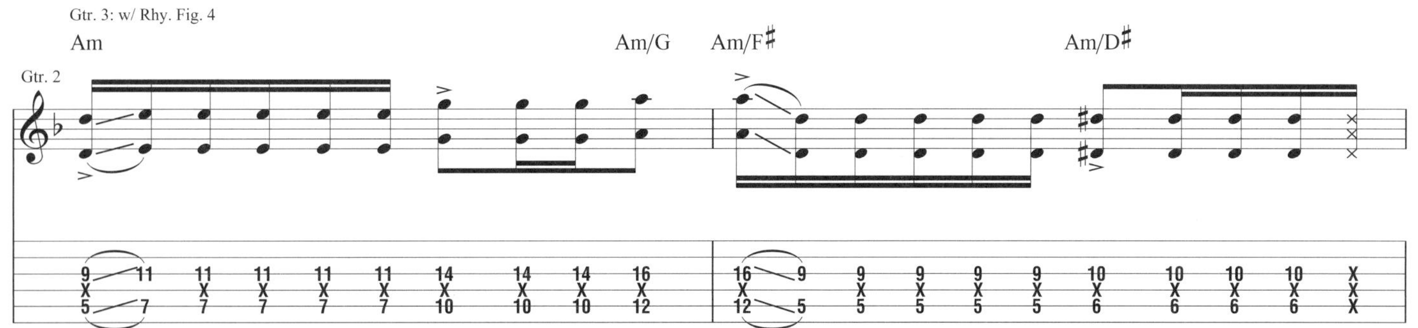
Gtr. 3: w/ Rhy. Fig. 4
Am
Am/G
Am/F♯
Am/D♯
Gtr. 2

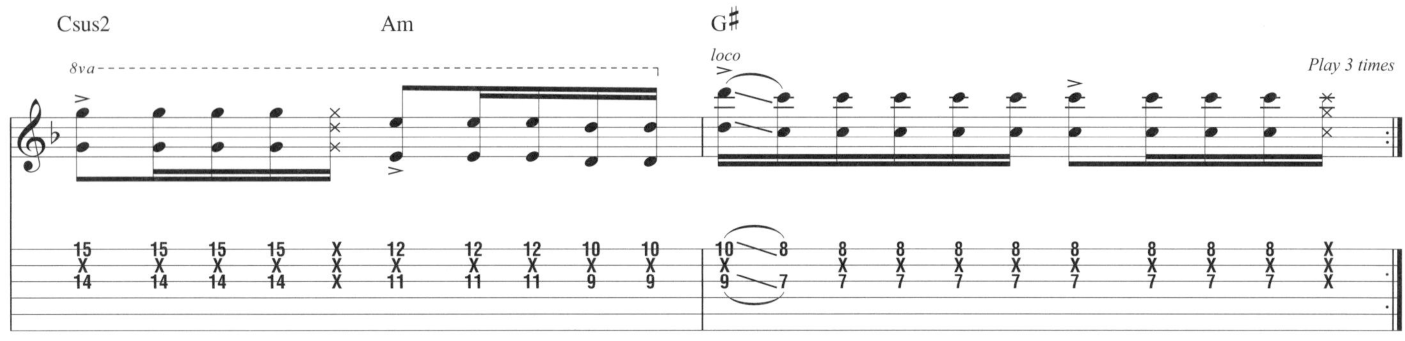
Csus2
Am
G♯
8va
loco
Play 3 times

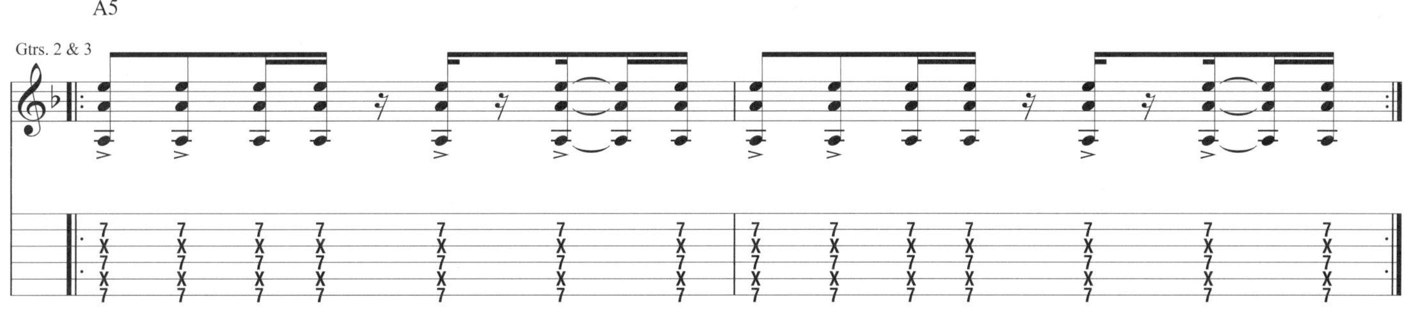
A5
Gtrs. 2 & 3

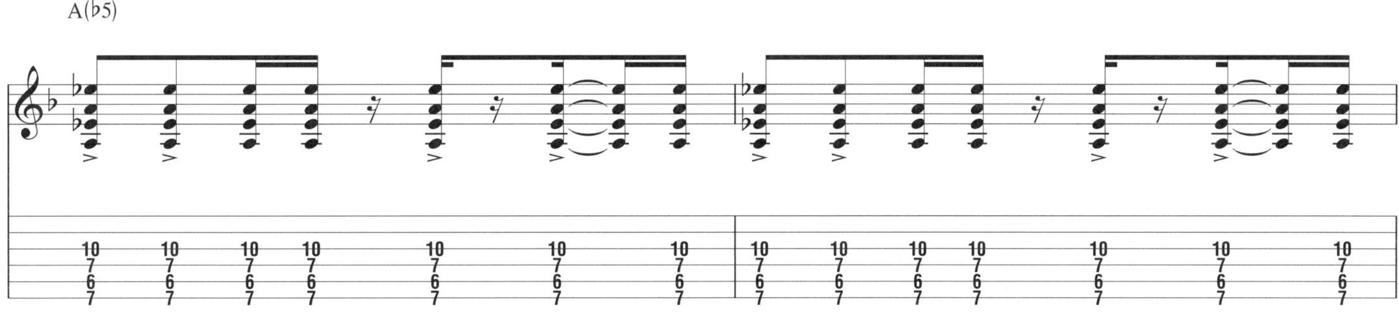
A(♭5)

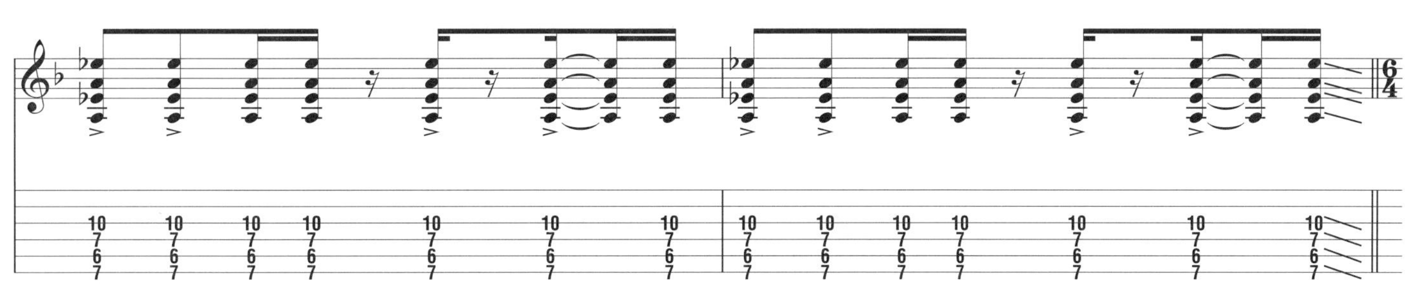

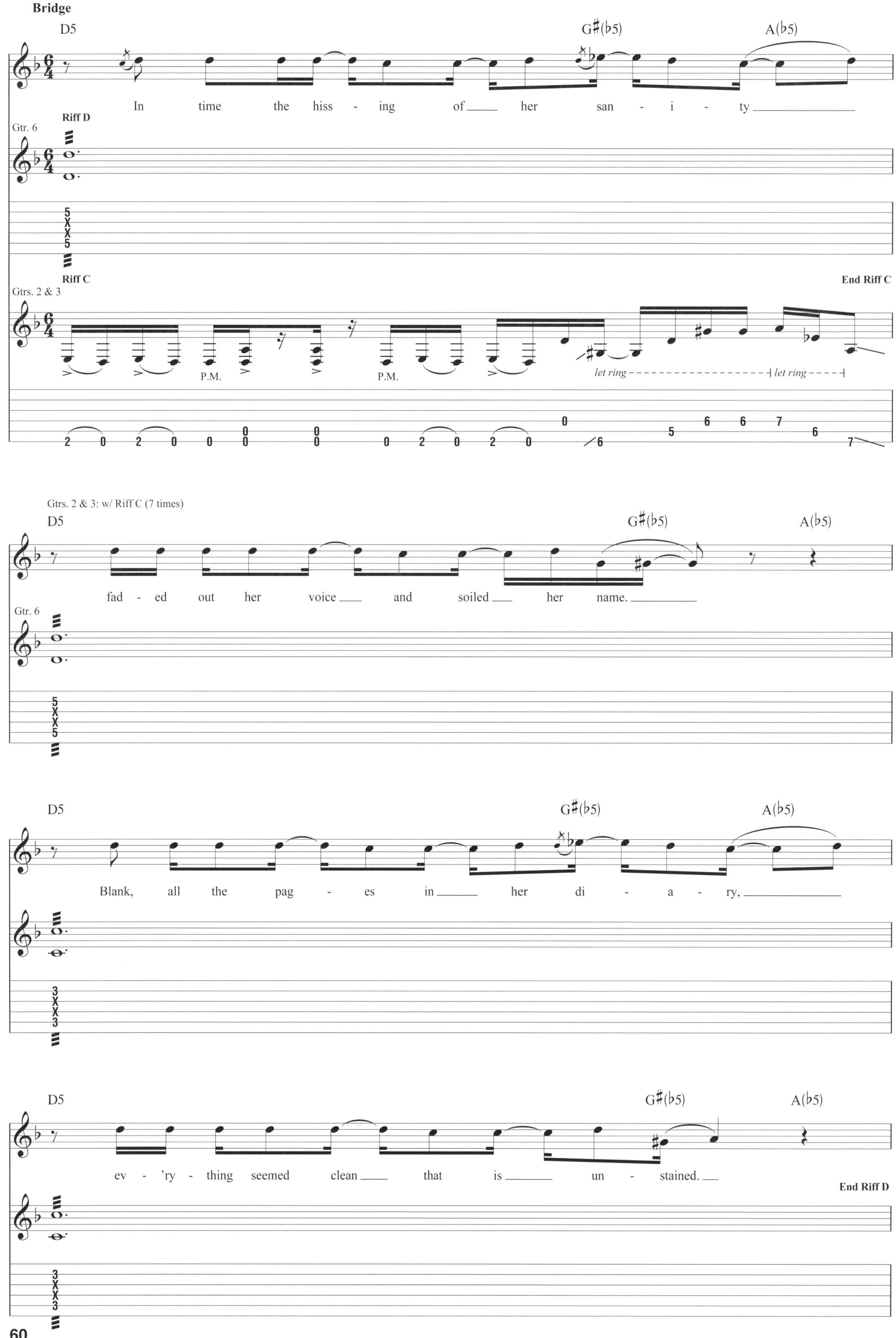
Bridge
D5
G♯(♭5)
A(♭5)
In time the hiss - ing of her san - i - ty
Riff D
Gtr. 6
Riff C
Gtrs. 2 & 3
End Riff C
P.M.
P.M.
let ring
let ring
Gtrs. 2 & 3: w/ Riff C (7 times)
fad - ed out her voice and soiled her name.
Blank, all the pag - es in her di - a - ry,
ev - 'ry - thing seemed clean that is un - stained.
End Riff D

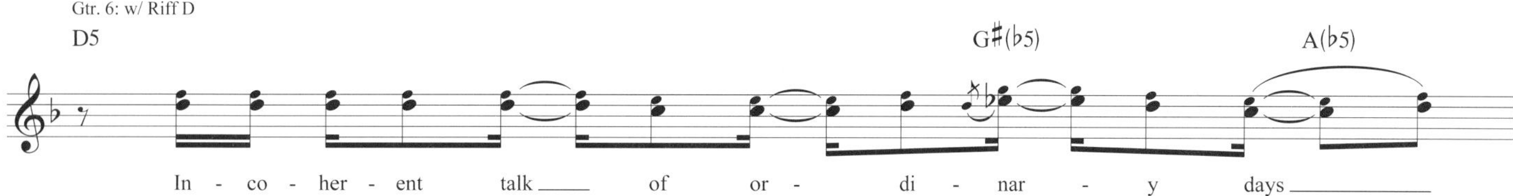
Gtr. 6: w/ Riff D
D5
G♯(♭5)
A(♭5)
In - co - her - ent talk of or - di - nar - y days

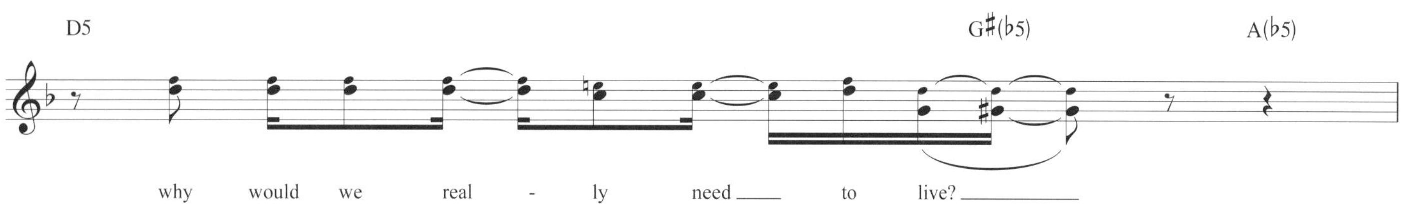
D5
G♯(♭5)
A(♭5)
why would we real - ly need to live?

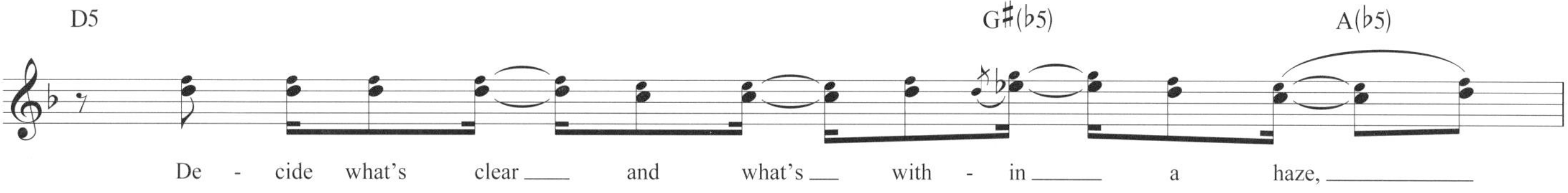
D5
G♯(♭5)
A(♭5)
De - cide what's clear and what's with - in a haze,

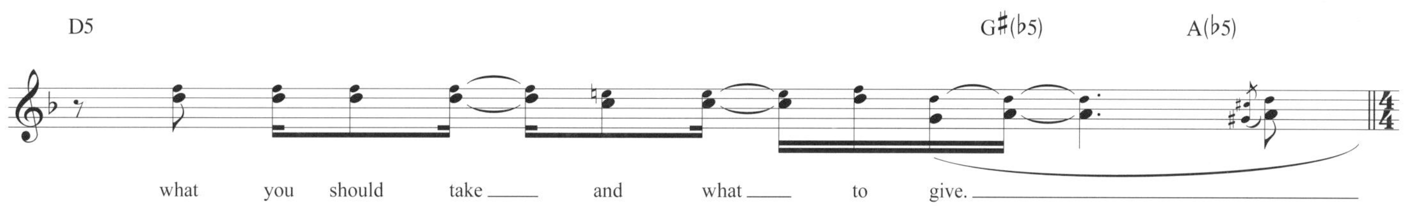
D5
G♯(♭5)
A(♭5)
what you should take and what to give.

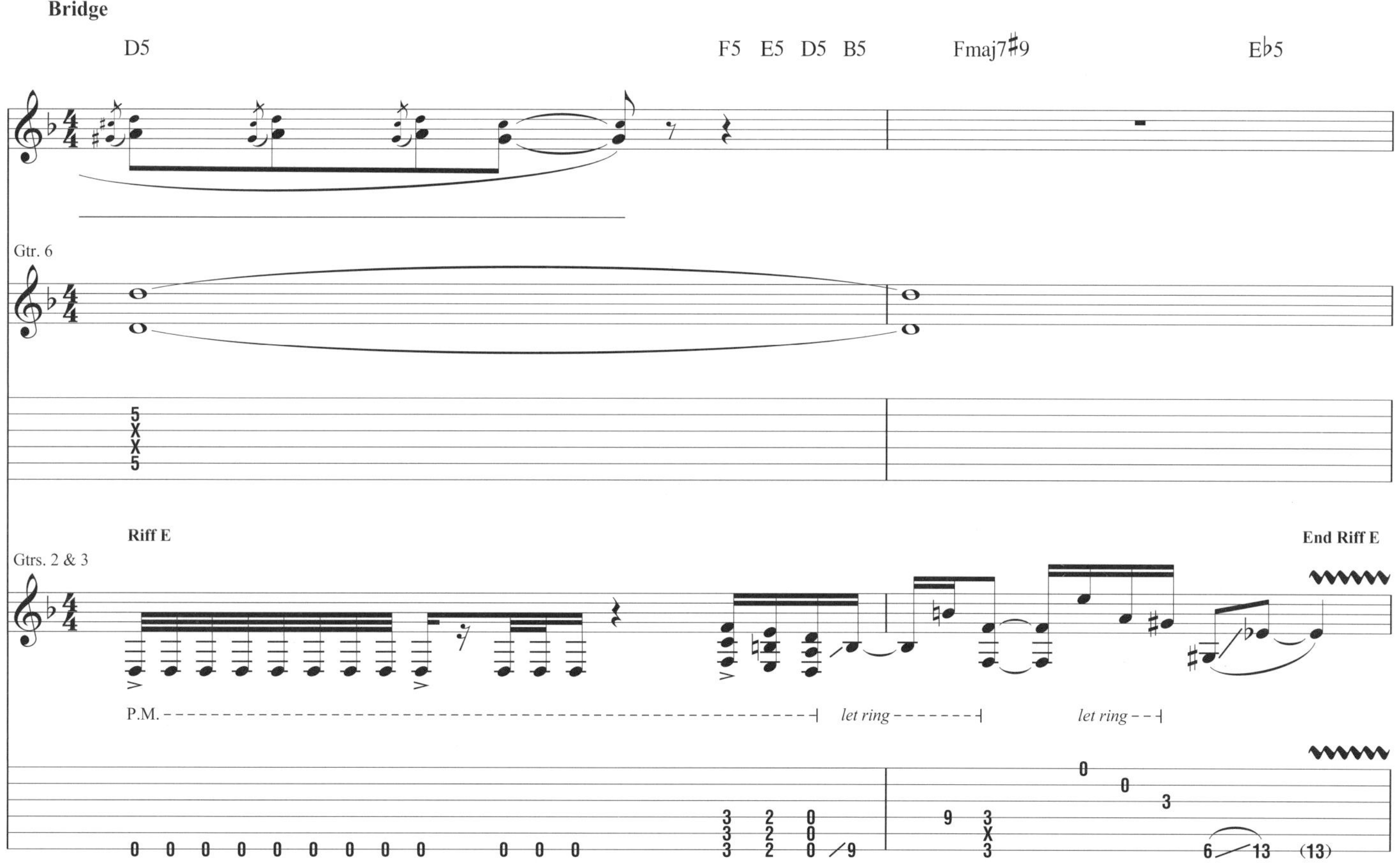
Bridge
D5
F5 E5 D5 B5
Fmaj7♯9
E♭5
Gtr. 6
Riff E
End Riff E
Gtrs. 2 & 3
P.M.
let ring
let ring

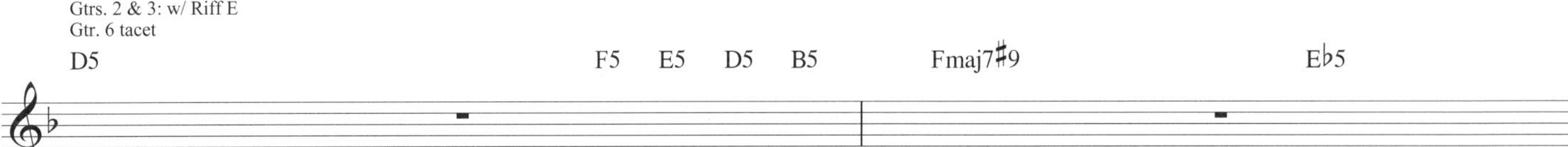
Gtrs. 2 & 3: w/ Riff E
Gtr. 6 tacet
D5
F5 E5 D5 B5
Fmaj7♯9
E♭5

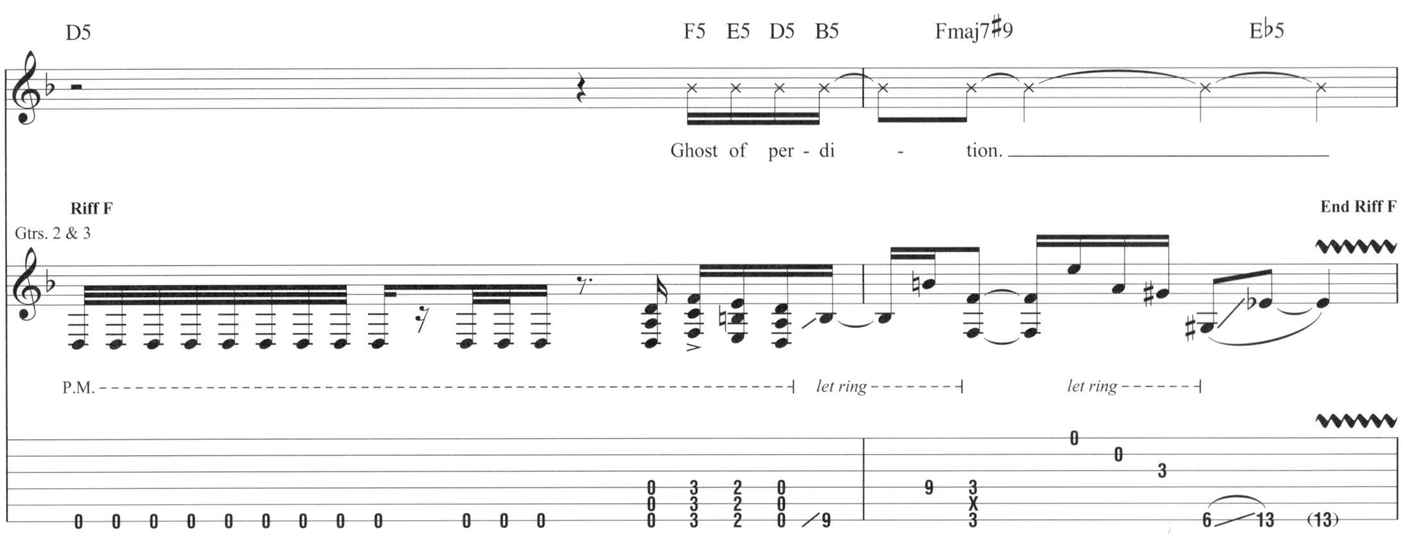
D5
F5 E5 D5 B5
Fmaj7♯9
E♭5
Ghost of per - di - tion.
Riff F
Gtrs. 2 & 3
End Riff F
P.M.
let ring
let ring

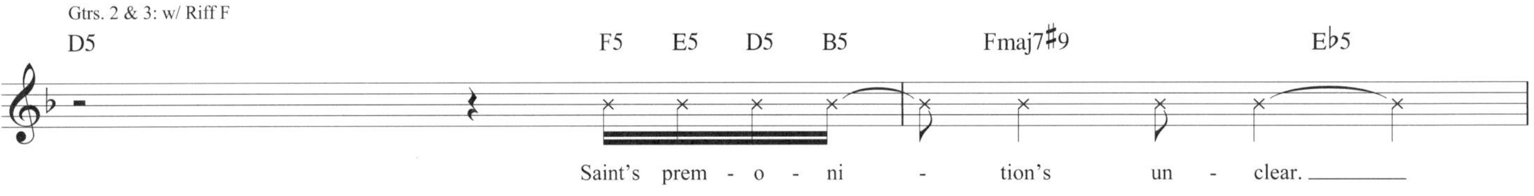
Gtrs. 2 & 3: w/ Riff F
D5
F5 E5 D5 B5
Fmaj7♯9
E♭5
Saint's prem - o - ni - tion's un - clear.

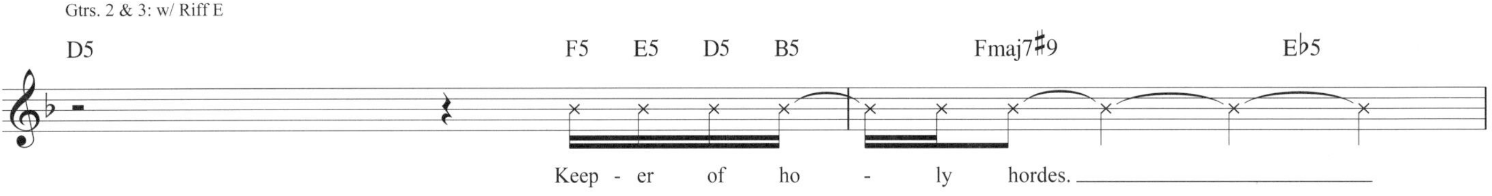
Gtrs. 2 & 3: w/ Riff E
D5
F5 E5 D5 B5
Fmaj7♯9
E♭5
Keep - er of ho - ly hordes.

D5
F5 E5 D5 B5
Fmaj7♯9
N.C.
Keep-er of ho - ly whores.
Gtrs. 2 & 3
P.M.
let ring
let ring
P.M.
P.M.

Interlude
Dm(add9)
Gm(add9) Gm
Huh!
Gtrs. 2 & 3
P.M.
Gtr. 4
F♯m9
Dm
Em/A
Fsus2/A
G/B
*T
*T = Thumb on 6th string
**T
**T = Thumb on 6th string
Gtrs. 2 & 3 tacet
Dm(add9)
Gm(add9) Gm
8va
***Gtr. 7
***Gtr. 8
divisi
mp
***Flute arr. for gtr.
Rhy. Fig. 5
Gtr. 4

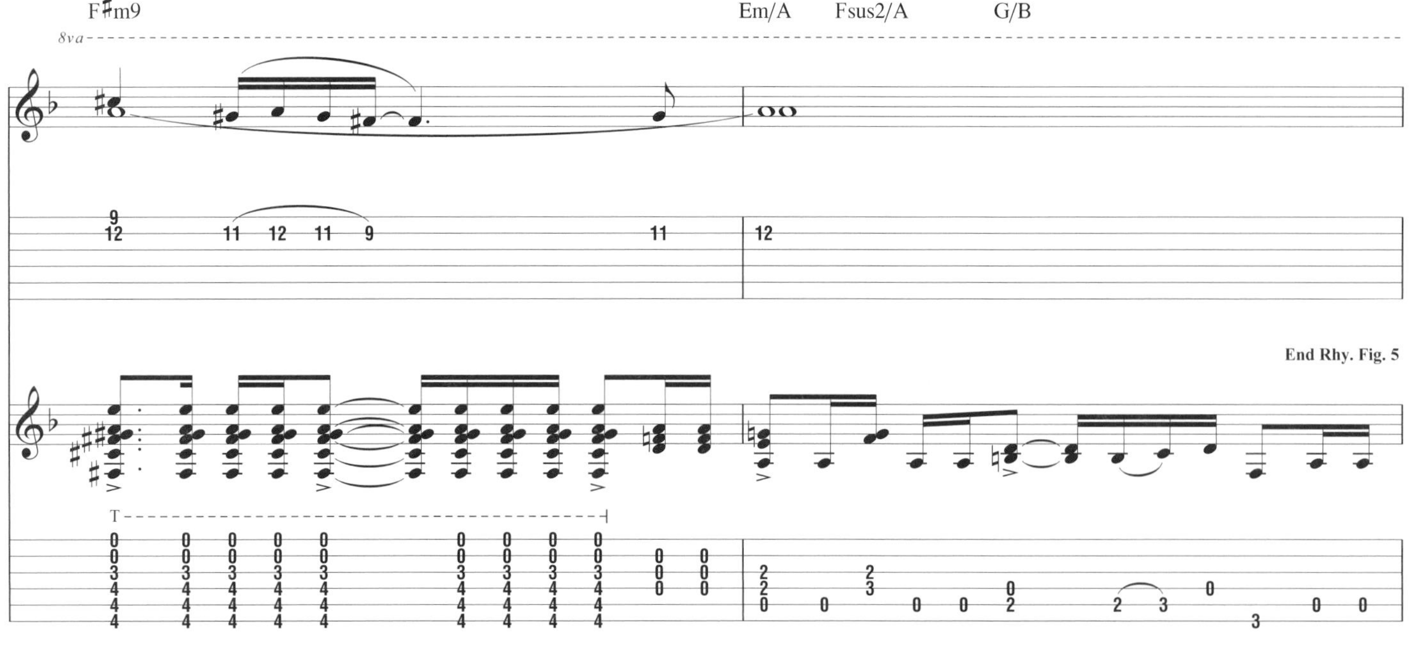
F♯m9
Em/A
Fsus2/A
G/B
8va
End Rhy. Fig. 5

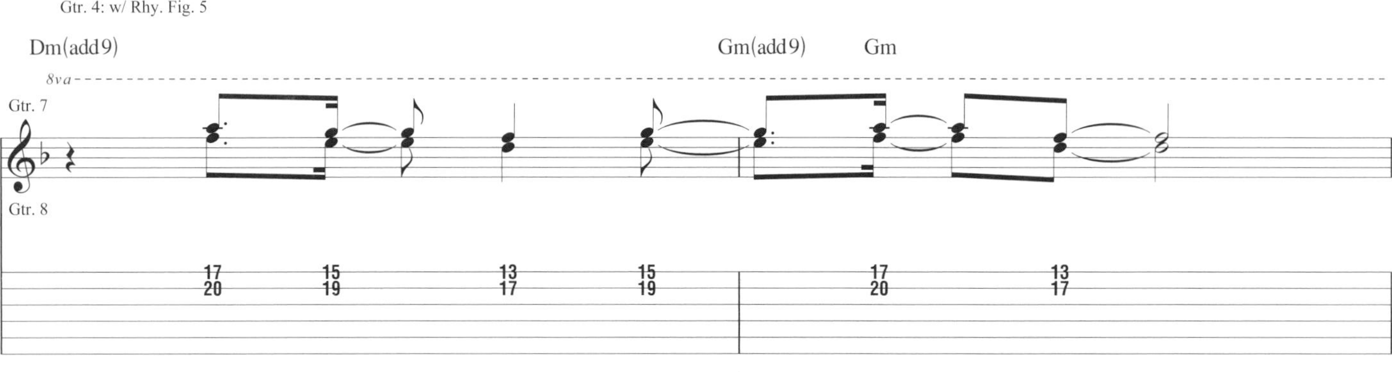
Gtr. 4: w/ Rhy. Fig. 5
Dm(add9)
Gm(add9)
Gm
8va
Gtr. 7
Gtr. 8

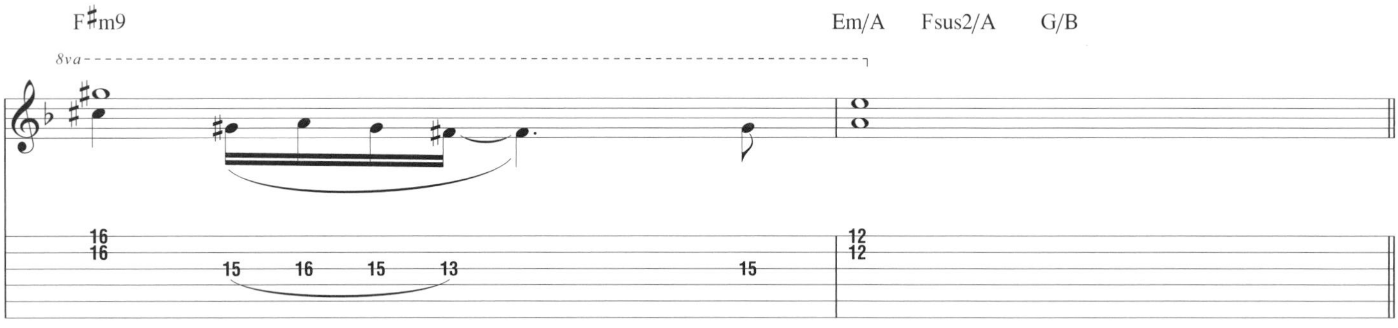
F♯m9
Em/A
Fsus2/A
G/B
8va

Bridge

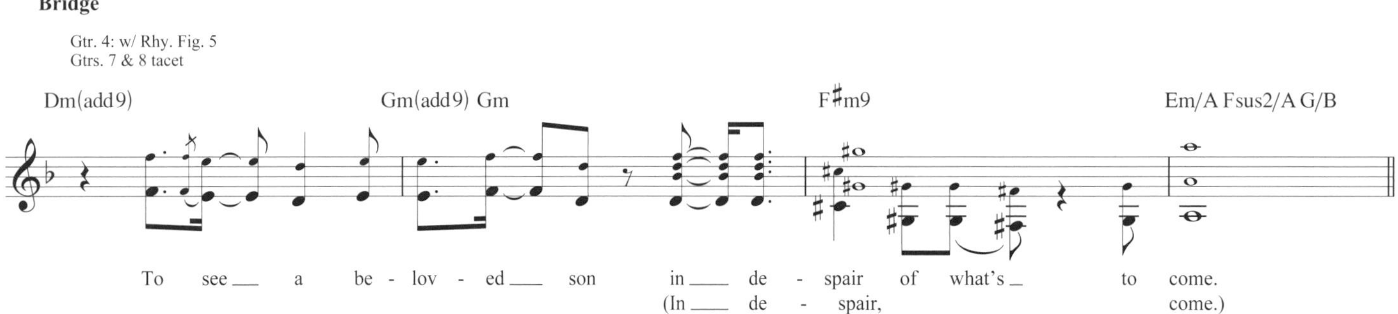
Gtr. 4: w/ Rhy. Fig. 5
Gtrs. 7 & 8 tacet
Dm(add9)
Gm(add9) Gm
F♯m9
Em/A Fsus2/A G/B
To see a be - lov - ed son in de - spair of what's to come.
(In de - spair, come.)

Interlude
Dm(add9)
Gm
Gtr. 9 (elec.)
mf
w/ dist.
Rhy. Fig. 6
Gtrs. 2 & 3
P.M.
Rhy. Fig. 6A
Gtr. 4
F#m9
1.
Em/G
Fsus2/A
G/B
End Rhy. Fig. 6
End Rhy. Fig. 6A

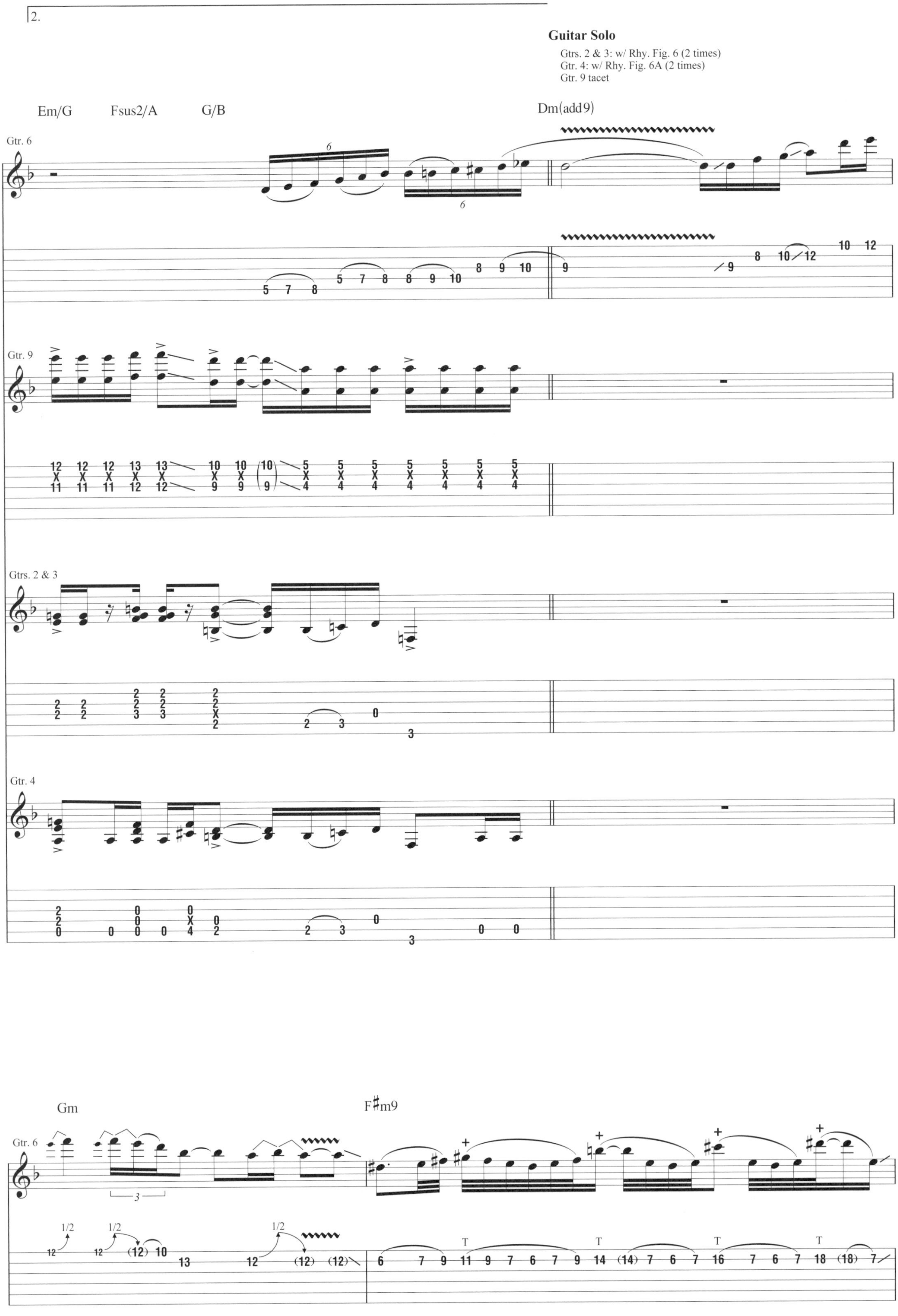

2.

Guitar Solo

Gtrs. 2 & 3: w/ Rhy. Fig. 6 (2 times)
Gtr. 4: w/ Rhy. Fig. 6A (2 times)
Gtr. 9 tacet

Em/G Fsus2/A G/B Dm(add9)

Gtr. 6

Gtr. 9

Gtrs. 2 & 3

Gtr. 4

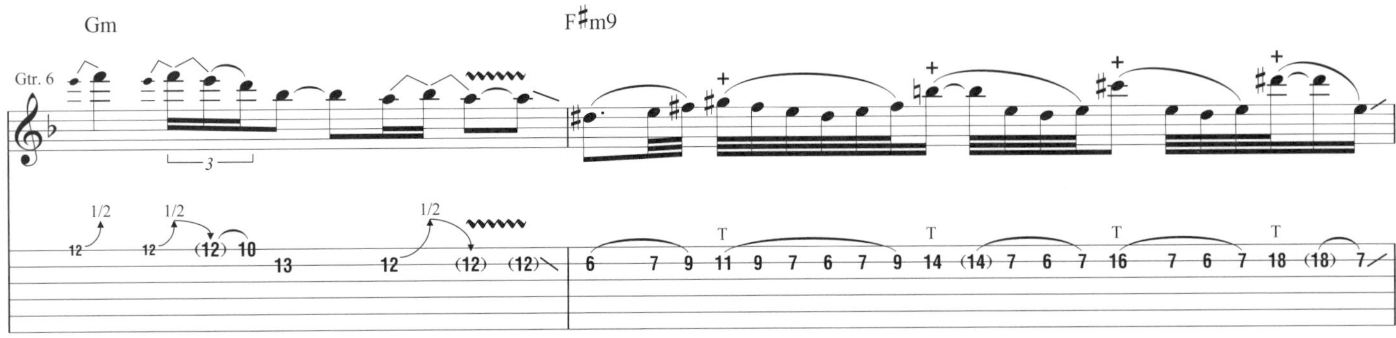

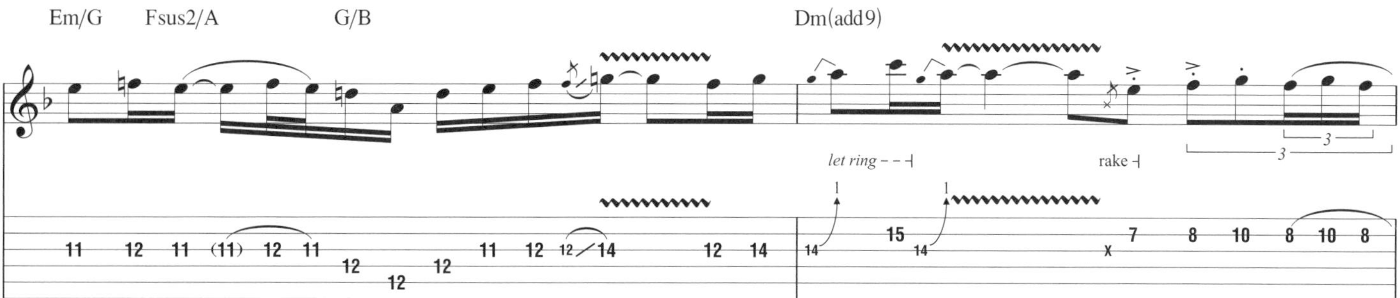
Em/G
Fsus2/A
G/B
Dm(add9)
let ring
rake

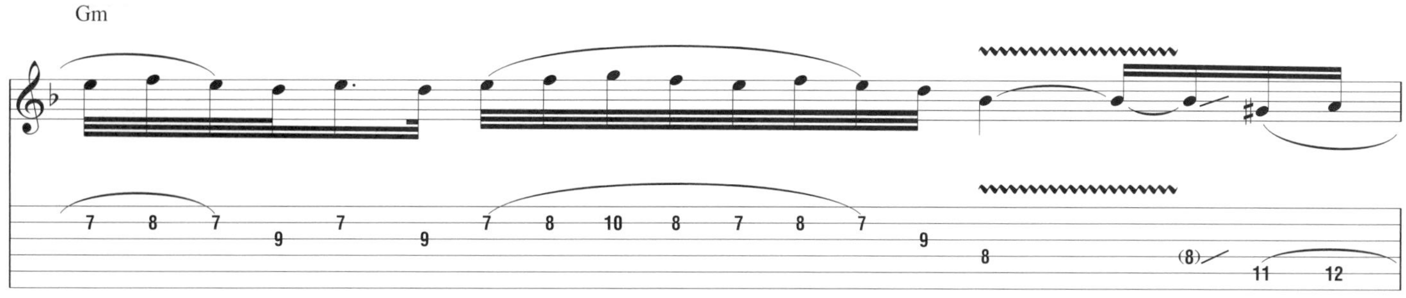
Gm

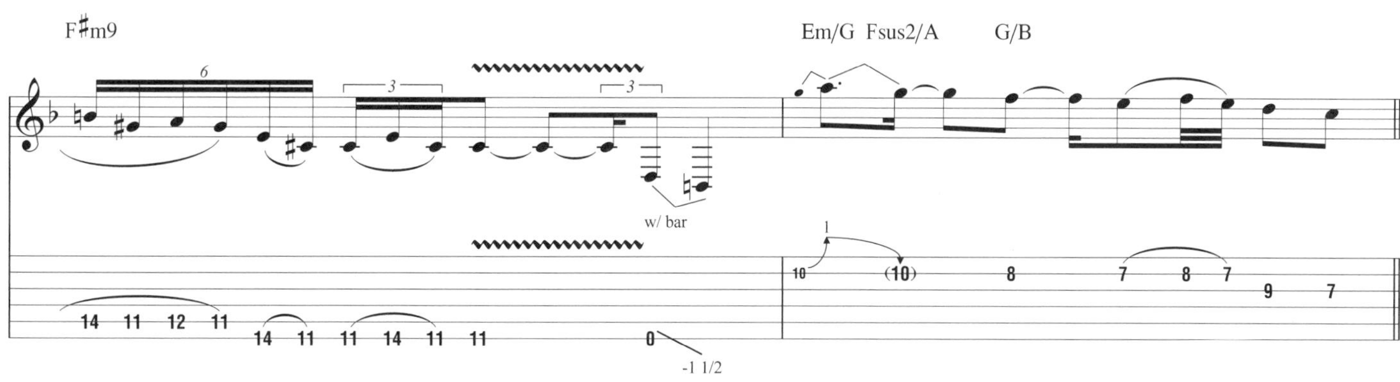
F#m9
w/ bar
Em/G Fsus2/A
G/B

Bridge

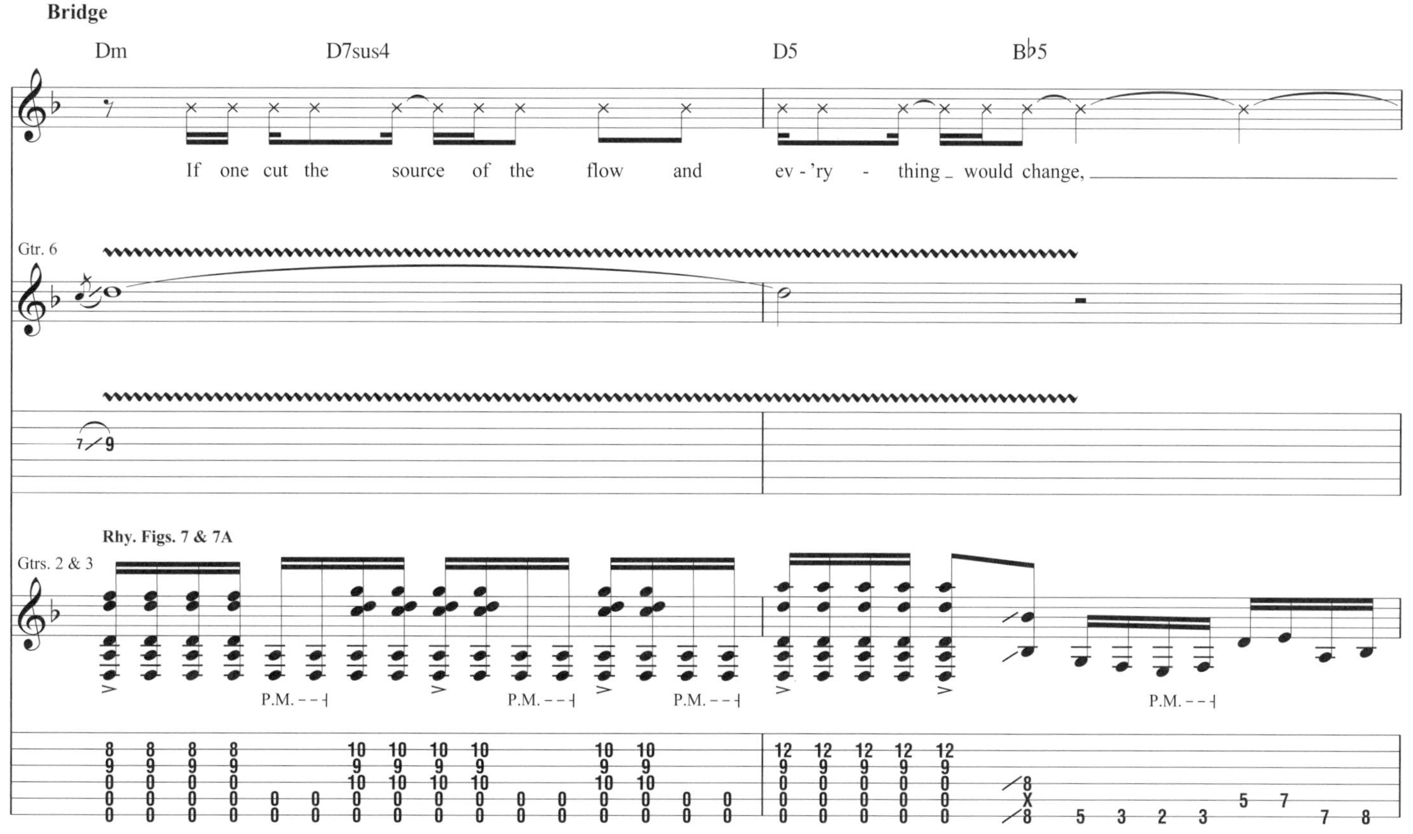
Dm
D7sus4
D5
B♭5
If one cut the source of the flow and ev-'ry - thing would change,
Gtr. 6
Rhy. Figs. 7 & 7A
Gtrs. 2 & 3
P.M.

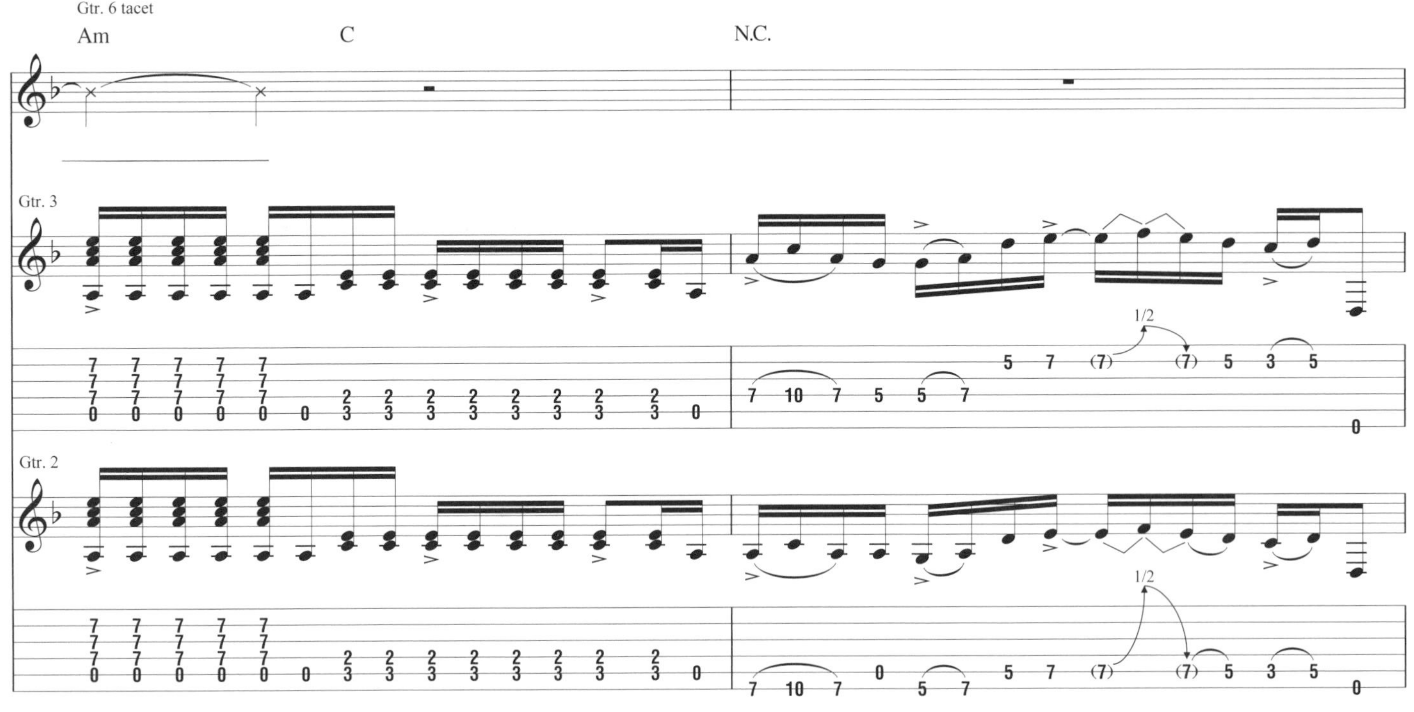
Gtr. 6 tacet
Am
C
N.C.
Gtr. 3
1/2
Gtr. 2
1/2

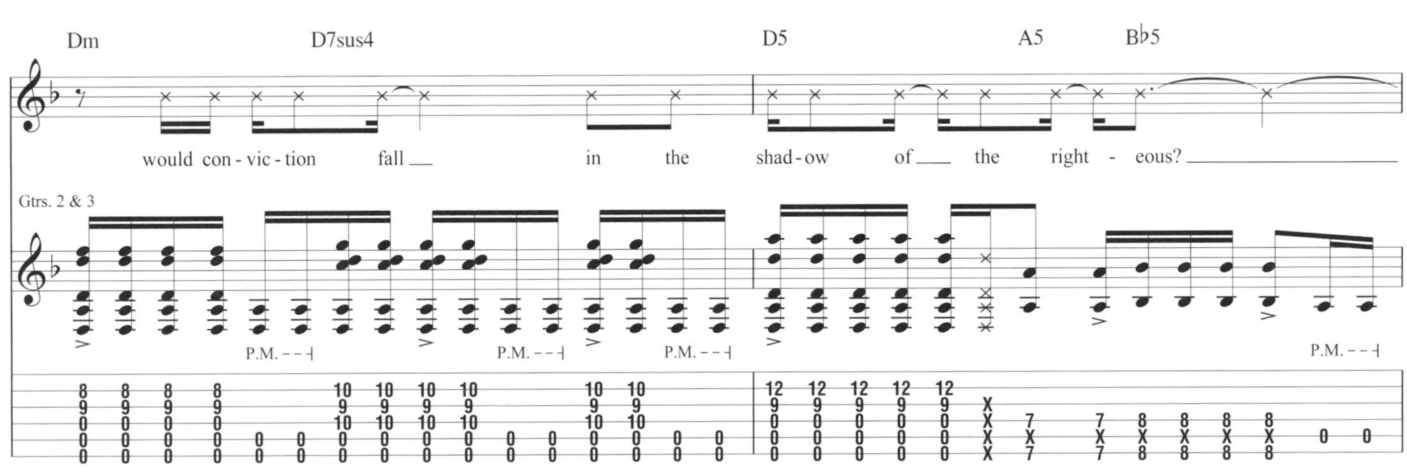
Dm
D7sus4
D5
A5
B♭5
would con - vic - tion fall in the shad - ow of the right - eous?
Gtrs. 2 & 3
P.M.
P.M.
P.M.
P.M.

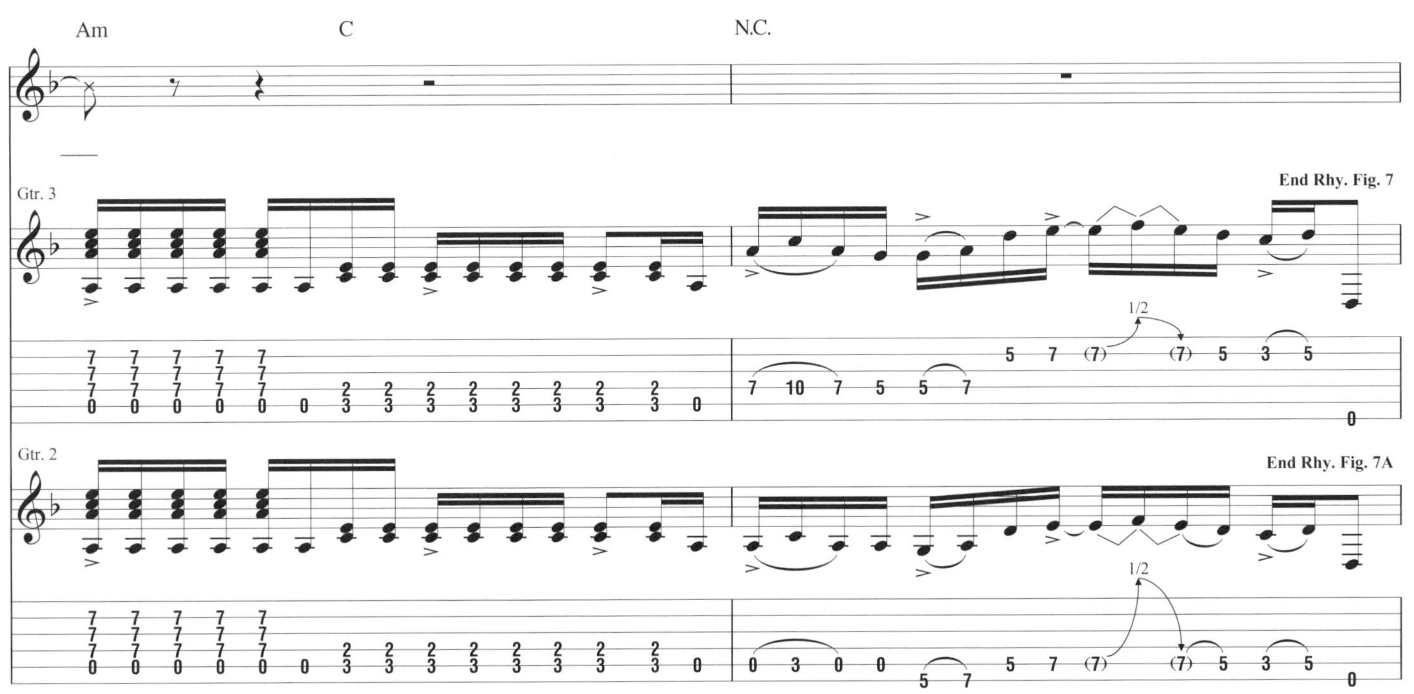
Am
C
N.C.
Gtr. 3
End Rhy. Fig. 7
1/2
Gtr. 2
End Rhy. Fig. 7A
1/2

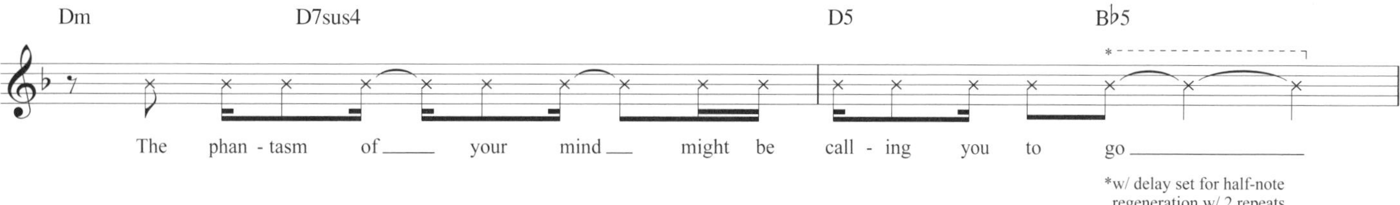
Gtrs. 2 & 3: w/ Rhy. Figs. 7 & 7A
Dm
D7sus4
D5
B♭5
The phan - tasm of your mind might be call - ing you to go
*w/ delay set for half-note regeneration w/ 2 repeats.

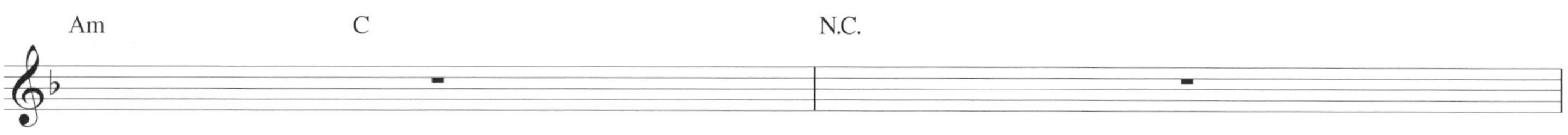
Am
C
N.C.

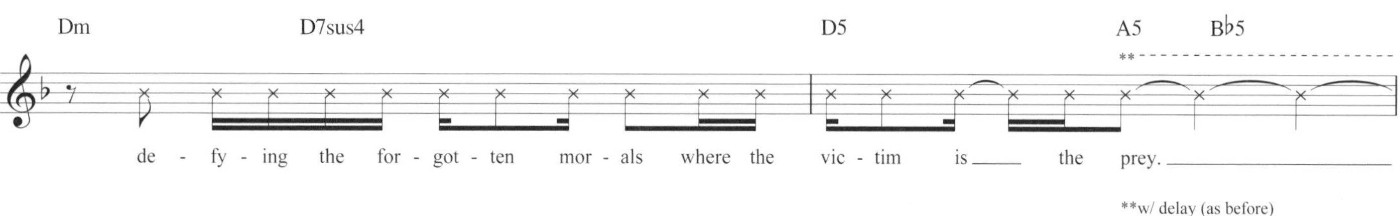
Dm
D7sus4
D5
A5
B♭5
de - fy - ing the for - got - ten mor - als where the vic - tim is the prey.
**w/ delay (as before)

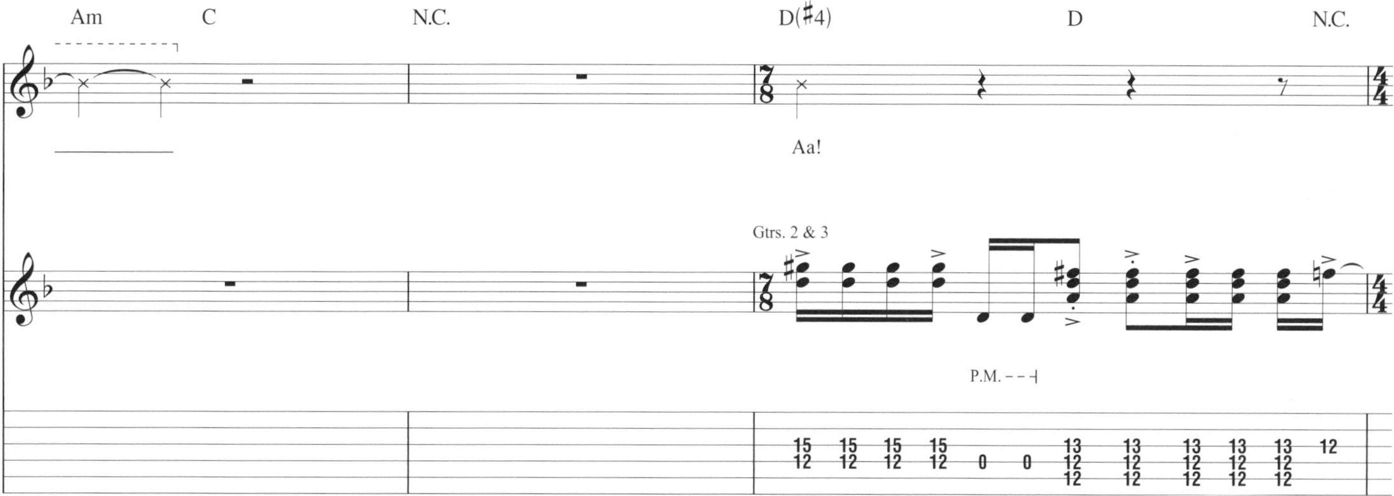
Am
C
N.C.
D(♯4)
D
N.C.
Aa!
Gtrs. 2 & 3
P.M.

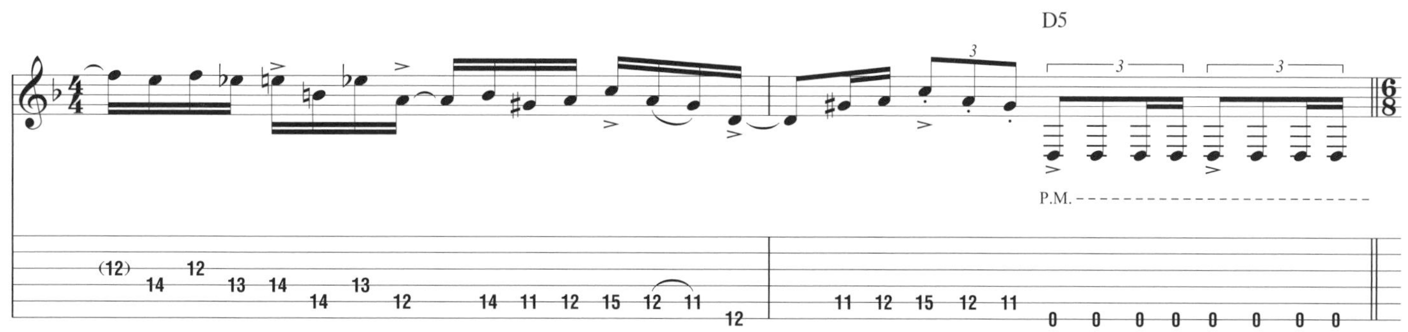
D5
P.M.

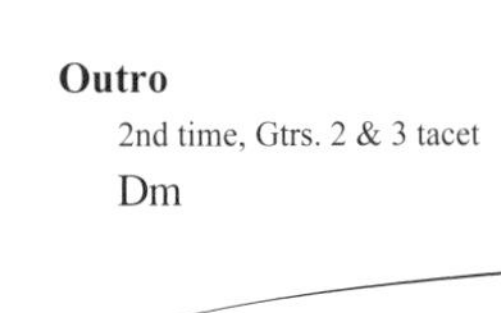

Outro
2nd time, Gtrs. 2 & 3 tacet
Dm

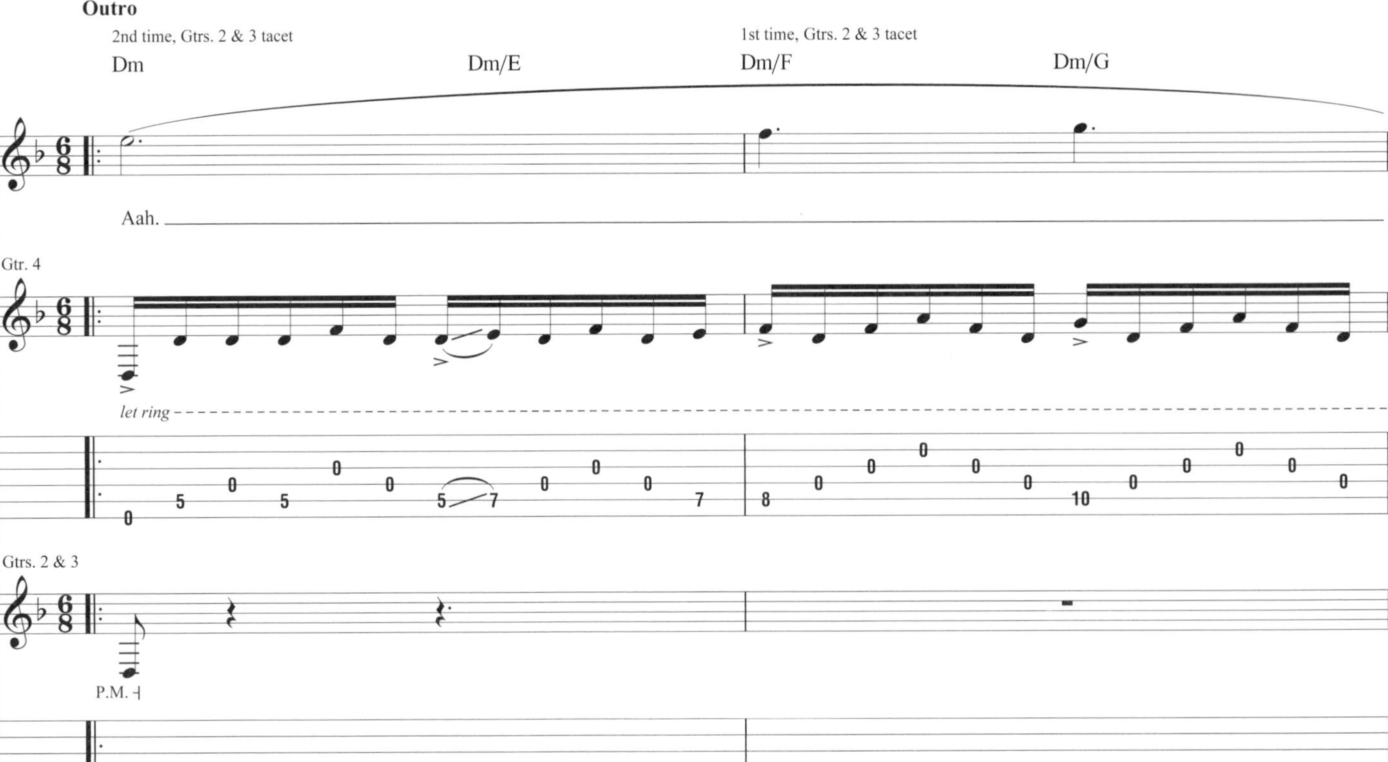

1st time, Gtrs. 2 & 3 tacet
Dm/E
Dm/F
Dm/G
Aah.
Gtr. 4
let ring
Gtrs. 2 & 3
P.M.

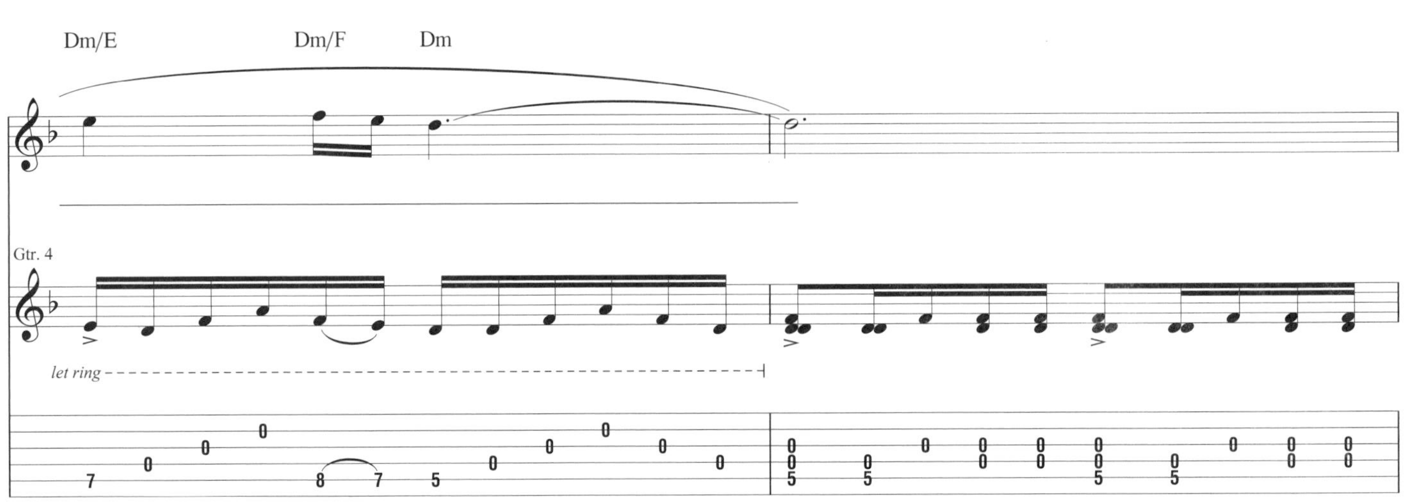

Dm/E
Dm/F
Dm
Gtr. 4
let ring

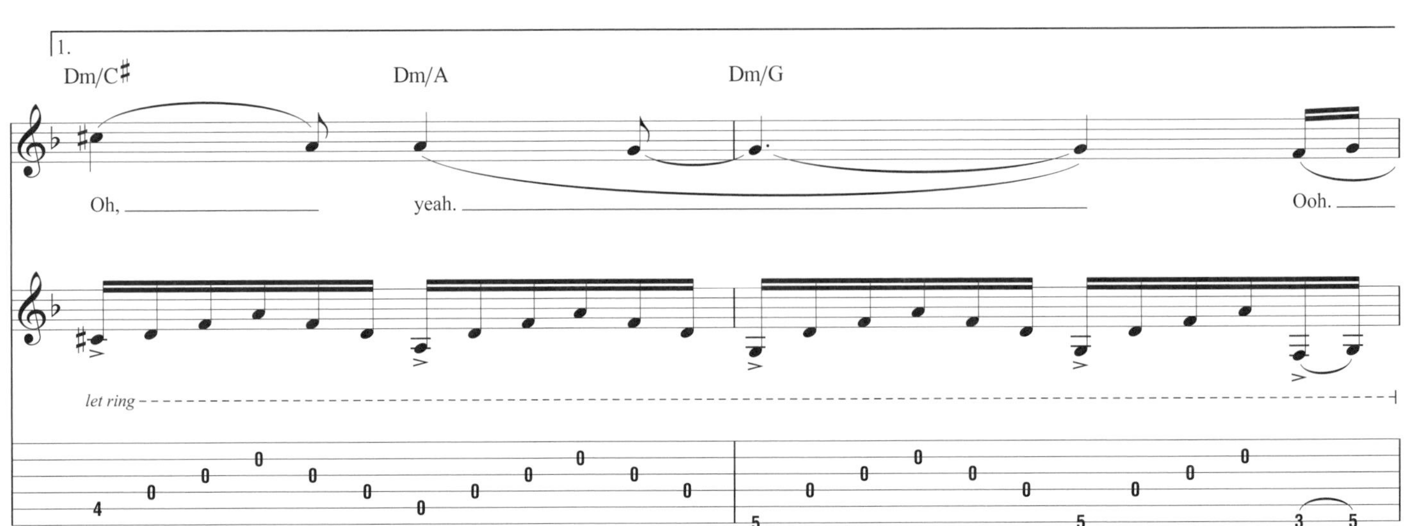

1.
Dm/C♯
Dm/A
Dm/G
Oh,
yeah.
Ooh.
let ring

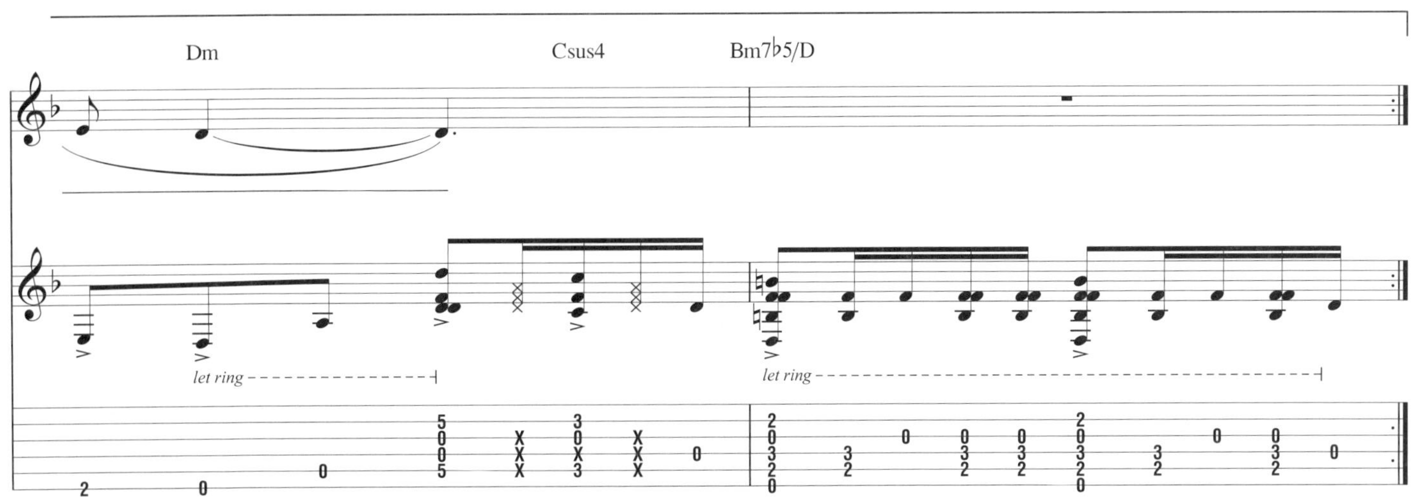
Dm
Csus4
Bm7♭5/D
let ring
let ring

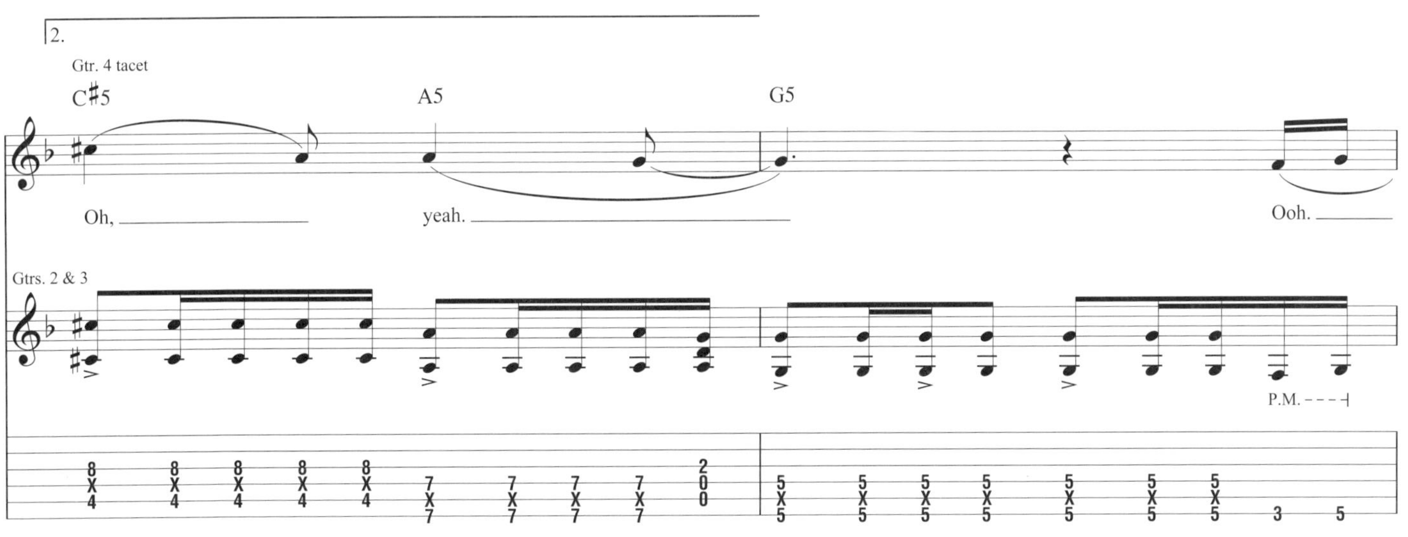
2.
Gtr. 4 tacet
C♯5
A5
G5
Oh,
yeah.
Ooh.
Gtrs. 2 & 3
P.M.

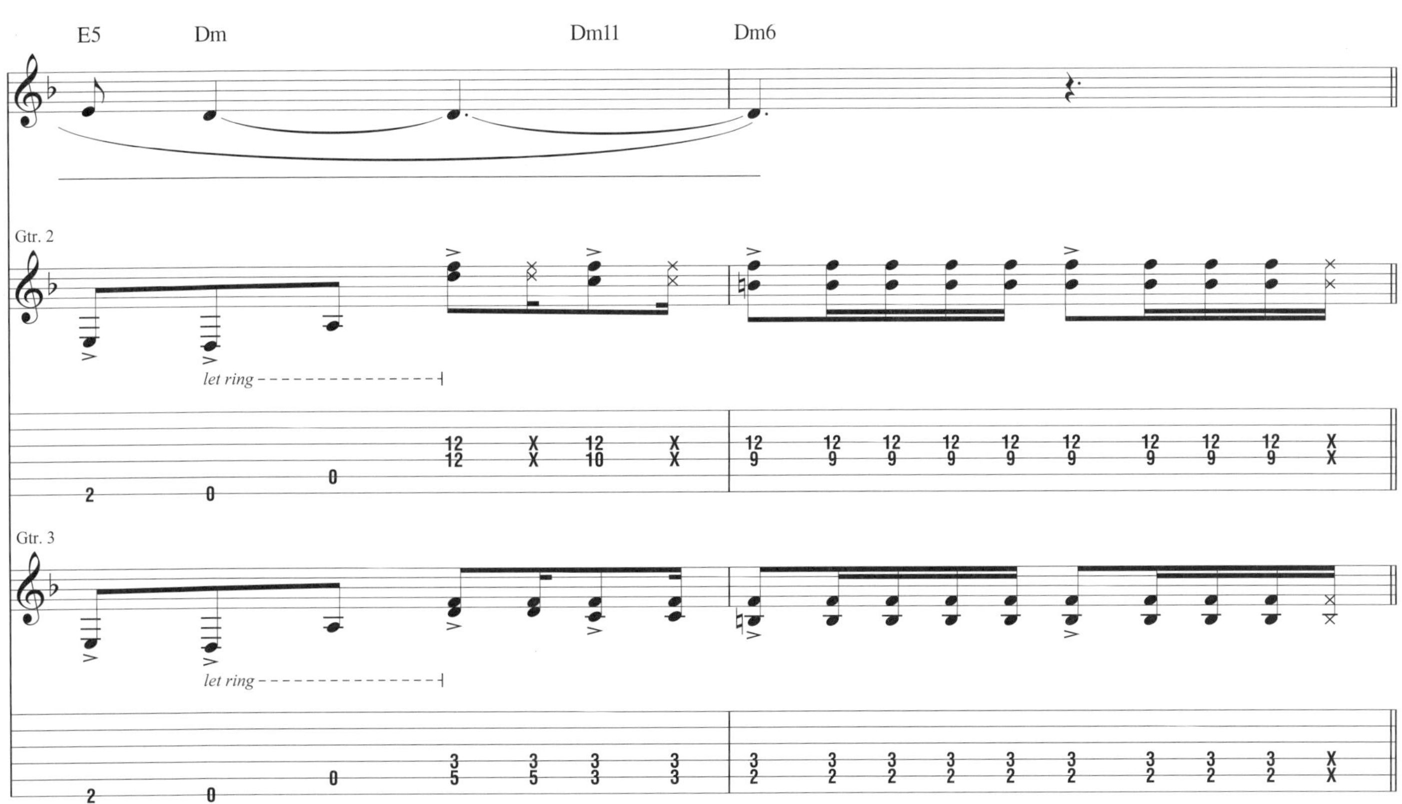
E5
Dm
Dm11
Dm6
Gtr. 2
let ring
Gtr. 3
let ring

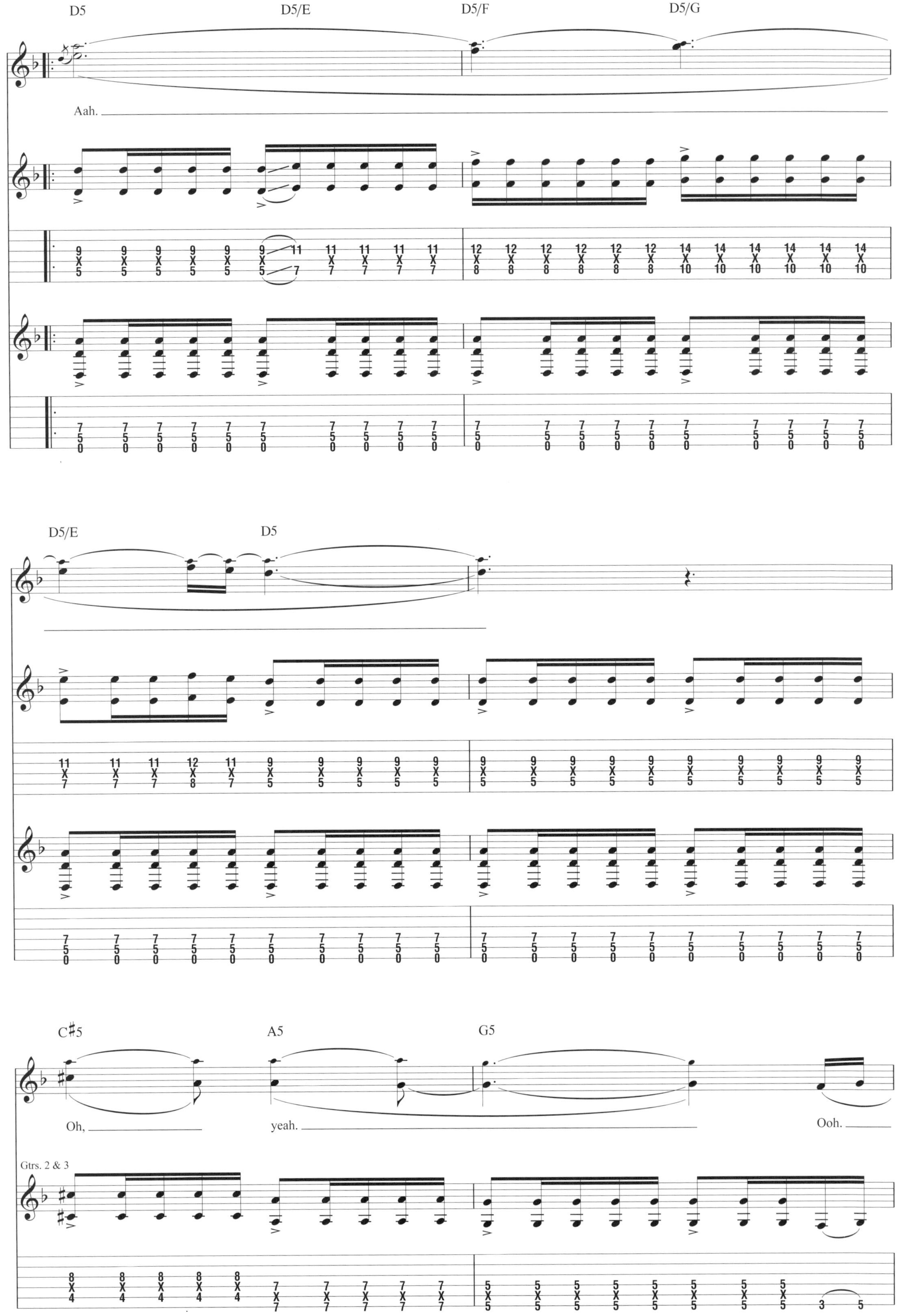
D5
D5/E
D5/F
D5/G
Aah.
D5/E
D5
C♯5
A5
G5
Oh,
yeah.
Ooh.
Gtrs. 2 & 3

1.

E5 Dm Dm11 Dm6

Gtr. 2

let ring

Gtr. 3

let ring

2.

E5 Dm A5 C/G

Ooh.

Gtr. 2

Rhy. Fig. 8

Gtr. 3

let ring

E5
Dm
A5
C
Ooh.
Riff G
End Riff G
End Rhy. Fig. 8
let ring
Gtr. 2: w/ Riff G (2 times)
Gtr. 3: w/ Rhy. Fig. 8
E5
Dm
A5
C/G
E5
Dm
A5
C
Ooh.
N.C.
Gtr. 3
Gtr. 10 (elec.)
w/ dist.
Gtr. 9
Gtr. 2

21 21 21 19 21 21 21 19 21
X X X X X X X X X
17 17 17 15 17 17 17 15 17
12 12 12 11 12 12 12 11 12
X X X X X X X X X
8 8 8 7 8 8 8 7 8
9 9 9 7 9 9 9 7 9
5 5 5 3 5 5 5 3 5

from *Still Life*

Godhead's Lament

Words and Music by Mikael Akerfeldt

F5 E5 D5 C♯5 C(♭5) Am6 F♯°

8va loco End Riff A

let ring

15 16 15 16
13 12 13 12 13 12 13 12
14 17 18 17 17 16

8va loco End Riff A1

let ring

15 16 15 16
13 12 13 12 13 12 13 12
13 16 17 16 16 15

Gtrs. 3 & 4: w/ Riffs A & A1

G5 A5 B♭5 D♭5 G5 F5 E5 D5 C♯5 C(♭5) B(♭5)

Aah! 1. Ma -

*Fade in

Verse

Gtrs. 1 & 2: w/ Rhy. Fig. 1 (1 3/4 times) Gtr. 3 tacet Gtr. 4 tacet

G5 A5 B♭5 D♭5 G5 F5 E5 D5 C♯5 C(♭5) Am6 F♯°

raud - er, stain - ing the soil, midst of still - ness. Be -

Gtr. 3

16

Gtr. 4

16

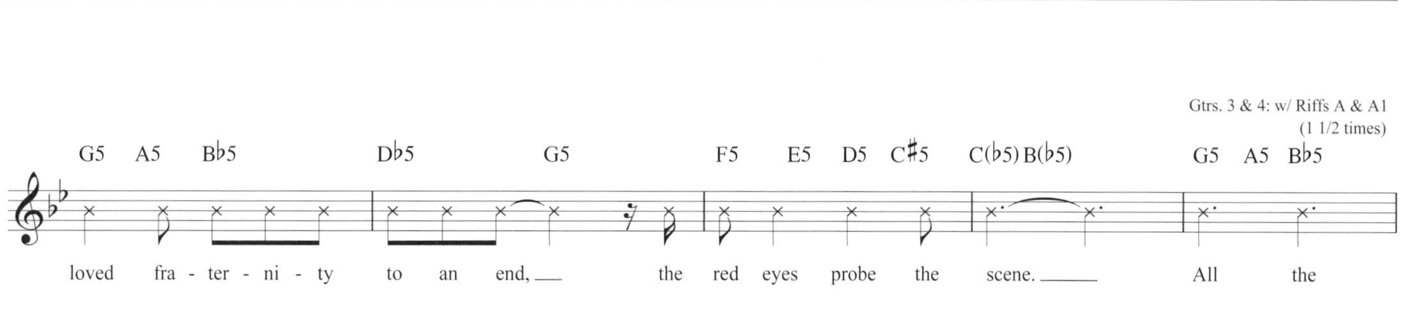

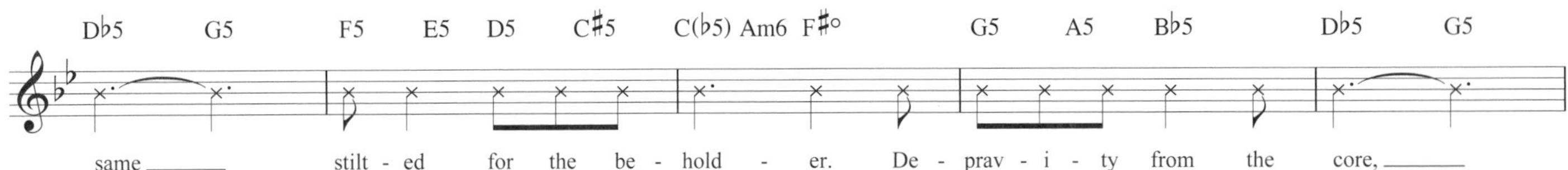

Db5 G5 F5 E5 D5 C#5 C(b5) Am6 F#o G5 A5 Bb5 Db5 G5
same stilt - ed for the be - hold - er. De - prav - i - ty from the core,

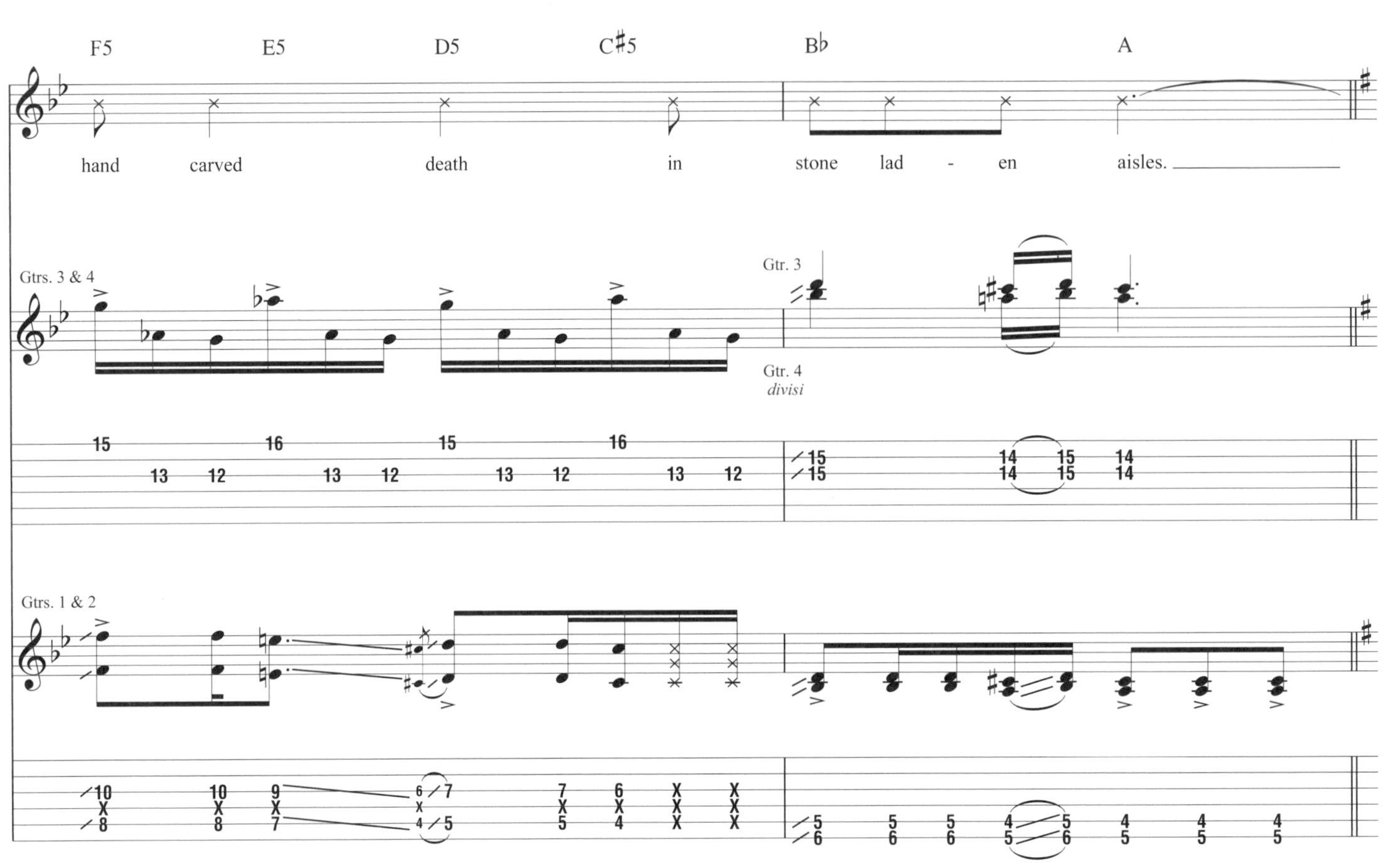

F5 E5 D5 C#5 Bb A
hand carved death in stone lad - en aisles.
Gtrs. 3 & 4
Gtr. 3
Gtr. 4
divisi
Gtrs. 1 & 2

Interlude

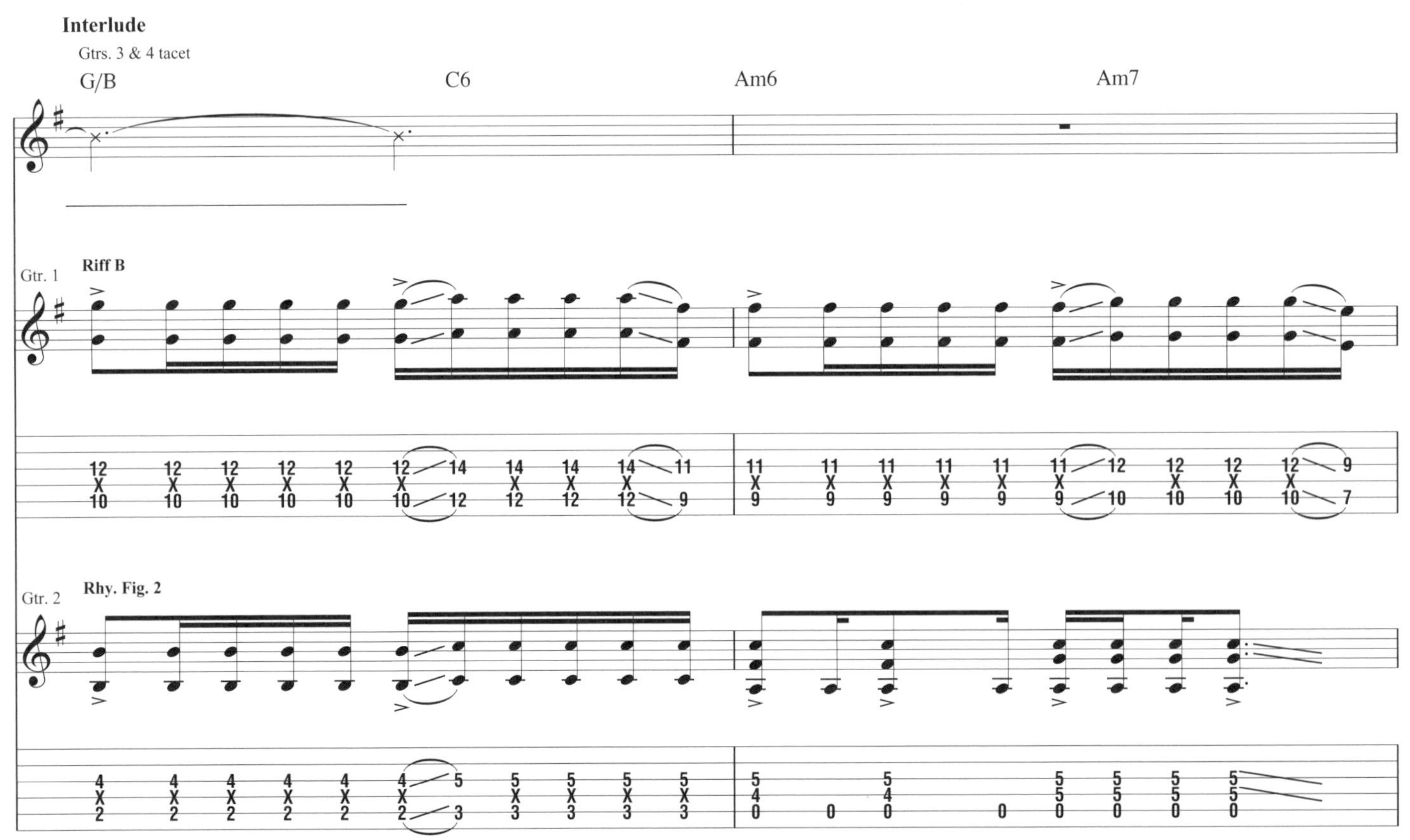

Gtrs. 3 & 4 tacet
G/B C6 Am6 Am7
Gtr. 1
Riff B
Gtr. 2
Rhy. Fig. 2

C♯m
F♯°
Am
Em(add9)
Fill 1
End Fill 1
Gtr. 3
P.M.
1/2
Gtr. 1
End Riff B
Gtr. 2
End Rhy. Fig. 2
P.M.
let ring
let ring
Gtr. 1: w/ Riff B
Gtr. 2: w/ Rhy. Fig. 2
Gtr. 3: w/ Fill 1
G/B
C6
Am6
Am7
Ooh!
Chorus
Gtr. 1: w/ Riff B (4 times)
Gtr. 2: w/ Rhy. Fig. 2 (4 times)
I hide the scars from my past,
yet they sense my dirge.
This is when it all falls a - part.
White hands grasp - ing for straws.

Interlude
N.C.
N.C.
Riff C1
Gtrs. 3 & 4
Gtrs. 1 & 2
Riff C
P.M.
End Riff C1
End Riff C
P.M.
P.M.
Gtrs. 1 & 2: w/ Riff C
Gtr. 4: w/ Riff C1
Riff D
Gtr. 3
End Riff D

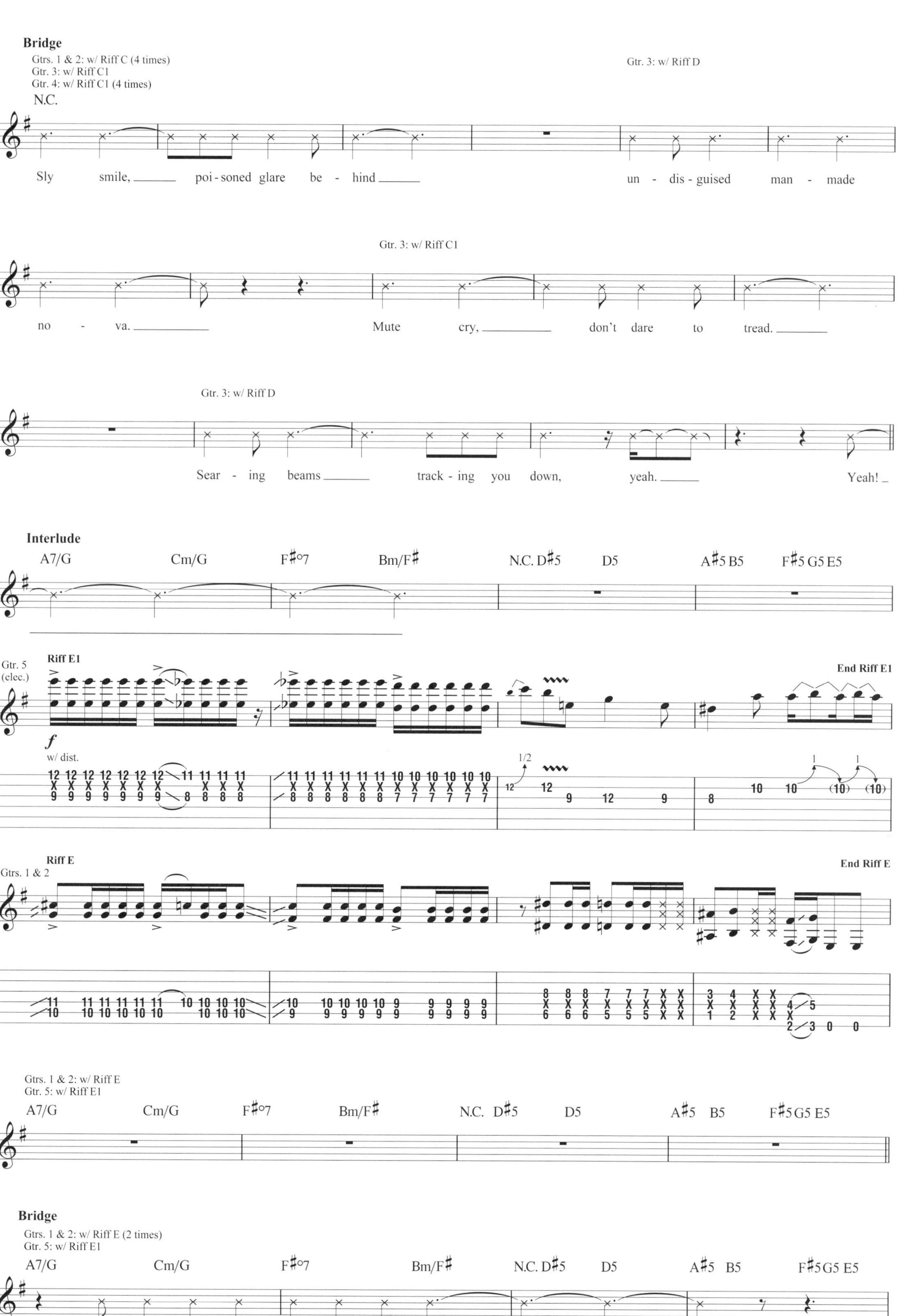
Bridge
Gtrs. 1 & 2: w/ Riff C (4 times)
Gtr. 3: w/ Riff C1
Gtr. 4: w/ Riff C1 (4 times)
N.C.
Gtr. 3: w/ Riff D
Sly smile, poi - soned glare be - hind un - dis - guised man - made
Gtr. 3: w/ Riff C1
no - va. Mute cry, don't dare to tread.
Gtr. 3: w/ Riff D
Sear - ing beams track - ing you down, yeah. Yeah!
Interlude
A7/G Cm/G F#°7 Bm/F# N.C. D#5 D5 A#5 B5 F#5 G5 E5
Gtr. 5 (elec.)
Riff E1
End Riff E1
w/ dist.
Riff E
Gtrs. 1 & 2
End Riff E
Gtrs. 1 & 2: w/ Riff E
Gtr. 5: w/ Riff E1
A7/G Cm/G F#°7 Bm/F# N.C. D#5 D5 A#5 B5 F#5 G5 E5
Bridge
Gtrs. 1 & 2: w/ Riff E (2 times)
Gtr. 5: w/ Riff E1
A7/G Cm/G F#°7 Bm/F# N.C. D#5 D5 A#5 B5 F#5 G5 E5
A - dor - ing what nev - er has been.

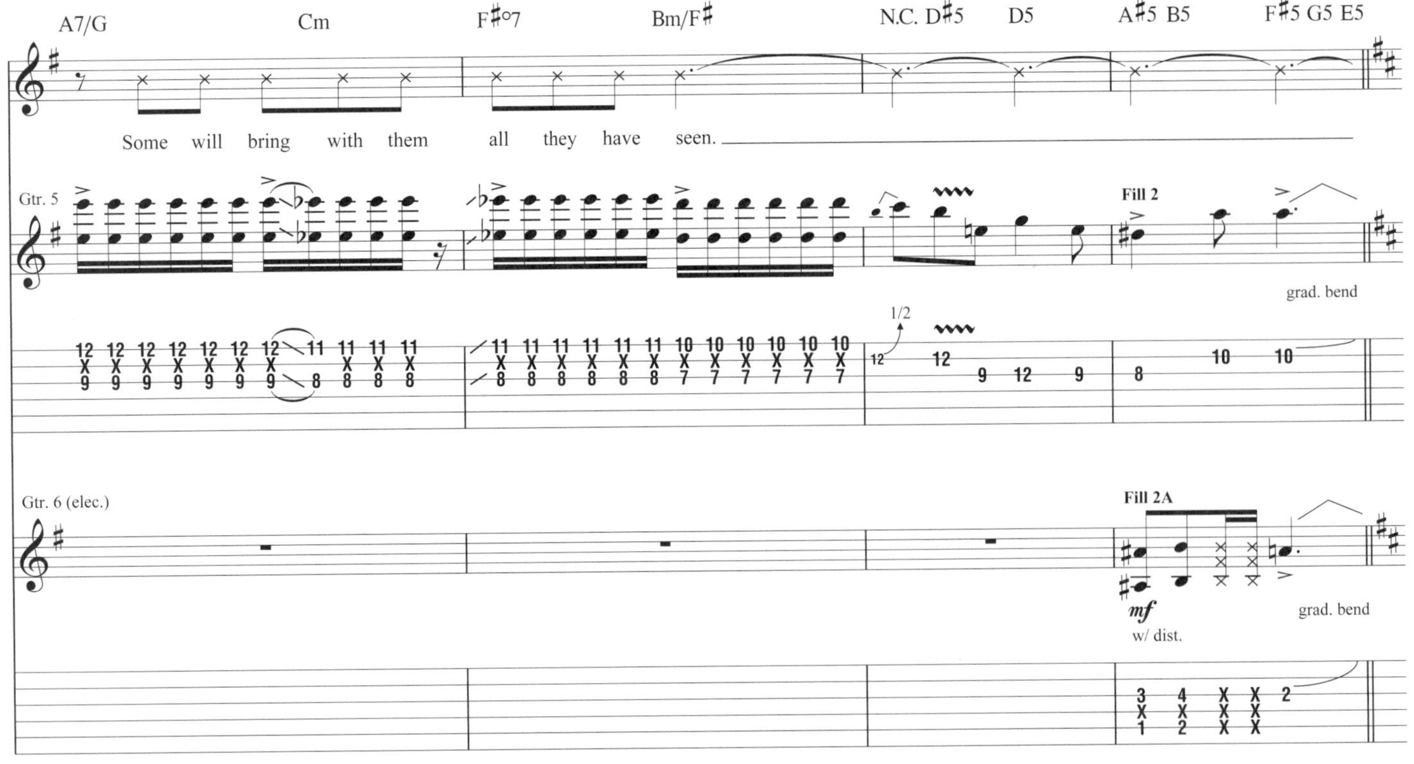

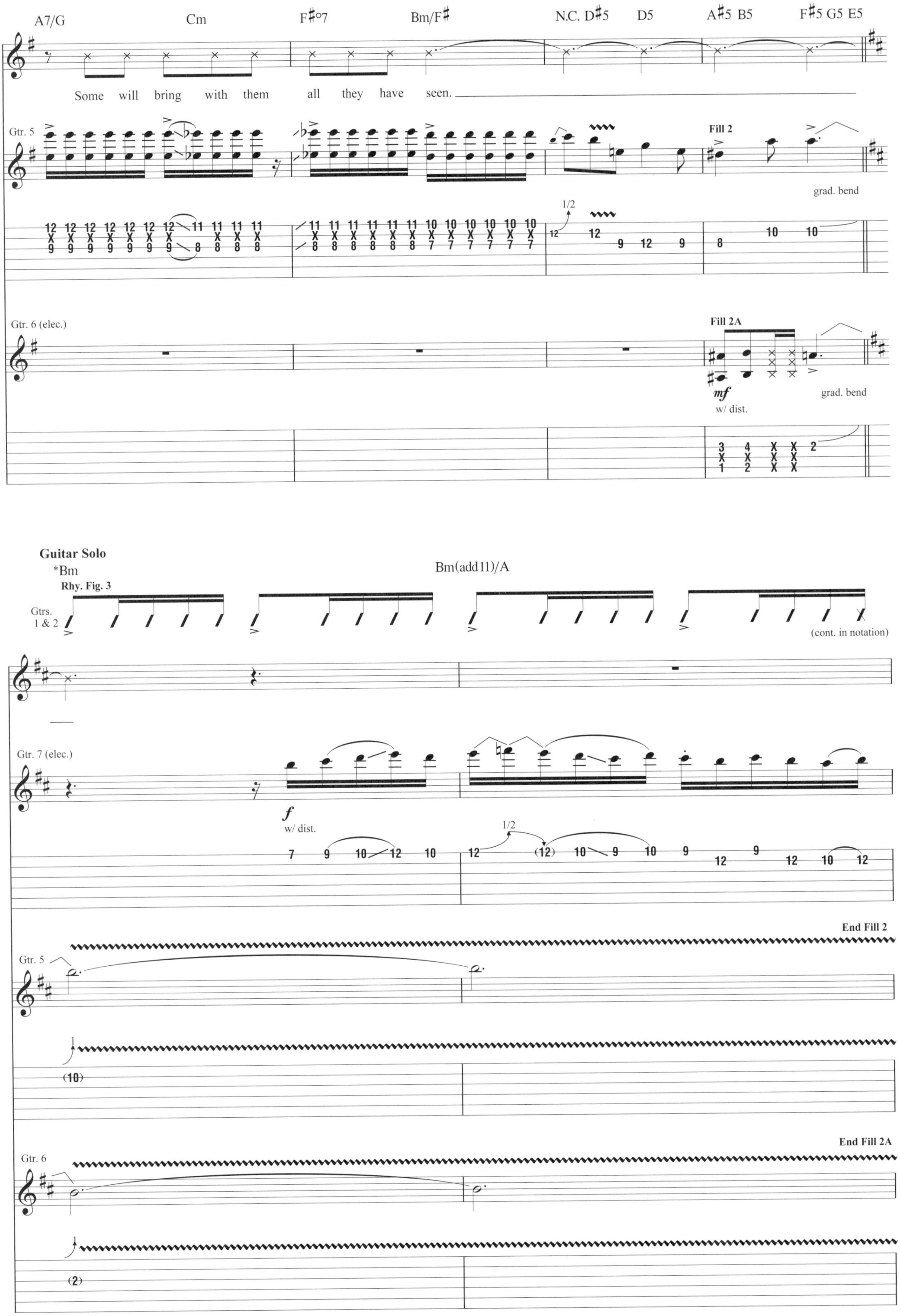

Guitar Solo

*Bm

Bm(add11)/A

Rhy. Fig. 3

Gtrs. 1 & 2

(cont. in notation)

Gtr. 7 (elec.)

f

w/ dist.

1/2

End Fill 2

Gtr. 5

End Fill 2A

Gtr. 6

*See top of first page of song for chord diagrams pertaining to rhythm slashes.

Gtrs. 5 & 6 tacet
Gmaj7
Dadd9
Em
Bm
Gtr. 7
P.M.
string noise
Gtrs. 1 & 2
Bm(add11)/A
Gmaj7
A
B5/F♯
G
grad. bend
let ring
End Rhy. Fig. 3
P.M.
Gtrs. 1 & 2: w/ Rhy. Fig. 3
Bm
Bm(add11)/A
Gmaj7
Dadd9
Em
Gtr. 5
Gtr. 7
Gtr. 3

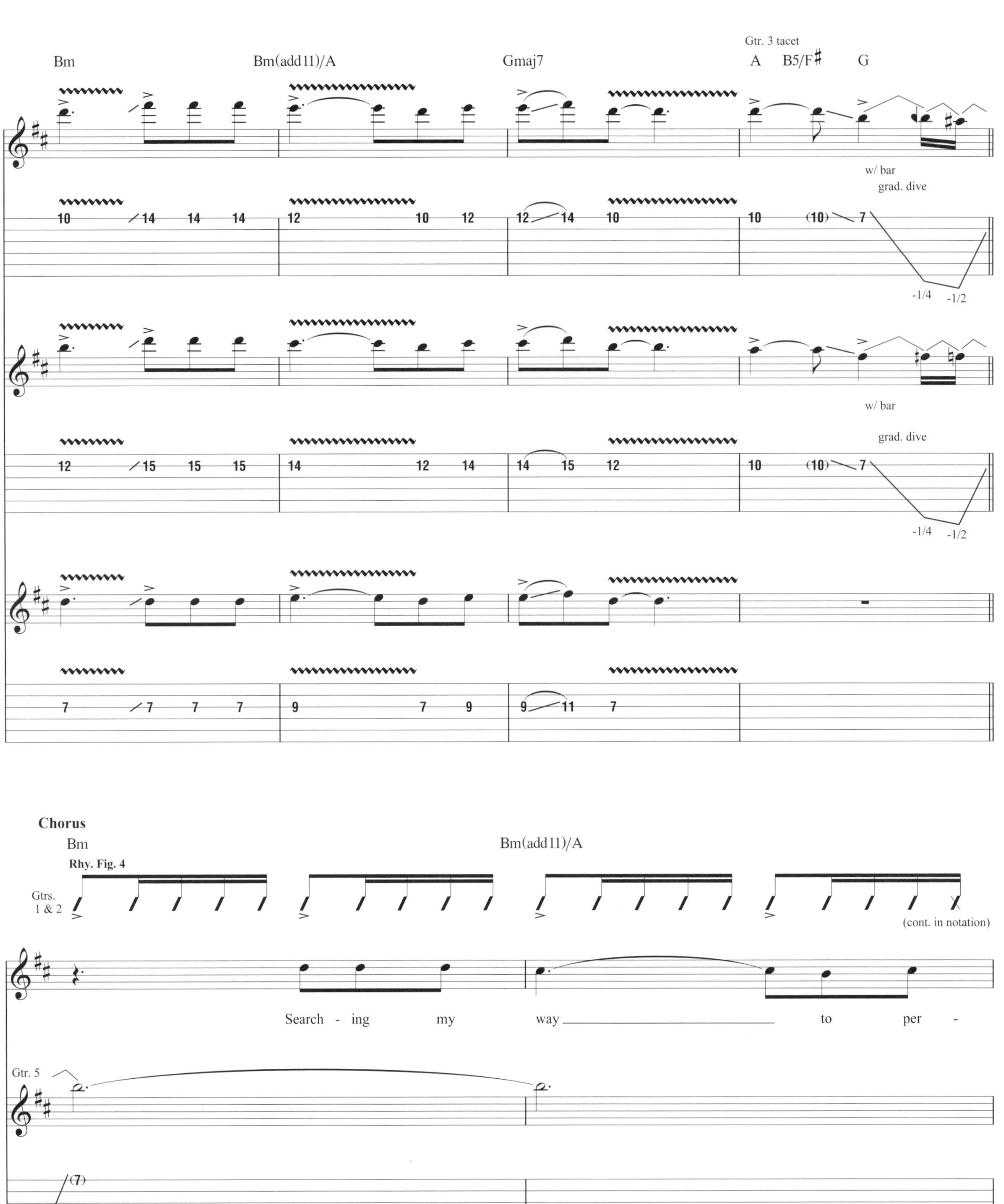
Gtr. 3 tacet
Bm
Bm(add11)/A
Gmaj7
A
B5/F♯
G
w/ bar
grad. dive
-1/4
-1/2
Chorus
Rhy. Fig. 4
Gtrs. 1 & 2
(cont. in notation)
Search - ing my way to per -
Gtr. 5
Gtr. 7
w/ bar
-1/2

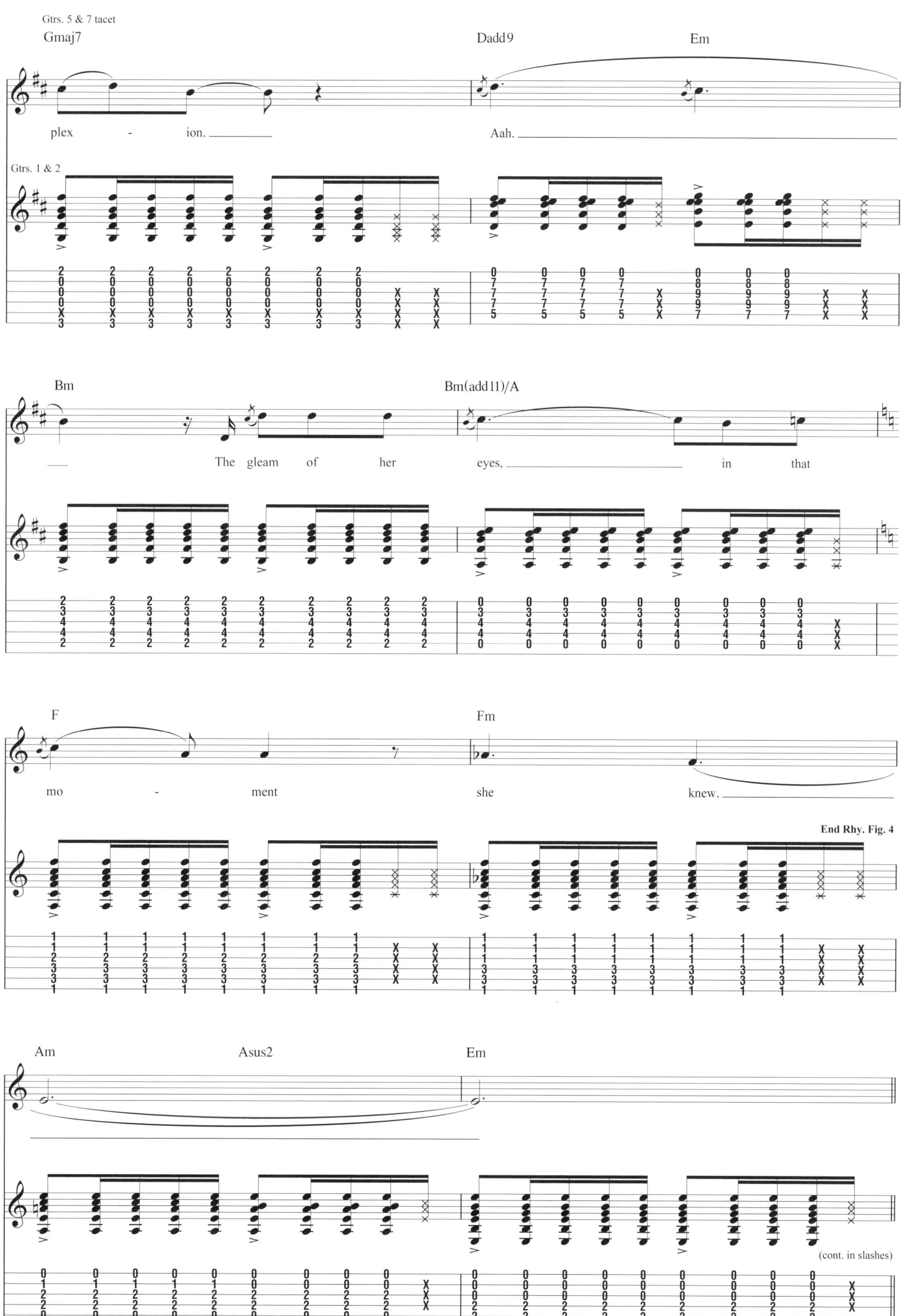
Gtrs. 5 & 7 tacet
Gmaj7
Dadd9
Em
plex - ion.
Aah.
Gtrs. 1 & 2
Bm
Bm(add11)/A
The gleam of her eyes, in that
F
Fm
mo - ment she knew.
End Rhy. Fig. 4
Am
Asus2
Em
(cont. in slashes)

Interlude
A5
Gtrs. 1 & 2
Riff F2
Gtr. 7
Riff F1
Gtr. 5
Riff F
Gtr. 8 (acous.)
End Riff F
mf
let ring throughout
Gtr. 8: w/ Riff F (5 times)
Gtrs. 1 & 2 tacet
Am
Am/G♯
Am/G
Am/F♯
End Riff F2
Gtr. 7
Gtr. 5
End Riff F1
Gtr. 3

Gtrs. 5 & 7: w/ Riffs F1 & F2
Am
Am/B
Am/C
Am/D
Am
Am/G♯
Am/G
Am/F♯
Gtr. 3
Gtr. 3 tacet
Gtr. 7
Gm
Gm/F♯
Gm/F
Gm/E
E♭maj7
Cm9(no3rd)
D
Dsus4
Gtr. 5
Gtr. 8
Riff G
End Riff G

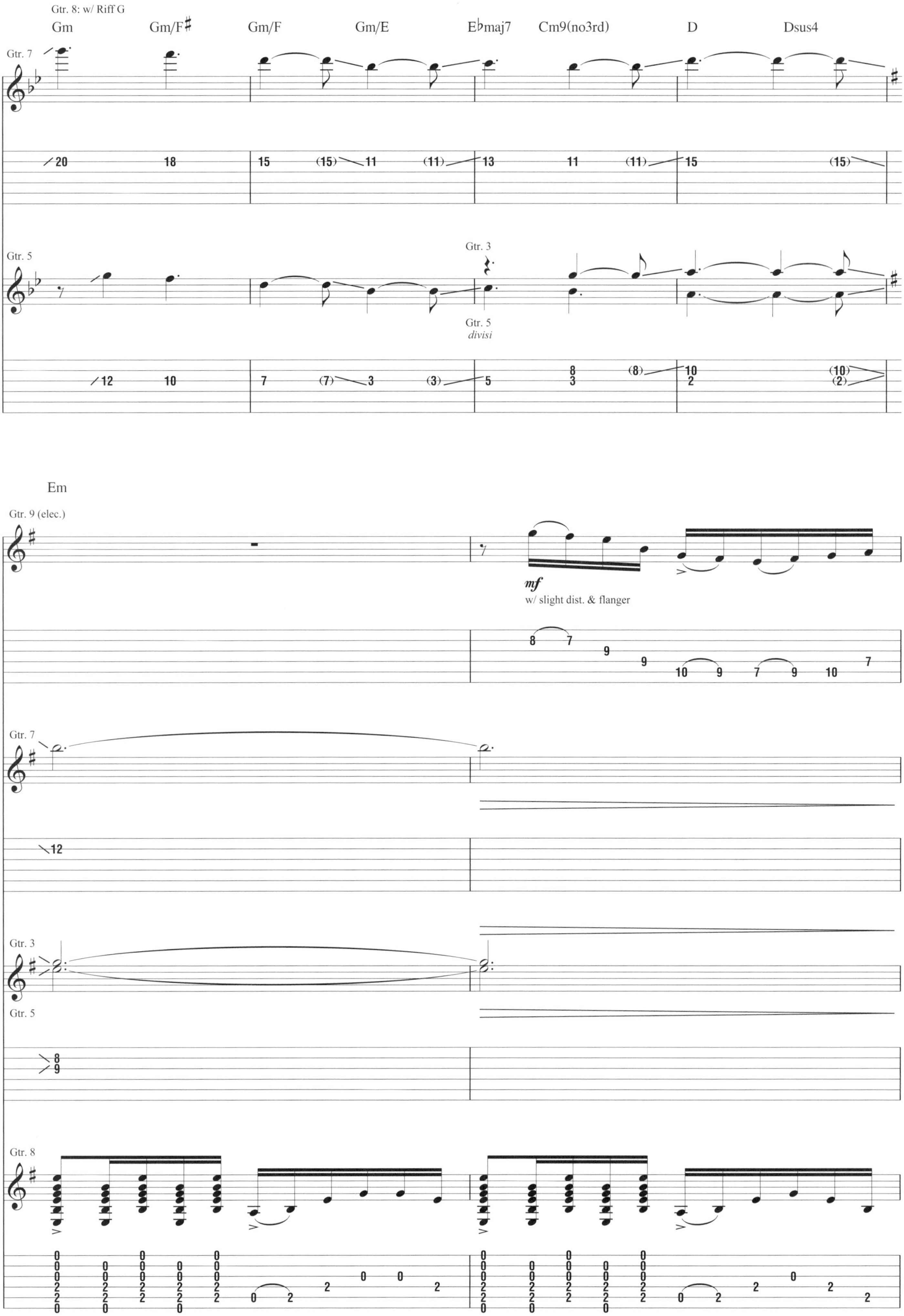

Gtr. 8: w/ Riff G

Gm Gm/F♯ Gm/F Gm/E E♭maj7 Cm9(no3rd) D Dsus4

Gtr. 7

Gtr. 5

Gtr. 3

Gtr. 5
divisi

Em

Gtr. 9 (elec.)

mf
w/ slight dist. & flanger

Gtr. 7

Gtr. 3

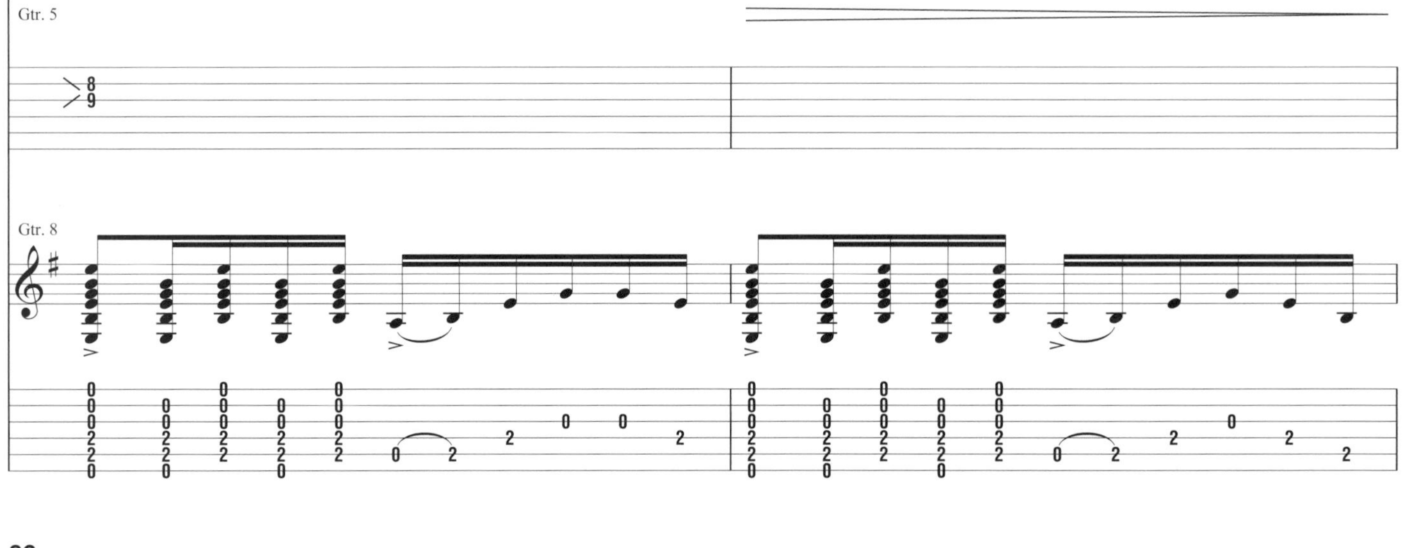

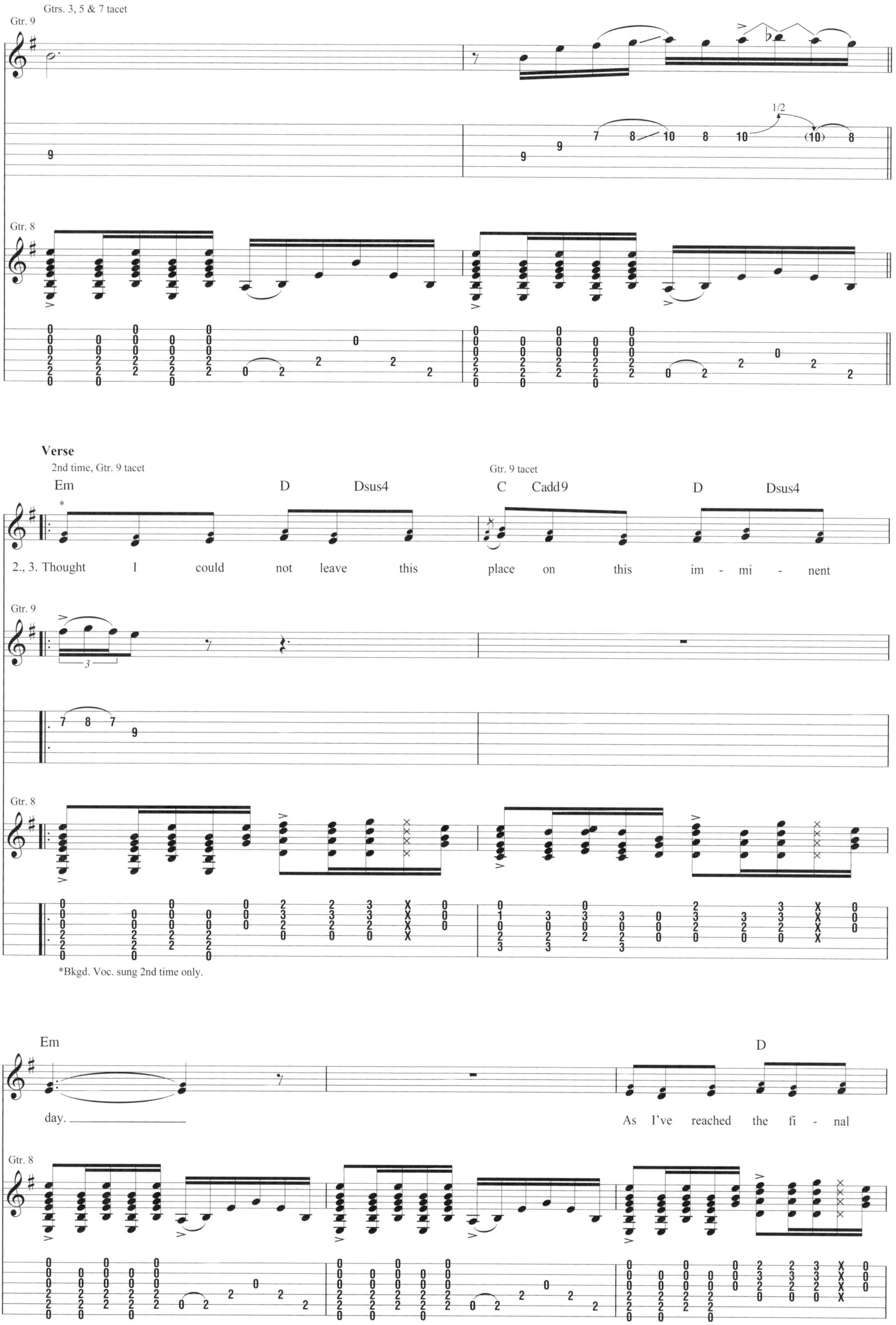
Gtrs. 3, 5 & 7 tacet
Gtr. 9
1/2
Gtr. 8
Verse
2nd time, Gtr. 9 tacet
Em
D
Dsus4
Gtr. 9 tacet
C
Cadd9
D
Dsus4
2., 3. Thought I could not leave this place on this im - mi - nent
Gtr. 9
Gtr. 8
*Bkgd. Voc. sung 2nd time only.
Em
D
day.
As I've reached the fi - nal
Gtr. 8

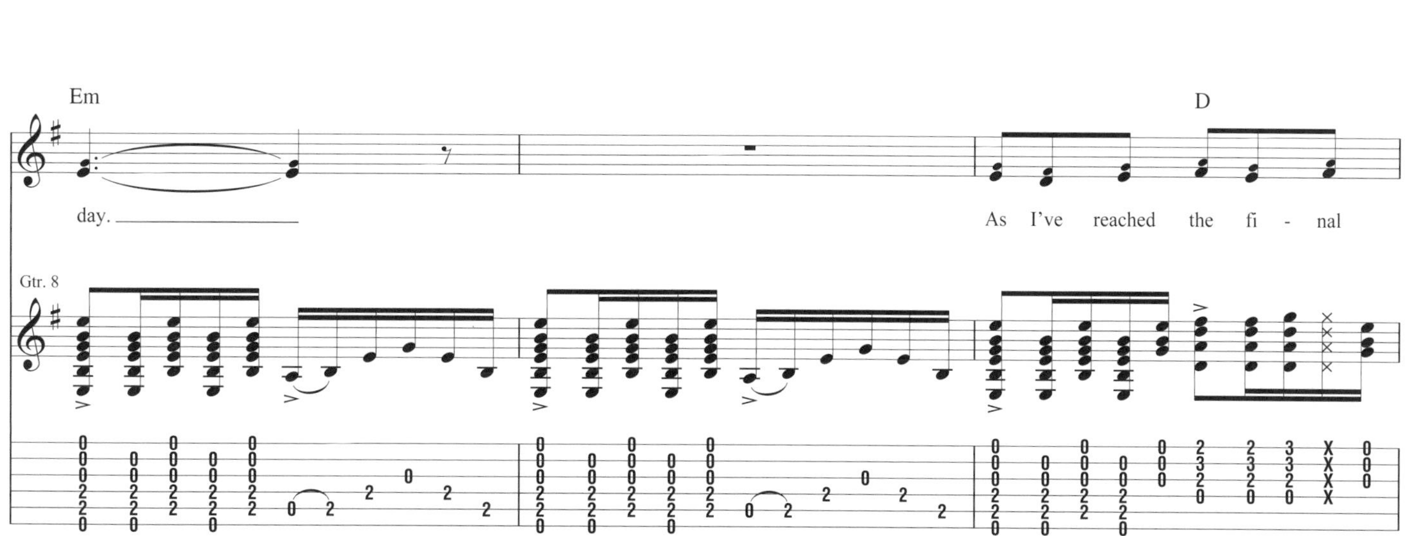

2nd time, Gtr. 8: w/ Rhy. Fill 1
C Cadd9
D
Em
dawn to what's gone a - stray.

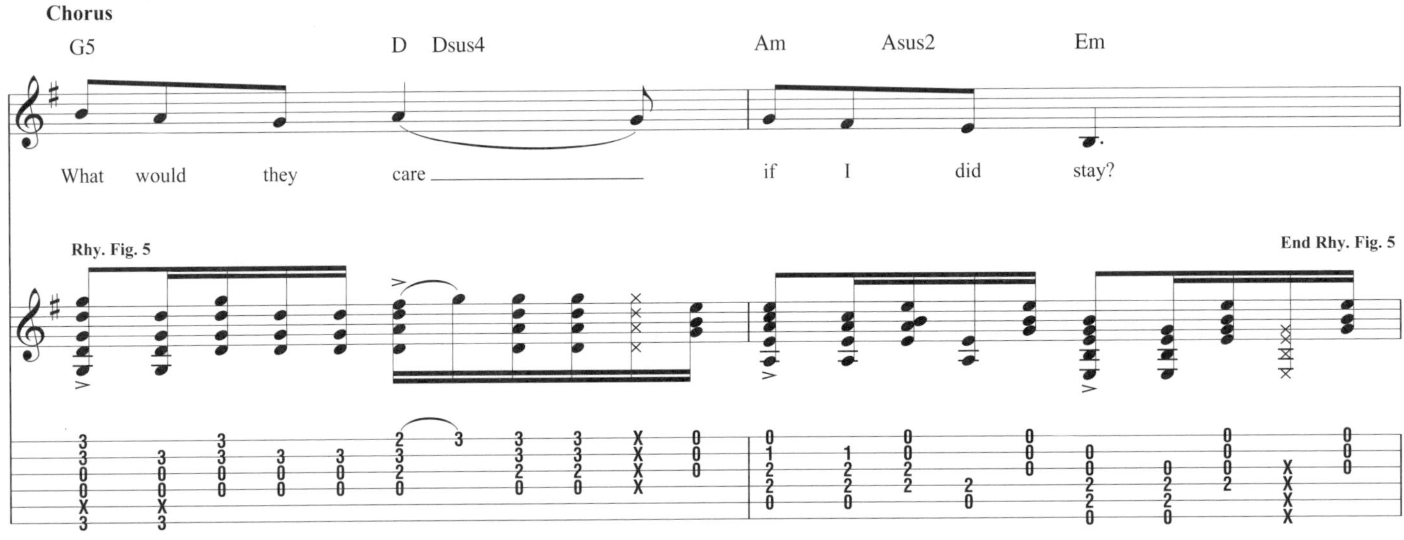
Chorus
G5
D Dsus4
Am
Asus2
Em
What would they care if I did stay?
Rhy. Fig. 5
End Rhy. Fig. 5

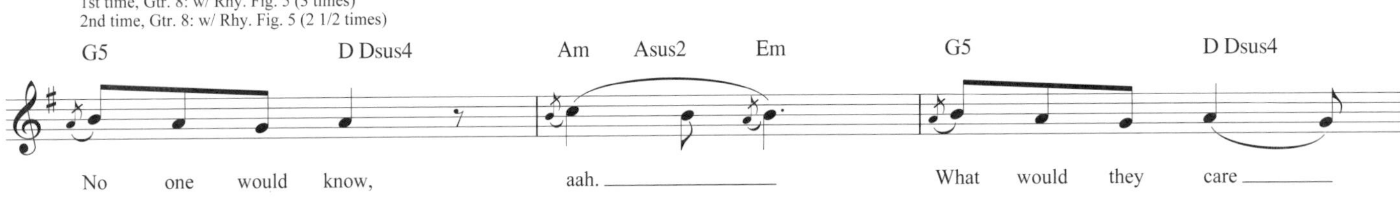
1st time, Gtr. 8: w/ Rhy. Fig. 5 (3 times)
2nd time, Gtr. 8: w/ Rhy. Fig. 5 (2 1/2 times)
G5
D Dsus4
Am
Asus2
Em
G5
D Dsus4
No one would know, aah. What would they care

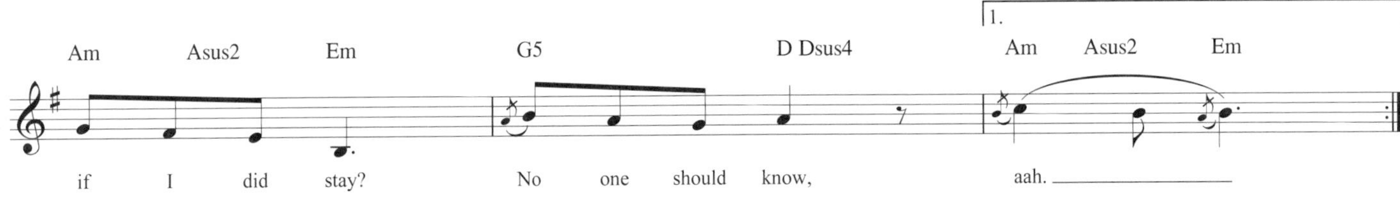
1.
Am
Asus2
Em
G5
D Dsus4
Am
Asus2
Em
if I did stay? No one should know, aah.

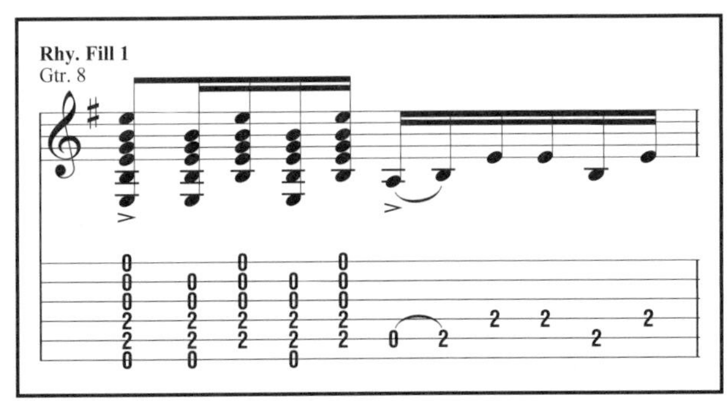
Rhy. Fill 1
Gtr. 8

2.
Am
Asus2
Em
N.C.
aah.
Gtr. 8

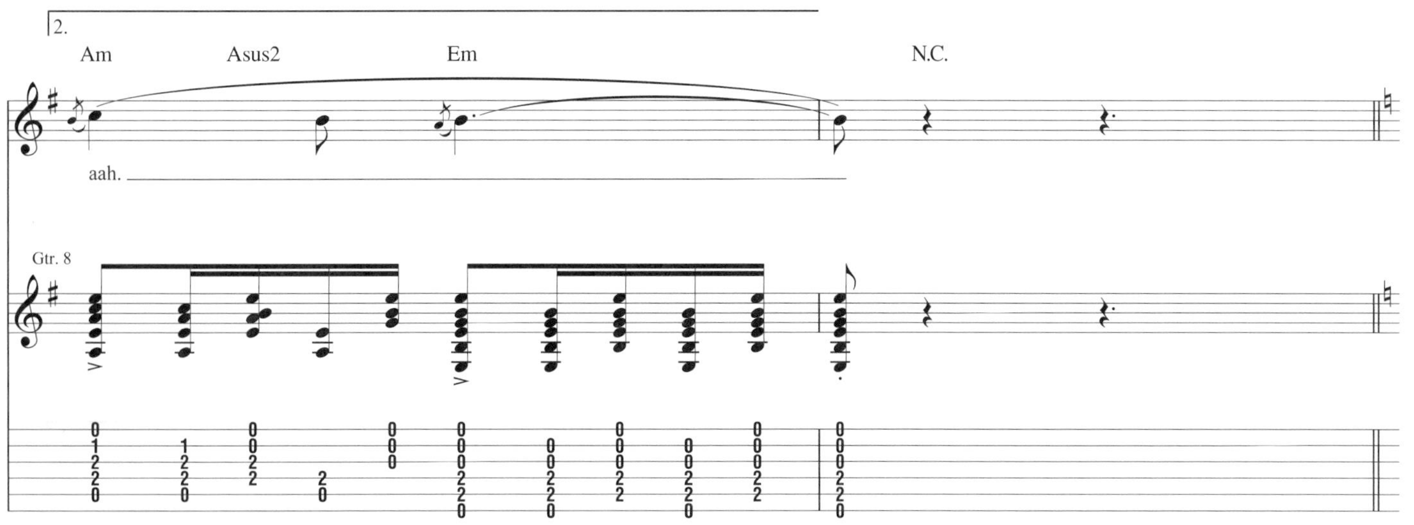

Interlude

Gtr. 8 tacet

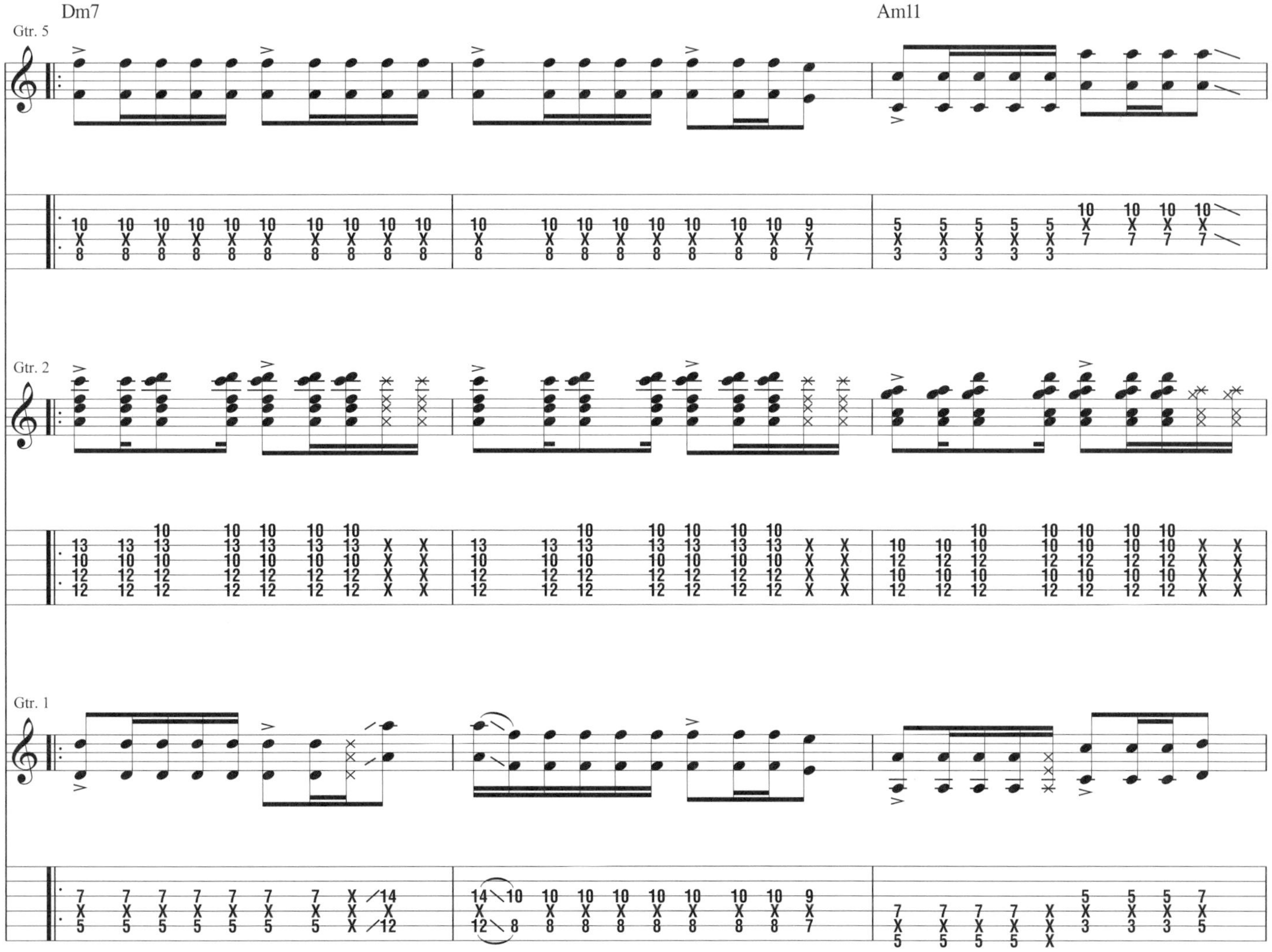

Dm7
Am11
Gtr. 5
Gtr. 2
Gtr. 1

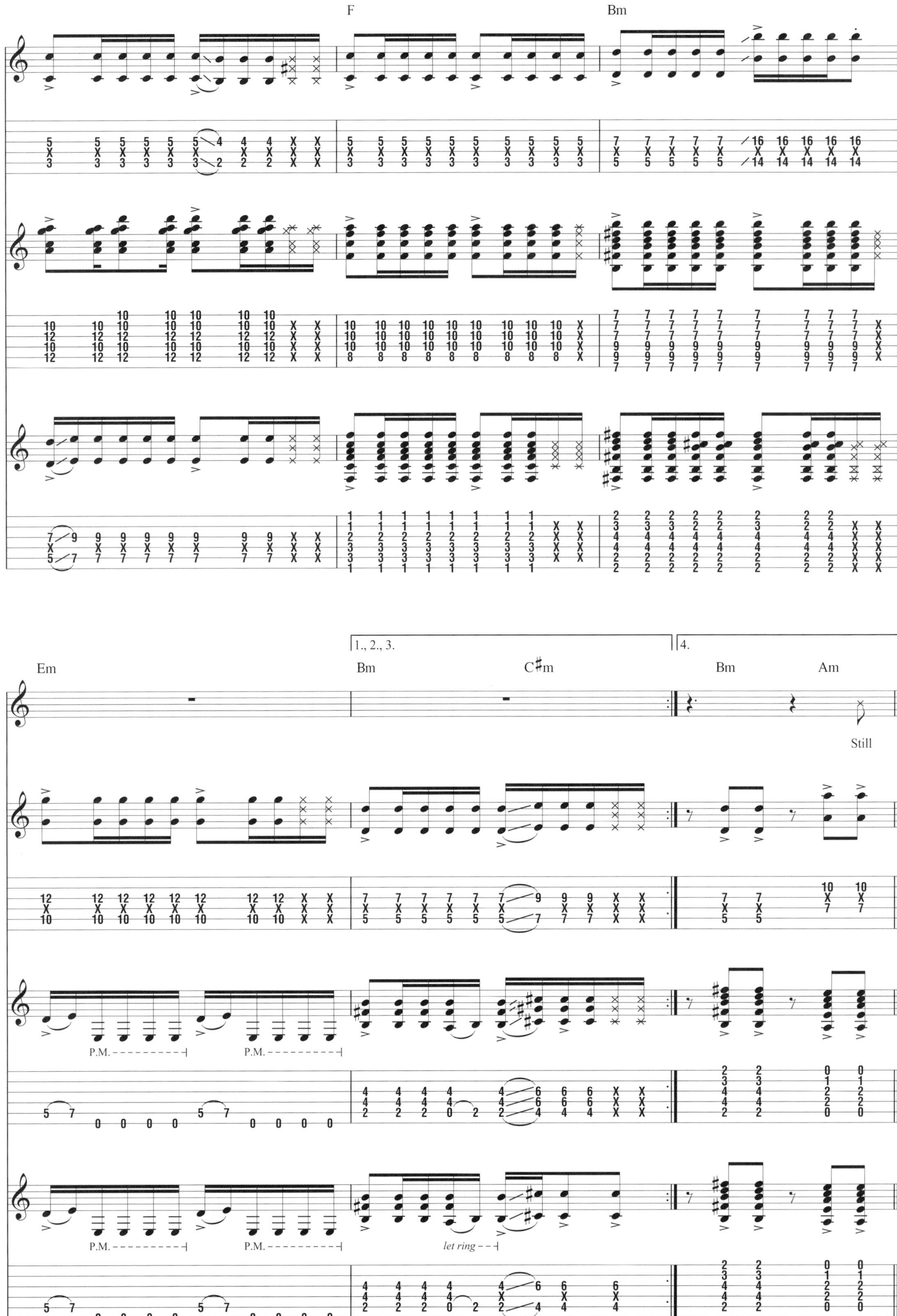
F
Bm
Em
1., 2., 3.
4.
Bm
C♯m
Bm
Am
Still
P.M.
let ring

Bridge
Gtr. 5 tacet
E5
N.C.
brood - ing,
sooth - ing
Riff H
Gtrs. 1 & 2
1/4
P.M.
P.M.
P.M.
E5
E♭5
Gm
calm.
That
End Riff H
let ring
Gtrs. 1 & 2: w/ Riff H (2 times)
E5
N.C.
E5
E♭5
Gm
rig - id,
twist - ed
face,
blank
god - head,
tear my
name,
uh.
Lost
vir - tue,
fran - tic
lust.
Gtrs. 1 & 2
1/4
P.M.
P.M.
P.M.
let ring

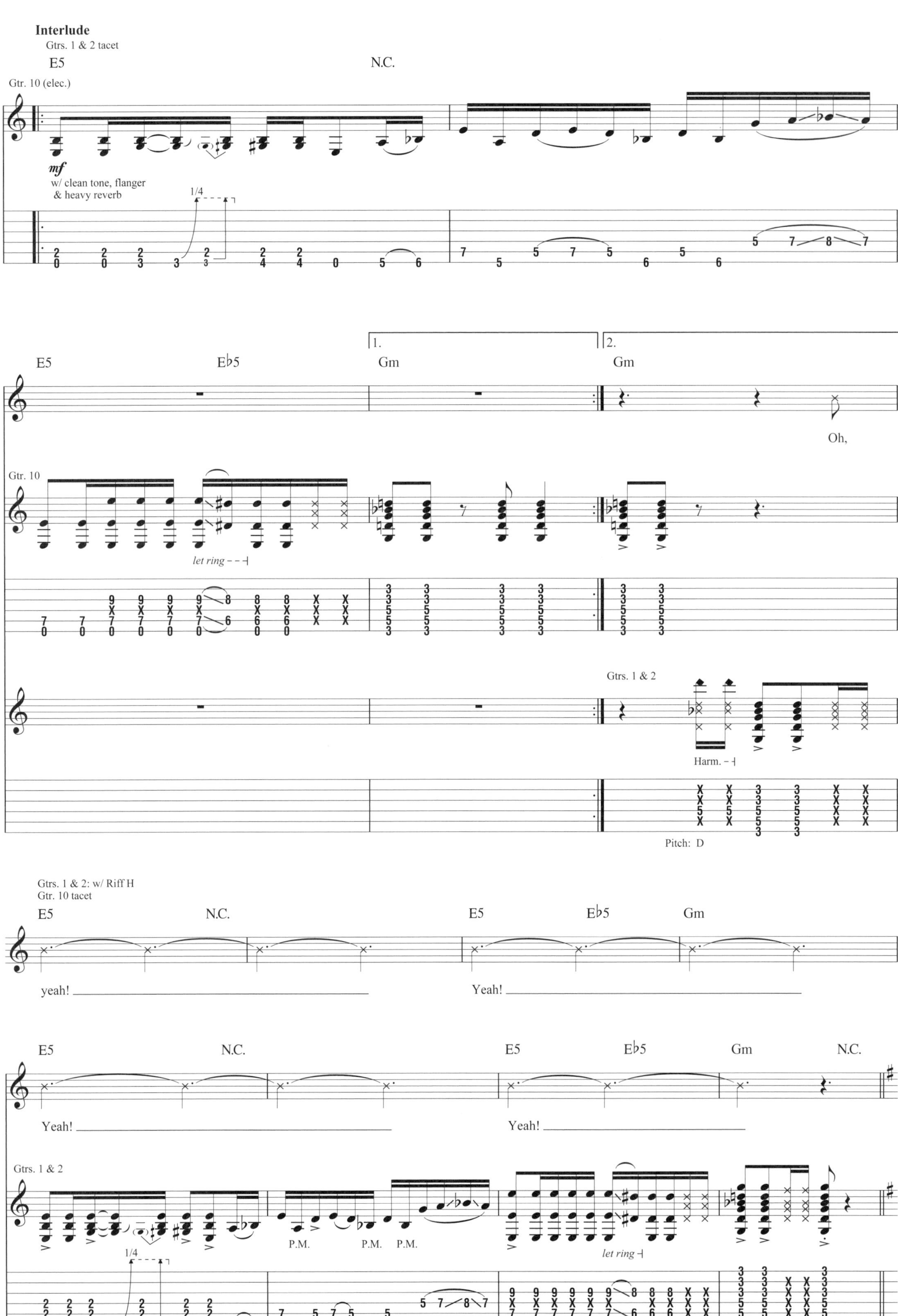

Interlude
Gtrs. 1 & 2 tacet
E5
N.C.
Gtr. 10 (elec.)
mf
w/ clean tone, flanger
& heavy reverb
1/4
E5
E♭5
1.
Gm
2.
Gm
Oh,
Gtr. 10
let ring
Gtrs. 1 & 2
Harm.
Pitch: D
Gtrs. 1 & 2: w/ Riff H
Gtr. 10 tacet
E5
N.C.
E5
E♭5
Gm
yeah!
Yeah!
E5
N.C.
E5
E♭5
Gm
N.C.
Yeah!
Yeah!
Gtrs. 1 & 2
P.M.
P.M.
P.M.
let ring
1/4

Bridge
Gtrs. 1 & 2: w/ Riff C (4 times)
Gtr. 3: w/ Riff C1
Gtr. 4: w/ Riff C1 (4 times)
N.C.
Sly smile, poi - soned glare be - hind,
Gtr. 3: w/ Riff D
un - dis - guised man - made no - va.
Gtr. 3: w/ Riff C1
Mute cry, don't dare to tread.
Gtr. 3: w/ Riff D
Sear - ing beams track - ing you down.
Interlude
Gtrs. 1 & 2: w/ Riff E1 (2 times)
Gtr. 5: w/ Riff E (2 times)
A7/G Cm/G F#°7 Bm/F# N.C. D#5 D5 A#5 B5 F#5 G5 E5
Voc. Fig. 1
End Voc. Fig. 1
(Aah. Aah.)
Bridge
Bkgd. Vocs.: w/ Voc. Fig. 1 (2 times)
Gtrs. 1 & 2: w/ Riff E (2 times)
Gtr. 5: w/ Riff E1 (1 3/4 times)
A7/G Cm/G F#°7 Bm/F# N.C. D#5 D5 A#5 B5 F#5 G5 E5
A - dor - ing what nev - er has been.
Gtrs. 5 & 6: w/ Fills 2 & 2A
A7/G Cm/G F#°7 Bm/F# N.C. D#5 D5 A#5 B5 F#5 G5 E5
Some will bring with them all they have seen, oh.
Chorus
Gtrs. 1 & 2: w/ Rhy. Fig. 3
Bm Bm(add11)/A Gmaj7 Dadd9 Em
Search - ing my way to per - plex - ion. Aah.

Bm
Bm(add11)/A
Gmaj7
A
B5/F♯
G
In crum - bling faith I saw her
Gtrs. 1 & 2: w/ Rhy. Fig. 4
Bm
Bm(add11)/A
Gmaj7
Dadd9
Em
bear - ing her pain in the wil - der - ness.
Aah.
Bm
Bm(add11)/A
F
Fm
The gleam of her eyes, in that mo - ment she knew.
Yeah!
Outro
G♯5
G5
F5
B5
A♯5
F5
E5
Gtrs. 1 & 2
Riff I
End Riff I
Gtrs. 1 & 2: w/ Riff I (4 times)
Yeah!
N.C.

from *Blackwater Park*

Harvest

Words and Music by Mikael Akerfeldt

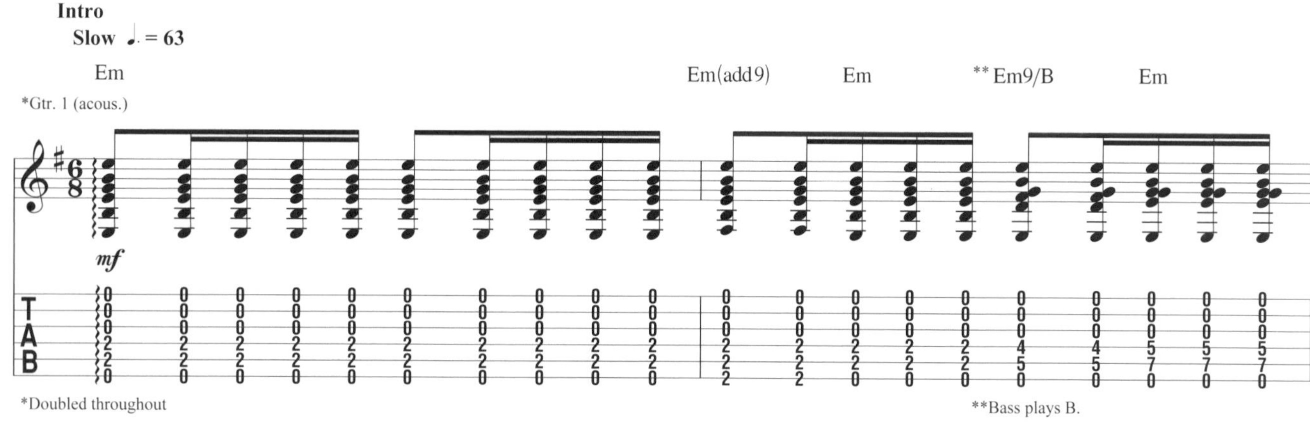

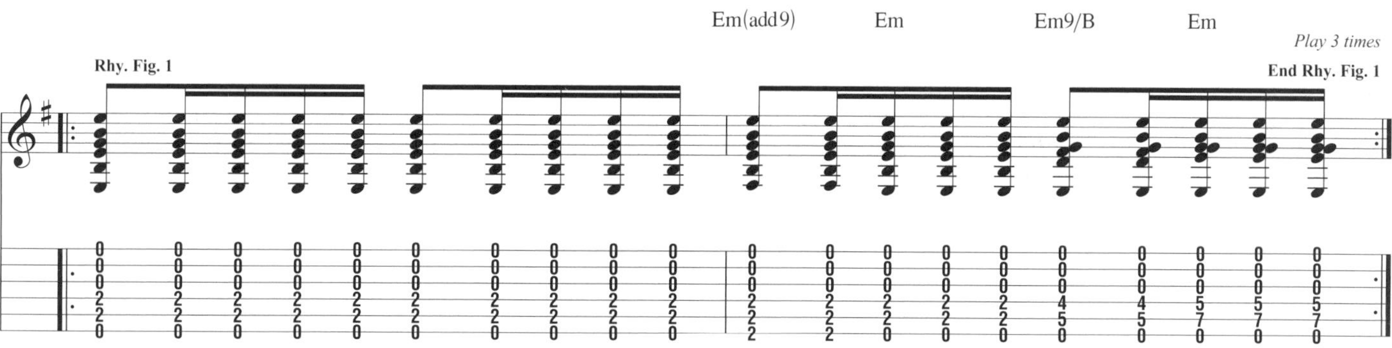

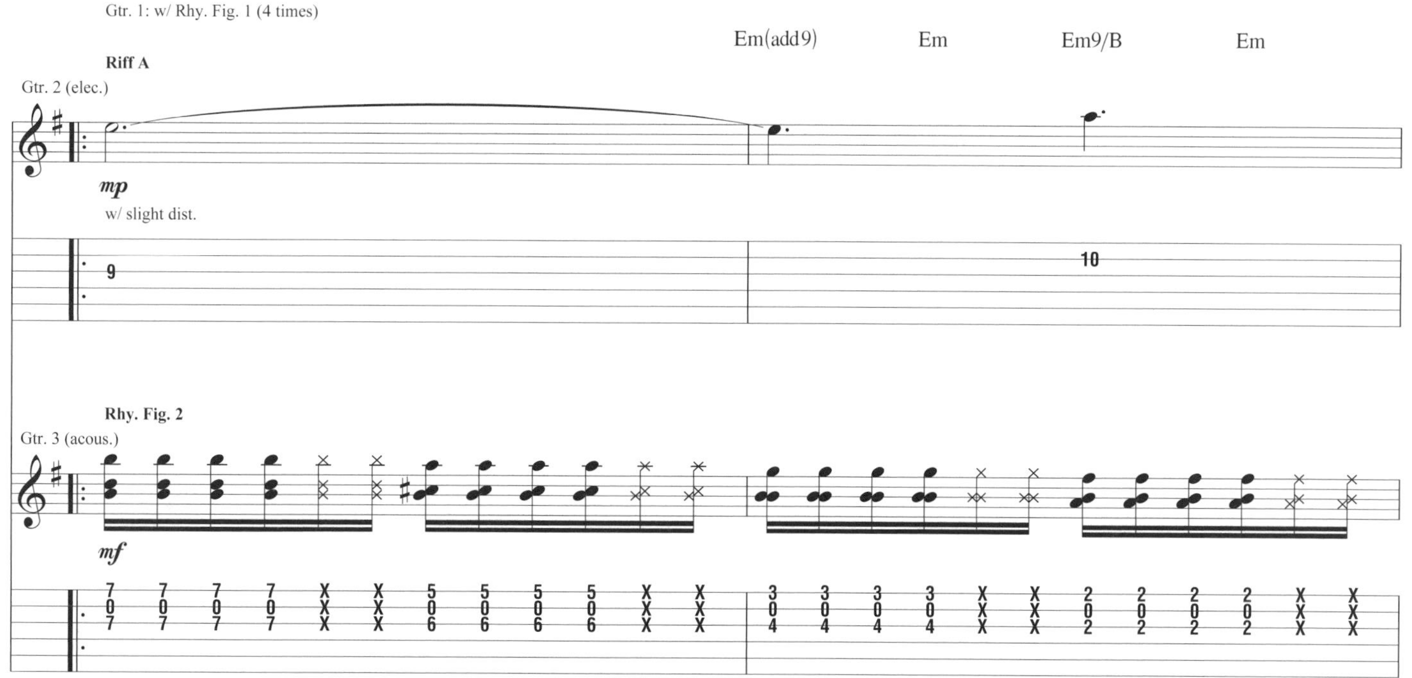

Em(add9)
Em
Em9/B
Em
End Rhy. Fig. 2
Gtr. 3: w/ Rhy. Fig. 2
Gtr. 2
Em(add9)
Em
Em9/B
Em
Em(add9)
Em
Em9/B
Em
End Riff A
let ring
Asus2
Bm
Em
Asus2
Bm
Gtr. 2
Rhy. Fig. 3
End Rhy. Fig. 3
Gtr. 1
Gtr. 1: w/ Rhy. Fig. 3 (3 times)
Gtr. 2 tacet
Em
Asus2
Bm
Em
Asus2
Bm
Gtr. 2

Verse
3rd time, Gtr. 2: w/ Fill 1
Cm
Csus2
A♭
1. Stay with me a
2. Pledge your - self to
3. Spir - it paint - ed
Rhy. Fig. 4
Gtr. 1
Gm
G
while.
me.
sin,
End Rhy. Fig. 4
let ring
Gtr. 1: w/ Rhy. Fig. 4 (3 times)
Cm
Csus2
A♭
Gm
G
Rise a - bove the vile.
Nev - er leave me be.
em - bers 'neath my skin.
Name my fi - nal rest,
Sweat breaks on my brow,
Veiled in pale em - brace,
Fill 1
Gtr. 2

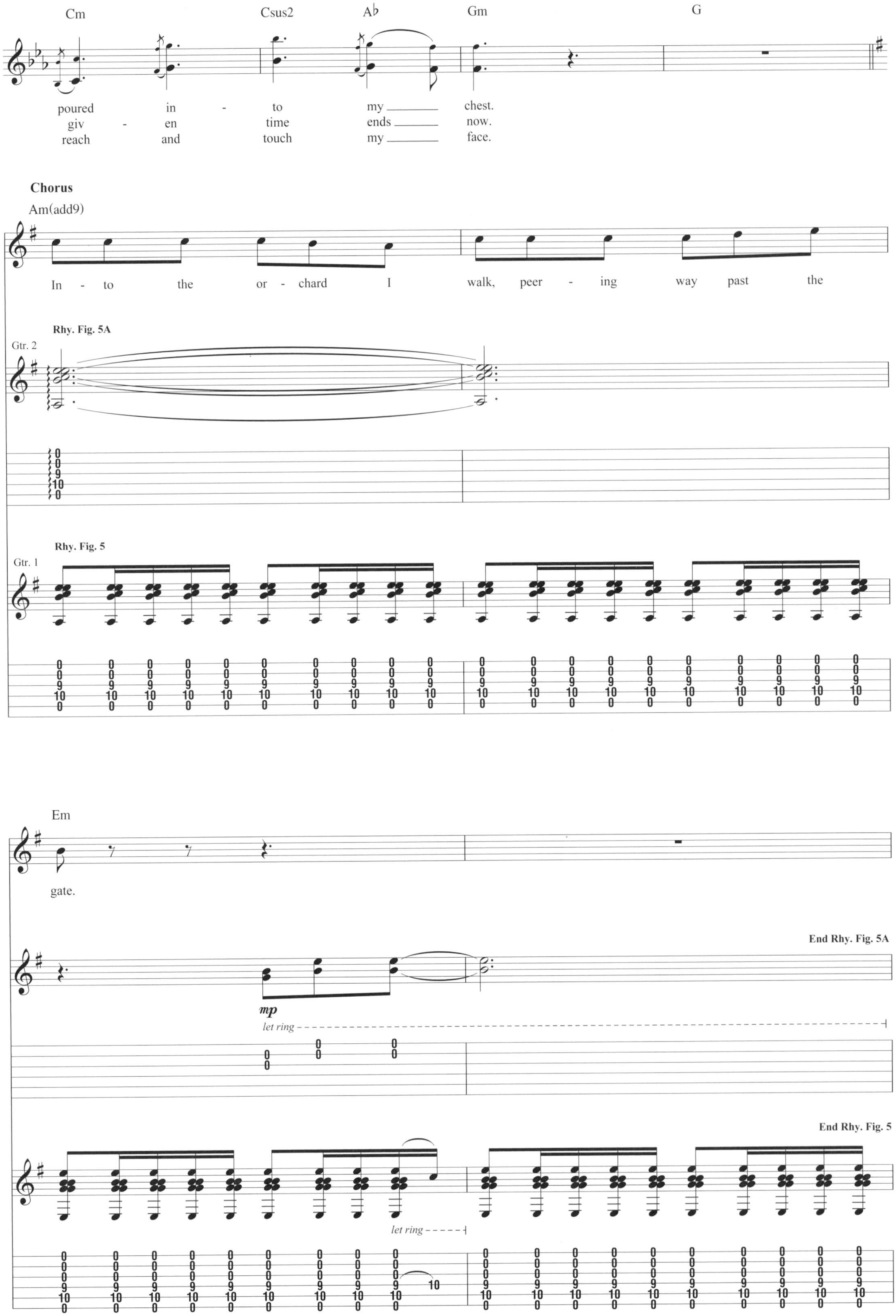

Cm Csus2 A♭ Gm G

poured in - to my chest.
giv - en time ends now.
reach and touch my face.

Chorus

Am(add9)

In - to the or - chard I walk, peer - ing way past the

Rhy. Fig. 5A

Gtr. 2

Rhy. Fig. 5

Gtr. 1

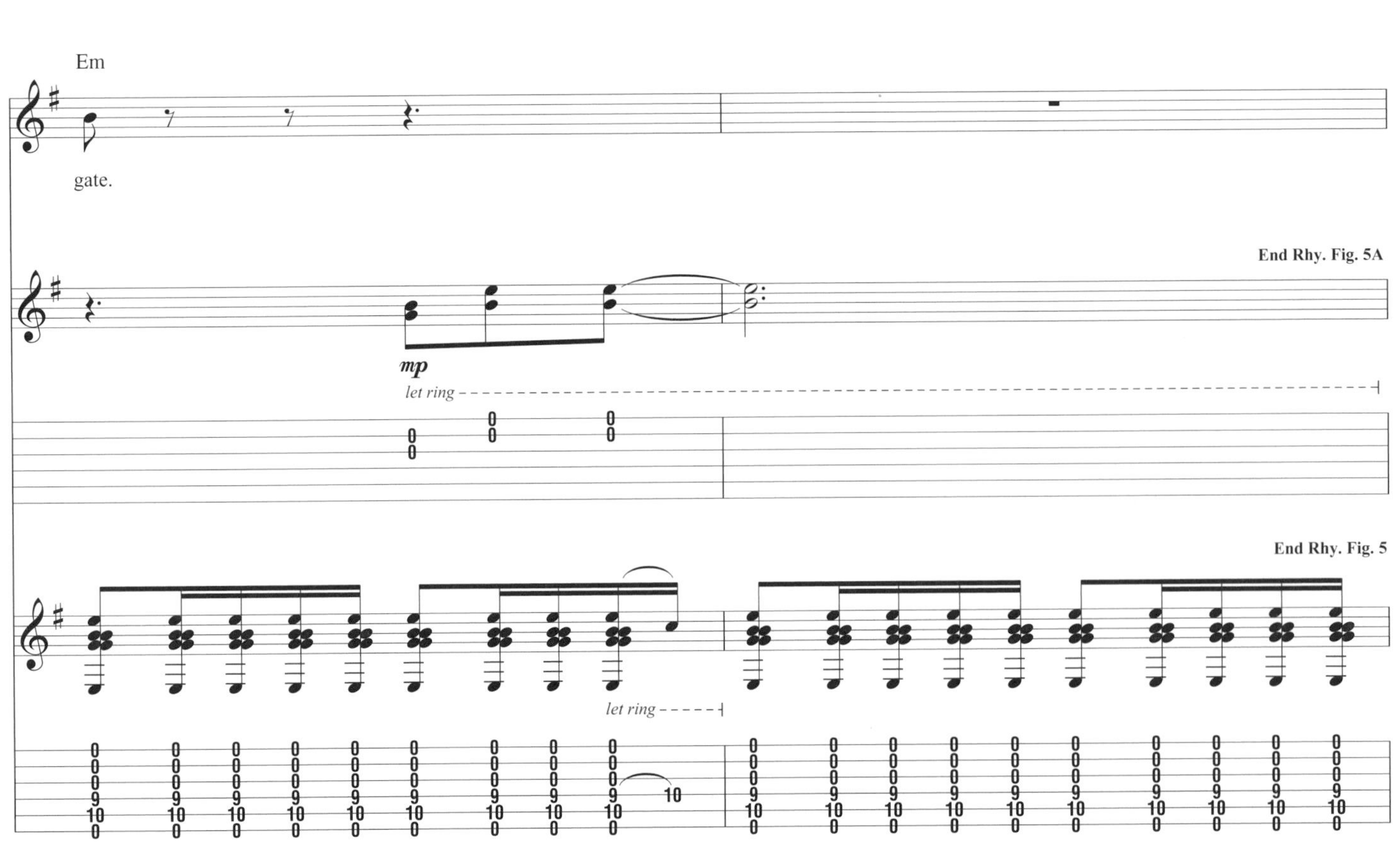

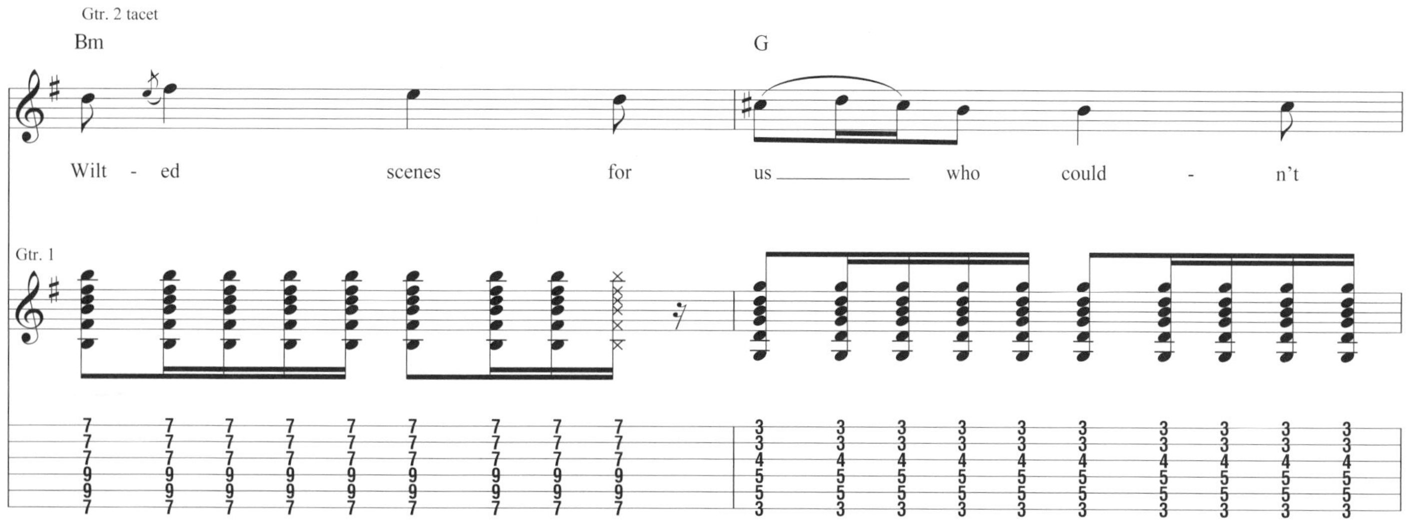
Gtr. 2 tacet
Bm
G
Wilt - ed scenes for us who could - n't
Gtr. 1

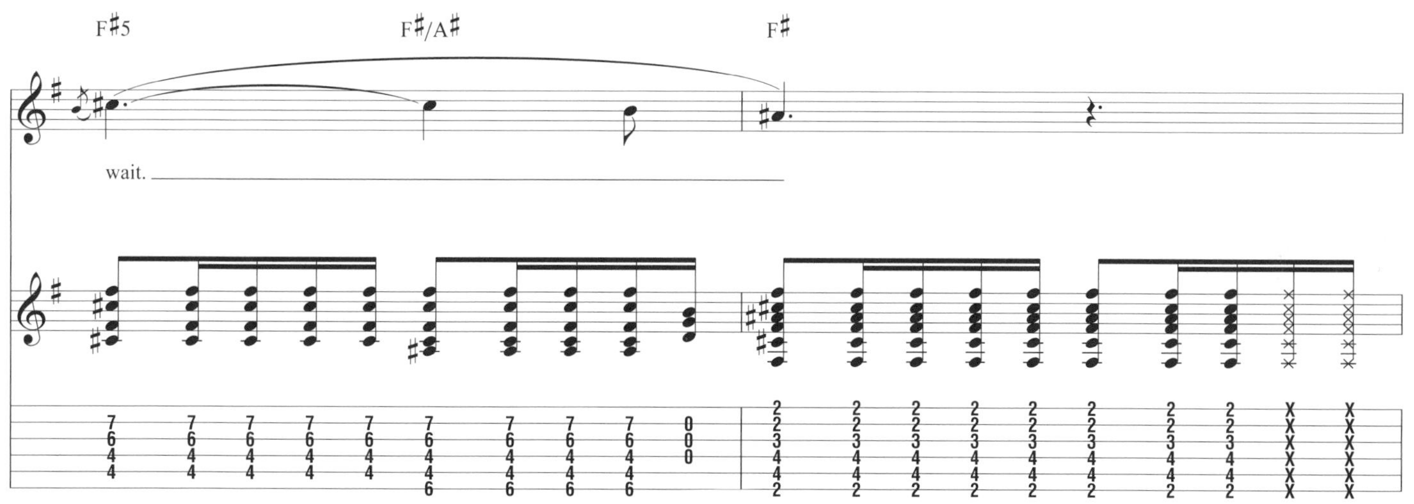
F#5
F#/A#
F#
wait.

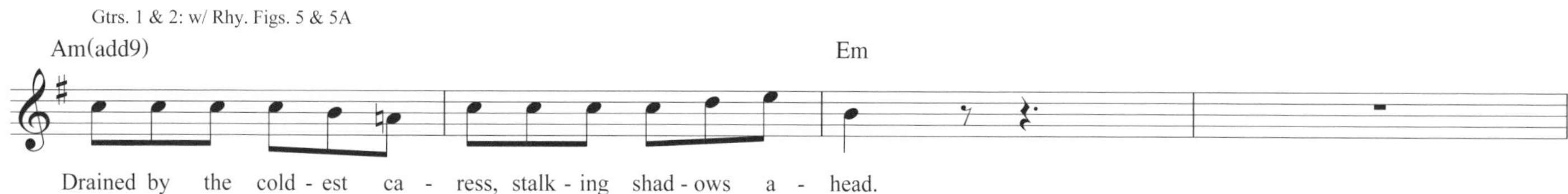
Gtrs. 1 & 2: w/ Rhy. Figs. 5 & 5A
Am(add9)
Em
Drained by the cold - est ca - ress, stalk - ing shad - ows a - head.

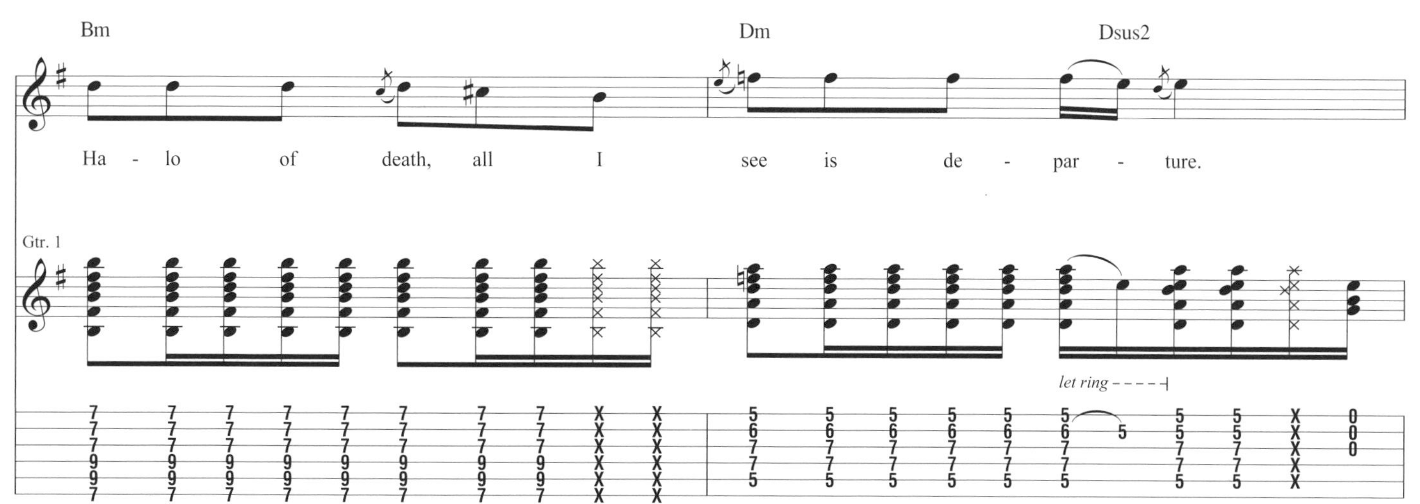
Bm
Dm
Dsus2
Ha - lo of death, all I see is de - par - ture.
Gtr. 1
let ring

1.
Am
A♭
Mourn - er's la - ment, but it's me who's the mar - tyr.

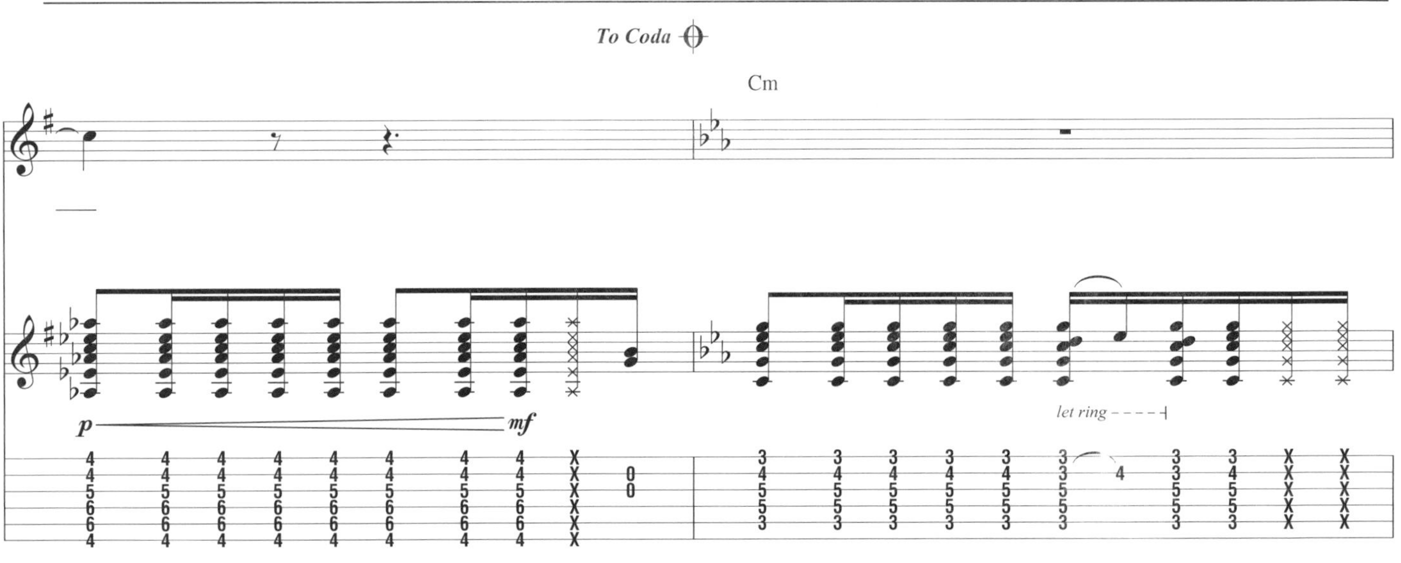
To Coda
Cm
p
mf
let ring

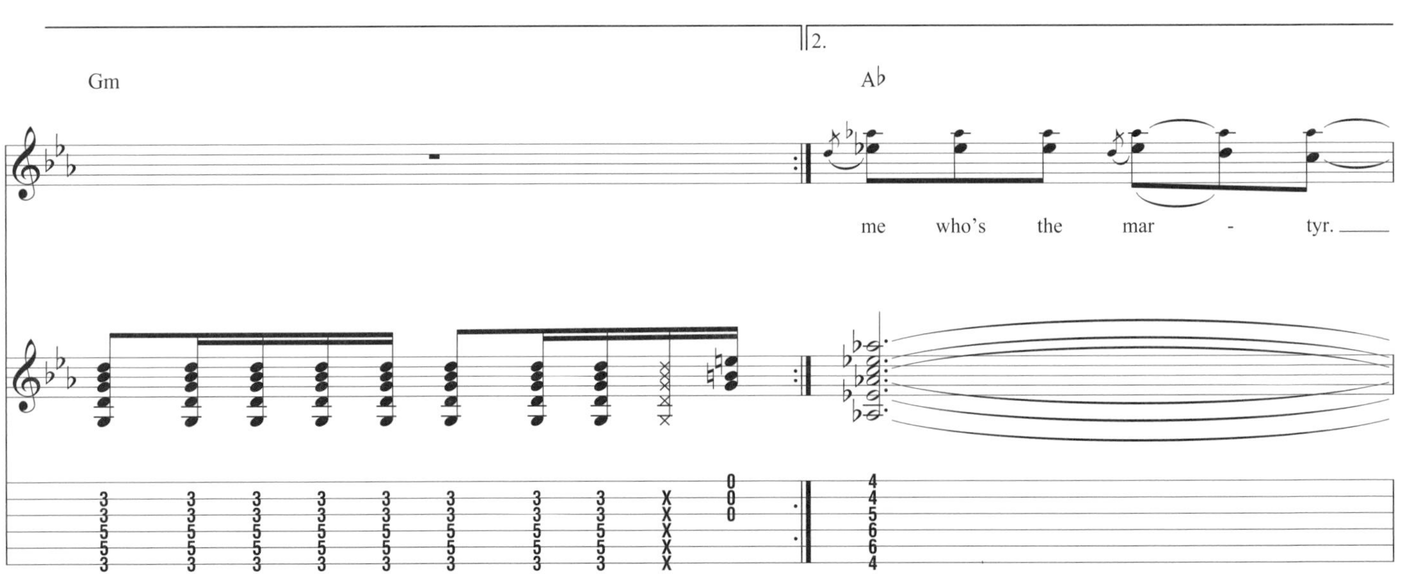
Gm
2.
A♭
me who's the mar - tyr.

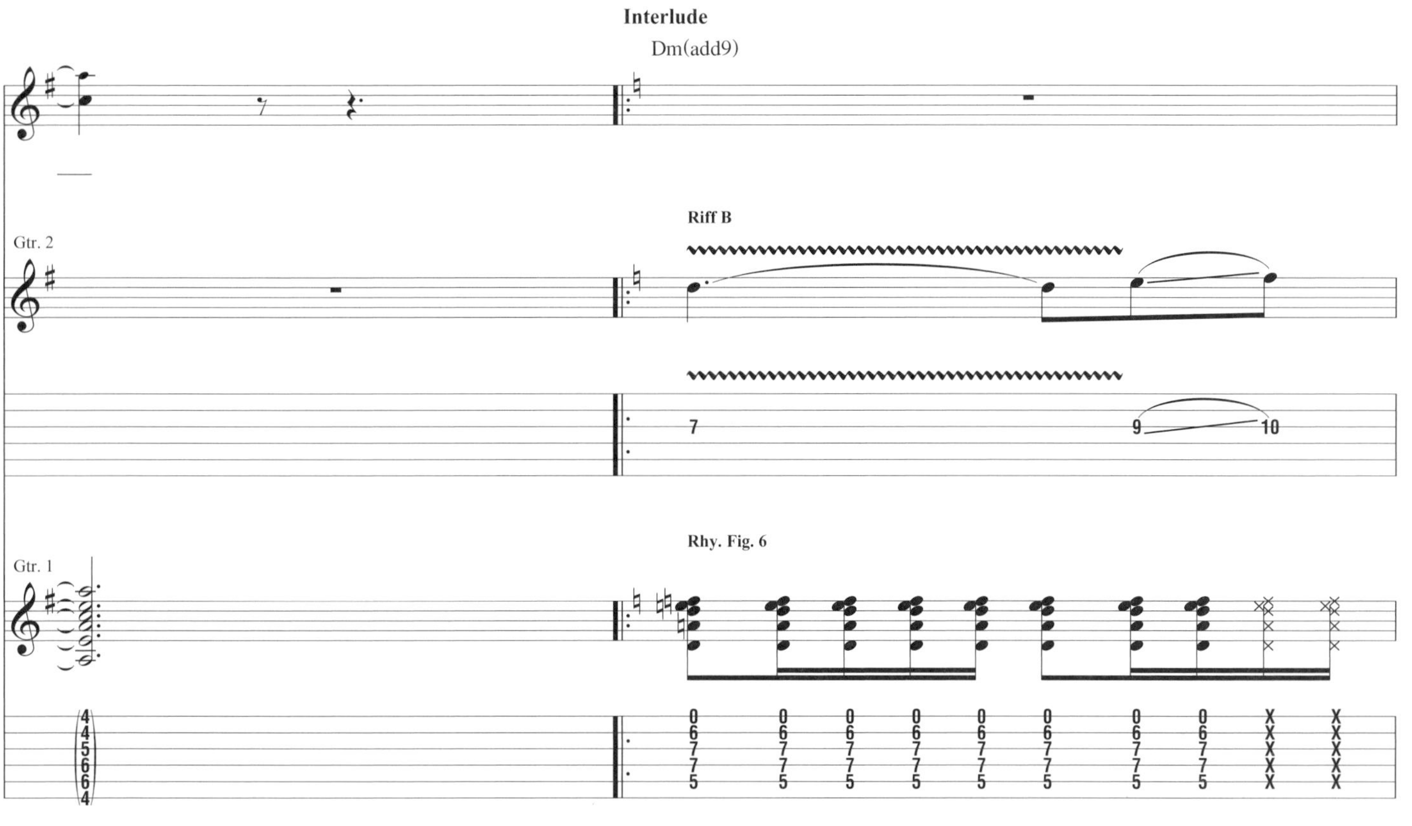
Interlude
Dm(add9)
Riff B
Gtr. 2
Rhy. Fig. 6
Gtr. 1

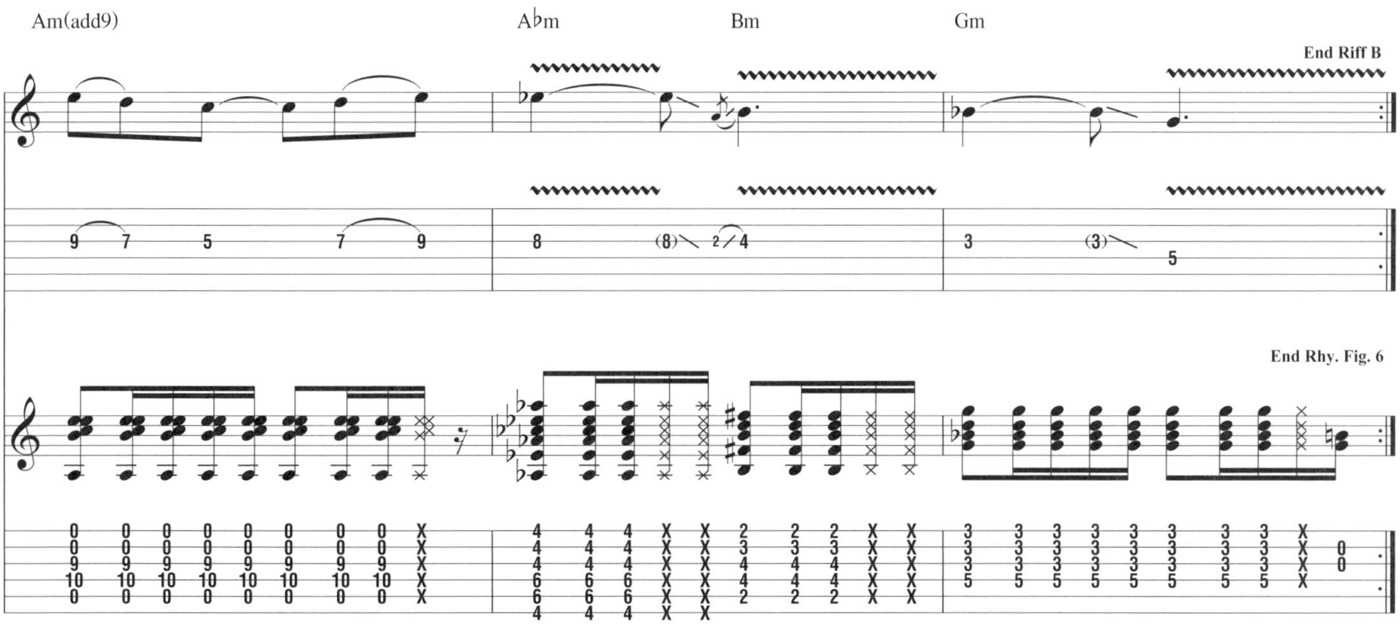
Am(add9)
A♭m
Bm
Gm
End Riff B
End Rhy. Fig. 6

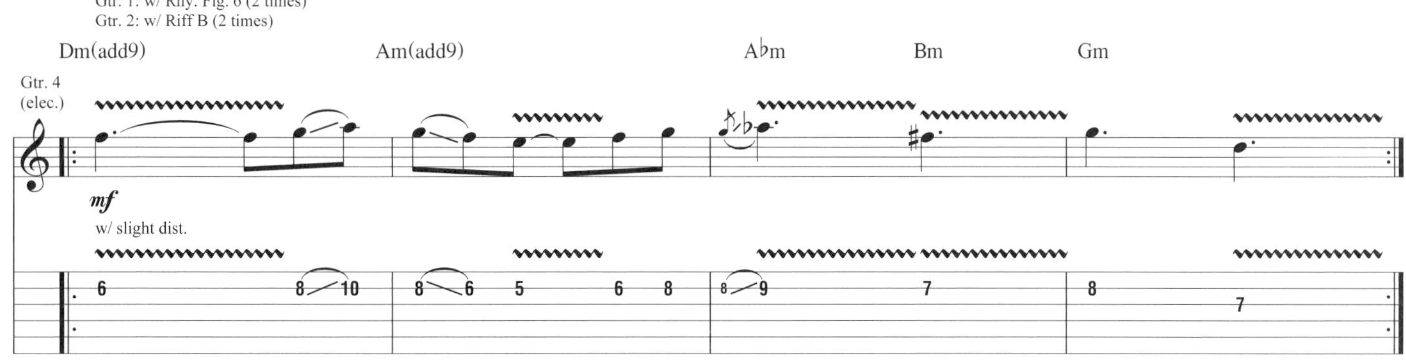
Gtr. 1: w/ Rhy. Fig. 6 (2 times)
Gtr. 2: w/ Riff B (2 times)
Dm(add9)
Am(add9)
A♭m
Bm
Gm
Gtr. 4
(elec.)
mf
w/ slight dist.

Guitar Solo

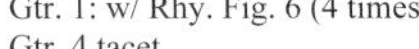
Gtr. 1: w/ Rhy. Fig. 6 (4 times)
Gtr. 4 tacet

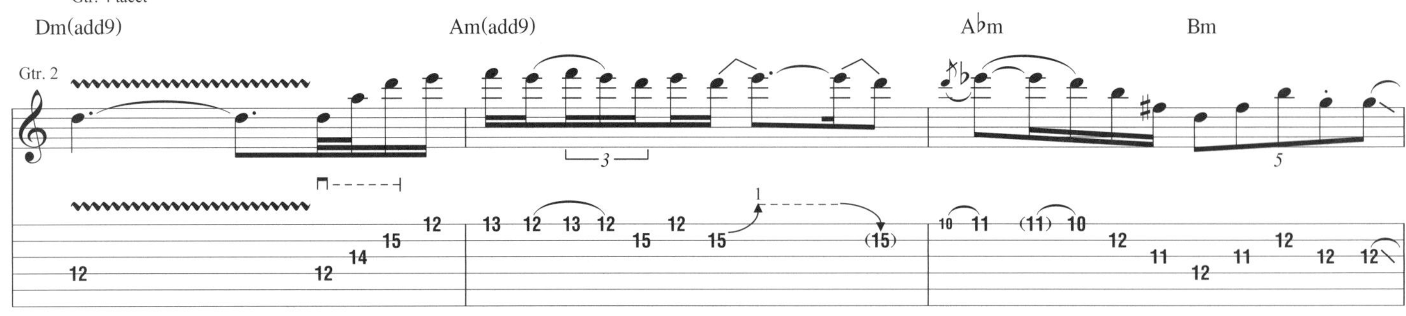
Dm(add9)
Am(add9)
A♭m
Bm
Gtr. 2

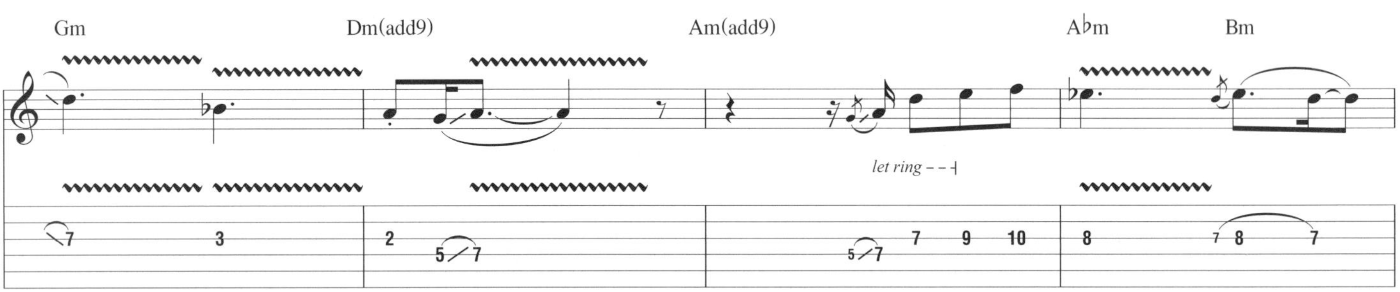
Gm
Dm(add9)
Am(add9)
A♭m
Bm
let ring

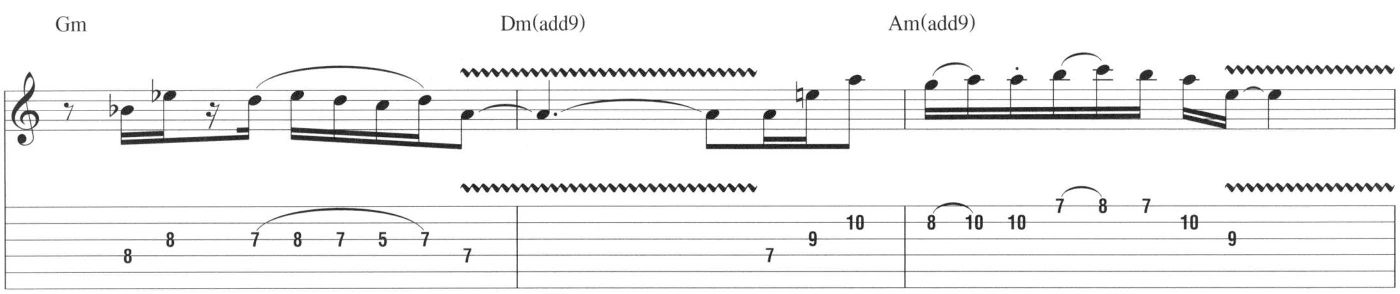
Gm
Dm(add9)
Am(add9)

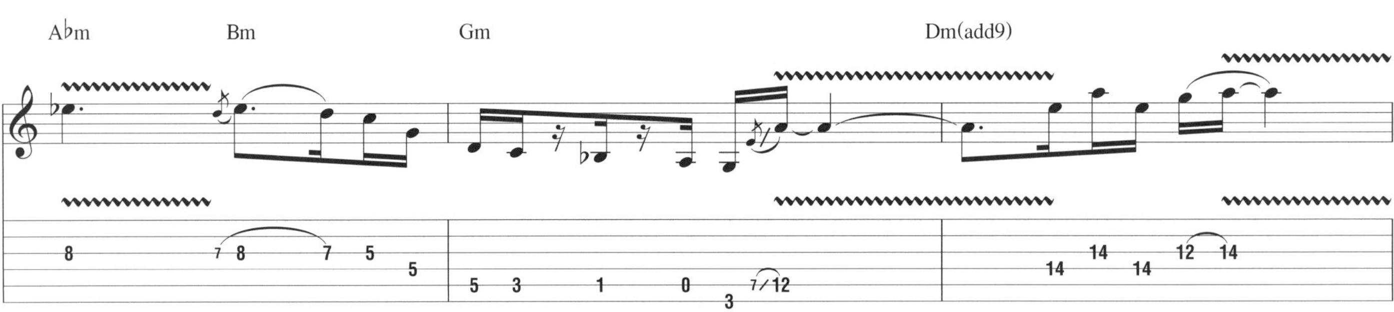
A♭m
Bm
Gm
Dm(add9)

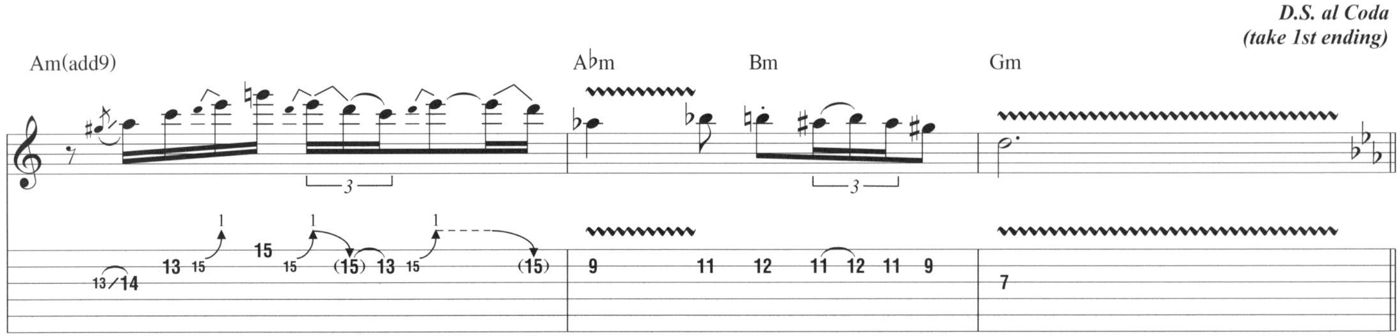
D.S. al Coda
(take 1st ending)
Am(add9)
A♭m
Bm
Gm

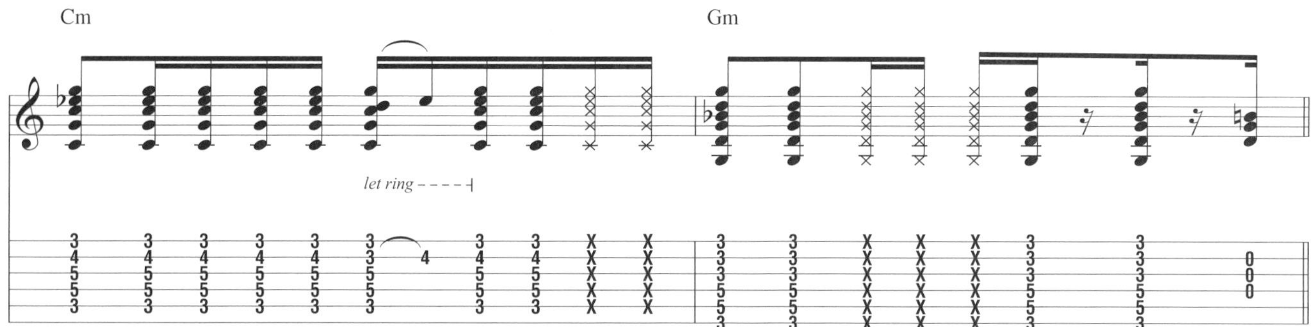

Outro

Gtr. 1: w/ Rhy. Fig. 1 (3 1/2 times)
Gtr. 2: w/ Riff A
Gtr. 3: w/ Rhy. Fig. 2 (1 3/4 times)

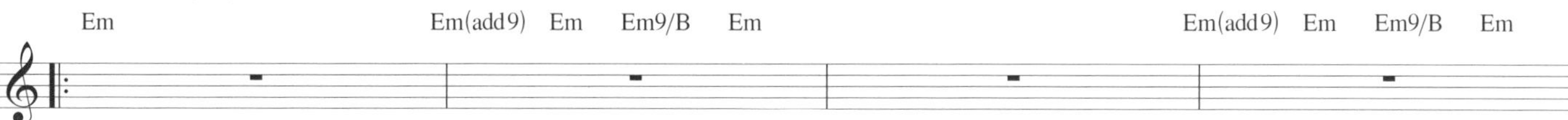

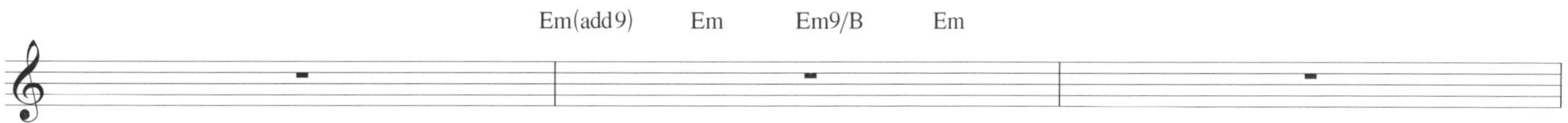

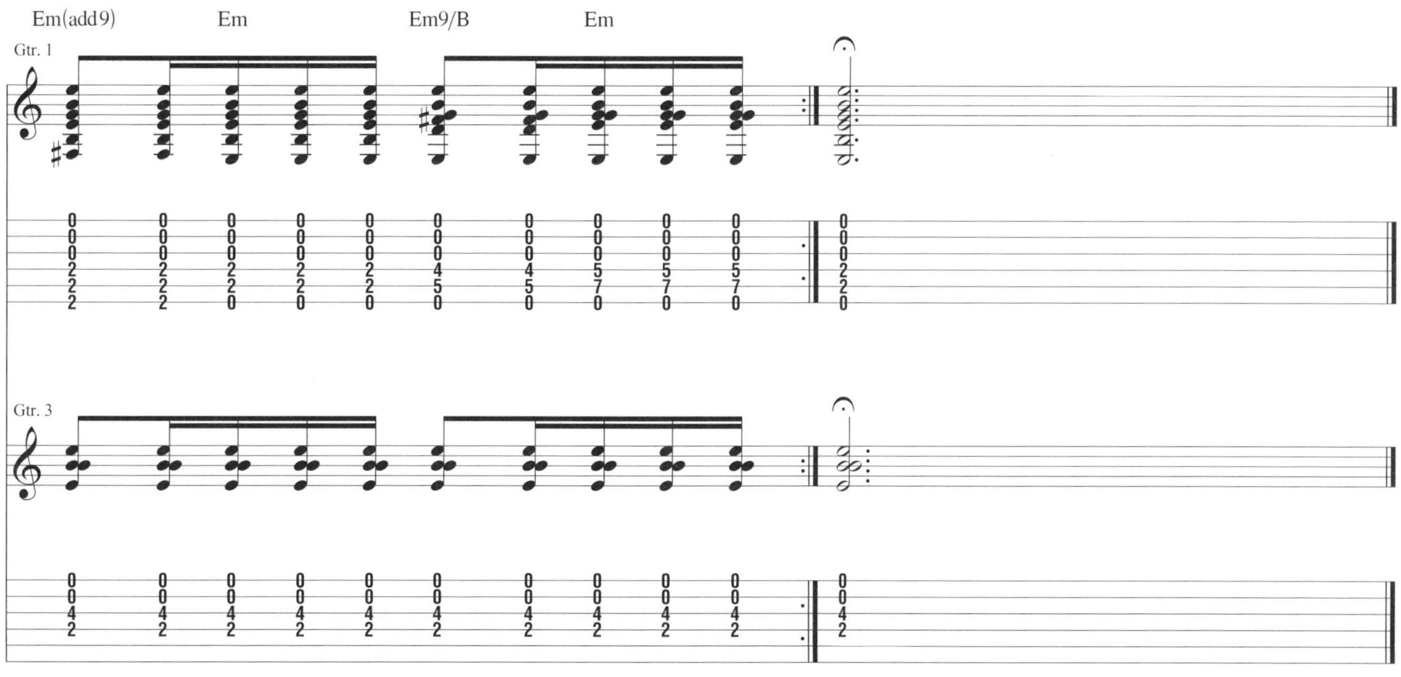

from *Damnation*

Hope Leaves

Words and Music by Mikael Akerfeldt

Capo II

Intro

Slow ♩ = 70

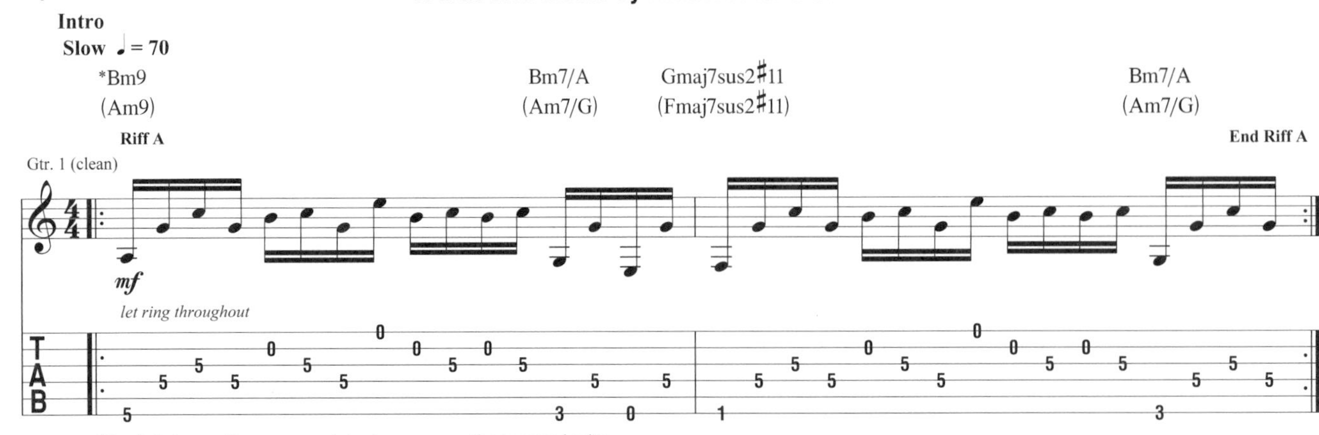

*Symbols in parentheses represent chord names respective to capoed guitar.
Symbols above reflect actual sounding chords. Capoed fret is "0" in tab. Chord symbols reflect implied harmony.

𝄋 Verse

Gtr. 1: w/ Riff A (3 1/2 times)
2nd & 3rd times, Gtr. 2 tacet
2nd & 3rd times, Gtr. 3: w/ Riff A (4 times)

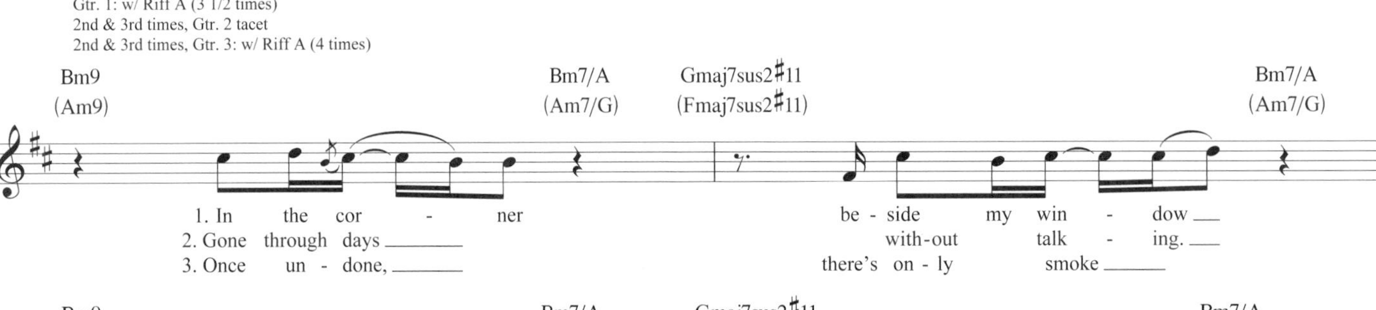

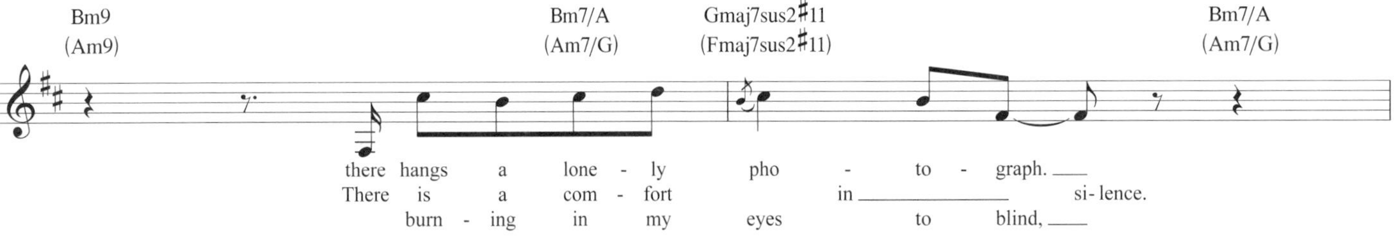

Chorus

2nd & 3rd times, Gtr. 3: w/ Riff B

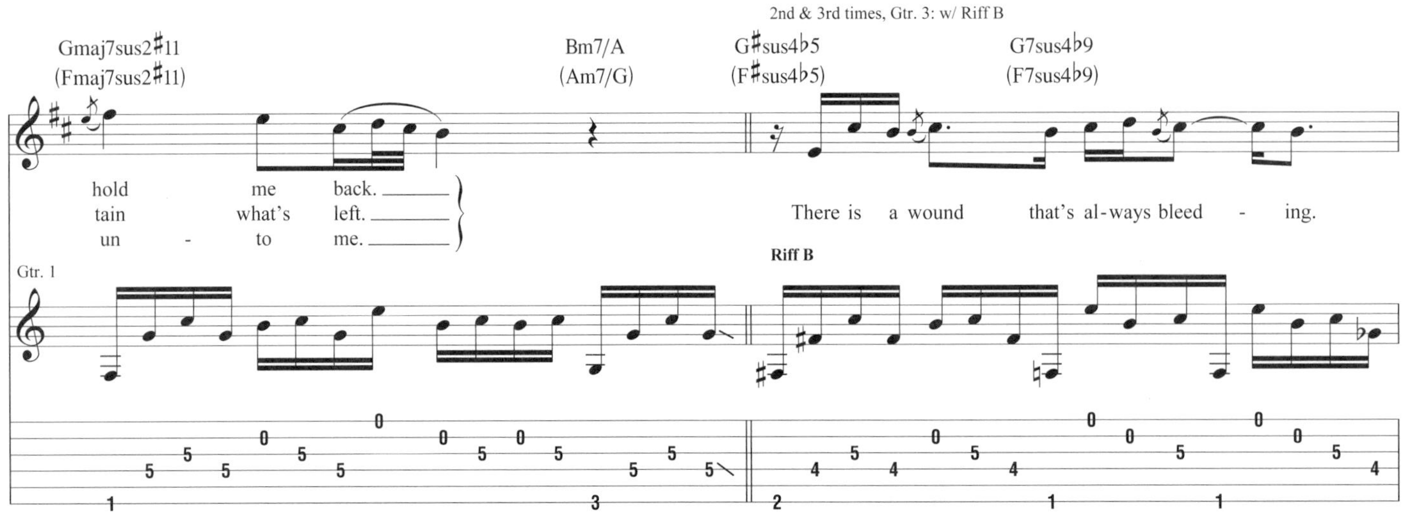

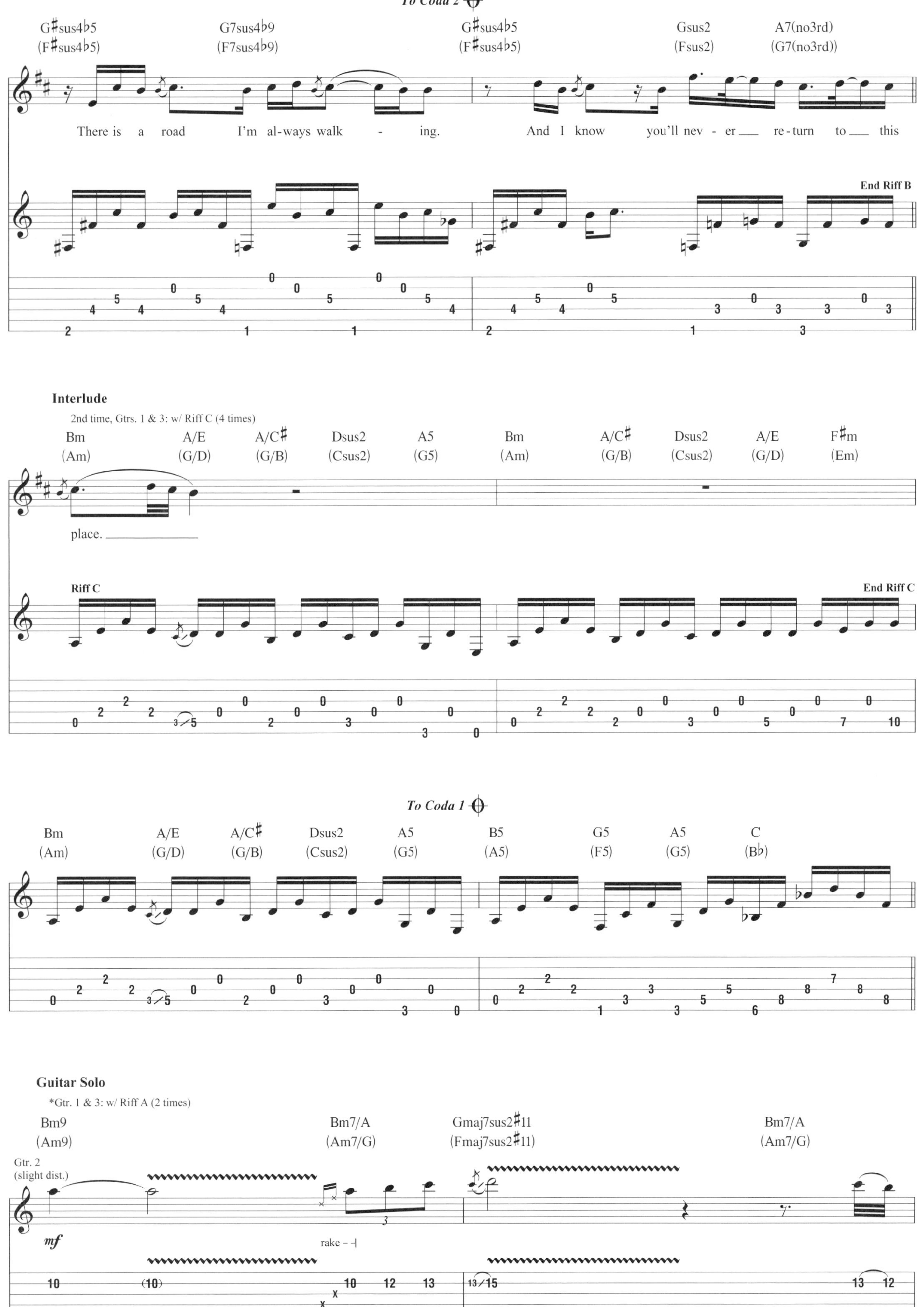
To Coda 2
G♯sus4♭5
(F♯sus4♭5)
G7sus4♭9
(F7sus4♭9)
G♯sus4♭5
(F♯sus4♭5)
Gsus2
(Fsus2)
A7(no3rd)
(G7(no3rd))
There is a road I'm al-ways walk - ing. And I know you'll nev - er re-turn to this
End Riff B
Interlude
2nd time, Gtrs. 1 & 3: w/ Riff C (4 times)
Bm
(Am)
A/E
(G/D)
A/C♯
(G/B)
Dsus2
(Csus2)
A5
(G5)
Bm
(Am)
A/C♯
(G/B)
Dsus2
(Csus2)
A/E
(G/D)
F♯m
(Em)
place.
Riff C
End Riff C
To Coda 1
Bm
(Am)
A/E
(G/D)
A/C♯
(G/B)
Dsus2
(Csus2)
A5
(G5)
B5
(A5)
G5
(F5)
A5
(G5)
C
(B♭)
Guitar Solo
*Gtr. 1 & 3: w/ Riff A (2 times)
Bm9
(Am9)
Bm7/A
(Am7/G)
Gmaj7sus2♯11
(Fmaj7sus2♯11)
Bm7/A
(Am7/G)
Gtr. 2
(slight dist.)
mf
rake
*Gtr. 3 (clean), played mf

D.S. al Coda 1
Bm9
(Am9)
Bm7/A
(Am7/G)
Gmaj7sus2♯11
(Fmaj7sus2♯11)
Bm7/A
(Am7/G)
Coda 1
Bm
(Am)
A/C♯
(G/B)
Dsus2
(Csus2)
A/E
(G/D)
F♯m
(Em)
A5
(G5)
Interlude
Bsus2
(Asus2)
Bsus2(♯11)
(Asus2(♯11))
B5
(A5)
C♯m7
(Bm7)
Gsus2
(Fsus2)
A
(G)
F♯/A♯
(E/G♯)
Gtr. 4 (clean)
mp
let ring throughout
string noise
D.S. al Coda 2
Interlude
Gtrs. 1 & 3: w/ Riff A (2 times)
Gtr. 4 tacet
Gtr. 2
*w/ delay
let ring
*Set for eighth-note regeneration w/ 1 repeat.
Coda 2
Outro
Gtr. 1: w/ Riff B (last meas.)
Gtrs. 1 & 3: w/ Riff C (till fade)
G♯sus4♭5
(F♯sus4♭5)
Gsus2
(Fsus2)
A7(no3rd)
(G7(no3rd))
And I know you'll nev - er re - turn to this place.
(Ah.)
4th time, begin fade
Fade out
Play 7 times

from *Damnation*

In My Time of Need

Words and Music by Mikael Akerfeldt

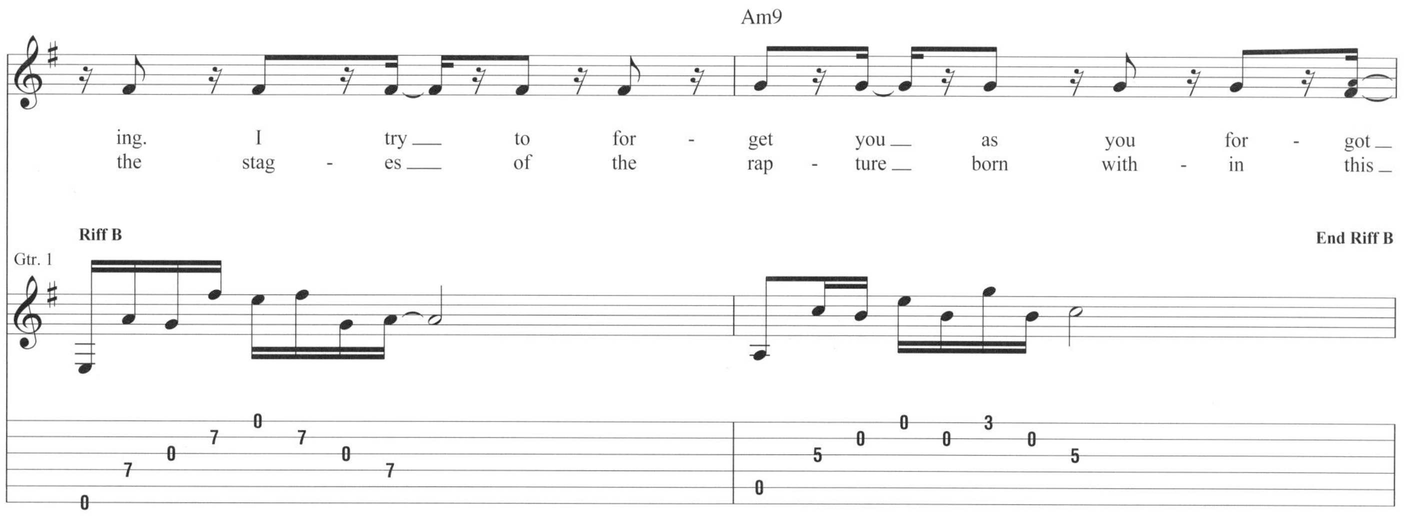

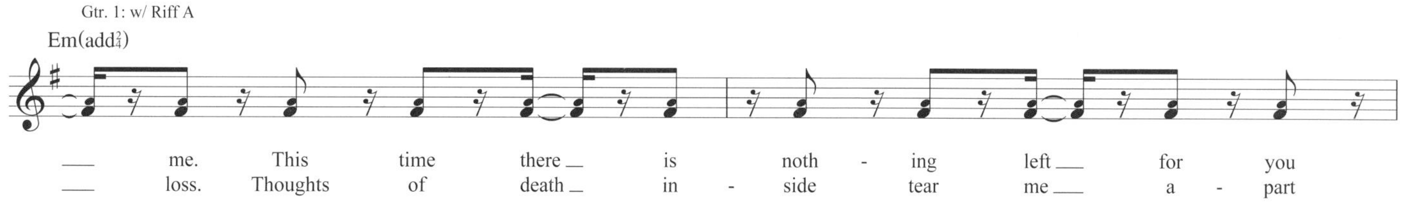

*Chord symbols reflect overall harmony.

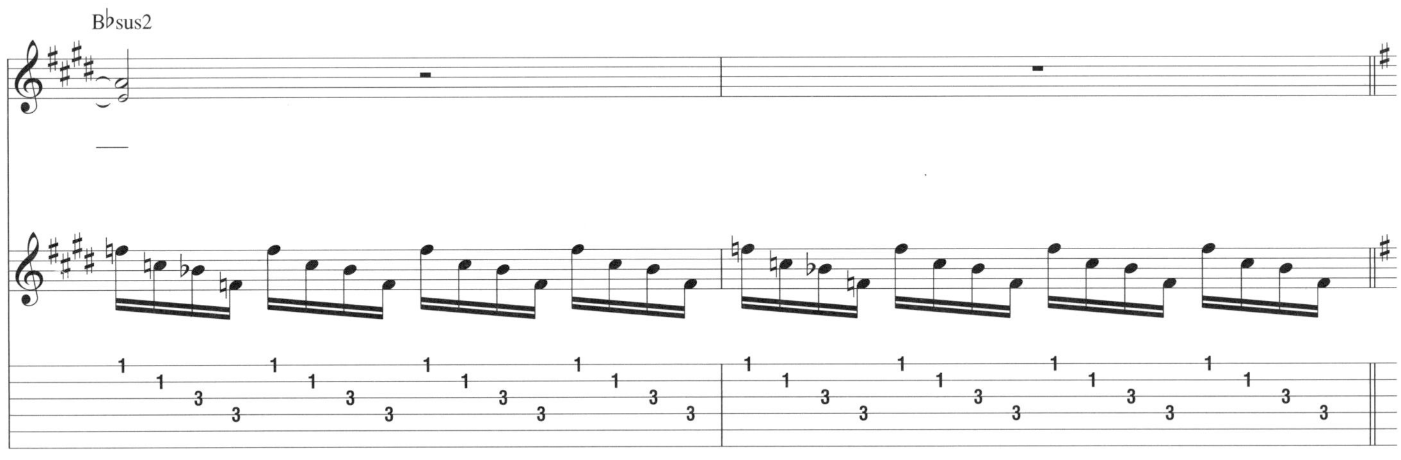

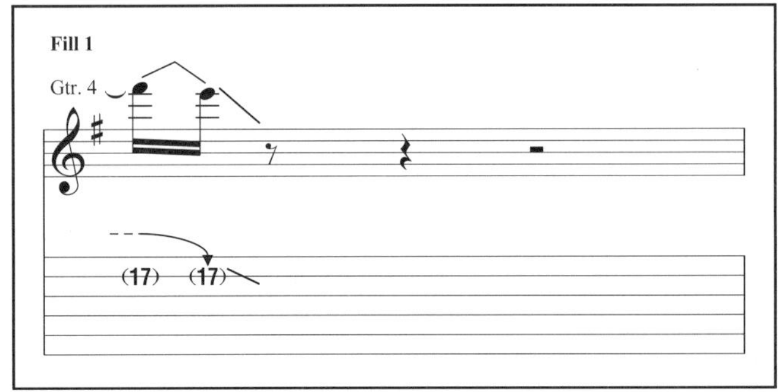

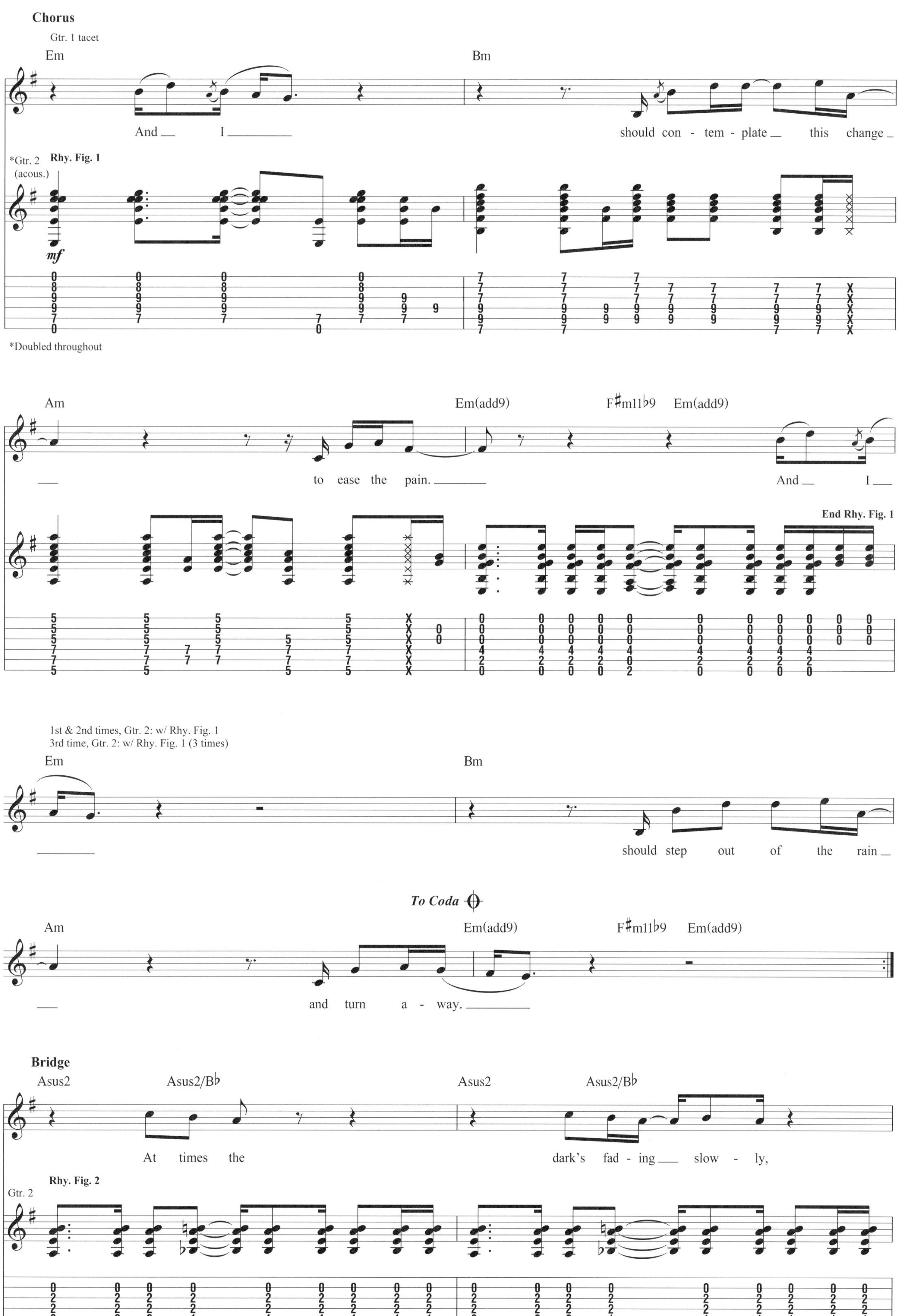

Chorus
Gtr. 1 tacet
Em
Bm
And I should con - tem - plate this change
*Gtr. 2 (acous.)
Rhy. Fig. 1
mf
*Doubled throughout
Am
Em(add9)
F♯m11♭9
Em(add9)
to ease the pain. And I
End Rhy. Fig. 1
1st & 2nd times, Gtr. 2: w/ Rhy. Fig. 1
3rd time, Gtr. 2: w/ Rhy. Fig. 1 (3 times)
Em
Bm
should step out of the rain
To Coda
Am
Em(add9)
F♯m11♭9
Em(add9)
and turn a - way.
Bridge
Asus2
Asus2/B♭
Asus2
Asus2/B♭
At times the dark's fad - ing slow - ly,
Rhy. Fig. 2
Gtr. 2

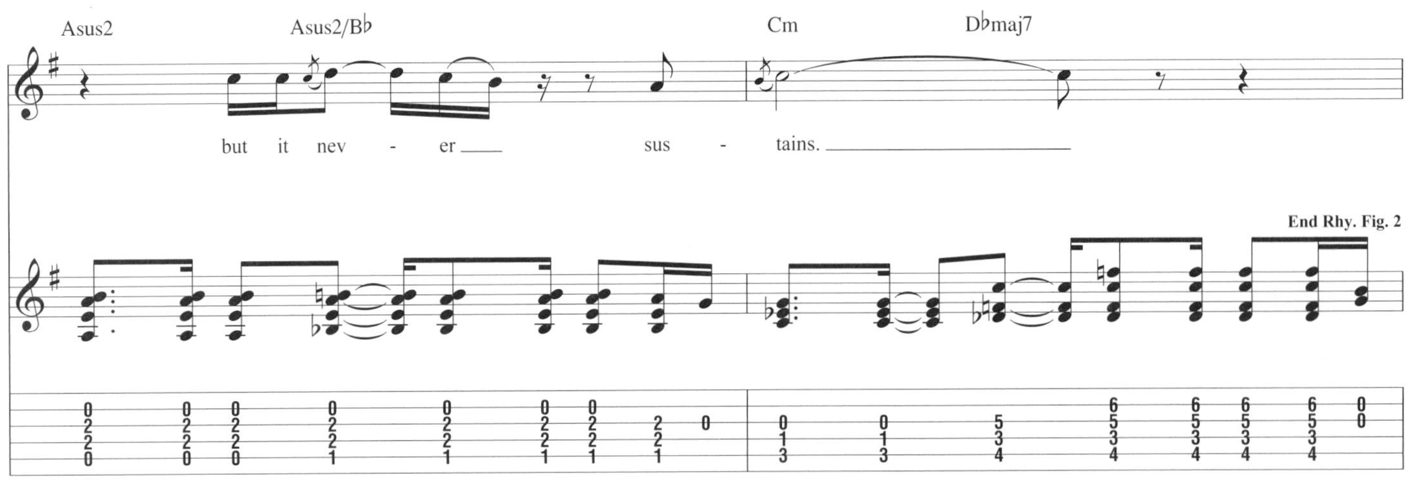
Asus2
Asus2/B♭
Cm
D♭maj7
but it nev - er sus - tains.
End Rhy. Fig. 2

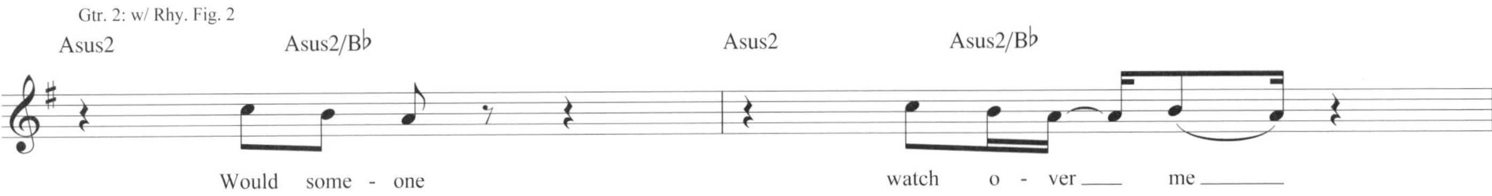
Gtr. 2: w/ Rhy. Fig. 2
Asus2
Asus2/B♭
Asus2
Asus2/B♭
Would some - one watch o - ver me

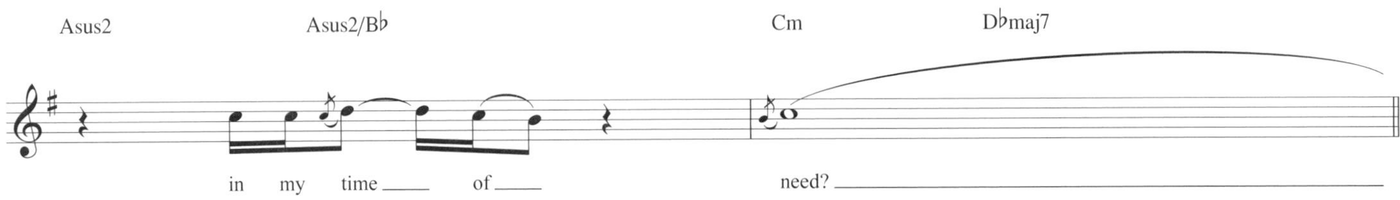
Asus2
Asus2/B♭
Cm
D♭maj7
in my time of need?

Guitar Solo

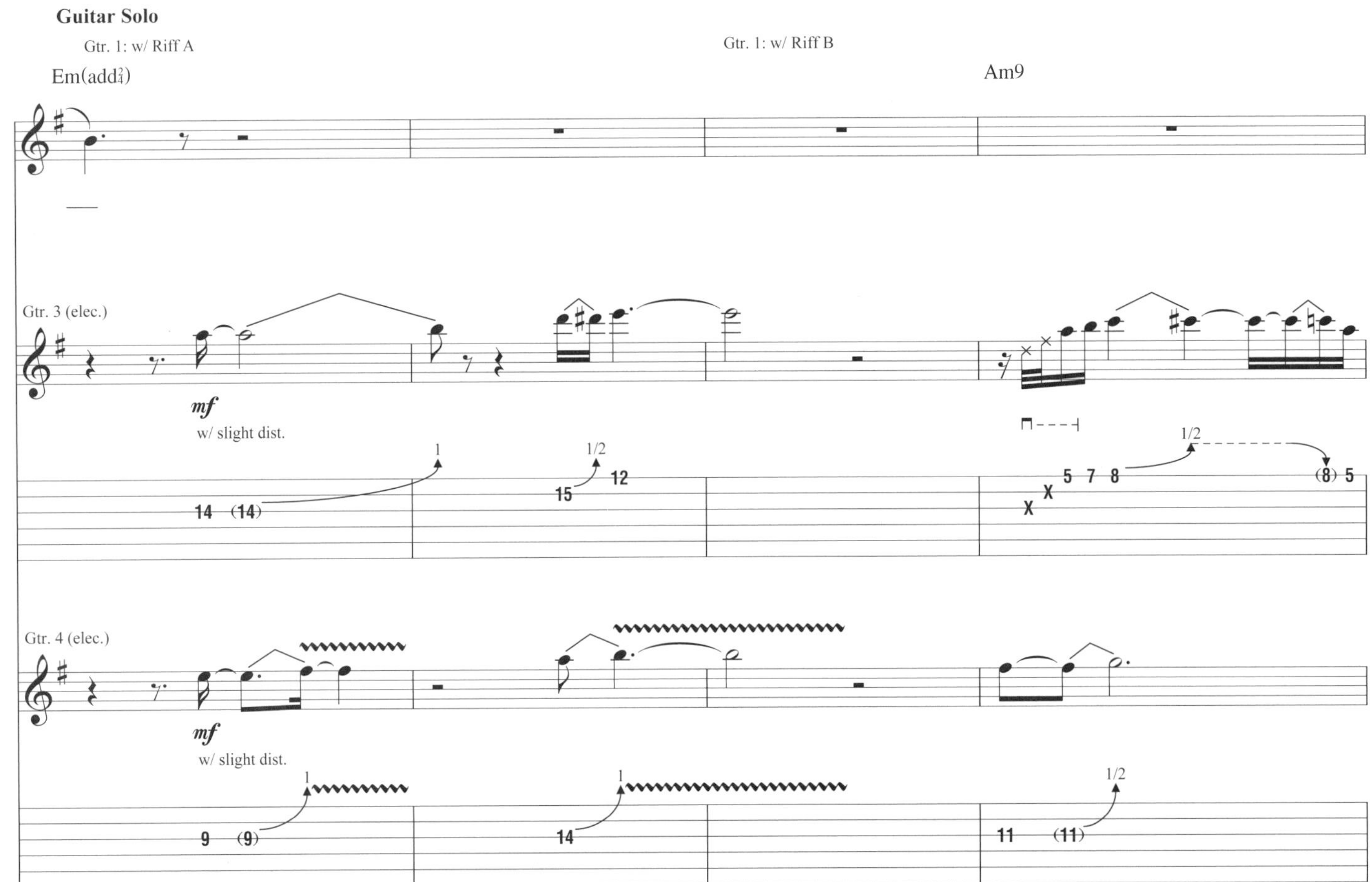
Gtr. 1: w/ Riff A
Gtr. 1: w/ Riff B
Em(add9)
Am9
Gtr. 3 (elec.)
mf
w/ slight dist.
Gtr. 4 (elec.)
mf
w/ slight dist.

D.S. al Coda

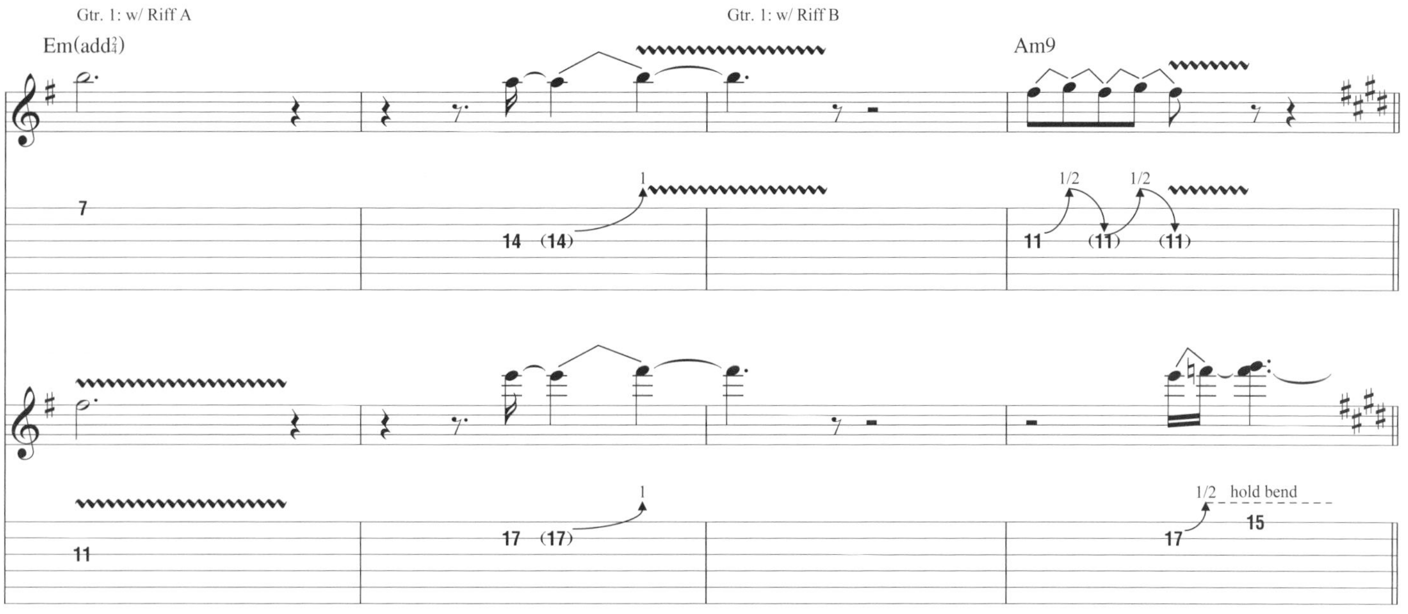

Coda

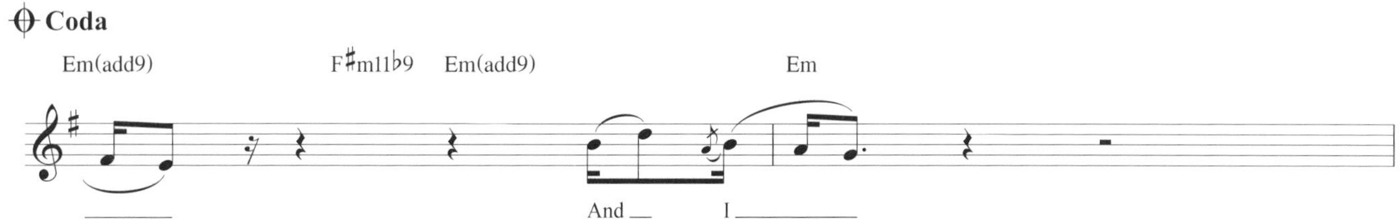

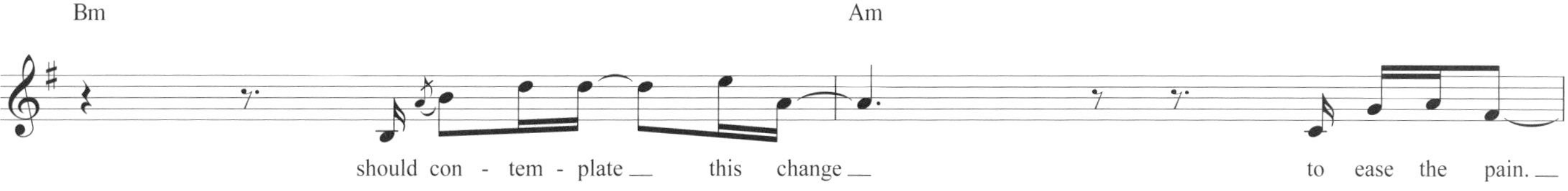

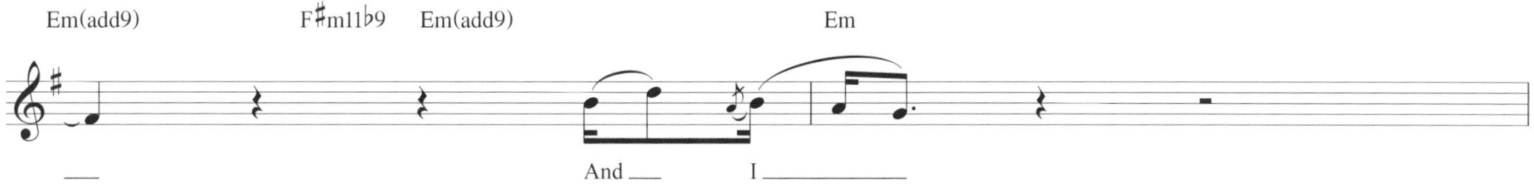

Outro

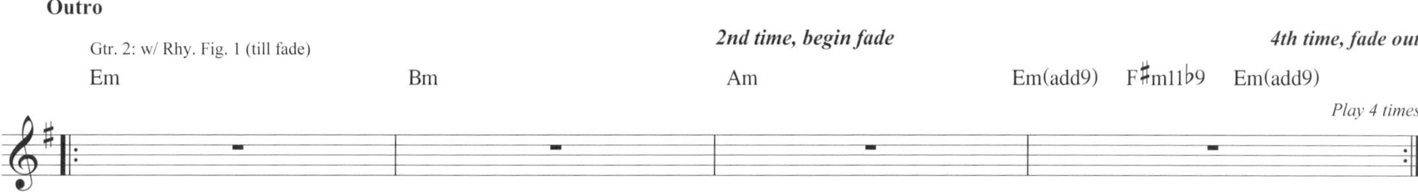

from *Blackwater Park*

Patterns in the Ivy

Words and Music by Mikael Akerfeldt

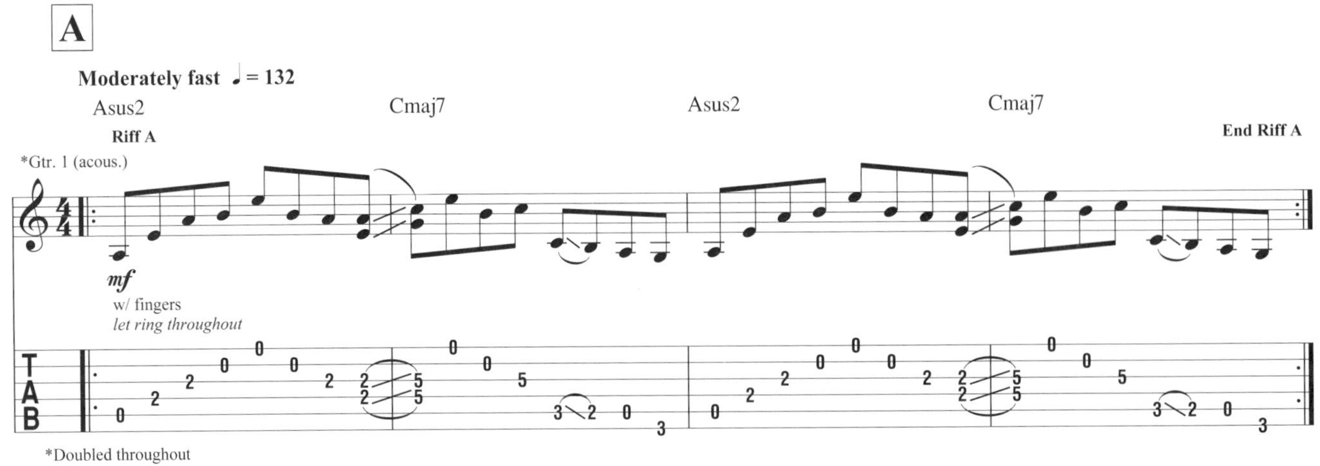

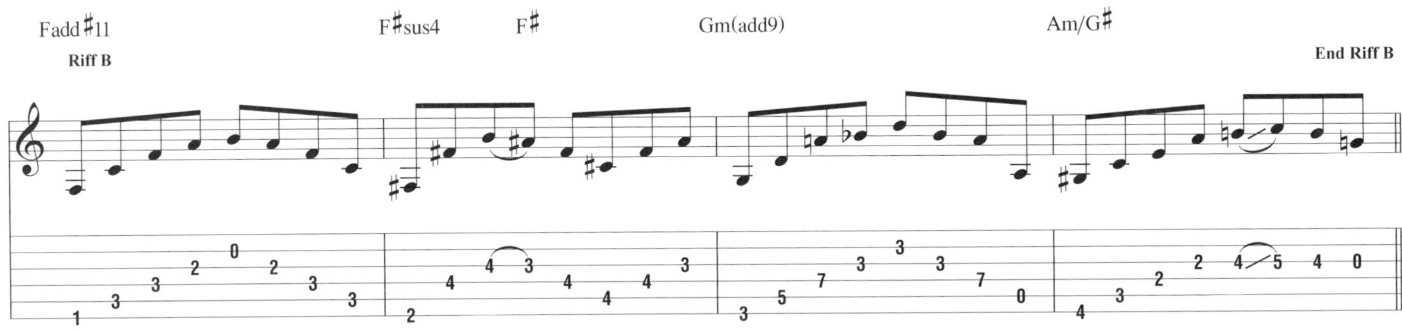

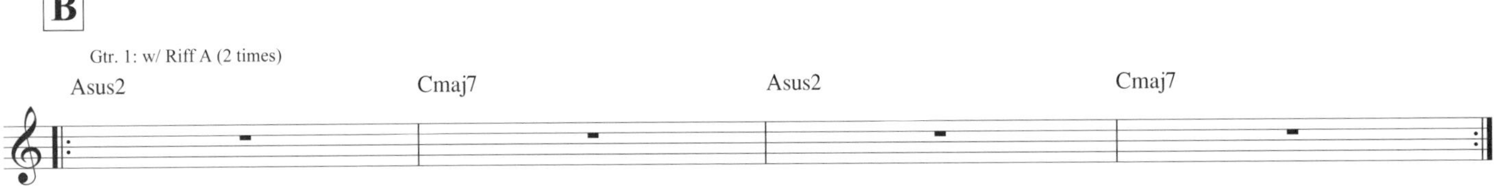

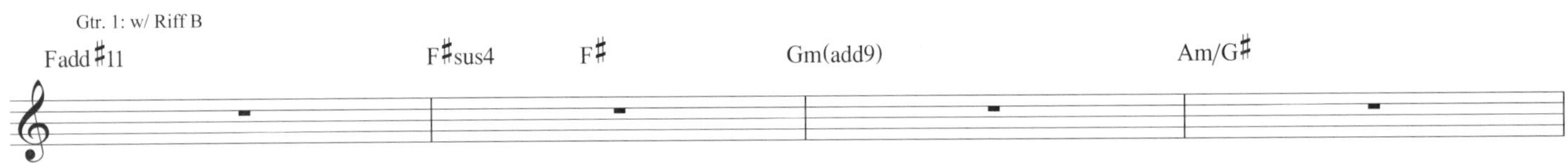

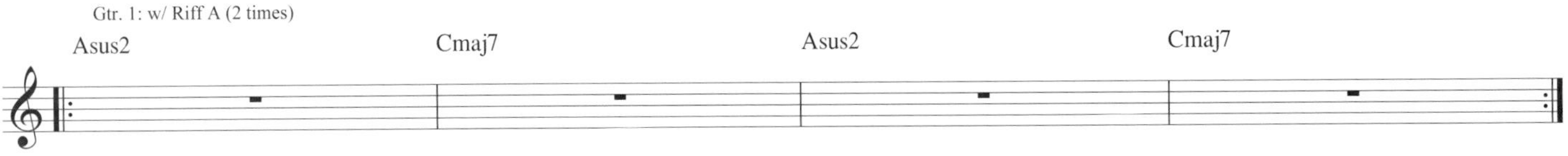

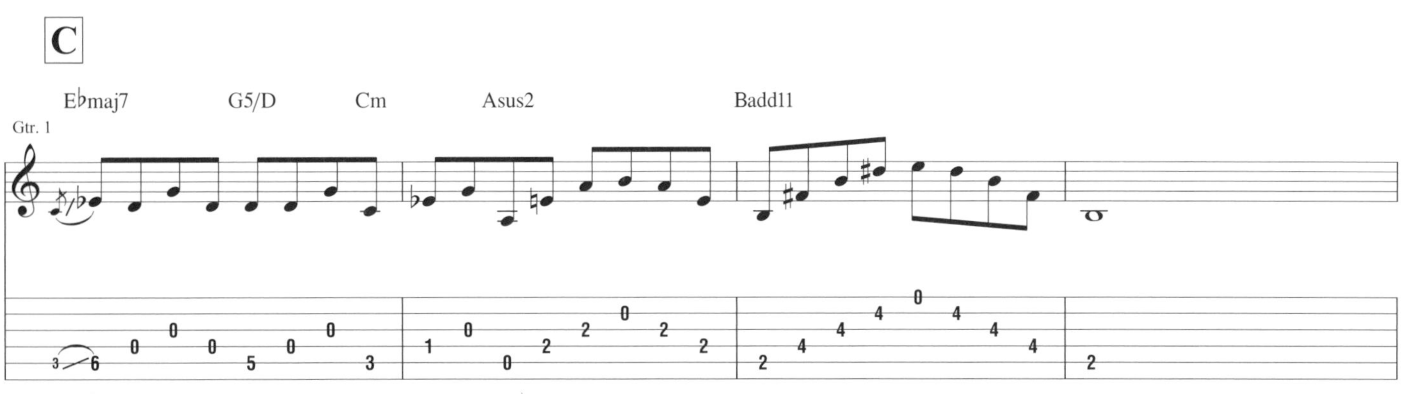
C
E♭maj7
G5/D
Cm
Asus2
Badd11
Gtr. 1

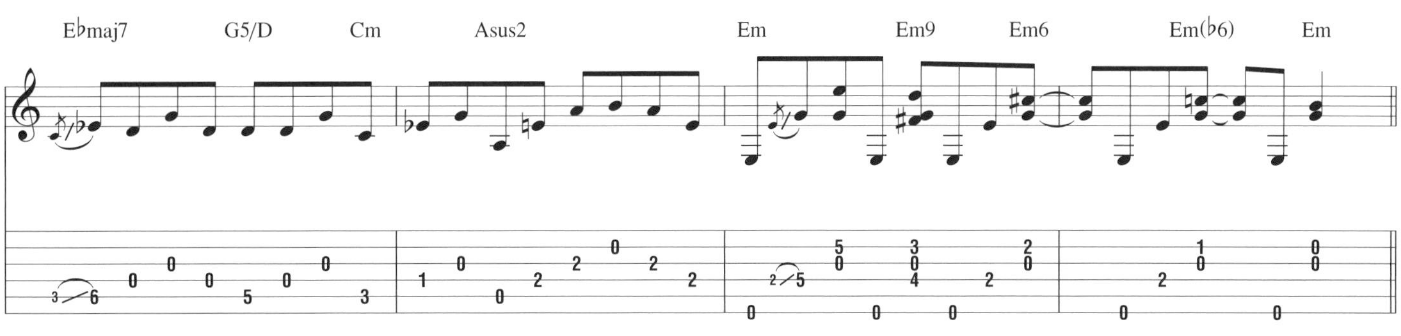
E♭maj7
G5/D
Cm
Asus2
Em
Em9
Em6
Em(♭6)
Em

D

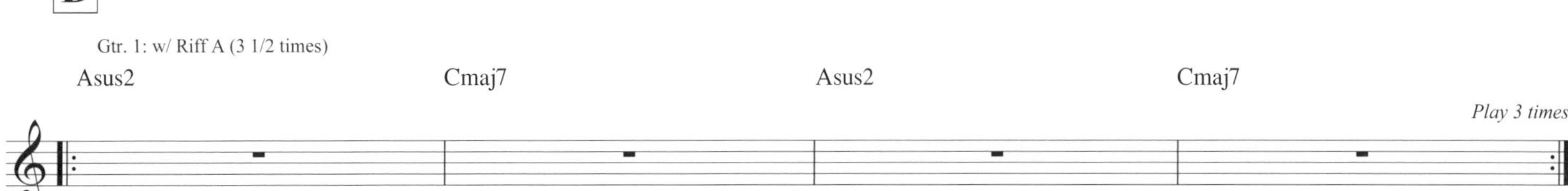
Gtr. 1: w/ Riff A (3 1/2 times)
Asus2
Cmaj7
Asus2
Cmaj7
Play 3 times

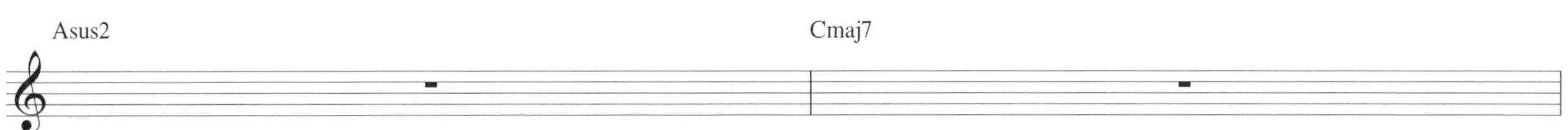
Asus2
Cmaj7

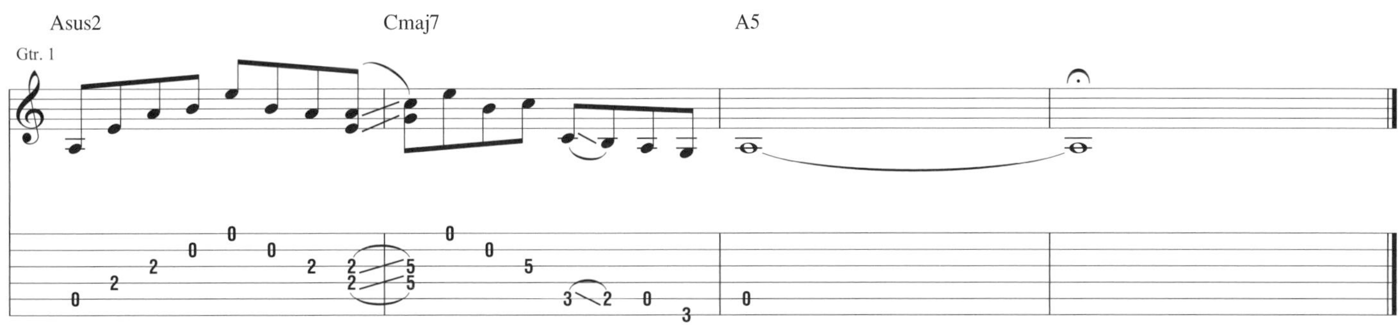
Asus2
Cmaj7
A5
Gtr. 1

from *Sorceress*

Sorceress

Words and Music by Mikael Akerfeldt

Drop A tuning:
(low to high) A-A-D-G-B-E

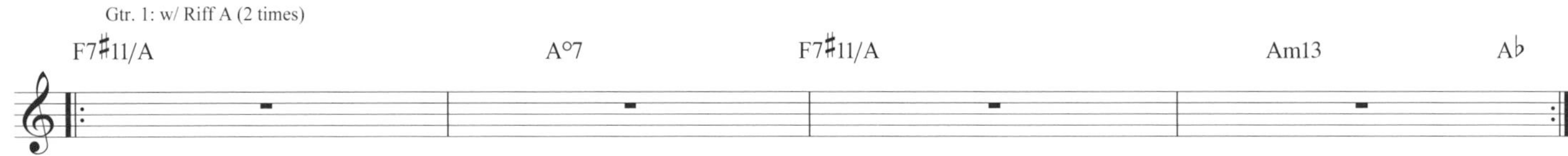

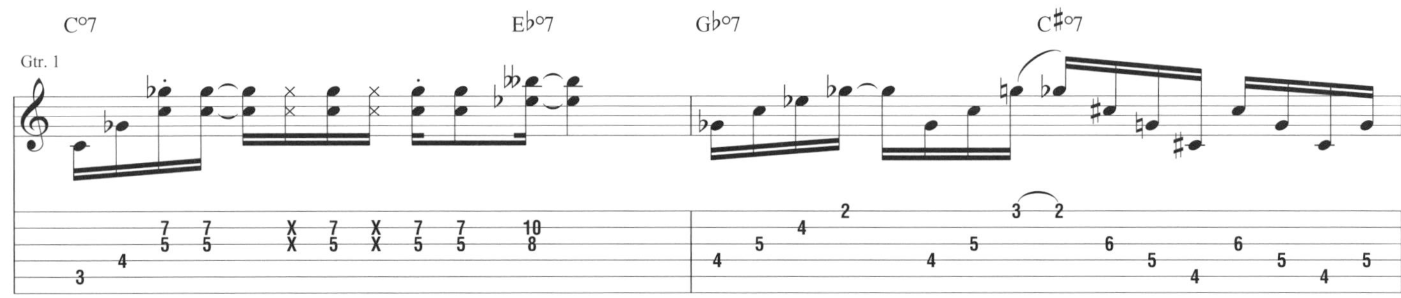

Gtr. 1 tacet
A5
Am
Gtr. 2 (dist.)
*Gtrs. 2 & 3
P.M.
*Gtr. 3 (dist.), played mf
1.
2.
D
Am
1. What a
Rhy. Fig. 1
End Rhy. Fig. 1
Verse
Gtrs. 2 & 3: w/ Rhy. Fig. 1 (3 times)
sin - ner when I wor - ship e - vil. Blood is thin - ner, but
you won't ev - er know. Can you con - fess that you thrive in cha - os? You're a
sor - cer - ess and your eye is on the lost.
But you're
A5
C5
B5
Rhy. Fill 1
Gtrs. 2 & 3
End Rhy. Fill 1

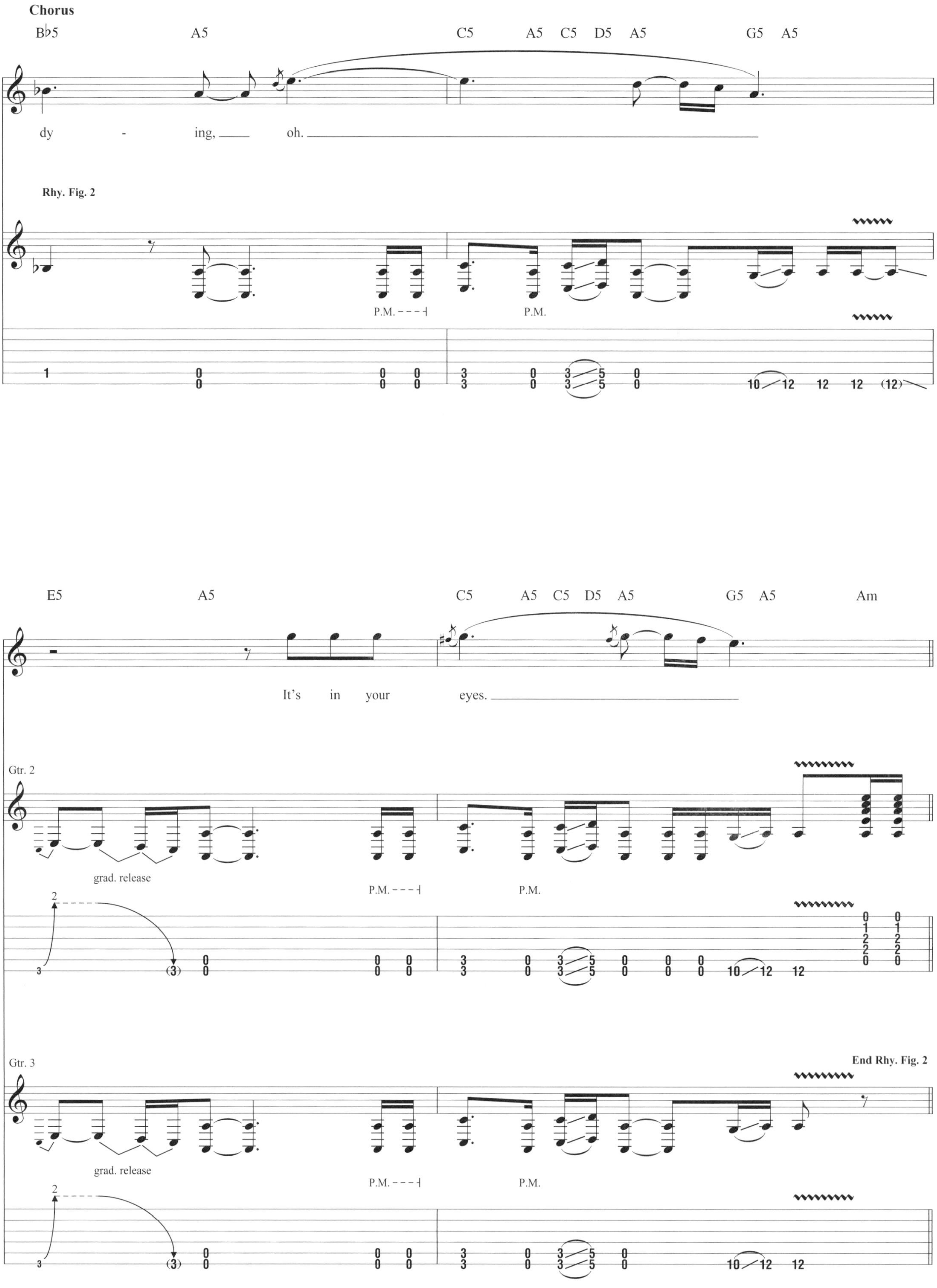

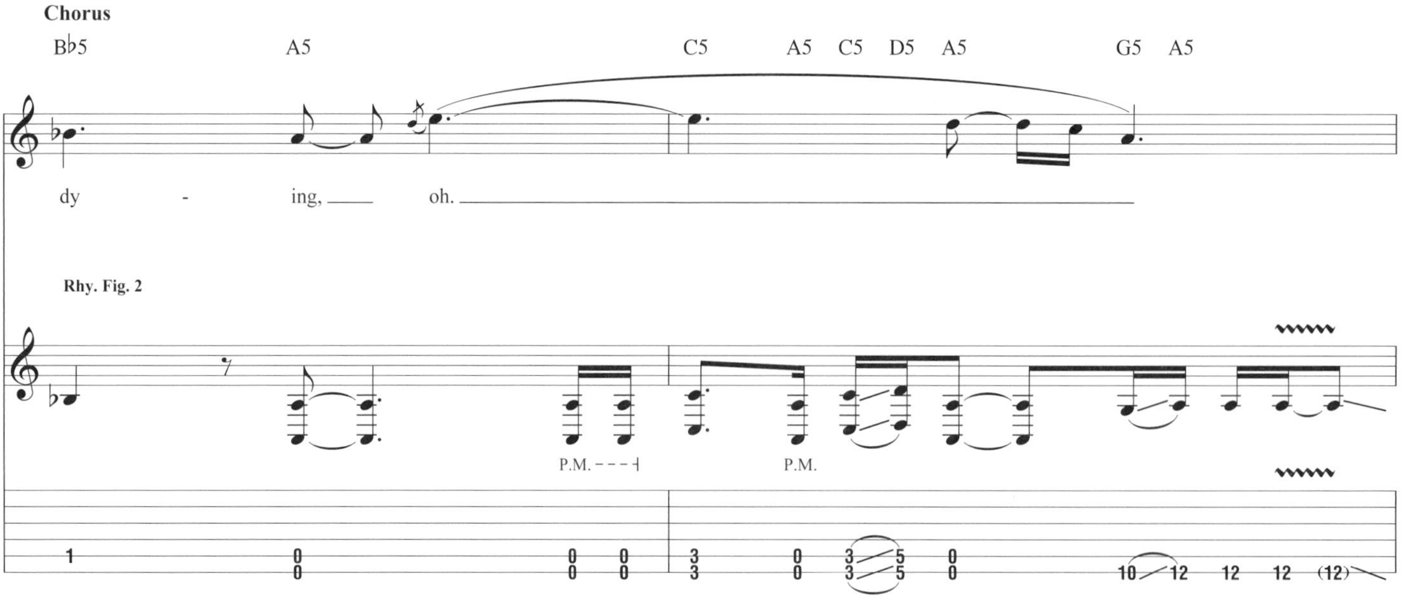

E5 A5 C5 A5 C5 D5 A5 G5 A5 Am

It's in your eyes.

Gtr. 2

grad. release

P.M.

P.M.

Gtr. 3

End Rhy. Fig. 2

grad. release

P.M.

P.M.

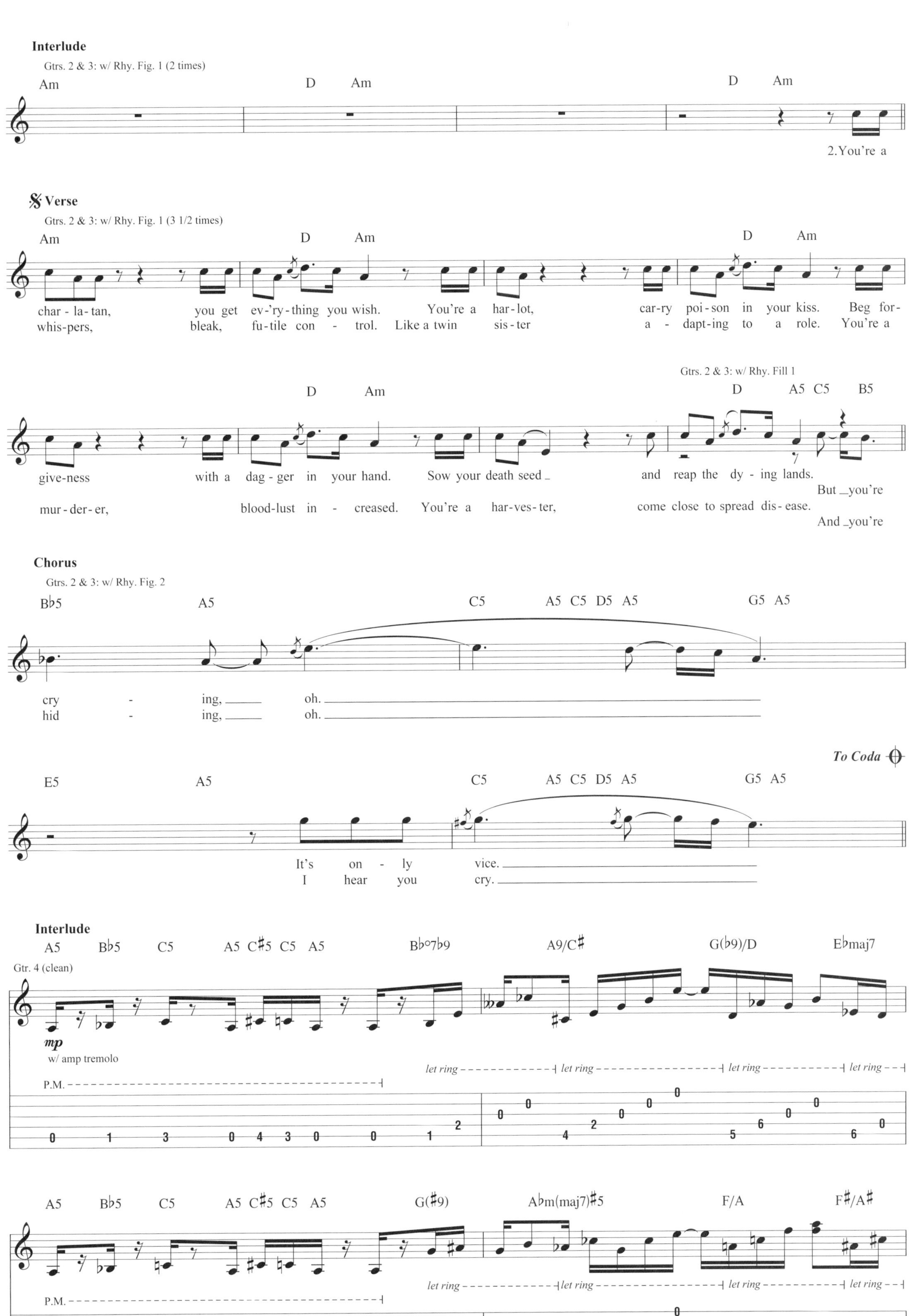
Interlude
Gtrs. 2 & 3: w/ Rhy. Fig. 1 (2 times)
Am
D Am
D Am
2.You're a
Verse
Gtrs. 2 & 3: w/ Rhy. Fig. 1 (3 1/2 times)
Am
D Am
D Am
char - la - tan, you get ev - 'ry - thing you wish. You're a har - lot, car - ry poi - son in your kiss. Beg for -
whis - pers, bleak, fu - tile con - trol. Like a twin sis - ter a - dapt - ing to a role. You're a
D Am
Gtrs. 2 & 3: w/ Rhy. Fill 1
D A5 C5 B5
give - ness with a dag - ger in your hand. Sow your death seed and reap the dy - ing lands.
But you're
mur - der - er, blood - lust in - creased. You're a har - ves - ter, come close to spread dis - ease.
And you're
Chorus
Gtrs. 2 & 3: w/ Rhy. Fig. 2
B♭5 A5 C5 A5 C5 D5 A5 G5 A5
cry - ing, oh.
hid - ing, oh.
To Coda
E5 A5 C5 A5 C5 D5 A5 G5 A5
It's on - ly vice.
I hear you cry.
Interlude
A5 B♭5 C5 A5 C♯5 C5 A5 B♭°7♭9 A9/C♯ G(♭9)/D E♭maj7
Gtr. 4 (clean)
mp
w/ amp tremolo
let ring
P.M.
A5 B♭5 C5 A5 C♯5 C5 A5 G(♯9) A♭m(maj7)♯5 F/A F♯/A♯
let ring
P.M.

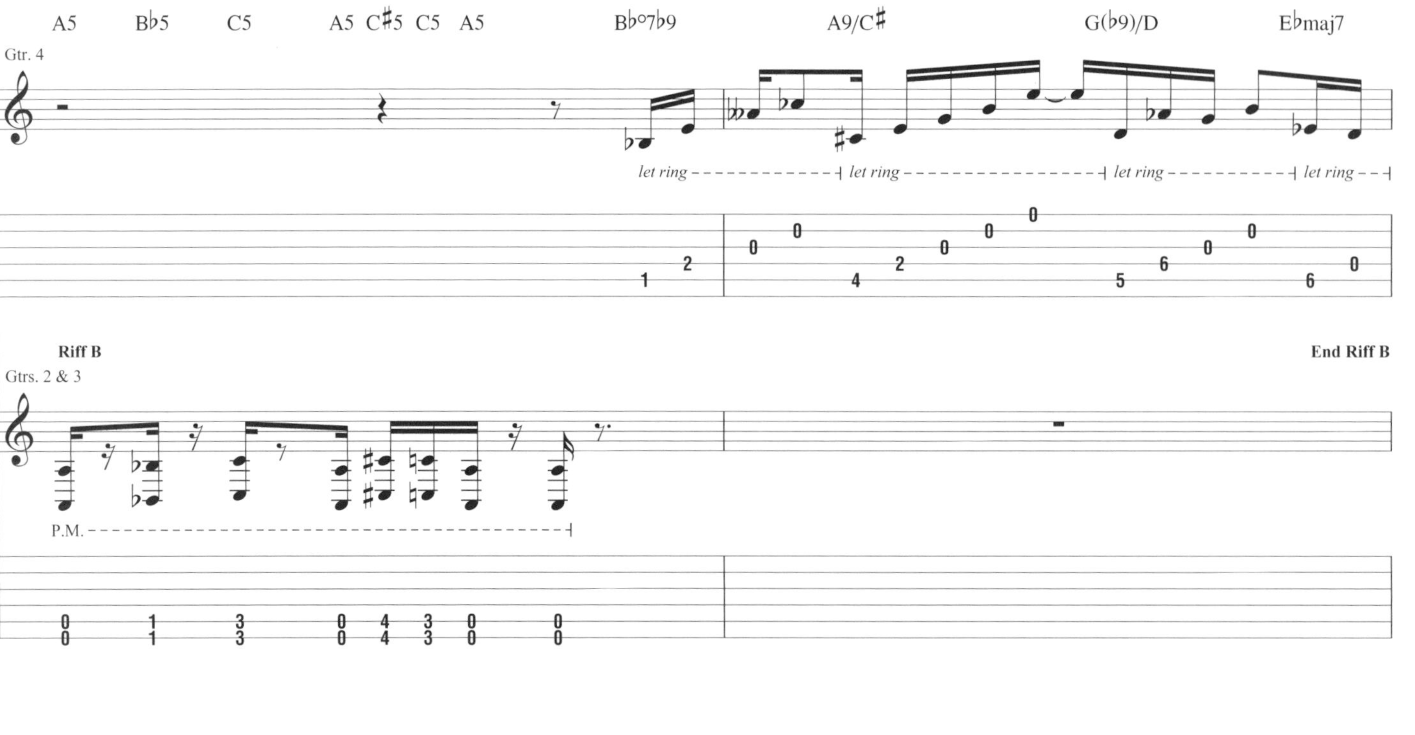
A5 B♭5 C5 A5 C♯5 C5 A5 B♭°7♭9 A9/C♯ G(♭9)/D E♭maj7
Gtr. 4
let ring
Riff B
End Riff B
Gtrs. 2 & 3
P.M.

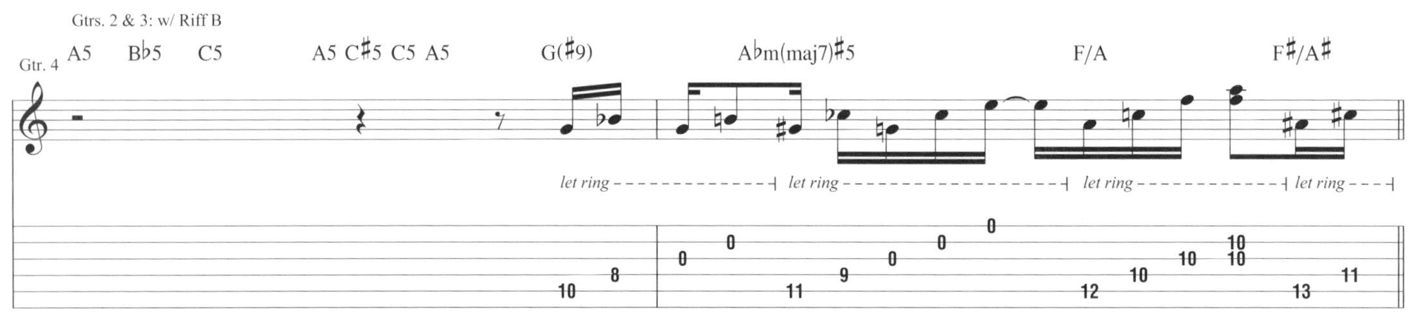
Gtrs. 2 & 3: w/ Riff B
A5 B♭5 C5 A5 C♯5 C5 A5 G(♯9) A♭m(maj7)♯5 F/A F♯/A♯
Gtr. 4
let ring

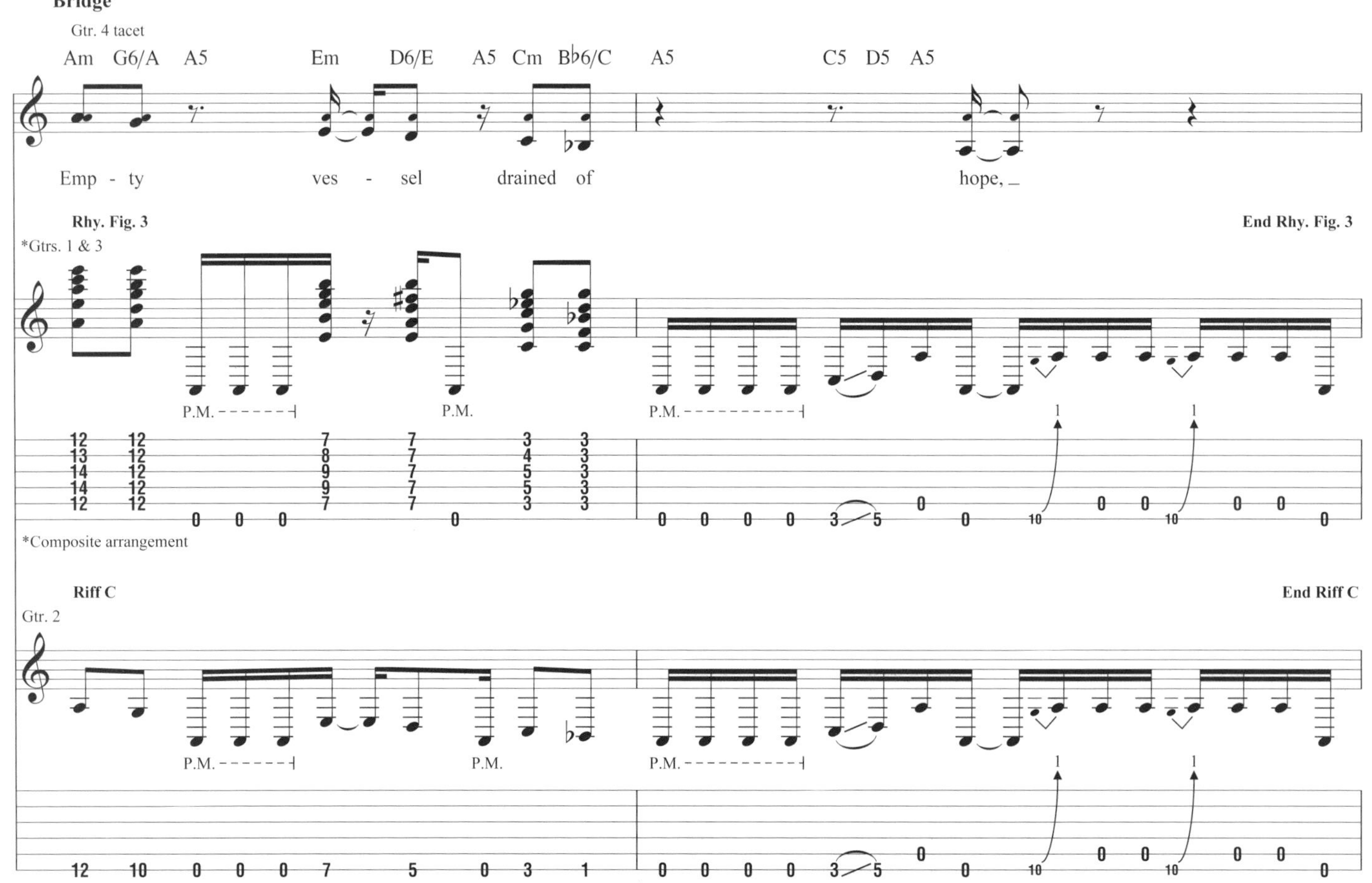
Bridge
Gtr. 4 tacet
Am G6/A A5 Em D6/E A5 Cm B♭6/C A5 C5 D5 A5
Emp - ty ves - sel drained of hope,
Rhy. Fig. 3
End Rhy. Fig. 3
*Gtrs. 1 & 3
P.M.
*Composite arrangement
Riff C
End Riff C
Gtr. 2

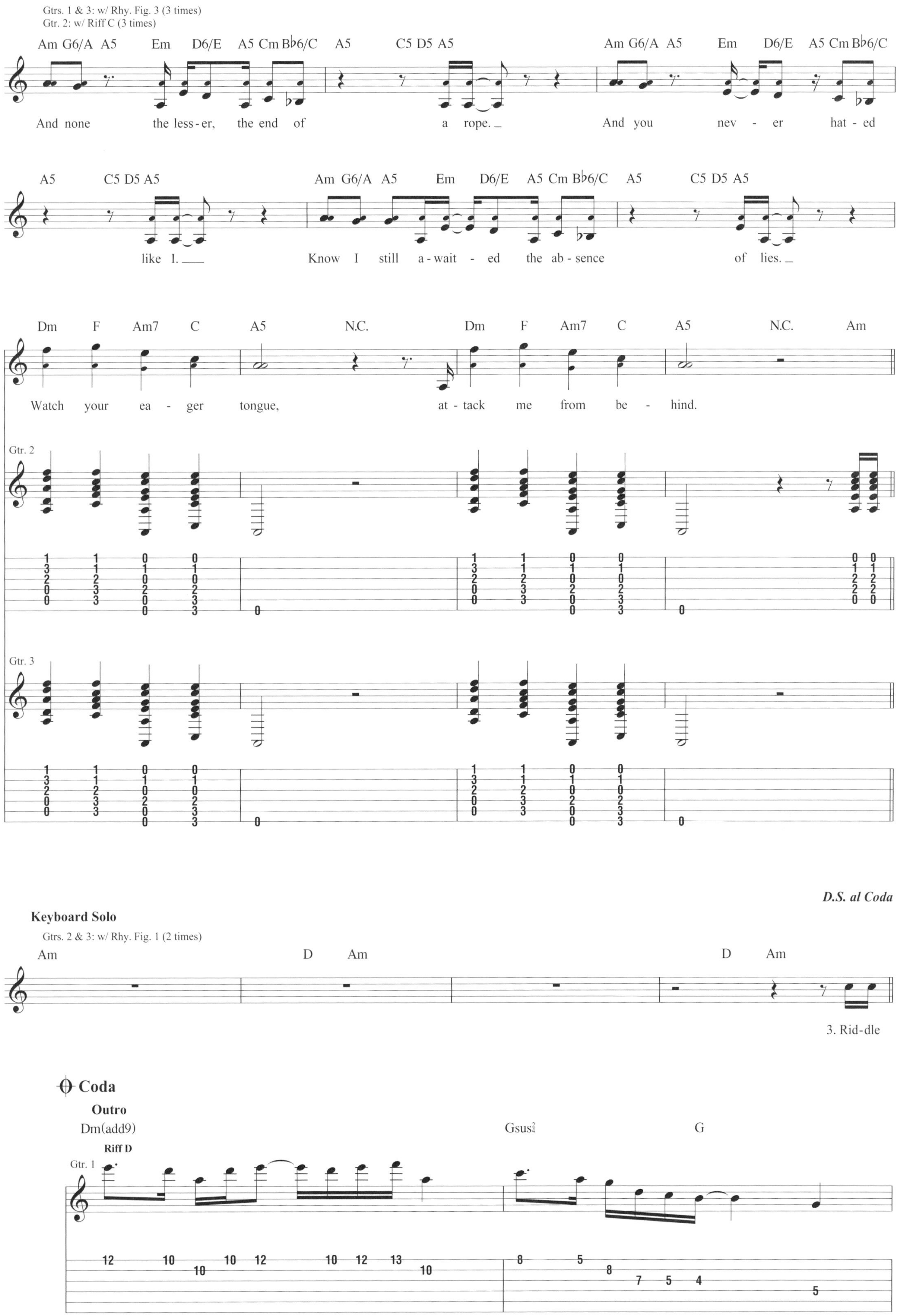

Gtrs. 1 & 3: w/ Rhy. Fig. 3 (3 times)
Gtr. 2: w/ Riff C (3 times)

Am G6/A A5 Em D6/E A5 Cm B♭6/C A5 C5 D5 A5 Am G6/A A5 Em D6/E A5 Cm B♭6/C

And none the less-er, the end of a rope. And you nev - er hat - ed

A5 C5 D5 A5 Am G6/A A5 Em D6/E A5 Cm B♭6/C A5 C5 D5 A5

like I. Know I still a-wait - ed the ab-sence of lies.

Dm F Am7 C A5 N.C. Dm F Am7 C A5 N.C. Am

Watch your ea - ger tongue, at-tack me from be - hind.

Gtr. 2

Gtr. 3

D.S. al Coda

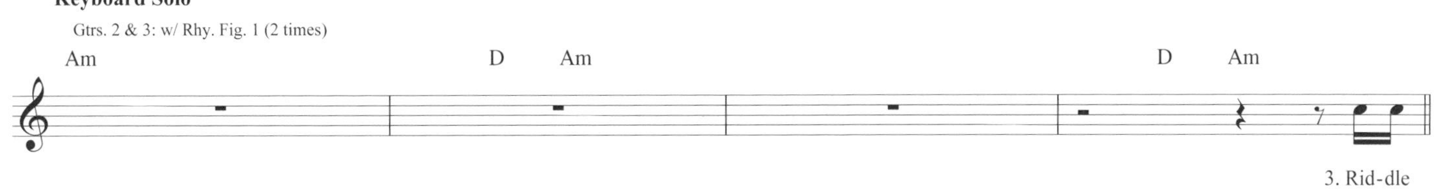

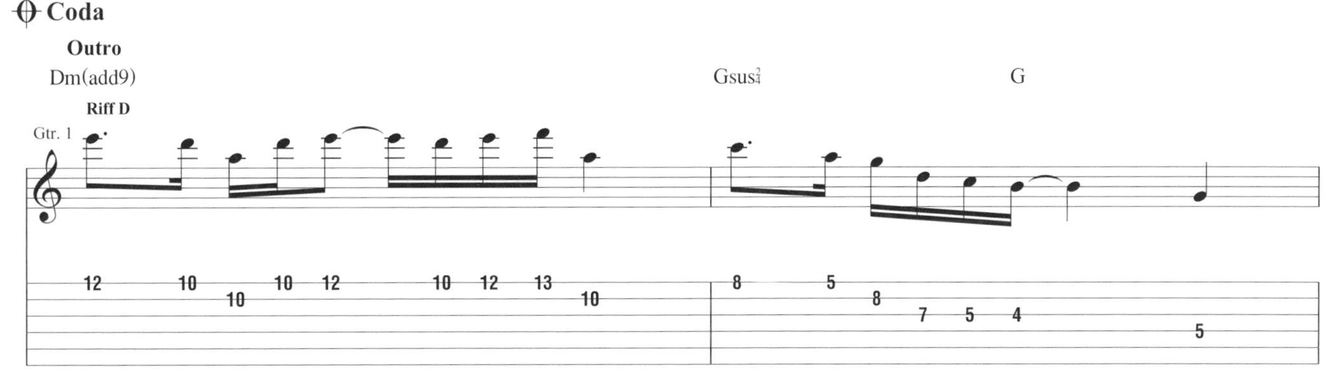

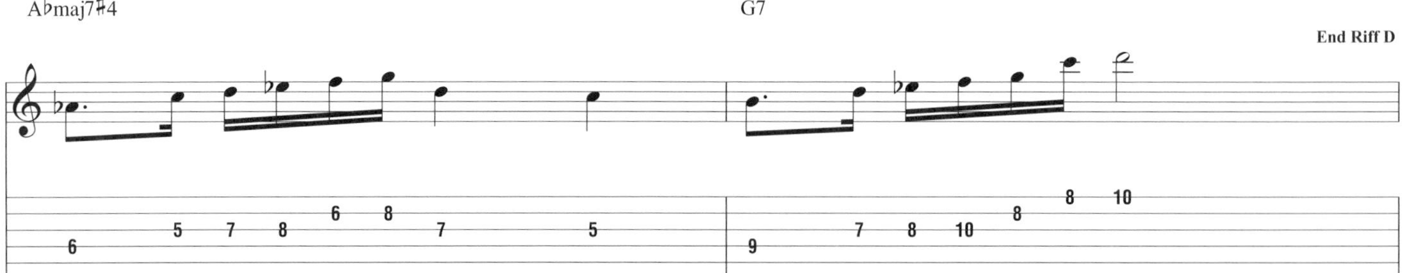

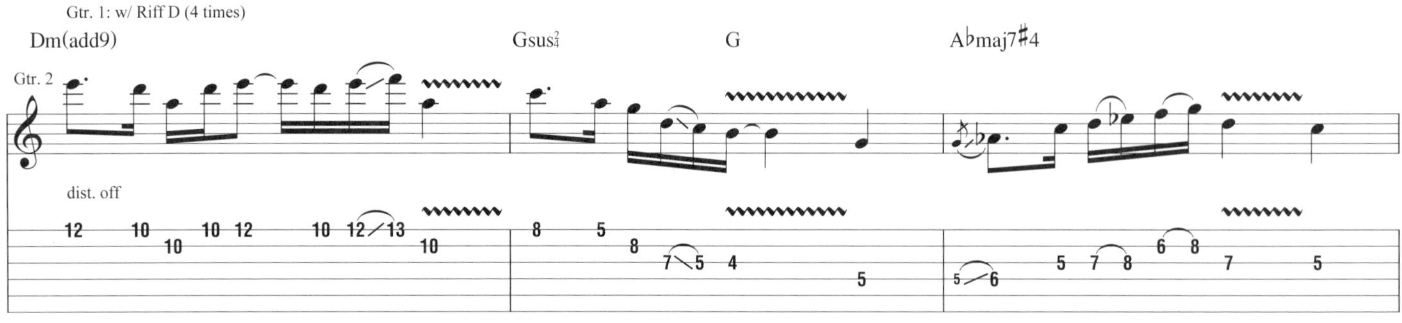

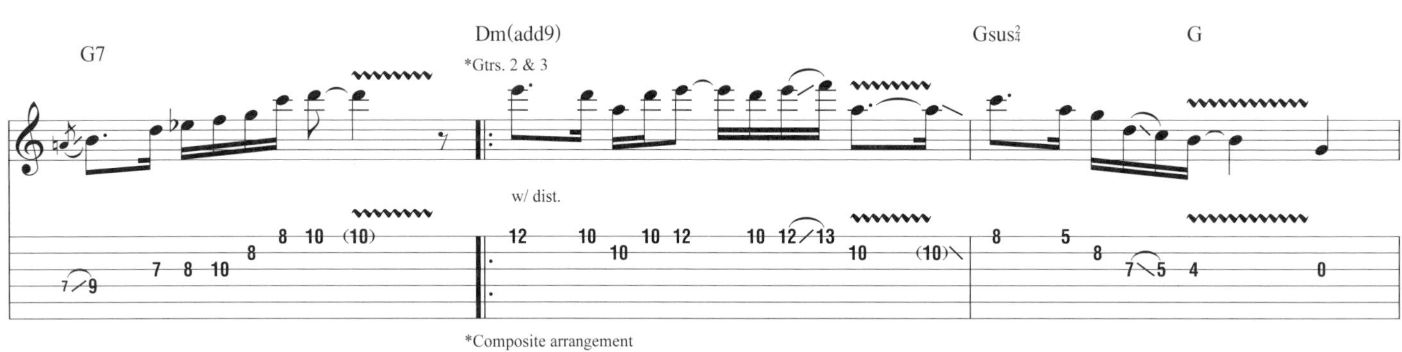

*Composite arrangement

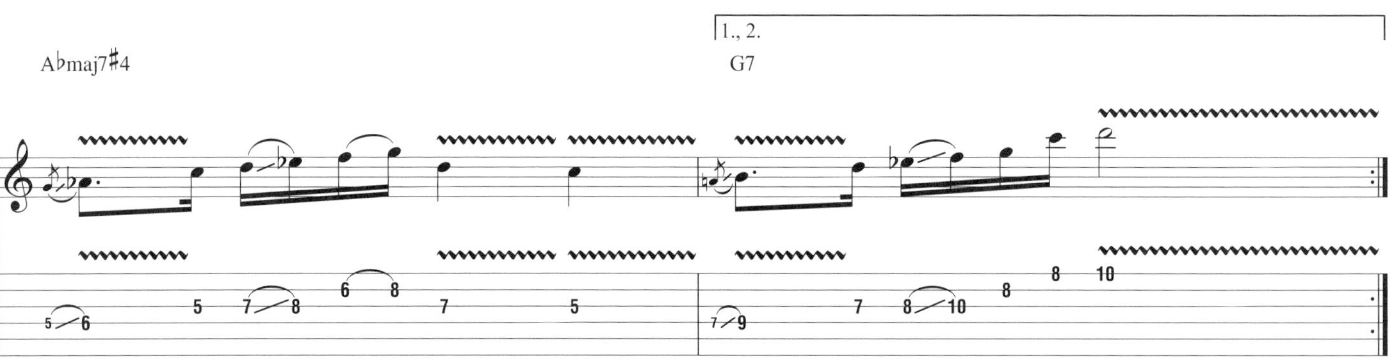

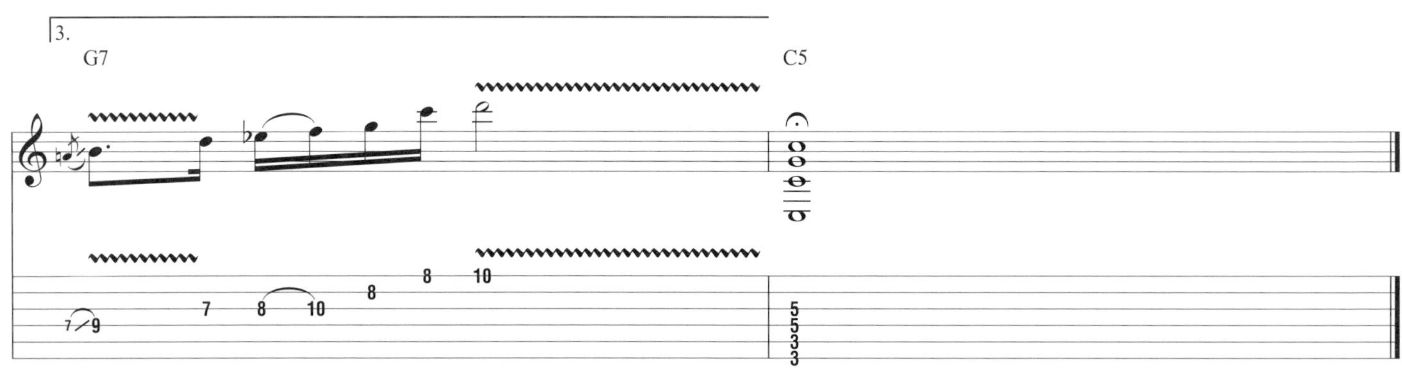

from *Morningrise*

To Bid You Farewell

Words and Music by Mikael Akerfeldt and Sven Peter Malcom Lindgren

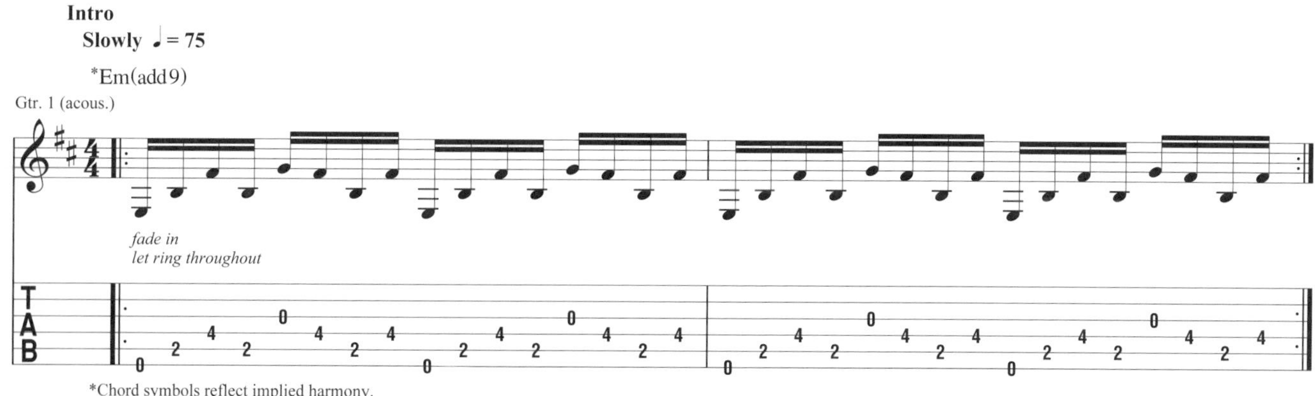

*Chord symbols reflect implied harmony.

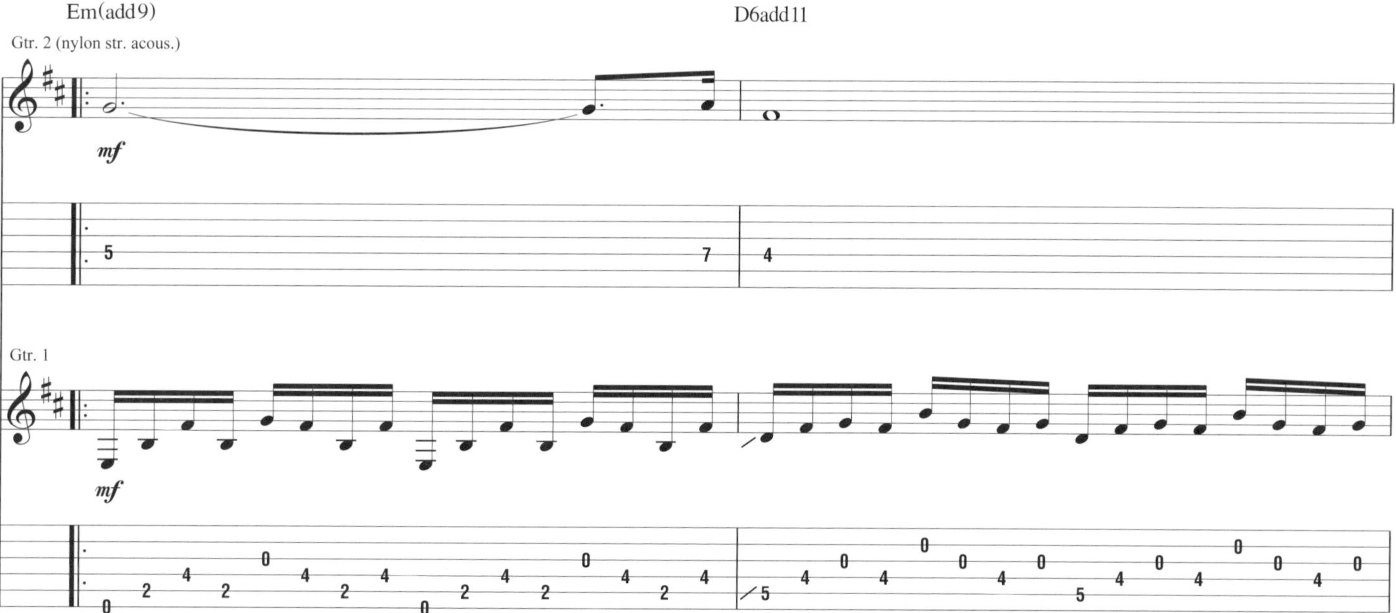

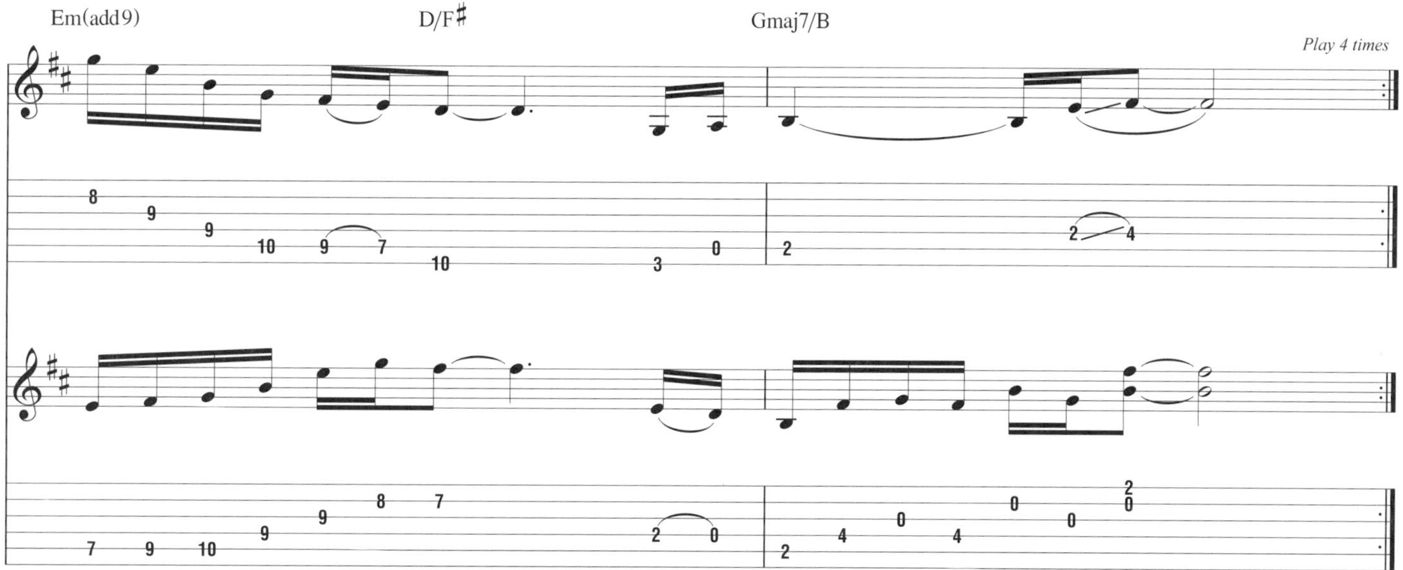

Bm
A
D
A/C♯
Riff A1
Riff A
w/ pick & fingers

Bm
A
D
A/C♯
End Riff A1
End Riff A

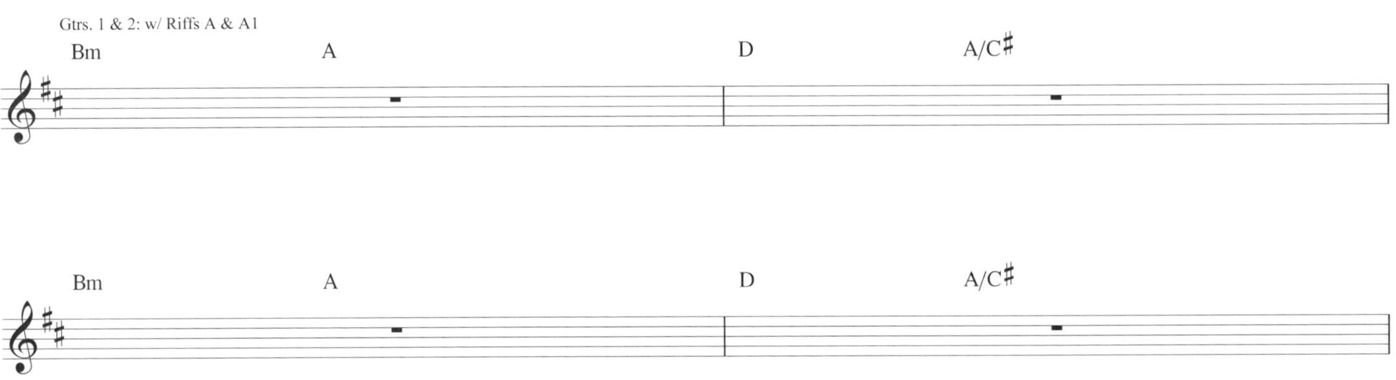
Gtrs. 1 & 2: w/ Riffs A & A1
Bm
A
D
A/C♯
Bm
A
D
A/C♯

2nd time, Gtrs. 1 & 2: w/ Fills 1 & 1A
Bm7
Aadd9
Gmaj7
A
Gtr. 2
Riff B1
let ring
Gtr. 1
Riff B
End Riff B

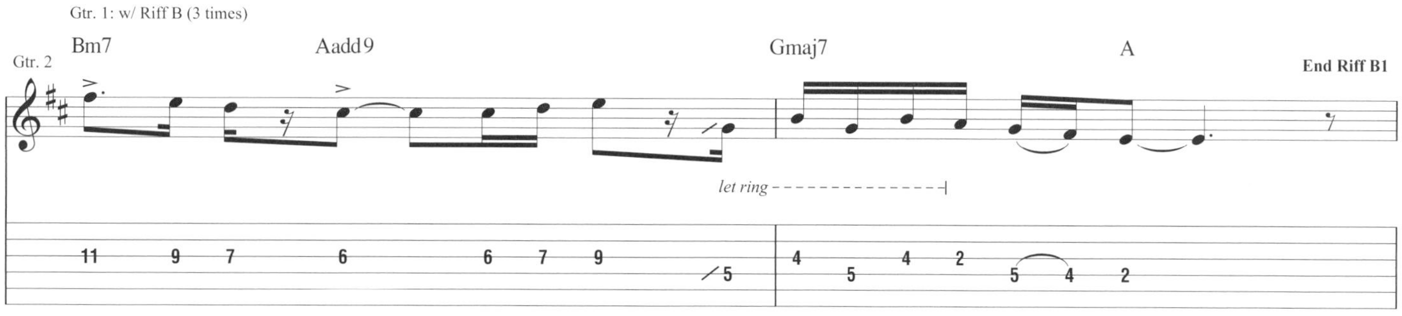

Gtr. 1: w/ Riff B (3 times)
Bm7
Aadd9
Gmaj7
A
Gtr. 2
End Riff B1
let ring

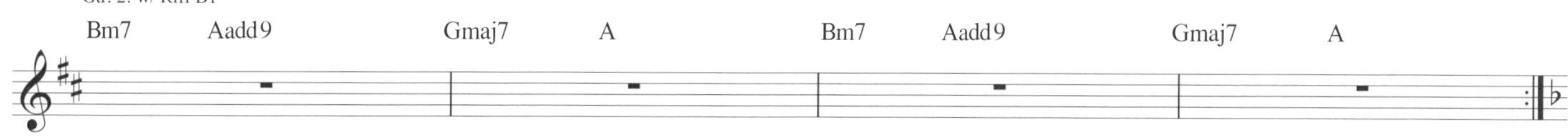

Gtr. 2: w/ Riff B1
Bm7
Aadd9
Gmaj7
A
Bm7
Aadd9
Gmaj7
A

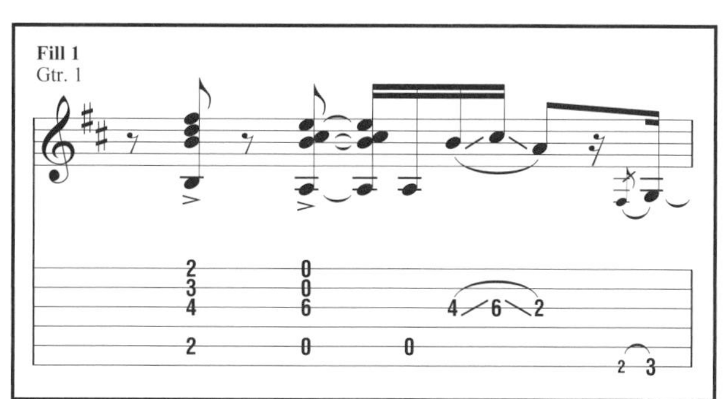

Fill 1
Gtr. 1

Fill 1A
Gtr. 2

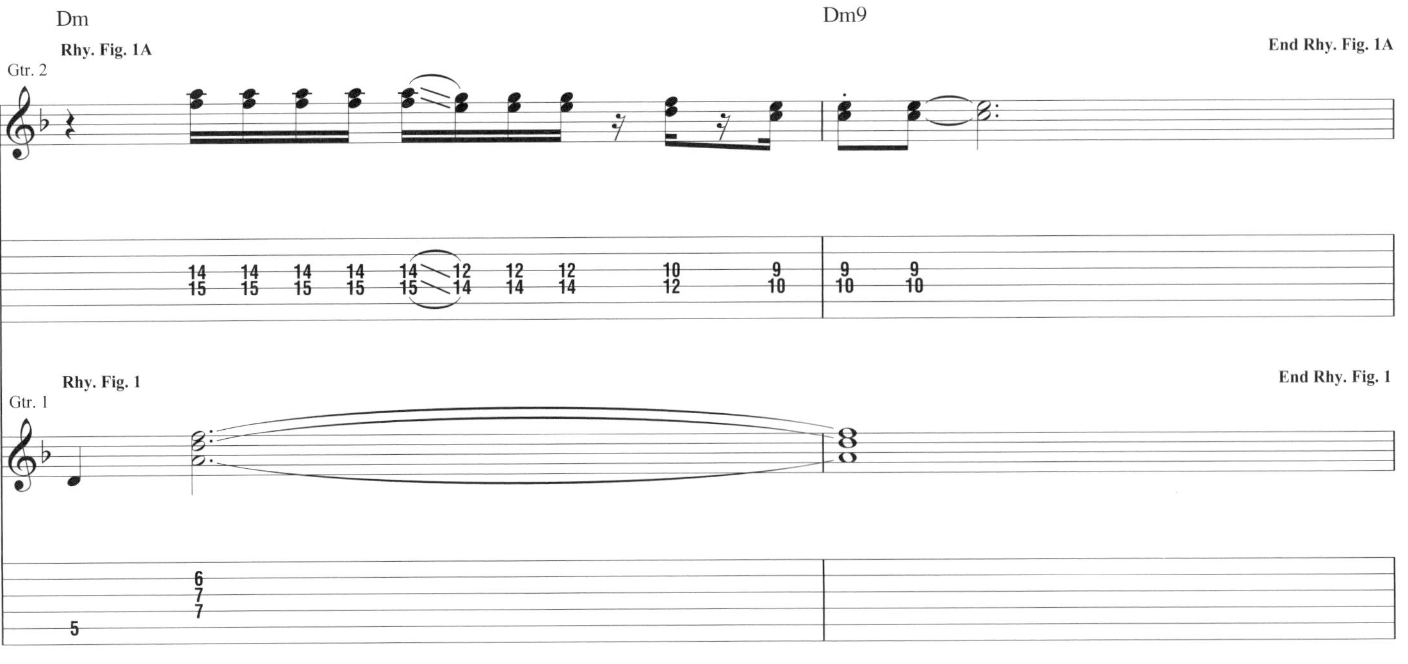

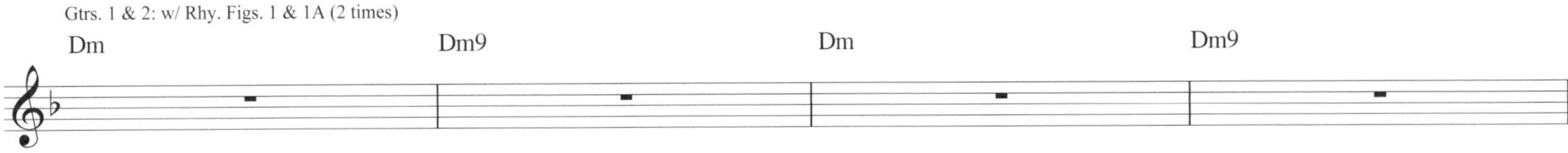

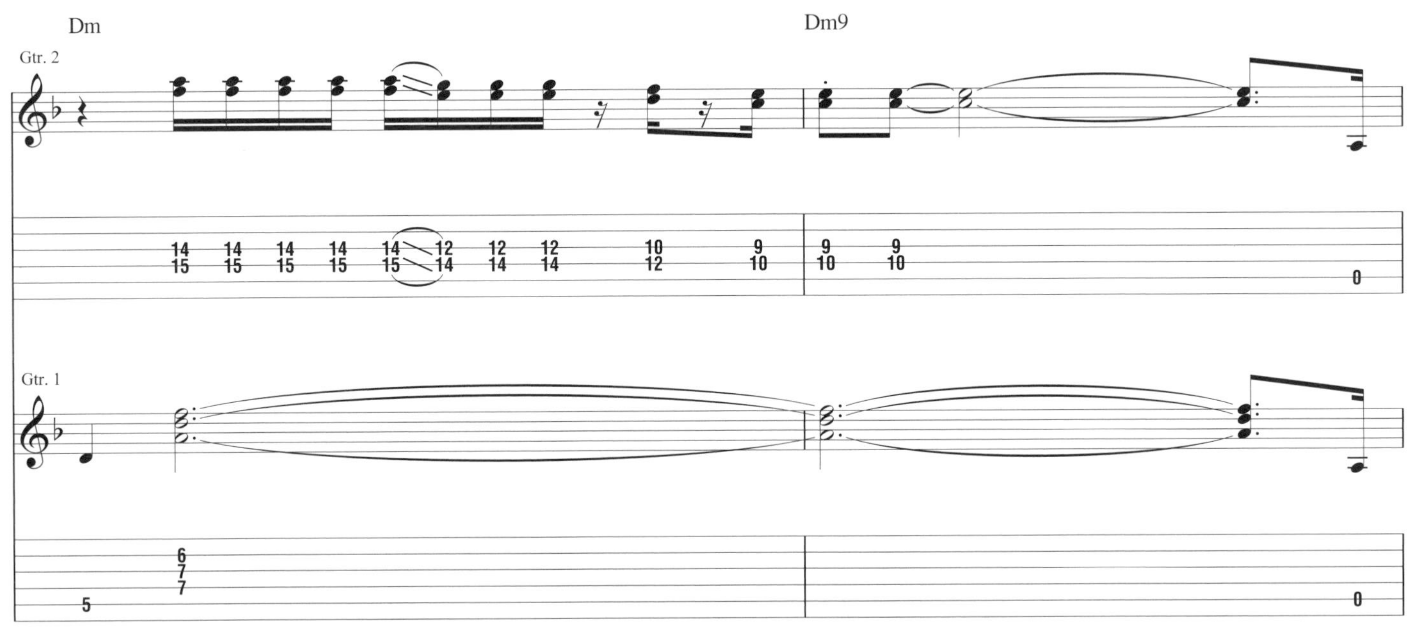

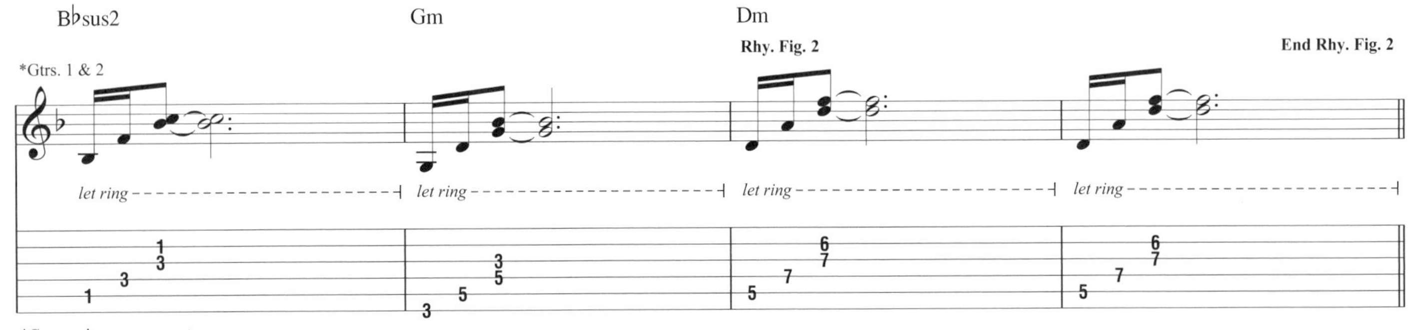

*Composite arrangement

Verse

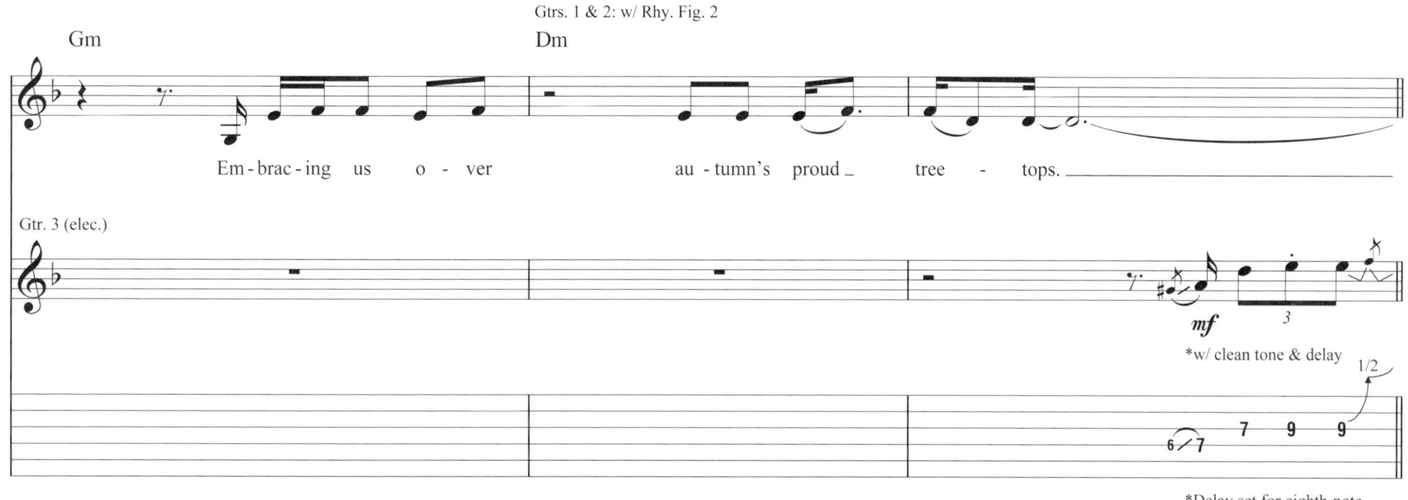

*Delay set for eighth-note regeneration w/ 3 repeats.

Guitar Solo

**Played behind the beat.

Gtr. 3 tacet
Gtrs. 1 & 2: w/ Rhy. Fig. 2
B♭sus2
Gm
Dm
Gtr. 4
grad. bend
let ring
1/2 hold bend
*Played behind the beat.
**Played ahead of the beat.
Verse
Gtrs. 1 & 2: w/ Rhy. Fig. 3 (2 times)
Gtr. 4 tacet
2. I stand motion - less in a pa-rade of fall - ing rain. Your voice I
can - not hear as I am fall - ing a - gain.
Interlude
Gtrs. 1 & 2: w/ Rhy. Figs. 1 & 1A (4 times)
Dm9
Em
mp
Gtrs. 1, 2 & 4 tacet
(Bass & drums)
Gtrs. 1 & 2

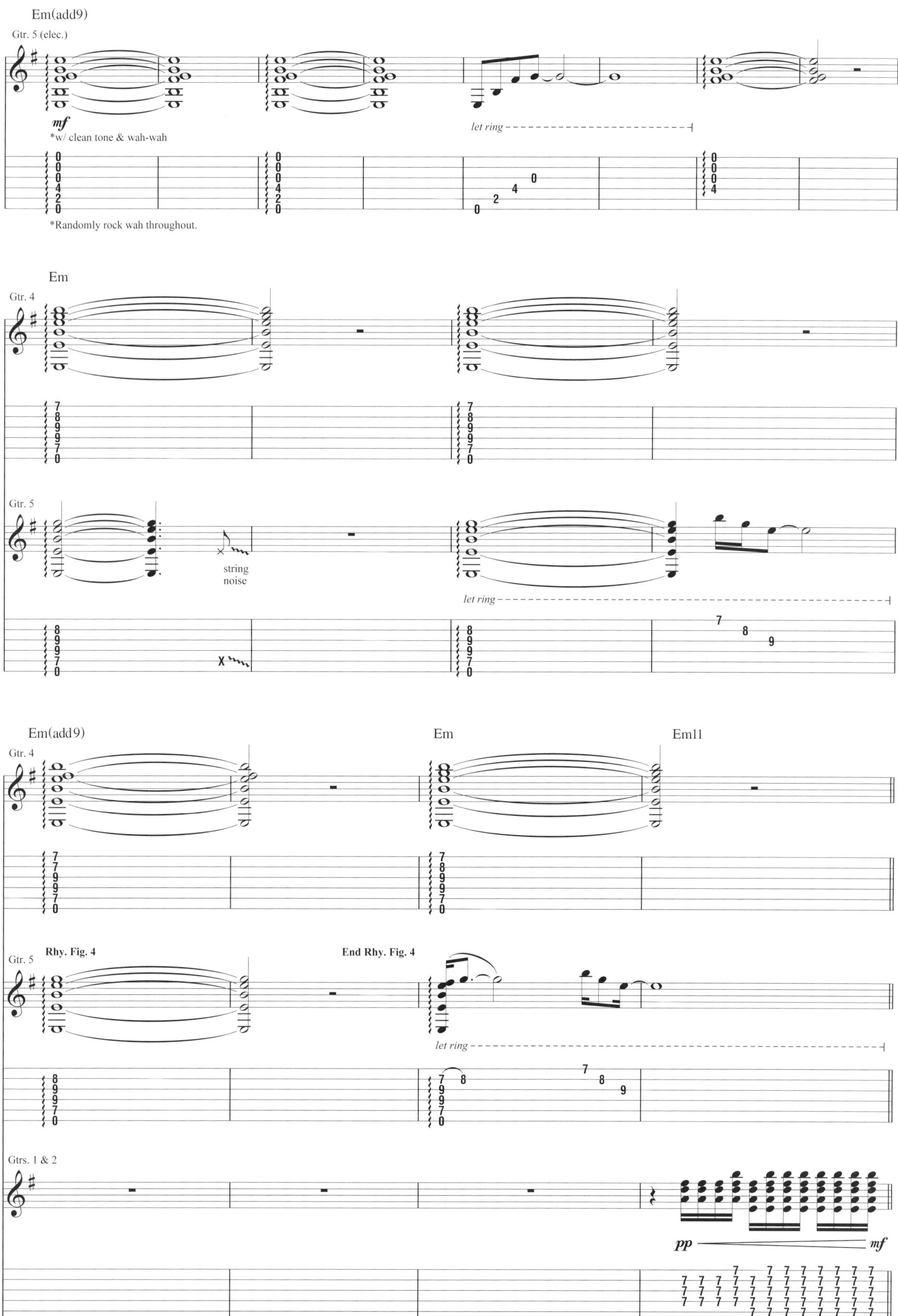
Em(add9)
Gtr. 5 (elec.)
mf
*w/ clean tone & wah-wah
let ring
*Randomly rock wah throughout.
Em
Gtr. 4
Gtr. 5
string noise
let ring
Em(add9)
Em
Em11
Gtr. 4
Rhy. Fig. 4
End Rhy. Fig. 4
Gtr. 5
let ring
Gtrs. 1 & 2
pp
mf

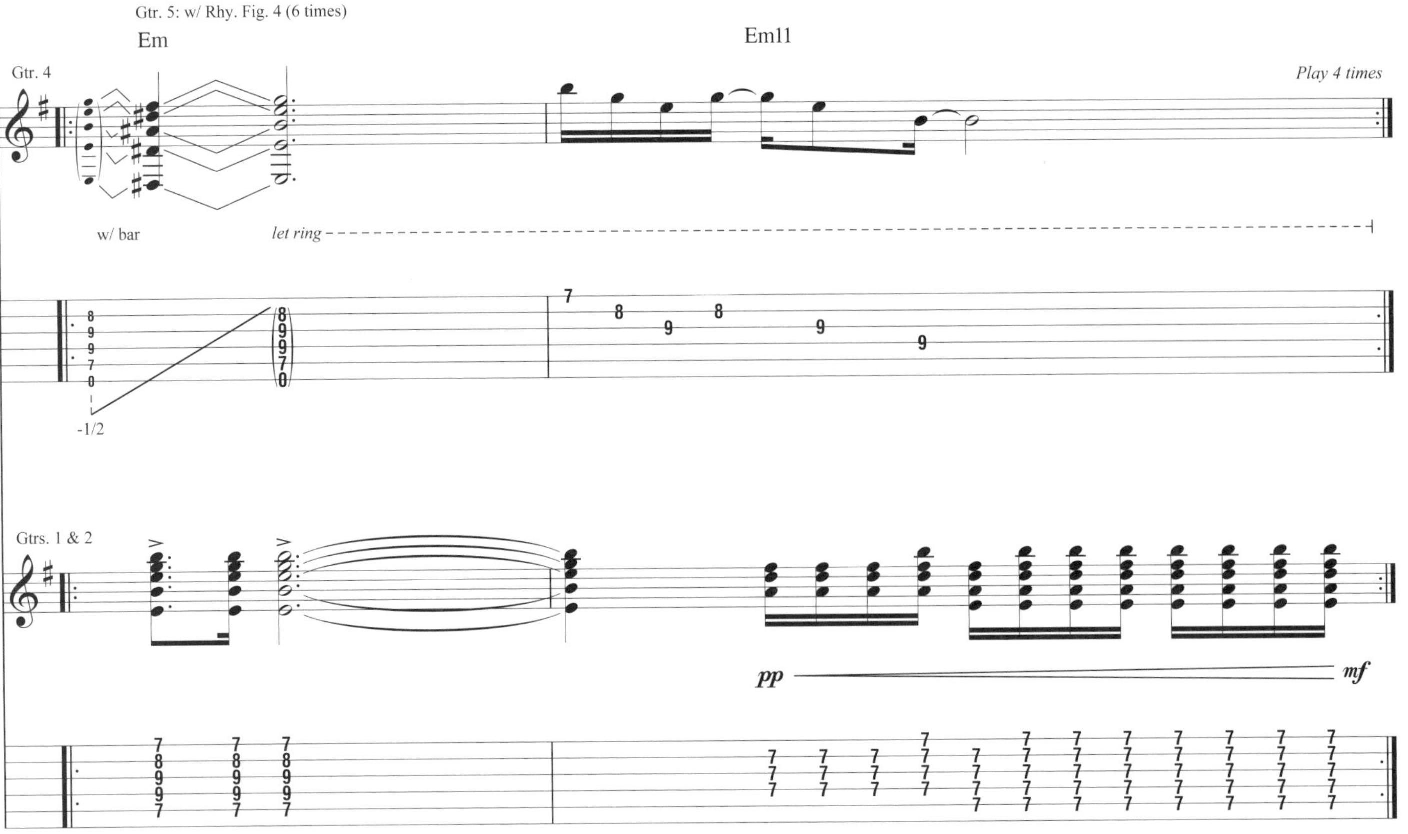
Gtr. 5: w/ Rhy. Fig. 4 (6 times)
Em
Em11
Gtr. 4
Play 4 times
w/ bar
let ring
-1/2
Gtrs. 1 & 2
pp
mf

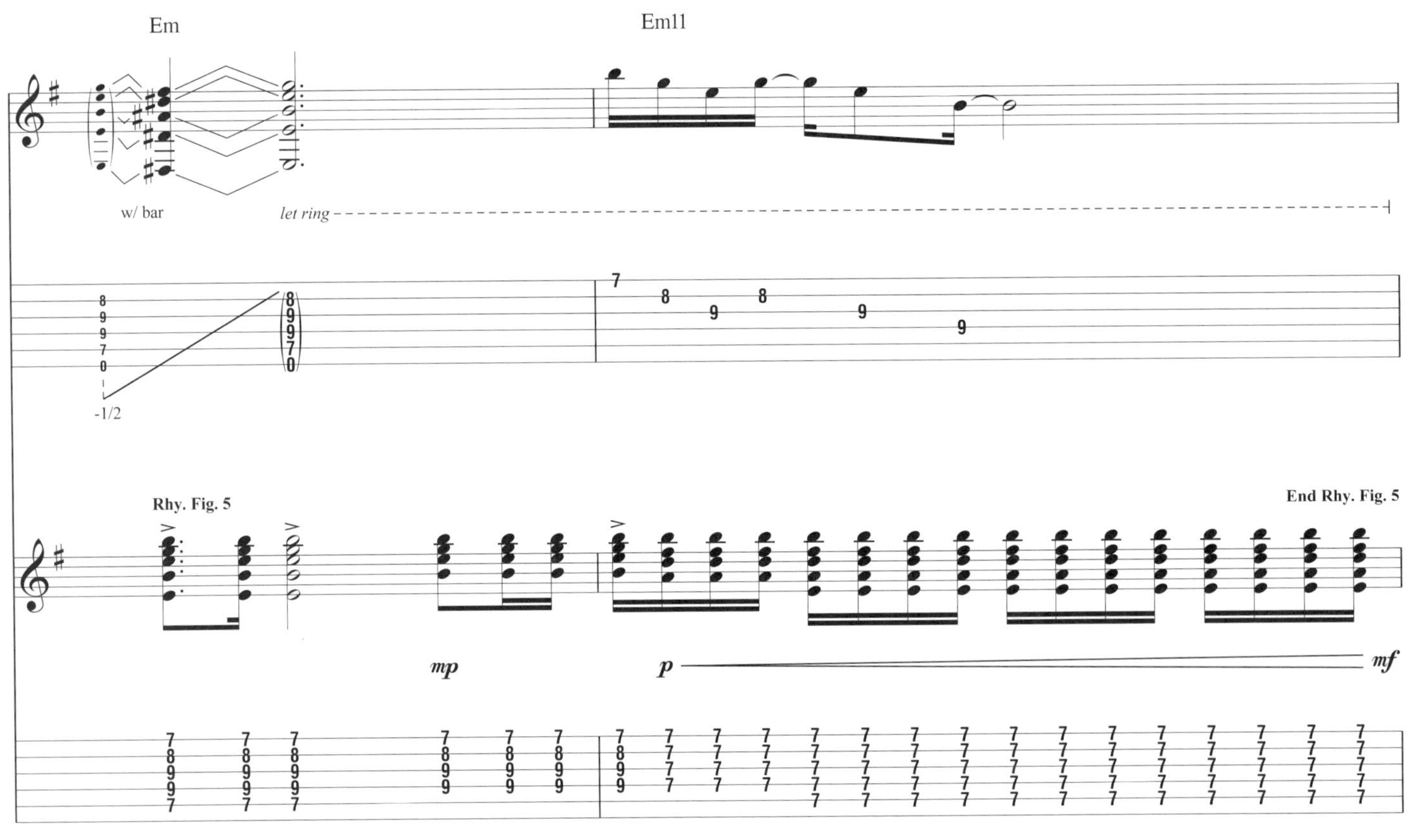
Em
Em11
w/ bar
let ring
-1/2
Rhy. Fig. 5
End Rhy. Fig. 5
mp
p
mf

Gtrs. 1 & 2: w/ Rhy. Fig. 5
Em
Em11
Gtr. 4
w/ bar
-1/2
Gtr. 6 (elec.)
*p
f
w/ dist.
*Vol. swell
Gtr. 4 tacet
Em
**G/E
Bm/E
Riff C1
Gtr. 7 (elec.)
f
w/ dist.
P.M.
Riff C
Gtr. 6
P.M.
**Bass plays E.
Em
G/D
C6(♭5)
C
End Riff C1
End Riff C
let ring
P.M.

Gtrs. 6 & 7: w/ Riffs C & C1
Em
G/E
Bm/E
Em
G/D C6(♭5) C
De -
Chorus
Gtr. 6: w/ Riff C (2 times)
Gtr. 7: w/ Riff C1 (1 1/2 times)
Em
G/E
Bm/E
Em
vo - tion e - ludes
and in sad - ness I lum - ber.
G/D C6(♭5) C
Em
G/E
Bm/E
In my own ash - es I am
Em
G/D C6(♭5) C
stand - ing with - out a soul.
Gtr. 7
P.M.
E5
D5
B
B/D♯
Whispered: She wept and whis - pered, "I
Gtr. 7
Gtr. 6

Interlude

Em Am D

know..."

Riff D

5 5 5 5 0 0 2 | 3 5 5 4

7 7 7 7 7 8 8 8 7 8 | 8 5 5 5 5 0 4 0 0 6

P.M. P.M.

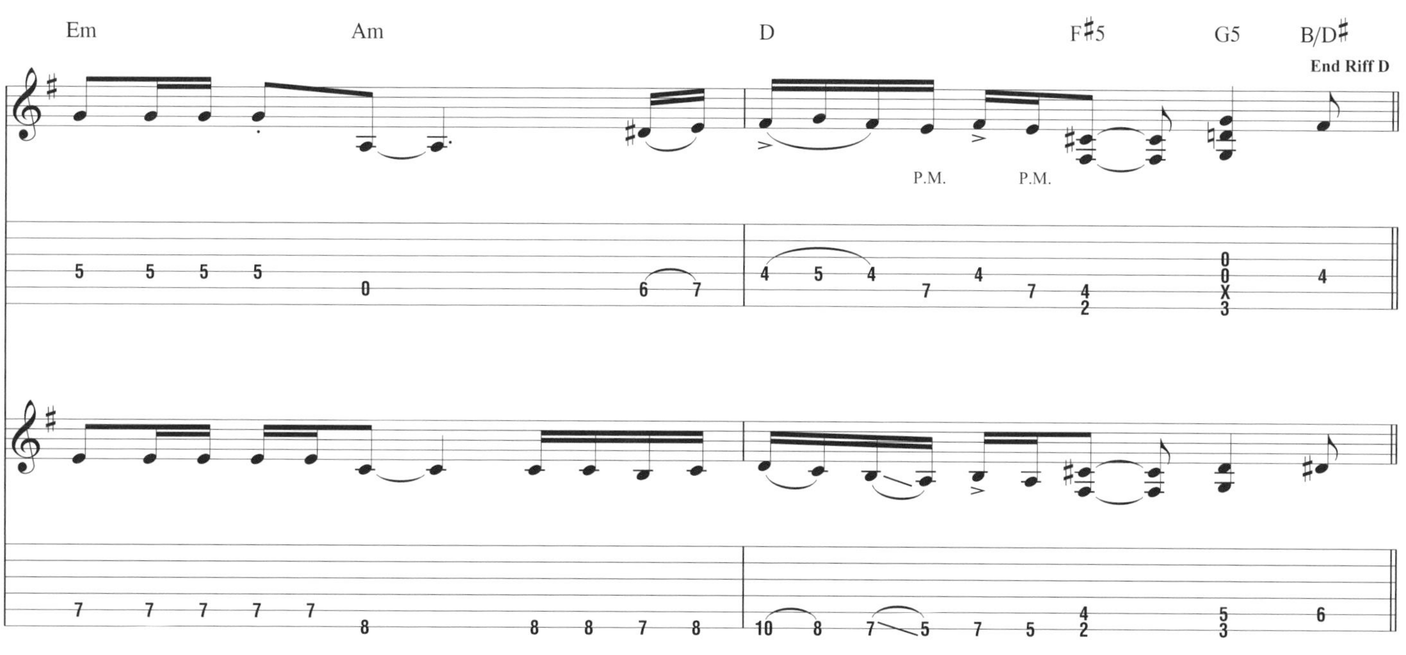

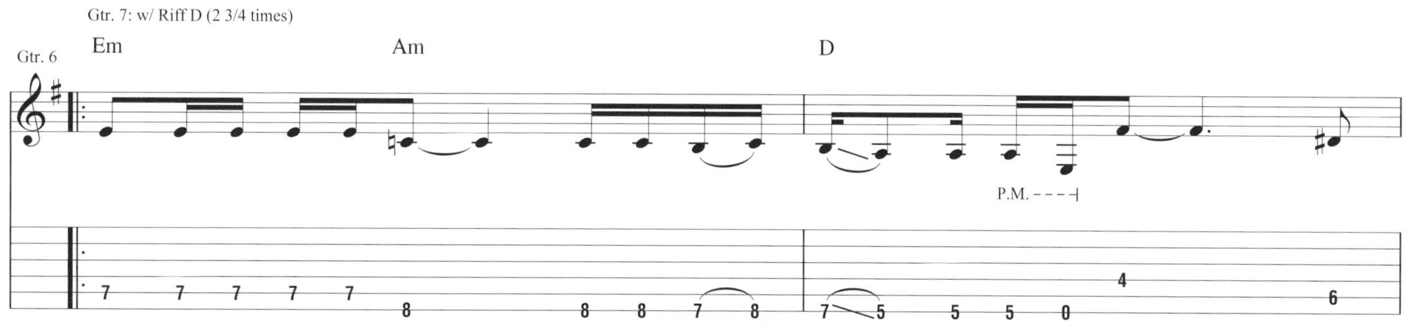

1., 2.
Em
Am
D
F#5
G5
B/D#
3.
Free time
Gtr. 2
D
Em
Dm
Am
Asus2
w/ fingers
Gtr. 6
pp
Gtr. 7
pp
Interlude
Slower ♩ = 63
Gtr. 2 tacet
Dm
Em
Am
Asus2
G
Fmaj7
Dm
Em
Am
Asus2
Gtr. 6
Gtr. 7

G
Fmaj7
Dm
Em
Am
Asus2
G
F
Dm
Em
Am
Asus2
G
F
Dm
Em
Am
Asus2
G
F
Riff E
Gtr. 8 (elec.)
mp
w/ clean tone & multiple reverb
let ring
Riff E1
Gtr. 9 (elec.)
mp
w/ clean tone & multiple reverb

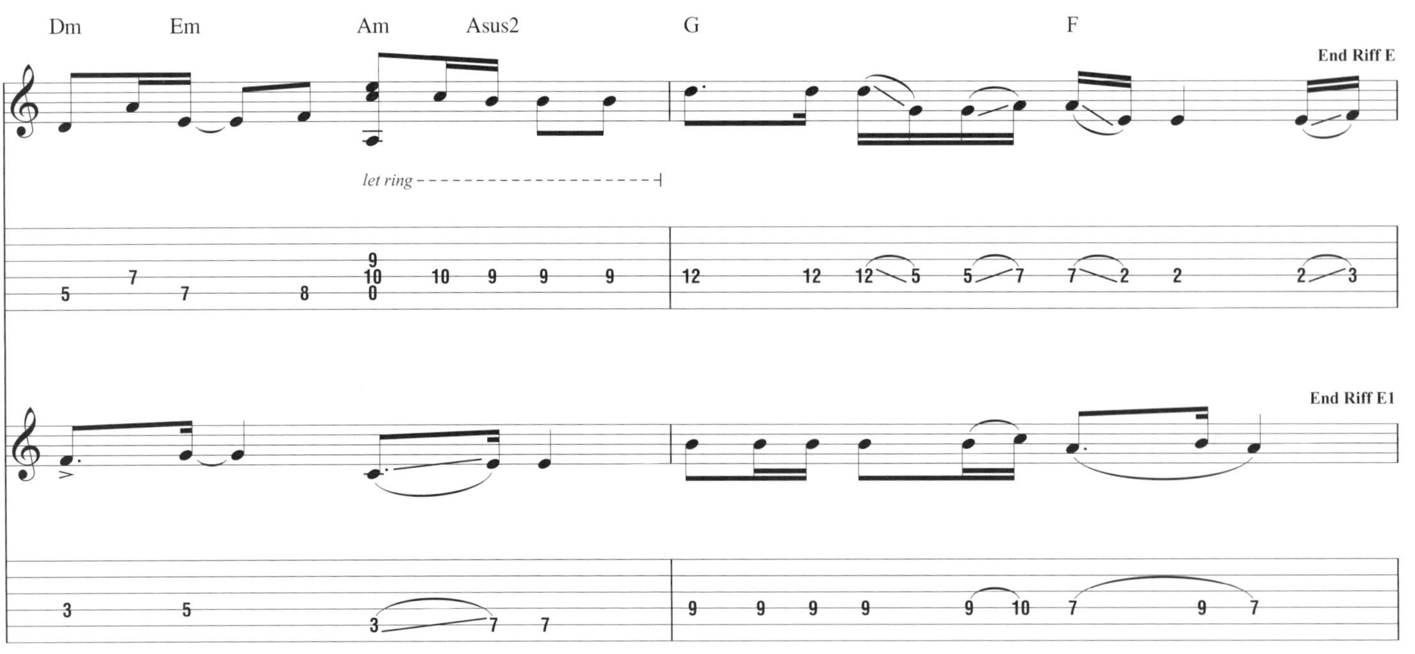
Dm
Em
Am
Asus2
G
F
End Riff E
let ring
End Riff E1

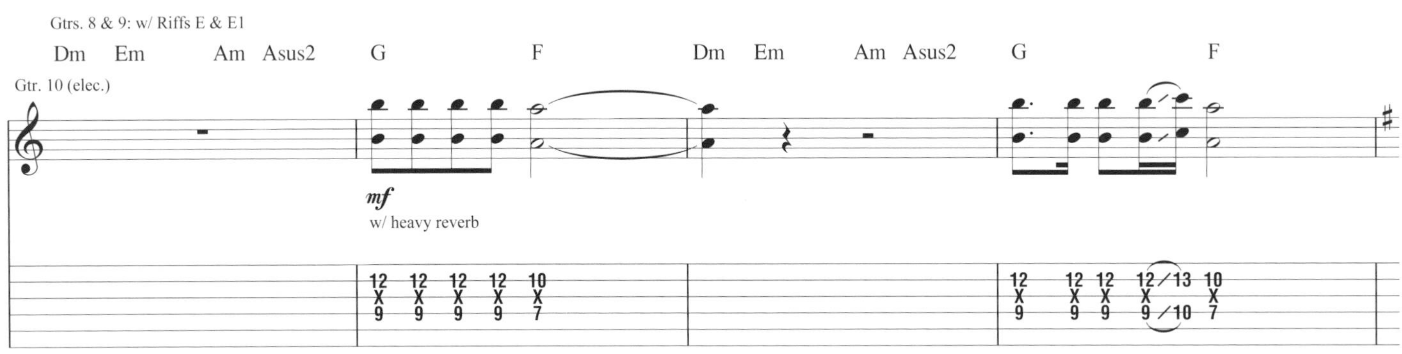
Gtrs. 8 & 9: w/ Riffs E & E1
Dm
Em
Am
Asus2
G
F
Dm
Em
Am
Asus2
G
F
Gtr. 10 (elec.)
mf
w/ heavy reverb

Gtr. 10 tacet
D/E
Em
N.C.
Bm
E5
A5
Riff F
Gtr. 2
Riff F1
Gtr. 11 (nylon str. acous.)
mp

D/E Em N.C. Bm E5 A5
We
End Riff F
End Riff F1
Outro
Gtrs. 2 & 11: w/ Riffs F & F1 (2 1/4 times)
D/E Em N.C. Bm E5 Am D/E Em N.C. Bm E5 A5
walked in - to the night. Am I to bid you fare - well?
D/E Em N.C. Bm E5 Am D/E Em N.C. Bm E5 A5 D/E Em N.C.
Why can't you see that I try when ev - 'ry tear I shed
Bm E5 Am D/E Em N.C. Bm E5 A5
is for you?
Gtr. 2
Gtr. 11

from *Sorceress*

Will O the Wisp

Words and Music by Mikael Akerfeldt

Gtrs. 1 & 2: Capo V

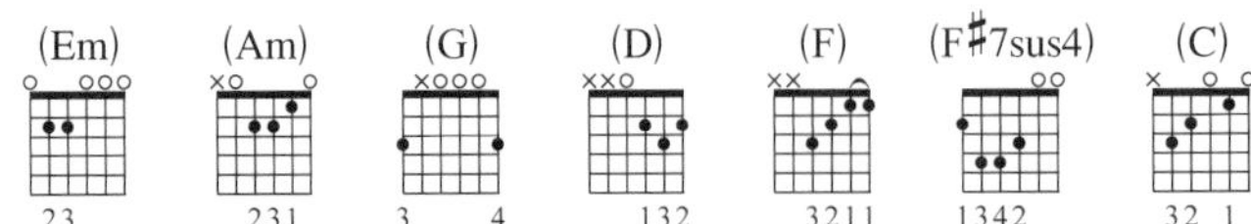

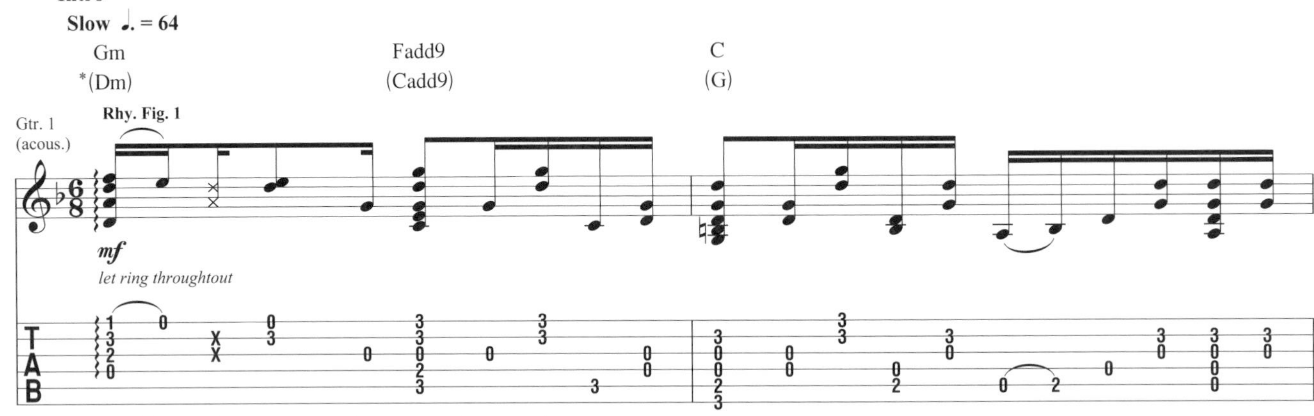

*Symbols in parentheses represent chord names respective to capoed guitar. Symbols above reflect actual sounding chords. Capoed fret is "0" in tab. Chord symbols reflect basic harmony.

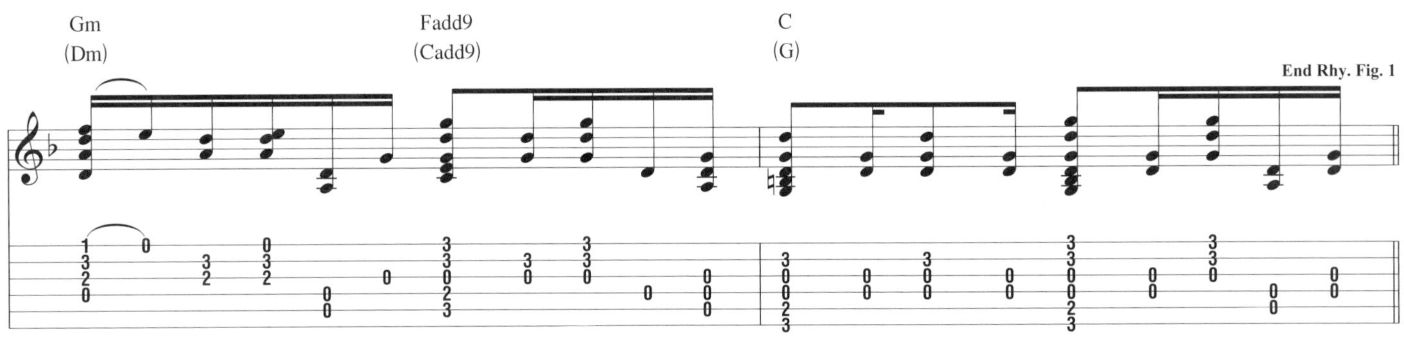

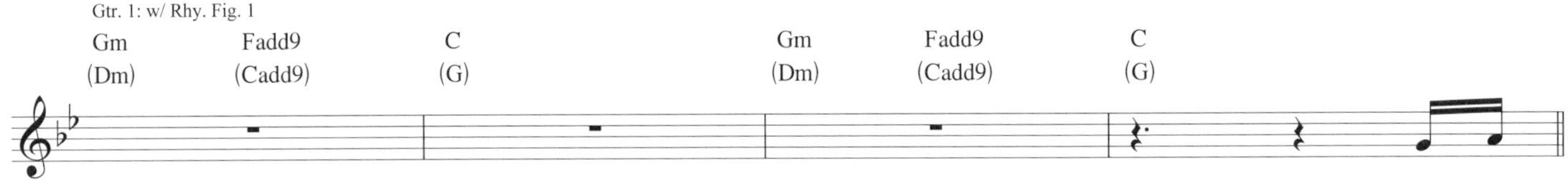

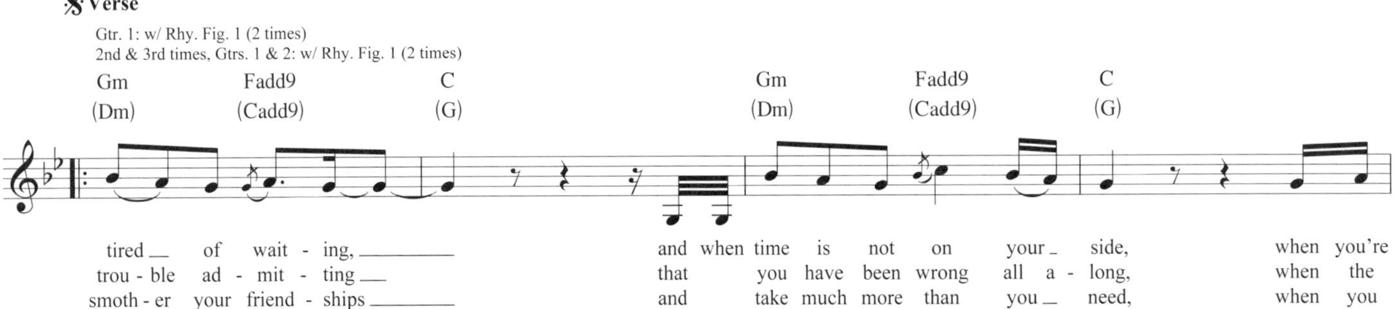

Gm
(Dm)
Fadd9
(Cadd9)
C
(G)
tired of hat - ing me, you no long - er want to hide.
words you have writ - ten down reads "ev - 'ry - thing is gone."
can't keep the se - cret to your - self and points to the source of the deed.
You're
Pre-Chorus
2nd & 3rd times, Gtr. 2: w/ Rhy. Fig. 2
B♭maj7/D
(Fmaj7/A)
Dm
(Am)
F
(C)
stuck to the fail - ures of your life,
Gtr. 1
Rhy. Fig. 2
To Coda
E♭sus2
(B♭sus2)
marred with the sor - rows of your strife.
End Rhy. Fig. 2
Chorus
Gsus2
**(Dsus2)
Gm(add9)/B♭
(Dm(add9)/F)
Fadd9/A
(Cadd9/E)
C6
(G6)
And time, it waits for no one; it heals them when you die.
*Gtrs. 1 & 2
Riff A
End Riff A
let ring throughout
*Gtr. 2 (12-str. acous.), played mf.
**Chord symbols reflect implied harmony.

Gtrs. 1 & 2: w/ Riff A
Gsus2 (Dsus2) Gm(add9)/B♭ (Dm(add9)/F) Fadd9/A (Cadd9/E) F (C) Gsus2 (Dsus2) Gm(add9)/B♭ (Dm(add9)/F) C6 (G6) Fadd9 (Cadd9)
And soon you are for - got - ten, a whis - per with - in a
1.
Interlude
Gtrs. 1 & 2: w/ Rhy. Fig. 1 (2 times)
Gm (Dm) Fadd9 (Cadd9) C (G) Gm (Dm) Fadd9 (Cadd9) C (G)
sigh.
Gm (Dm) Fadd9 (Cadd9) C (G) Gm (Dm) Fadd9 (Cadd9) C (G)
2. When there's
2.
Gtrs. 1 & 2: w/ Riff A (2 times)
Gsus2 (Dsus2) Gm(add9)/B♭ (Dm(add9)/F) Fadd9/A (Cadd9/E) F (C) Gsus2 (Dsus2) Gm(add9)/B♭ (Dm(add9)/F) C6 (G6) Fadd9 (Cadd9)
sigh. And time, it waits for no one; it heals them when you die.
Gsus2 (Dsus2) Gm(add9)/B♭ (Dm(add9)/F) Fadd9/A (Cadd9/E) F (C) Gsus2 (Dsus2) Gm(add9)/B♭ (Dm(add9)/F) C6 (G6) Fadd9 (Cadd9)
And soon you are for - got - ten, a whis - per with - in a
Interlude
Gtrs. 1 & 2: w/ Rhy. Fig. 1 (2 times)
Gm (Dm) Fadd9 (Cadd9) C (G) Gm (Dm) Fadd9 (Cadd9) C (G)
sigh. Hm.
D.S. al Coda
Gm (Dm) Fadd9 (Cadd9) C (G) Gm (Dm) Fadd9 (Cadd9) C (G)
3. When you

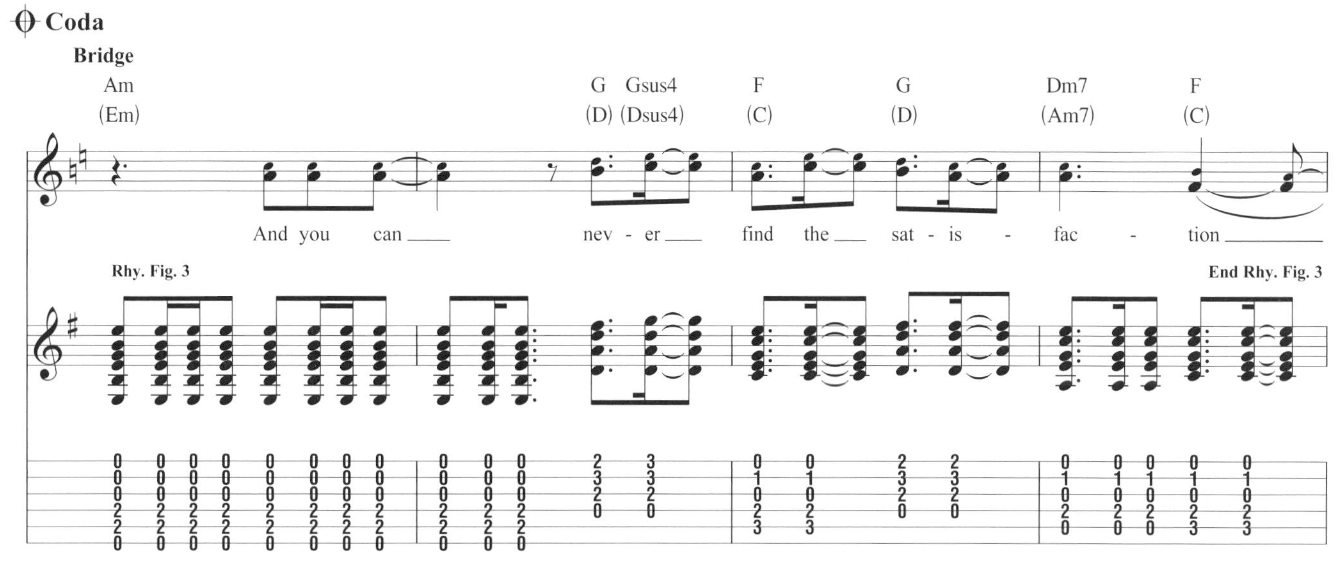

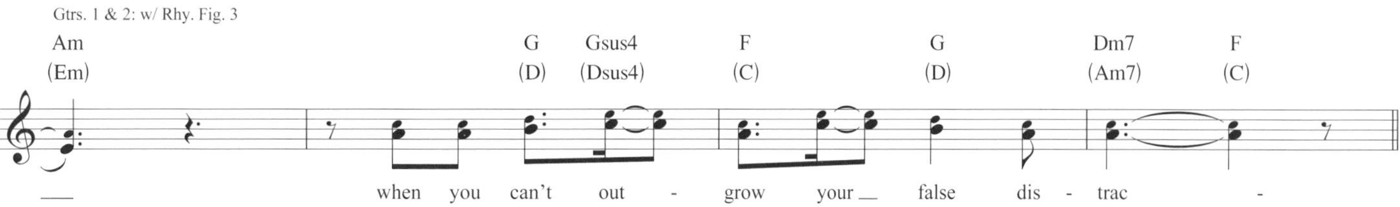

*See top of first page of song for chord diagrams pertaining to rhythm slashes.

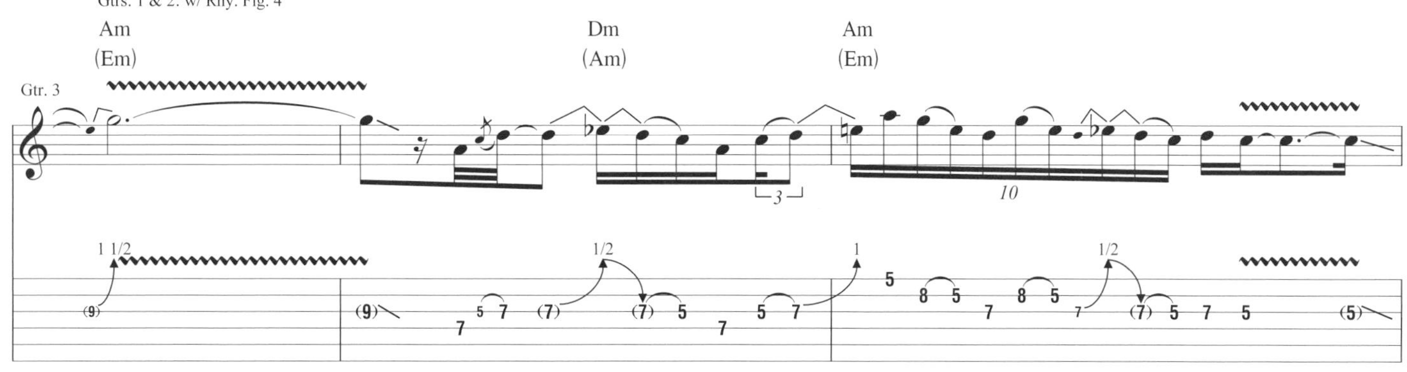

Bridge
Dm
(Am)
(G)
(Am)
(D)
(F)
Gtrs. 1 & 2
You know your soul is weighed on the sil - ver
Gtr. 3
1 1/2
Gtr. 3 tacet
(F♯7add4)
(C)
(D)
Gtrs. 1 & 2
scale
of de - ceit and lies.
Outro-Guitar Solo
Gtrs. 1 & 2: w/ Riff A (till fade)
Gsus2
(Dsus2)
Gm(add9)/B♭
(Dm(add9)/F)
Fadd9/A
(Cadd9/E)
F
(C)
Gsus2
(Dsus2)
Gm(add9)/B♭
(Dm(add9)/F)
C6
(G6)
Fadd9
(Cadd9)
Gtr. 3
mf
w/ dist.
Gsus2
(Dsus2)
Gm(add9)/B♭
(Dm(add9)/F)
Fadd9/A
(Cadd9/E)
F
(C)
Gsus2
(Dsus2)
Gm(add9)/B♭
(Dm(add9)/F)
C6
(G6)
Fadd9
(Cadd9)

Gtr. 3 tacet
Gsus2 (Dsus2) Gm(add9)/B♭ (Dm(add9)/F) Fadd9/A (Cadd9/E) F (C) Gsus2 (Dsus2) Gm(add9)/B♭ (Dm(add9)/F) C6 (G6) Fadd9 (Cadd9)
Gtr. 4 (elec.)
mf
w/ dist.
2nd time, Begin fade
Gsus2 (Dsus2) Gm(add9)/B♭ (Dm(add9)/F) Fadd9/A (Cadd9/E) F (C) Gsus2 (Dsus2) Gm(add9)/B♭ (Dm(add9)/F) C6 (G6) Fadd9 (Cadd9)
Gtr. 4 tacet
Gsus2 (Dsus2) Gm(add9)/B♭ (Dm(add9)/F) Fadd9/A (Cadd9/E) F (C) Gsus2 (Dsus2) Gm(add9)/B♭ (Dm(add9)/F) C6 (G6) Fadd9 (Cadd9)
Gtr. 3
Gsus2 (Dsus2) Gm(add9)/B♭ (Dm(add9)/F) Fadd9/A (Cadd9/E) F (C) Gsus2 (Dsus2) Gm(add9)/B♭ (Dm(add9)/F) C6 (G6) Fadd9 (Cadd9)
Fade out
Gtr. 3 tacet
Gsus2 (Dsus2) Gm(add9)/B♭ (Dm(add9)/F) Fadd9/A (Cadd9/E) F (C) Gsus2 (Dsus2) Gm(add9)/B♭ (Dm(add9)/F)
Gtr. 4

from *Damnation*

Windowpane

Words and Music by Mikael Akerfeldt

Gtrs. 1, 2 & 9: Capo II

Intro

Moderately ♩. = 56

F♯m(add9)
* (Em(add9))
F♯m7
(Em7)
Play 8 times
Riff A
End Riff A
Gtr. 1 (elec.)
mp
w/ pick & fingers
let ring
let ring

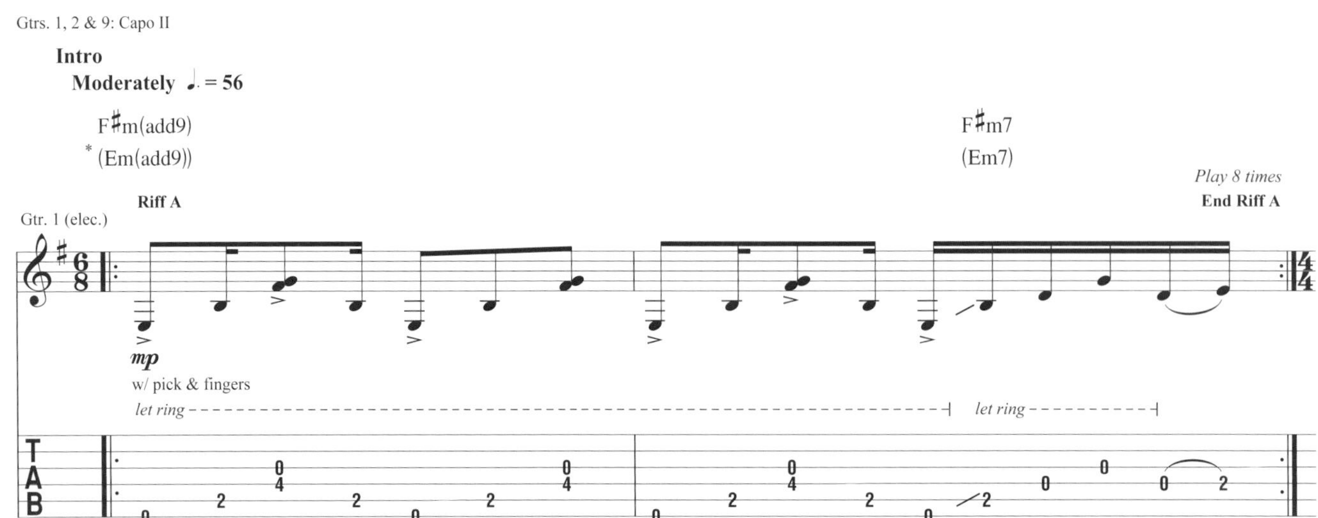

*Symbols in parentheses represent chord names respective to capoed guitars. Symbols above reflect actual sounding chords. Capoed fret is "0" in tab. Chord symbols reflect implied harmony.

Verse

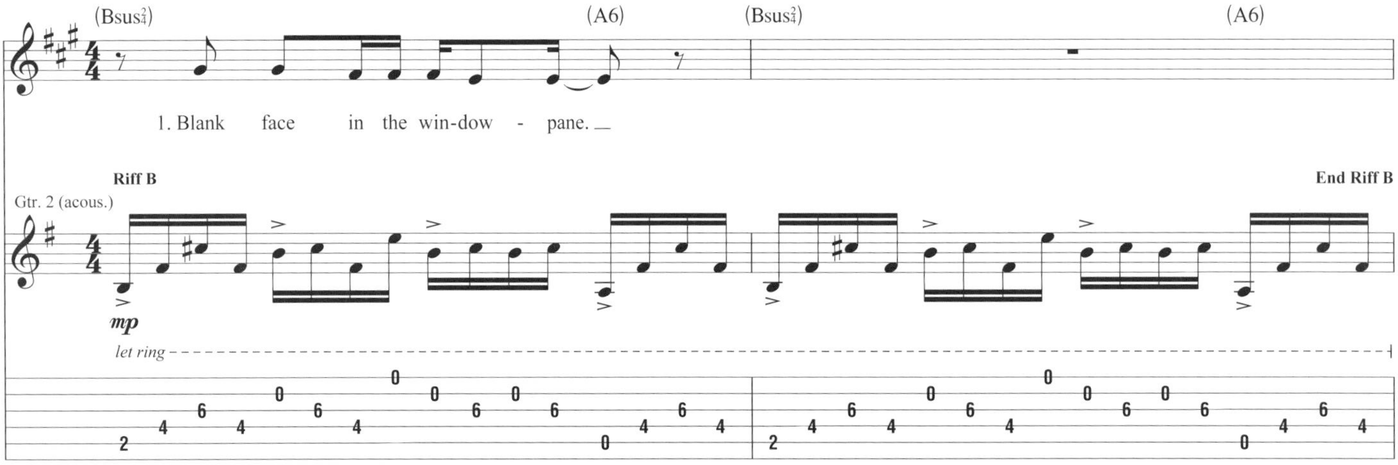

Gtr. 1 tacet
C♯sus2/4
(Bsus2/4)
B6
(A6)
C♯sus2/4
(Bsus2/4)
B6
(A6)
1. Blank face in the win-dow - pane.
Riff B
End Riff B
Gtr. 2 (acous.)
mp
let ring

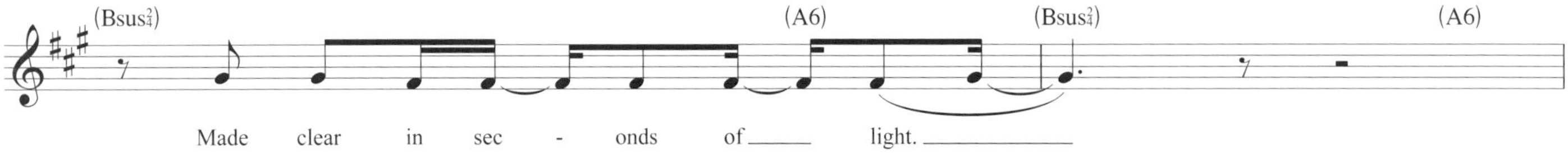

Gtr. 2: w/ Riff B (5 times)
C♯sus2/4
(Bsus2/4)
B6
(A6)
C♯sus2/4
(Bsus2/4)
B6
(A6)
Made clear in sec - onds of light.

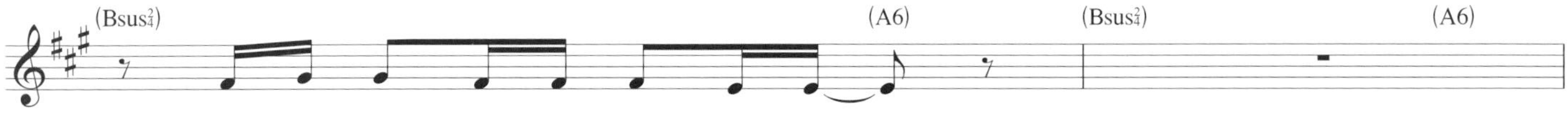

C♯sus2/4
(Bsus2/4)
B6
(A6)
C♯sus2/4
(Bsus2/4)
B6
(A6)
Dis - ap - pears and re - turns a - gain.

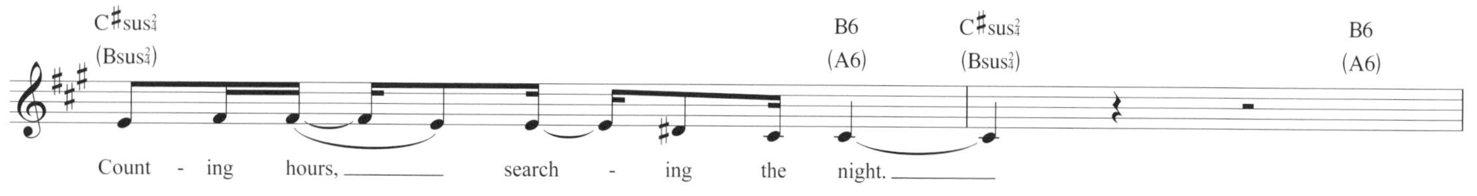

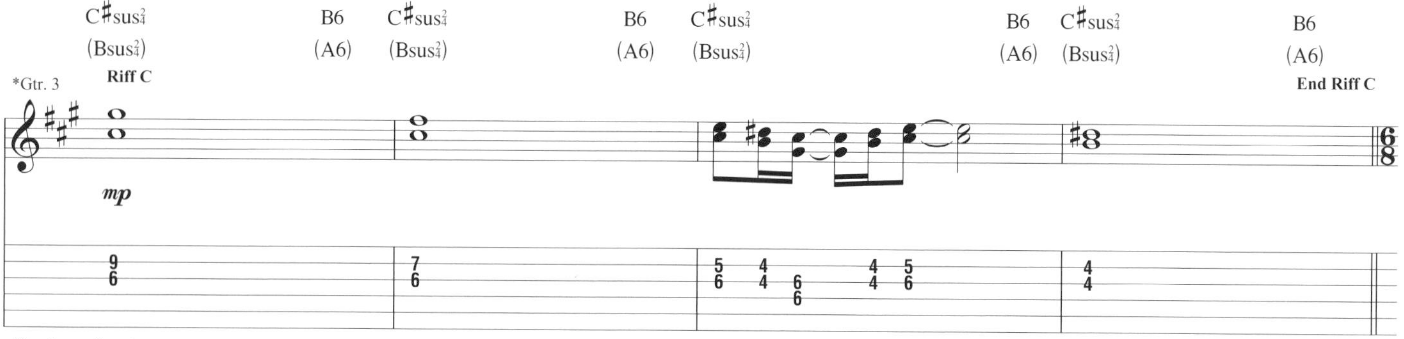

*Synth. arr. for gtr.

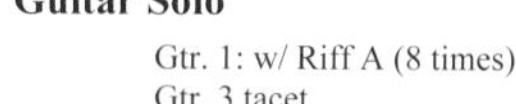

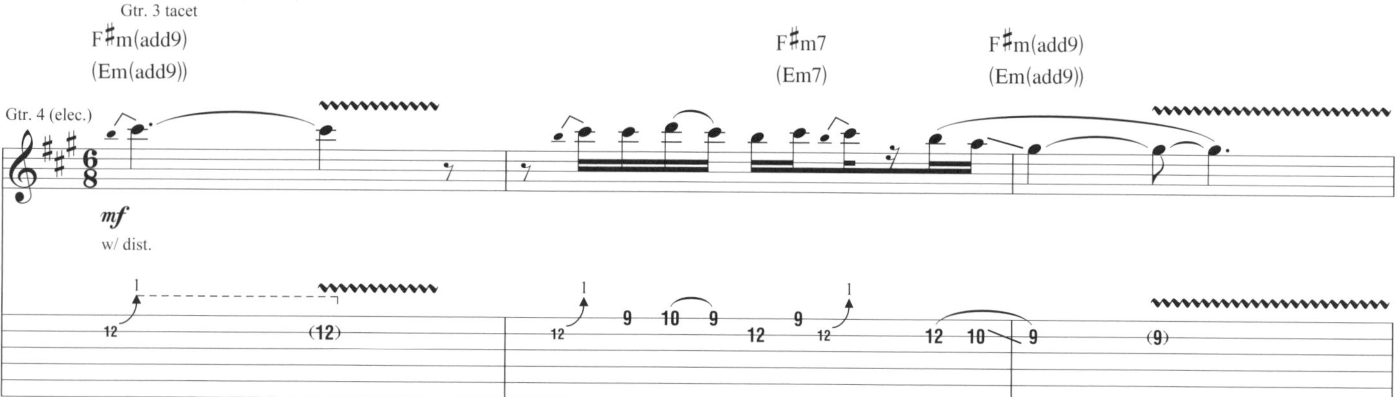

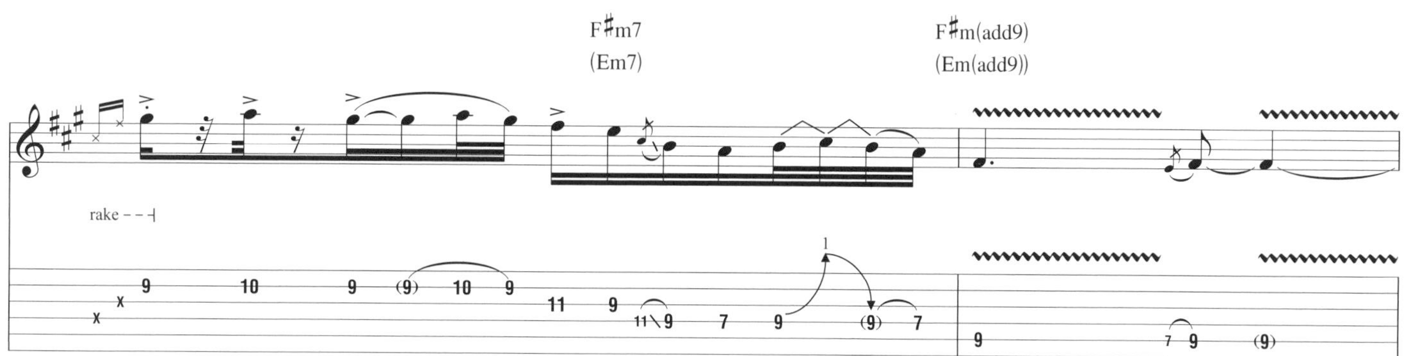

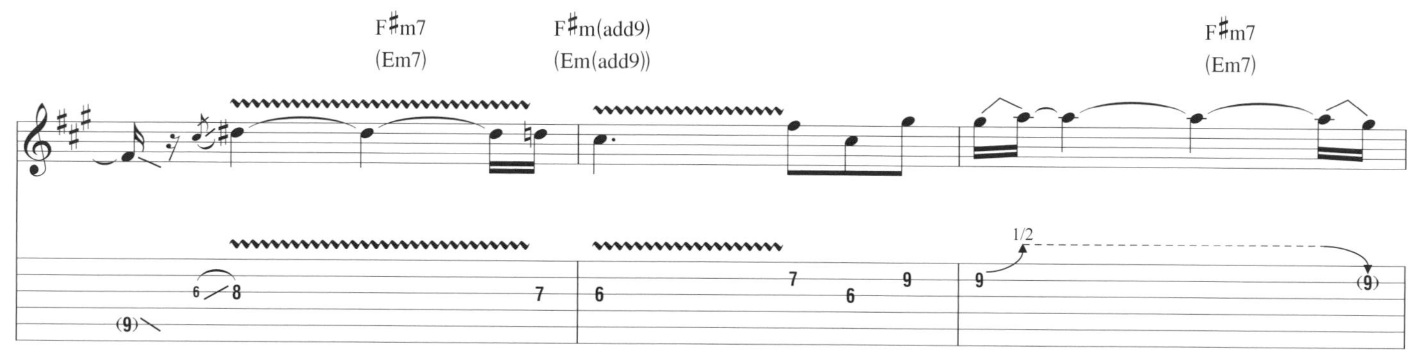

F♯m(add9)
(Em(add9))
F♯m7
(Em7)
F♯m(add9)
(Em(add9))
string noise
rake
Verse
Gtr. 2: w/ Riff B (6 times)
Gtr. 4 tacet
C♯sus2/4
(Bsus2/4)
B6
(A6)
2. Might be wait - ing for some - one.
Might be there for us to see.
fdbk.
Pitch: G♯

Gtr. 4 tacet
C♯sus2/4
(Bsus2/4)
B6
(A6)
Might be in need of talk - ing.
Might be star - ing di - rect - ly at me.
Gtr. 3: w/ Riff C
Am
(Gm)
Am/B
(Gm/A)
Am/C
(Gm/B♭)
Riff D
Gtr. 5 (elec.)
mf
w/ slight dist.
Riff D1
Gtr. 6 (elec.)
Rhy. Fig. 1
Gtr. 2
let ring

Am
(Gm)
Am/C
(Gm/B♭)
B♭m
(G♯m)
G♭maj7
(Emaj7)
B♭m
(G♯m)
G♭maj7
(Emaj7)
let ring
Am
(Gm)
Am/B
(Gm/A)
Am
(Gm)
Am/C
(Gm/B♭)
Bridge
Gtr. 2: w/ Rhy. Fig. 1
Am
(Gm)
Am/B
(Gm/A)
In - side plays a lul -
End Riff D
End Riff D1
End Rhy. Fig. 1

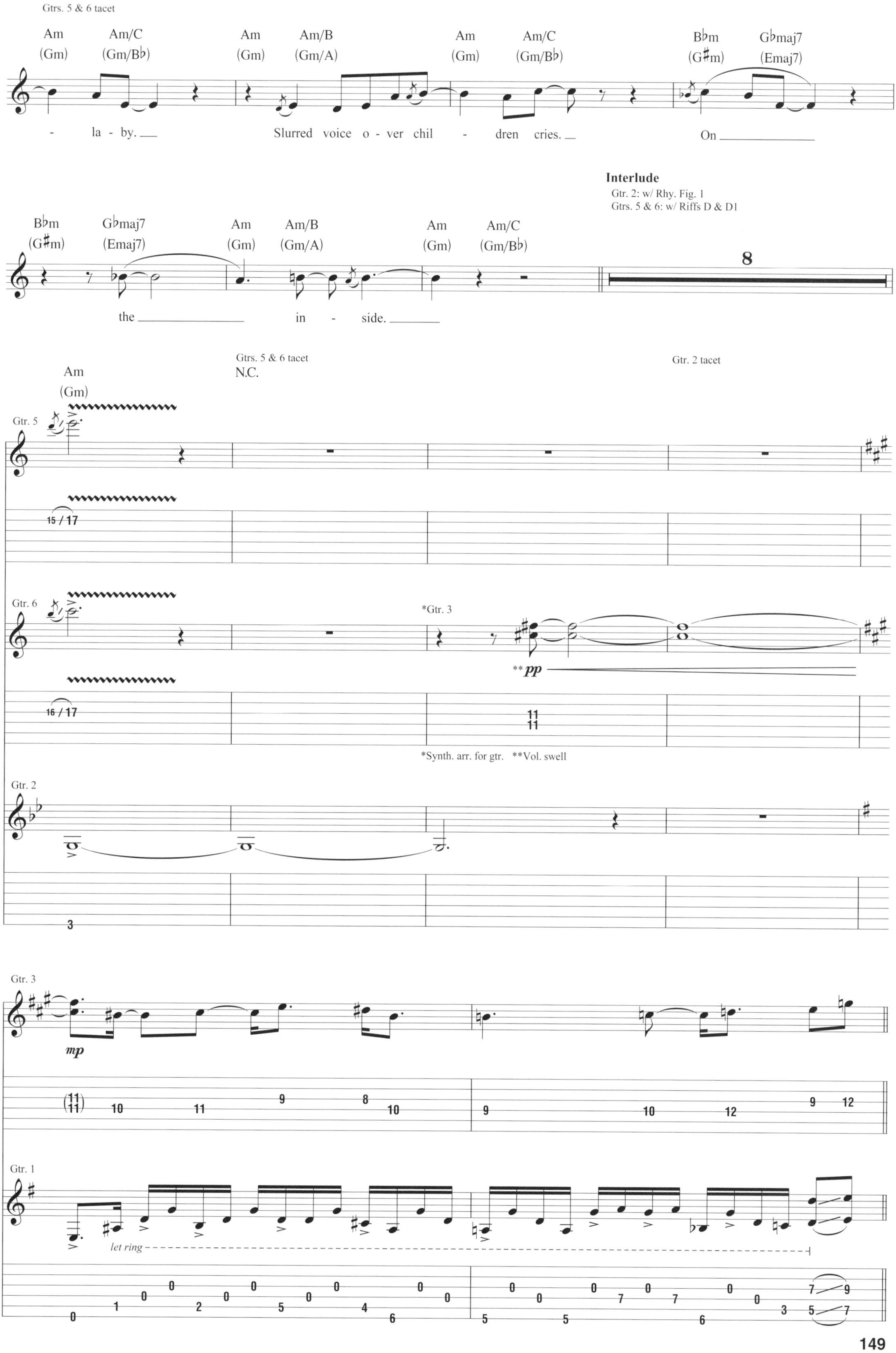

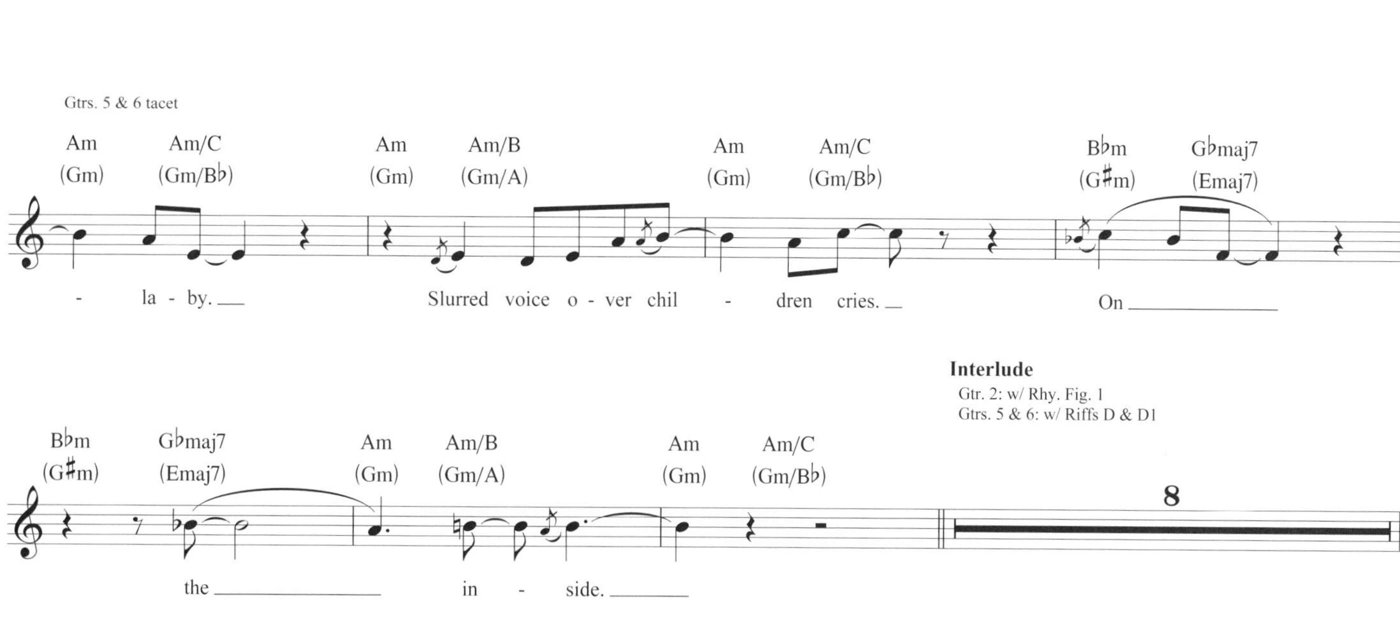

Am
(Gm)

Gtrs. 5 & 6 tacet
N.C.

Gtr. 2 tacet

Gtr. 5

15 / 17

Gtr. 6

*Gtr. 3

**pp

16 / 17

11
11

*Synth. arr. for gtr. **Vol. swell

Gtr. 2

3

Play 7 times
Gtr. 3 tacet
F♯m9
(Em9)
Riff E
Dmaj7
(Cmaj7)
Gtr. 7 (elec.)
mf
w/ clean tone
Gtr. 1
w/ fingers
let ring

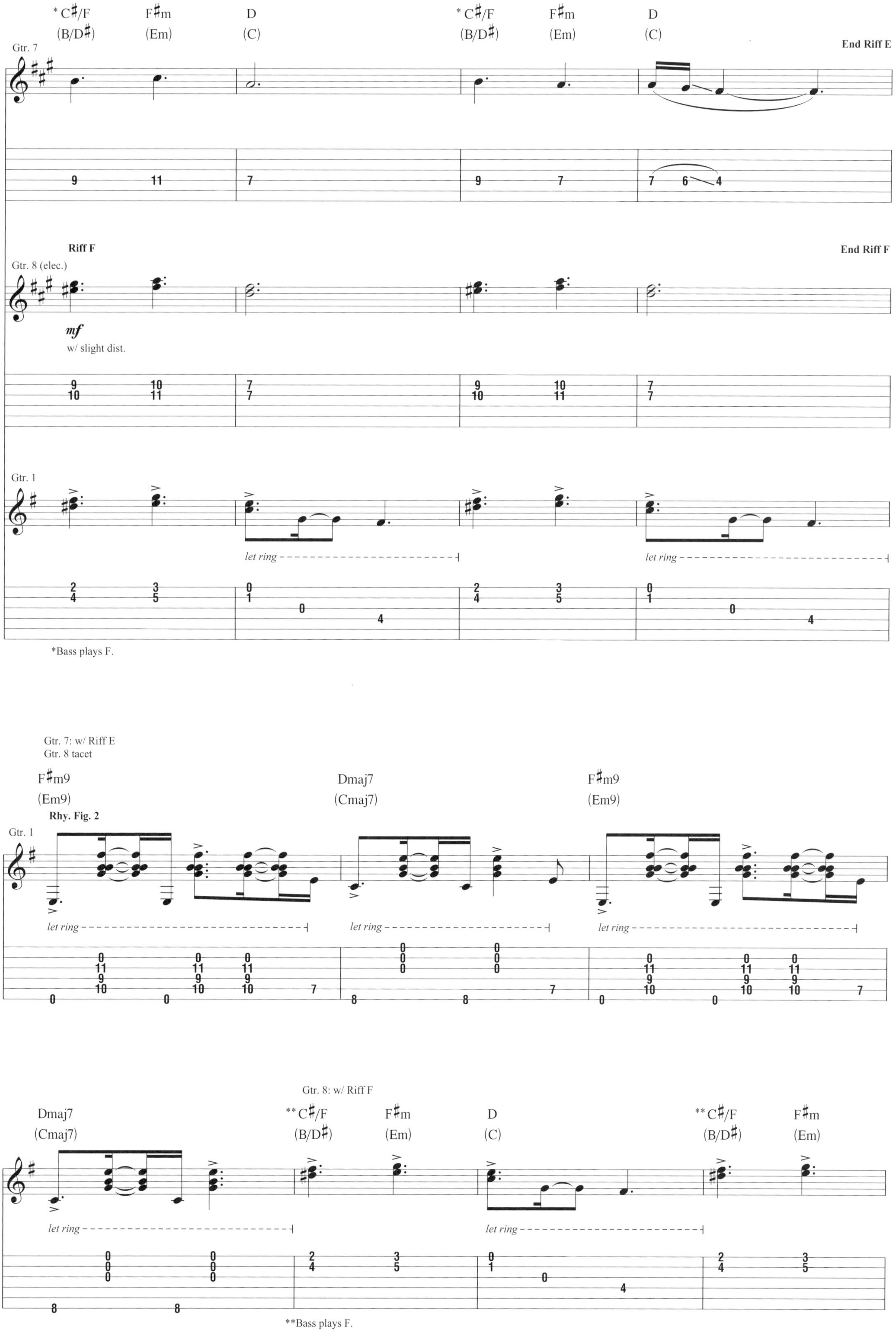

*C♯/F (B/D♯) F♯m (Em) D (C) *C♯/F (B/D♯) F♯m (Em) D (C)

Gtr. 7

End Riff E

Riff F

Gtr. 8 (elec.)

End Riff F

mf

w/ slight dist.

Gtr. 1

let ring

let ring

*Bass plays F.

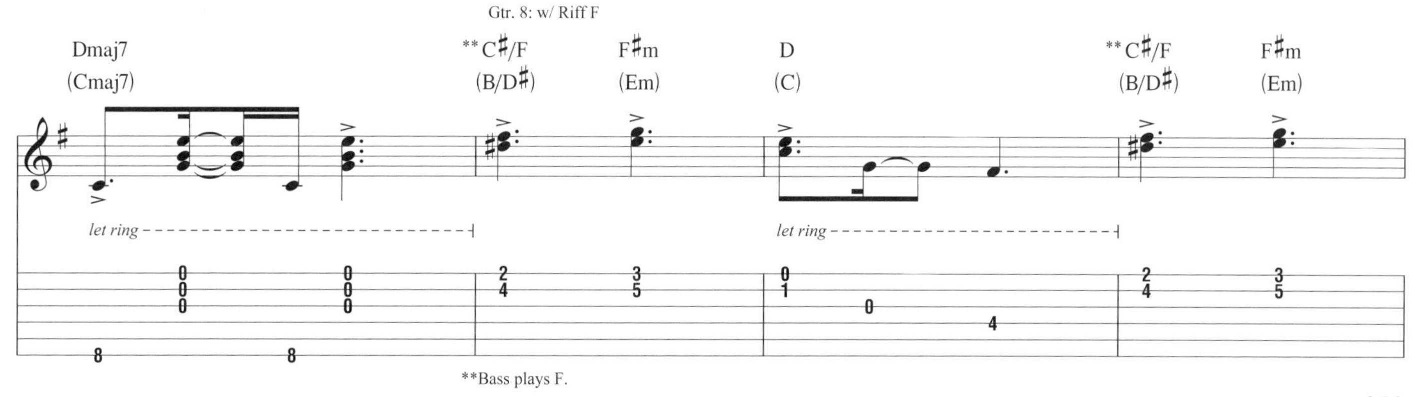

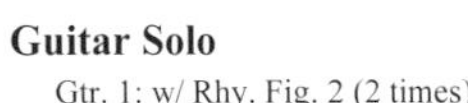
Guitar Solo
Gtr. 1: w/ Rhy. Fig. 2 (2 times)

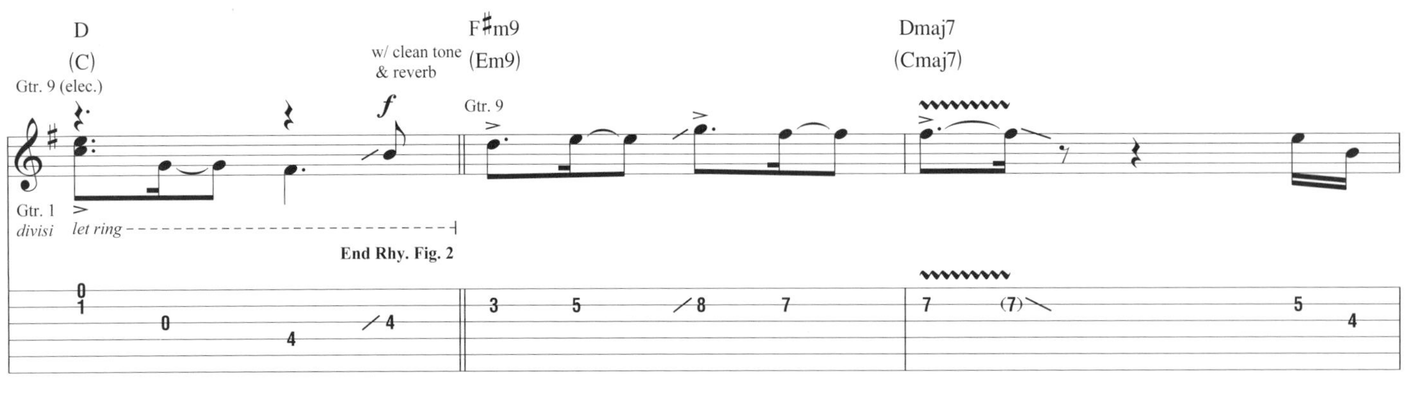
D
(C)
F♯m9
(Em9)
Dmaj7
(Cmaj7)
Gtr. 9 (elec.)
w/ clean tone
& reverb
Gtr. 9
Gtr. 1
divisi
let ring
End Rhy. Fig. 2

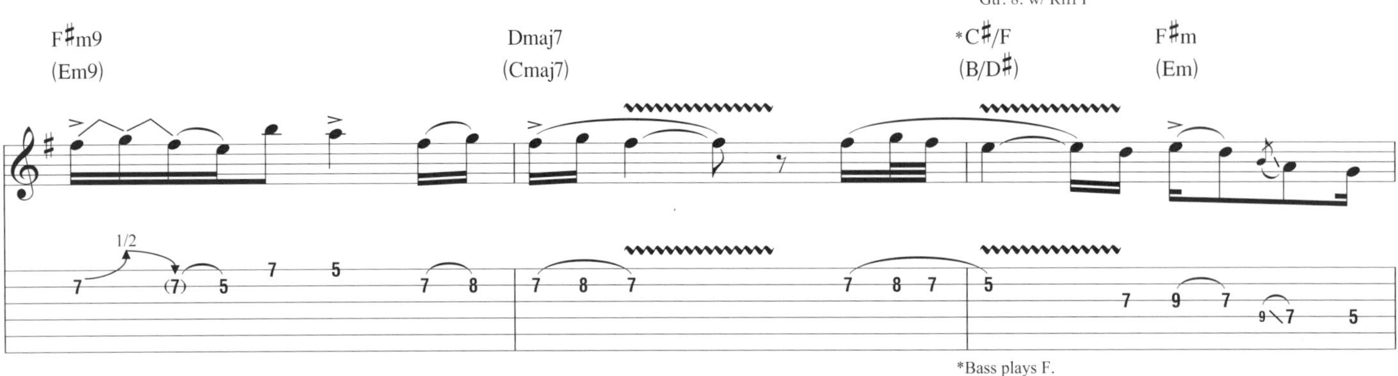
Gtr. 8: w/ Riff F
F♯m9
(Em9)
Dmaj7
(Cmaj7)
*C♯/F
(B/D♯)
F♯m
(Em)
*Bass plays F.

D
(C)
**C♯/F
(B/D♯)
F♯m
(Em)
D
(C)
**Bass plays F.

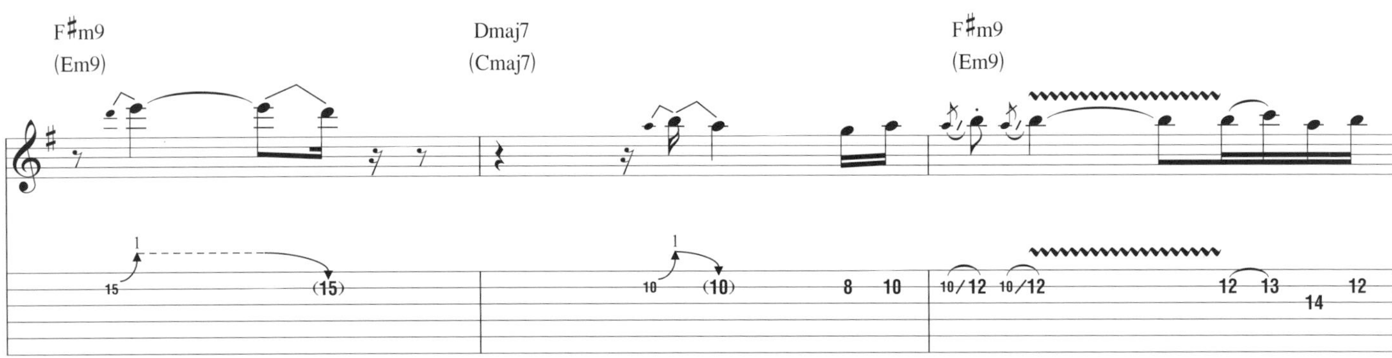
F♯m9
(Em9)
Dmaj7
(Cmaj7)
F♯m9
(Em9)

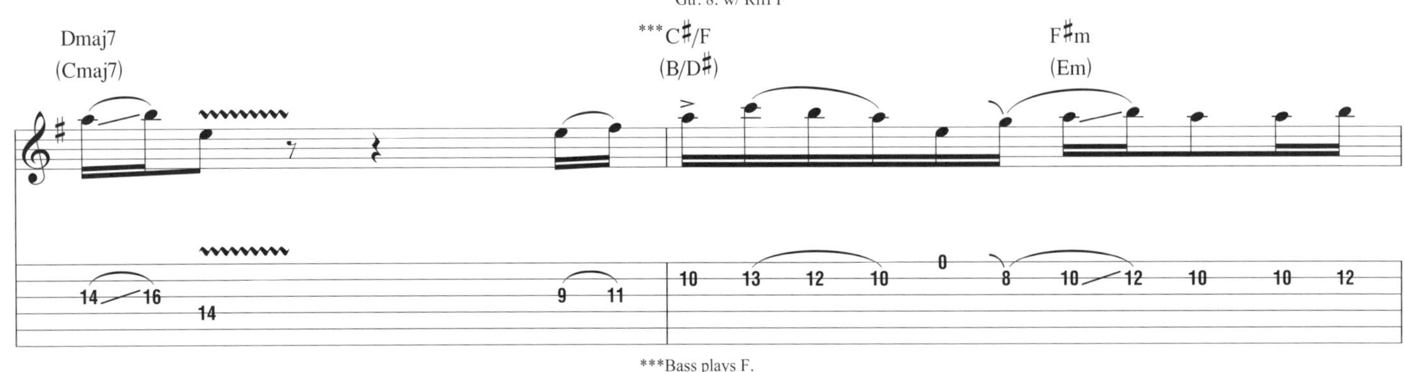
Gtr. 8: w/ Riff F
Dmaj7
(Cmaj7)
***C♯/F
(B/D♯)
F♯m
(Em)
***Bass plays F.

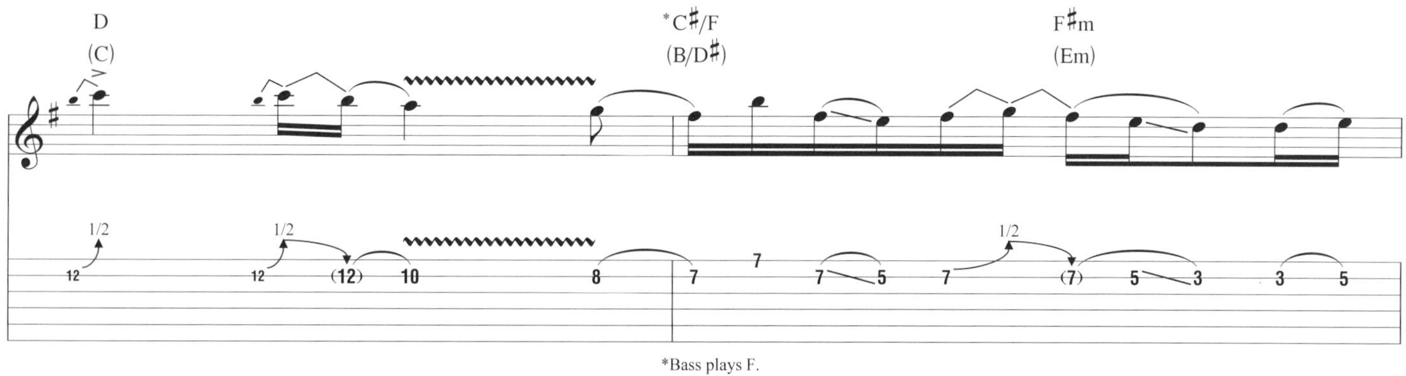
D
(C)
*C♯/F
(B/D♯)
F♯m
(Em)
1/2
*Bass plays F.

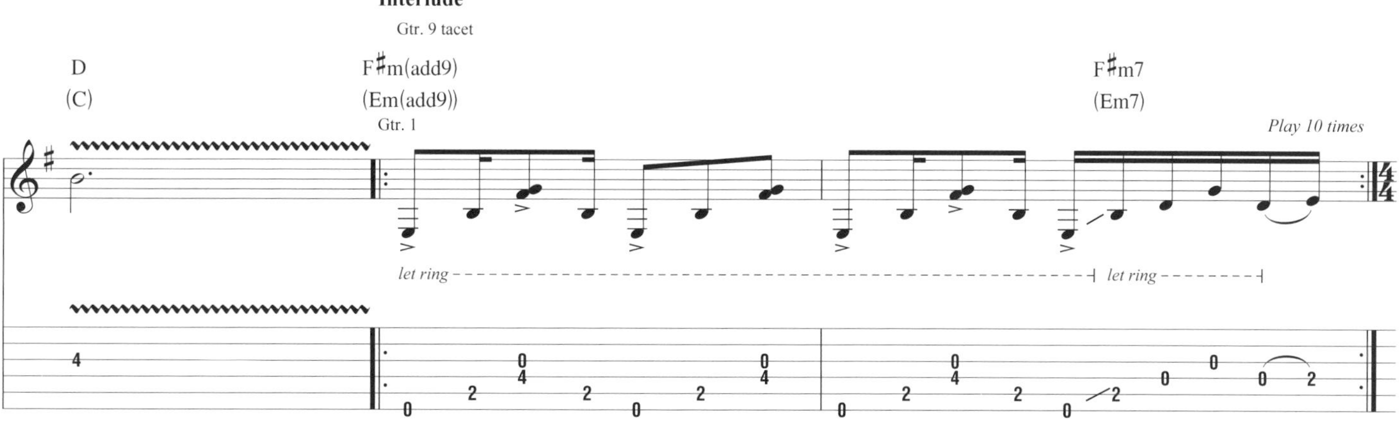
Interlude
Gtr. 9 tacet
D
(C)
F♯m(add9)
(Em(add9))
Gtr. 1
F♯m7
(Em7)
Play 10 times
let ring
let ring

Verse

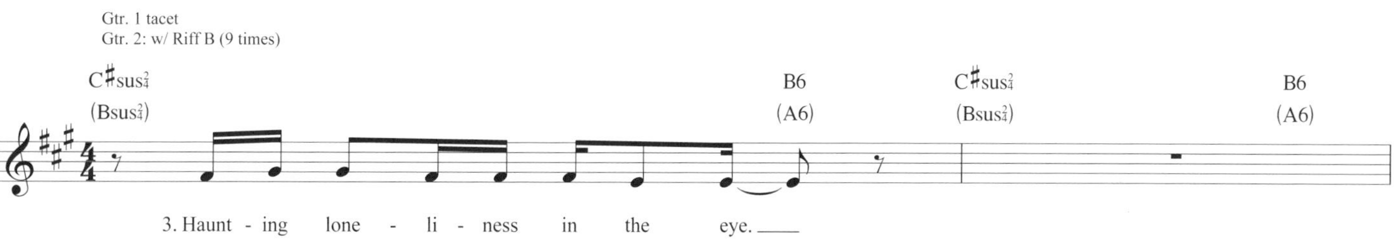
Gtr. 1 tacet
Gtr. 2: w/ Riff B (9 times)
C♯sus2/4
(Bsus2/4)
B6
(A6)
3. Haunt - ing lone - li - ness in the eye.

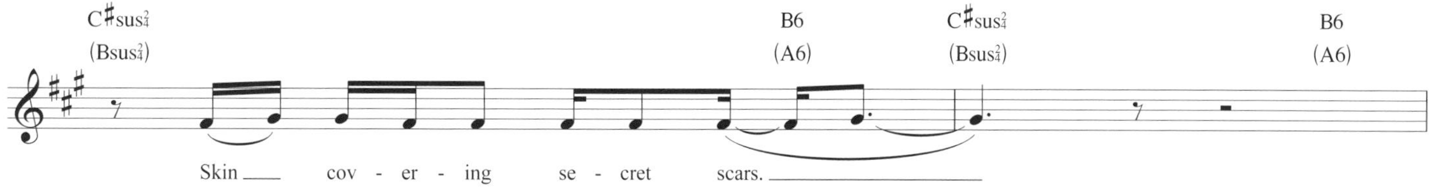
C♯sus2/4
(Bsus2/4)
B6
(A6)
Skin cov - er - ing se - cret scars.

C♯sus2/4
(Bsus2/4)
B6
(A6)
His hand is wav - ing a good - bye.
There's

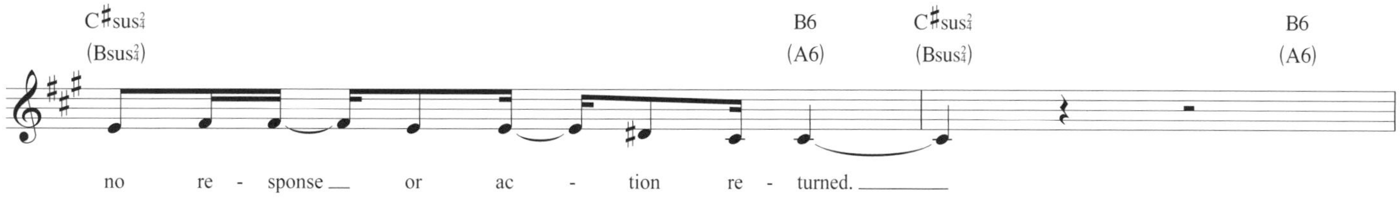
C♯sus2/4
(Bsus2/4)
B6
(A6)
no re - sponse or ac - tion re - turned.

Gtr. 3: w/ Riff C (2 1/2 times)
C♯sus2/4 (Bsus2/4) B6 (A6) C♯sus2/4 (Bsus2/4) B6 (A6)
There is deep prej - u - dice in me.
Out - shines all rea - son in - side.
Giv - en dreams all rid - den with pain.
And pro - ject - ed un - to the lost.
Gtr. 3
Gtr. 2
let ring

GUITAR NOTATION LEGEND

Guitar music can be notated three different ways: on a *musical staff*, in *tablature*, and in *rhythm slashes*.

RHYTHM SLASHES are written above the staff. Strum chords in the rhythm indicated. Use the chord diagrams found at the top of the first page of the transcription for the appropriate chord voicings. Round noteheads indicate single notes.

THE MUSICAL STAFF shows pitches and rhythms and is divided by bar lines into measures. Pitches are named after the first seven letters of the alphabet.

TABLATURE graphically represents the guitar fingerboard. Each horizontal line represents a string, and each number represents a fret.

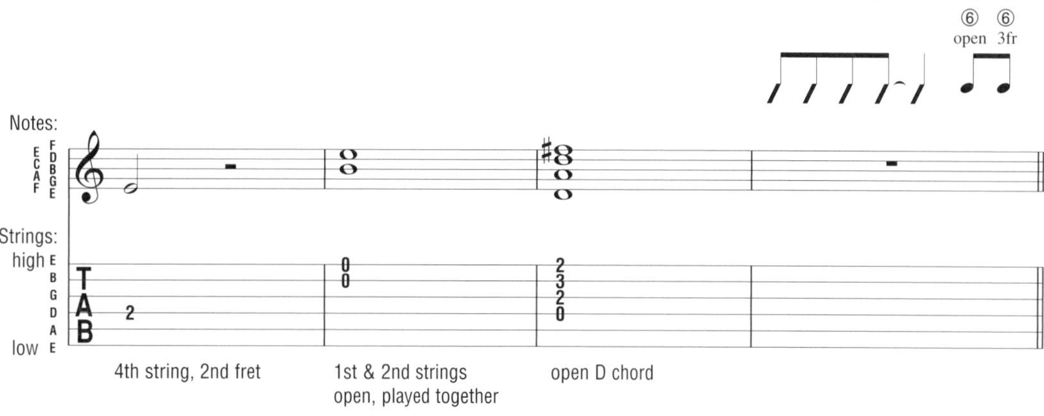

Definitions for Special Guitar Notation

HALF-STEP BEND: Strike the note and bend up 1/2 step.

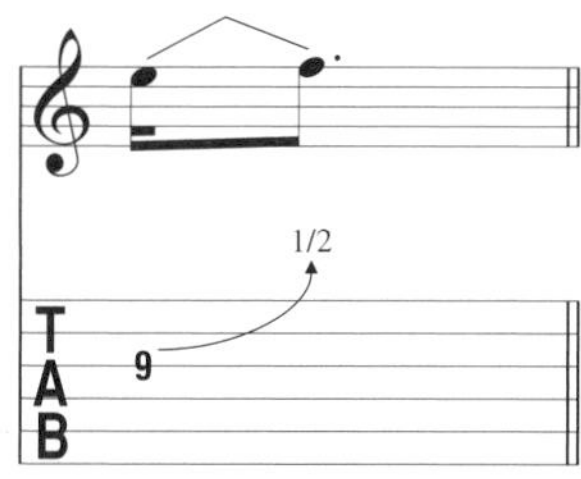

WHOLE-STEP BEND: Strike the note and bend up one step.

GRACE NOTE BEND: Strike the note and immediately bend up as indicated.

SLIGHT (MICROTONE) BEND: Strike the note and bend up 1/4 step.

BEND AND RELEASE: Strike the note and bend up as indicated, then release back to the original note. Only the first note is struck.

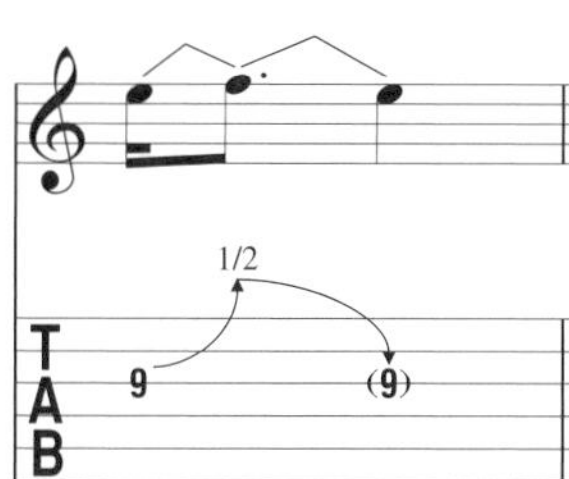

PRE-BEND: Bend the note as indicated, then strike it.

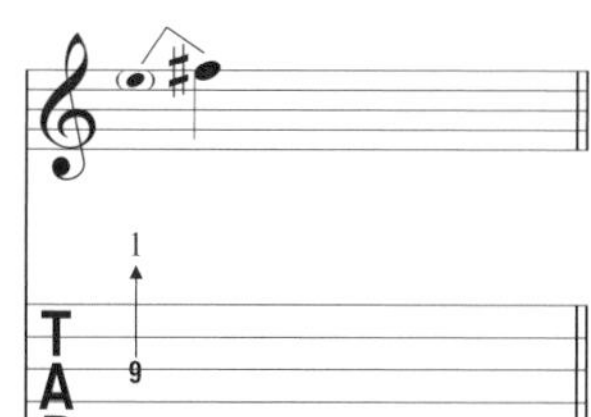
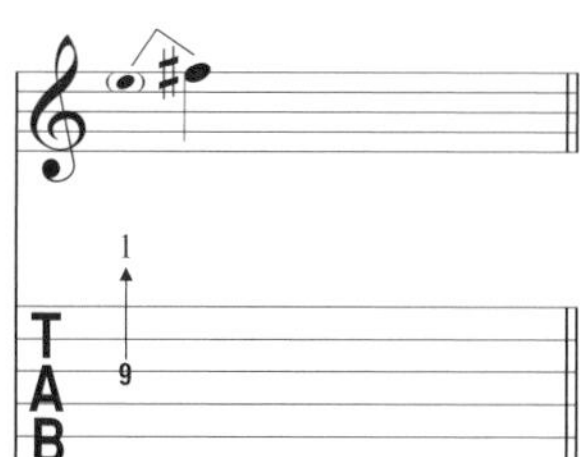

PRE-BEND AND RELEASE: Bend the note as indicated. Strike it and release the bend back to the original note.

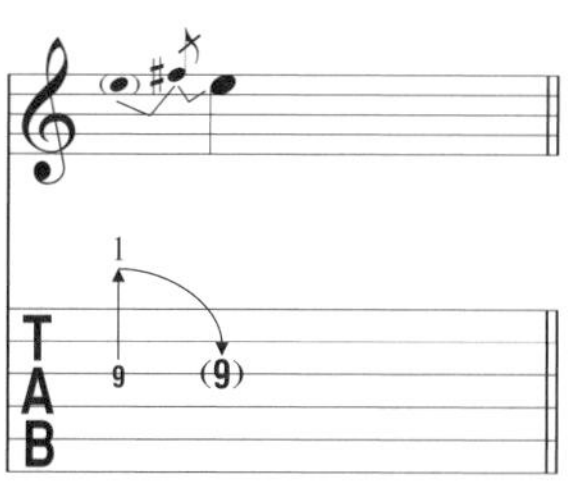

UNISON BEND: Strike the two notes simultaneously and bend the lower note up to the pitch of the higher.

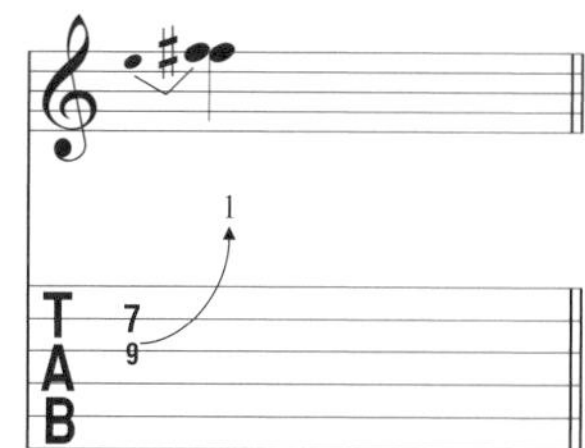

VIBRATO: The string is vibrated by rapidly bending and releasing the note with the fretting hand.

WIDE VIBRATO: The pitch is varied to a greater degree by vibrating with the fretting hand.

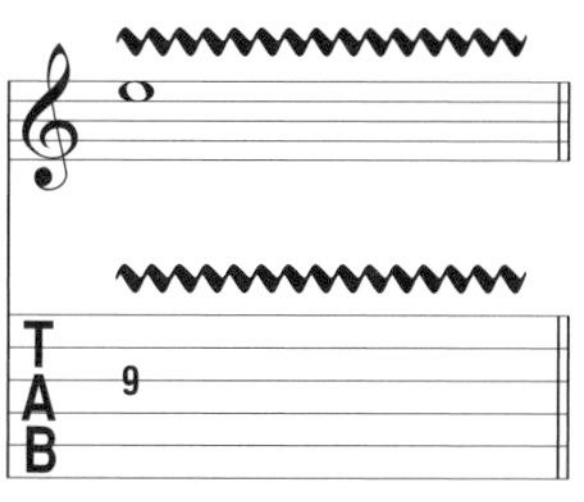

HAMMER-ON: Strike the first (lower) note with one finger, then sound the higher note (on the same string) with another finger by fretting it without picking.

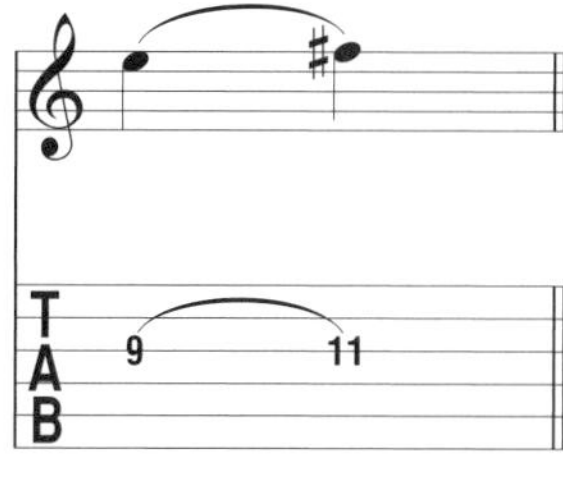

PULL-OFF: Place both fingers on the notes to be sounded. Strike the first note and without picking, pull the finger off to sound the second (lower) note.

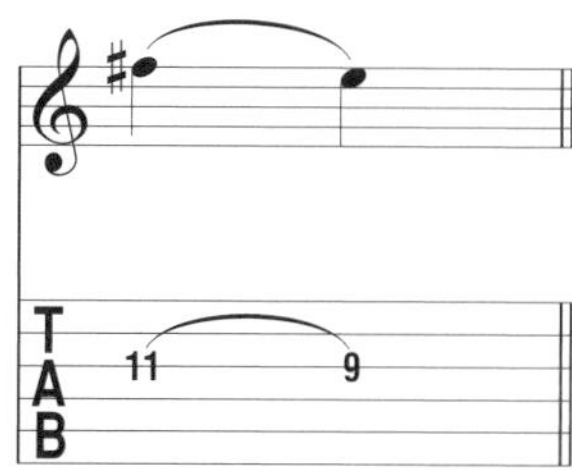

LEGATO SLIDE: Strike the first note and then slide the same fret-hand finger up or down to the second note. The second note is not struck.

SHIFT SLIDE: Same as legato slide, except the second note is struck.

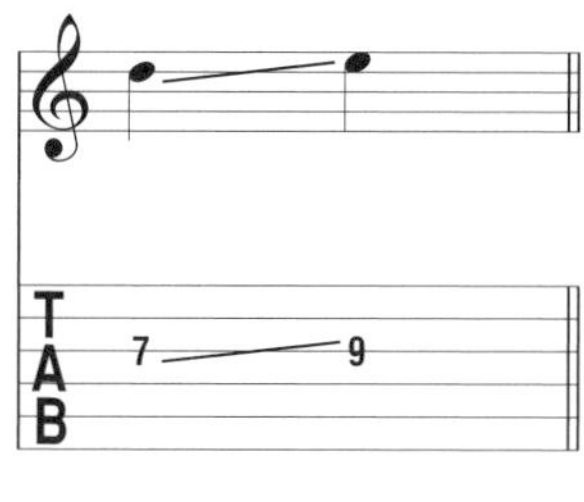

TRILL: Very rapidly alternate between the notes indicated by continuously hammering on and pulling off.

TAPPING: Hammer ("tap") the fret indicated with the pick-hand index or middle finger and pull off to the note fretted by the fret hand.

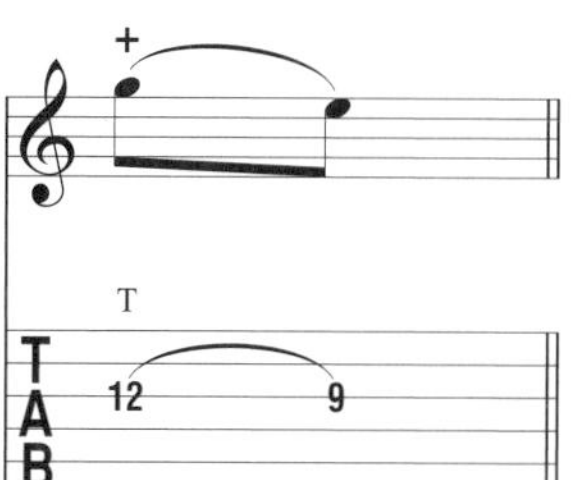

NATURAL HARMONIC: Strike the note while the fret-hand lightly touches the string directly over the fret indicated.

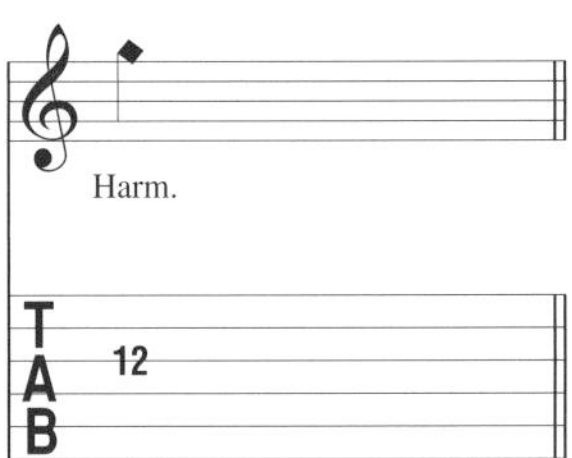

PINCH HARMONIC: The note is fretted normally and a harmonic is produced by adding the edge of the thumb or the tip of the index finger of the pick hand to the normal pick attack.

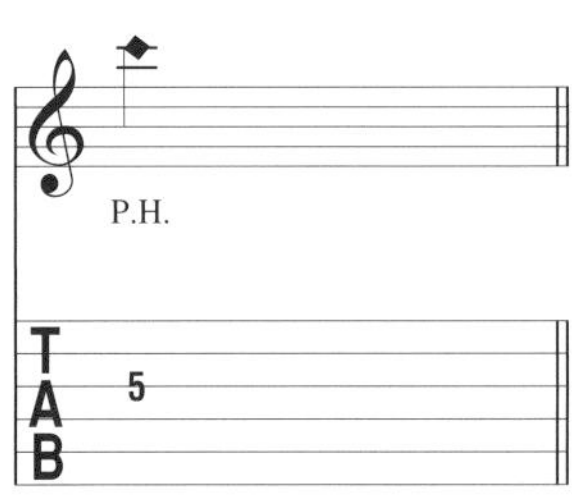

HARP HARMONIC: The note is fretted normally and a harmonic is produced by gently resting the pick hand's index finger directly above the indicated fret (in parentheses) while the pick hand's thumb or pick assists by plucking the appropriate string.

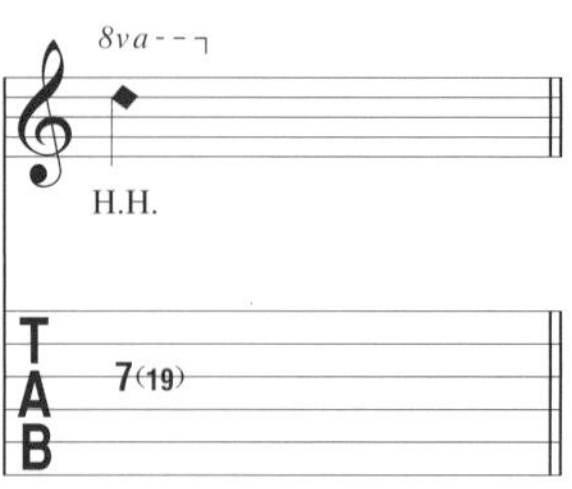

PICK SCRAPE: The edge of the pick is rubbed down (or up) the string, producing a scratchy sound.

MUFFLED STRINGS: A percussive sound is produced by laying the fret hand across the string(s) without depressing, and striking them with the pick hand.

PALM MUTING: The note is partially muted by the pick hand lightly touching the string(s) just before the bridge.

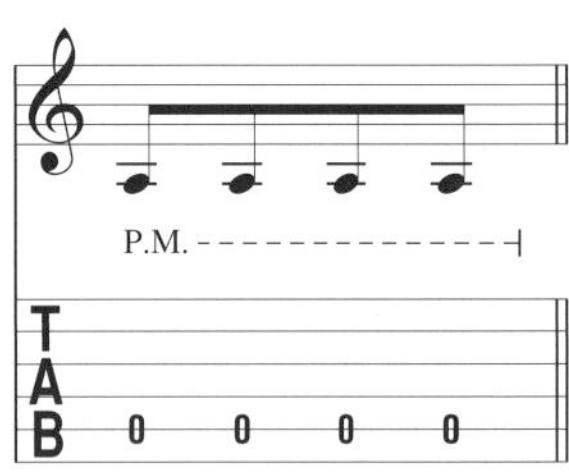

RAKE: Drag the pick across the strings indicated with a single motion.

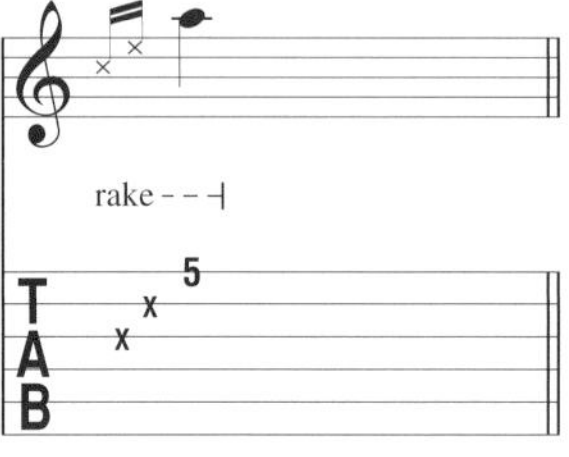

TREMOLO PICKING: The note is picked as rapidly and continuously as possible.

ARPEGGIATE: Play the notes of the chord indicated by quickly rolling them from bottom to top.

VIBRATO BAR DIVE AND RETURN: The pitch of the note or chord is dropped a specified number of steps (in rhythm), then returned to the original pitch.

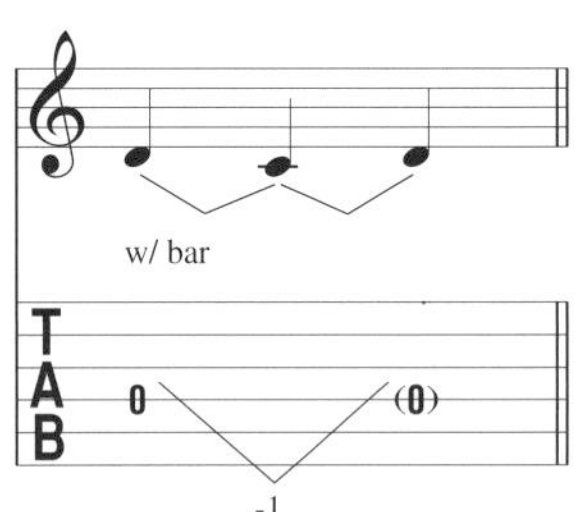

VIBRATO BAR SCOOP: Depress the bar just before striking the note, then quickly release the bar.

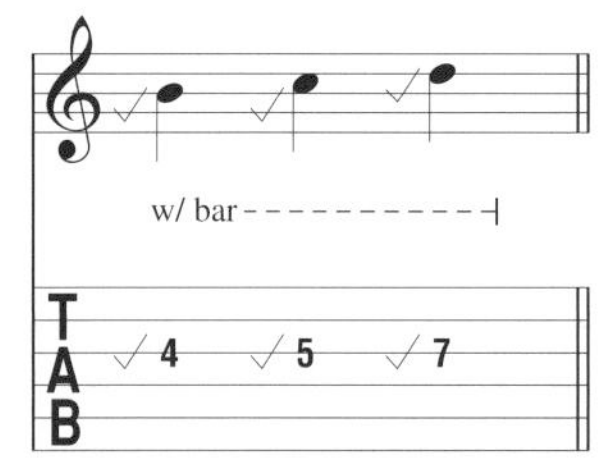

VIBRATO BAR DIP: Strike the note and then immediately drop a specified number of steps, then release back to the original pitch.

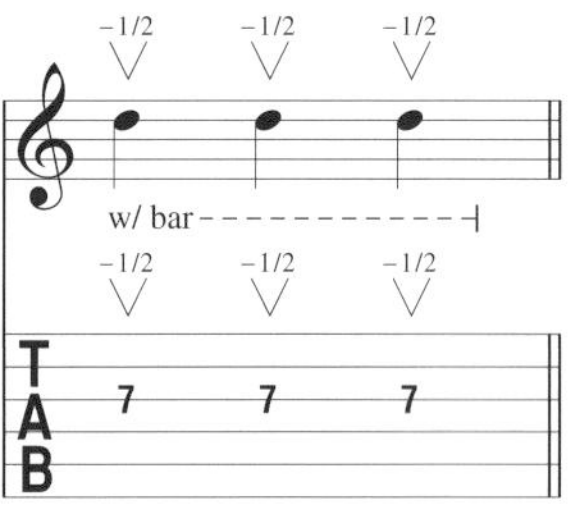

Additional Musical Definitions

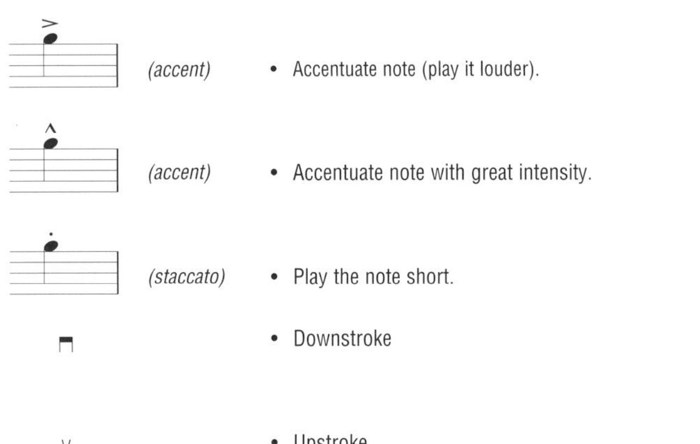

(accent) • Accentuate note (play it louder).

(accent) • Accentuate note with great intensity.

(staccato) • Play the note short.

• Downstroke

• Upstroke

D.S. al Coda • Go back to the sign (𝄋), then play until the measure marked "***To Coda***," then skip to the section labelled "**Coda**."

D.C. al Fine • Go back to the beginning of the song and play until the measure marked "***Fine***" (end).

Rhy. Fig. • Label used to recall a recurring accompaniment pattern (usually chordal).

Riff • Label used to recall composed, melodic lines (usually single notes) which recur.

Fill • Label used to identify a brief melodic figure which is to be inserted into the arrangement.

Rhy. Fill • A chordal version of a Fill.

tacet • Instrument is silent (drops out).

• Repeat measures between signs.

1. 2.

• When a repeated section has different endings, play the first ending only the first time and the second ending only the second time.

NOTE: Tablature numbers in parentheses mean:

1. The note is being sustained over a system (note in standard notation is tied), or
2. The note is sustained, but a new articulation (such as a hammer-on, pull-off, slide or vibrato) begins, or
3. The note is a barely audible "ghost" note (note in standard notation is also in parentheses).

GUITAR RECORDED VERSIONS®

Guitar Recorded Versions® are note-for-note transcriptions of guitar music taken directly off recordings. This series, one of the most popular in print today, features some of the greatest guitar players and groups from blues and rock to country and jazz.

Guitar Recorded Versions are transcribed by the best transcribers in the business. Every book contains notes and tablature unless otherwise marked. Visit **www.halleonard.com** for our complete selection.

14041344 The Definitive AC/DC Songbook $45.99
00690016 The Will Ackerman Collection $19.95
00690501 Bryan Adams – Greatest Hits $19.95
00690603 Aerosmith – O Yeah! (Ultimate Hits) $24.95
00690178 Alice in Chains – Acoustic $19.99
00694865 Alice in Chains – Dirt $19.99
00660225 Alice in Chains – Facelift $19.95
00694925 Alice in Chains – Jar of Flies/Sap $19.99
00690387 Alice in Chains – Nothing Safe: Best of the Box $19.95
00694932 Allman Brothers Band – Definitive Collection for Guitar Volume 1 $24.95
00694933 Allman Brothers Band – Definitive Collection for Guitar Volume 2 $24.95
00694934 Allman Brothers Band – Definitive Collection for Guitar Volume 3 $24.95
00690958 Duane Allman Guitar Anthology $24.99
00691071 Alter Bridge – AB III $22.99
00690945 Alter Bridge – Blackbird $22.99
00690755 Alter Bridge – One Day Remains $22.99
00123558 Arctic Monkeys – AM $22.99
00114564 As I Lay Dying – Awakened $22.99
00690158 Chet Atkins – Almost Alone $19.95
00694876 Chet Atkins – Contemporary Styles $19.95
00694878 Chet Atkins – Vintage Fingerstyle $19.95
00690609 Audioslave $19.95
00690884 Audioslave – Revelations $19.95
00690926 Avenged Sevenfold $22.95
00214869 Avenged Sevenfold – The Best of 2005-2013 $24.99
00690820 Avenged Sevenfold – City of Evil $24.95
00123216 Avenged Sevenfold – Hail to the King $22.99
00222486 Avenged Sevenfold – The Stage $24.99
00691065 Avenged Sevenfold – Waking the Fallen $22.99
00123140 The Avett Brothers Guitar Collection $22.99
00694918 Randy Bachman Collection $22.95
00690503 Beach Boys – Very Best of $19.99
00694929 Beatles: 1962-1966 $24.99
00694930 Beatles: 1967-1970 $24.99
00690489 Beatles – 1 $24.99
00694880 Beatles – Abbey Road $19.95
00691066 Beatles – Beatles for Sale $22.99
00690110 Beatles – Book 1 (White Album) $19.99
00690111 Beatles – Book 2 (White Album) $19.95
00690902 Beatles – The Capitol Albums, Volume 1 $24.99
00694832 Beatles – For Acoustic Guitar $22.99
00691031 Beatles – Help! $19.99
00690482 Beatles – Let It Be $17.95
00691067 Beatles – Meet the Beatles! $22.99
00691068 Beatles – Please Please Me $22.99
00694891 Beatles – Revolver $19.95
00694914 Beatles – Rubber Soul $22.99
00694863 Beatles – Sgt. Pepper's Lonely Hearts Club Band $22.99
00110193 Beatles – Tomorrow Never Knows $22.99
00691044 Jeff Beck – Best of Beck $24.99
00690632 Beck – Sea Change $19.95
00691041 Jeff Beck – Truth $19.99
00694884 Best of George Benson $19.95
00692385 Chuck Berry $22.99
00690835 Billy Talent $19.95
00690879 Billy Talent II $19.95
00147787 Best of the Black Crowes $19.99
00129737 The Black Keys – Turn Blue $22.99
00690149 Black Sabbath $16.99
00690901 Best of Black Sabbath $19.95
00691010 Black Sabbath – Heaven and Hell $22.99
00690148 Black Sabbath – Master of Reality $16.99
00690142 Black Sabbath – Paranoid $16.99
14042759 Black Sabbath – 13 $19.99
00692200 Black Sabbath – We Sold Our Soul for Rock 'N' Roll $22.99
00690389 blink-182 – Enema of the State $19.95
00690831 blink-182 – Greatest Hits $19.95
00691179 blink-182 – Neighborhoods $22.99
00148544 Michael Bloomfield Guitar Anthology $24.99
00690028 Blue Oyster Cult – Cult Classics $19.95
00691074 Bon Jovi – Greatest Hits $22.99
00158600 Joe Bonamassa – Blues of Desperation $22.99
00139086 Joe Bonamassa – Different Shades of Blue $22.99
00690913 Boston $19.95
00690829 Boston Guitar Collection $19.99
00690491 Best of David Bowie $19.99
00690583 Box Car Racer $19.95
00691023 Breaking Benjamin – Dear Agony $22.99
00690873 Breaking Benjamin – Phobia $19.95
00690764 Breaking Benjamin – We Are Not Alone $19.95
00141446 Best of Lenny Breau $19.99
00690451 Jeff Buckley Collection $24.95
00690957 Bullet for My Valentine – Scream Aim Fire $22.99
00119629 Bullet for My Valentine – Temper Temper $22.99
00690678 Best of Kenny Burrell $19.95
00691077 Cage the Elephant – Thank You, Happy Birthday $22.99
00691159 The Cars – Complete Greatest Hits $22.99
00690261 Carter Family Collection $19.95
00691079 Best of Johnny Cash $22.99
00690043 Best of Cheap Trick $19.95
00690171 Chicago – The Definitive Guitar Collection $22.95
00691011 Chimaira Guitar Collection $24.99
00690567 Charlie Christian – The Definitive Collection $19.95
00101916 Eric Church – Chief $22.99
00129545 The Civil Wars $19.99
00138731 Eric Clapton & Friends – The Breeze $22.99
00690590 Eric Clapton – Anthology $29.95
00692391 Best of Eric Clapton – 2nd Edition $22.95
00691055 Eric Clapton – Clapton $22.99
00690936 Eric Clapton – Complete Clapton $29.99
00690010 Eric Clapton – From the Cradle $19.95
00192383 Eric Clapton – I Still Do* $19.99
00690363 Eric Clapton – Just One Night $24.99
00694873 Eric Clapton – Timepieces $19.95
00694869 Eric Clapton – Unplugged $22.95
00690415 Clapton Chronicles – Best of Eric Clapton $18.95
00694896 John Mayall/Eric Clapton – Bluesbreakers $19.99
00690162 Best of the Clash $19.95
00690828 Coheed & Cambria – Good Apollo I'm Burning Star, IV, Vol. 1: From Fear Through the Eyes of Madness $19.95
00130786 Coldplay – Ghost Stories $19.99
00690593 Coldplay – A Rush of Blood to the Head $19.95
00690806 Coldplay – X & Y $19.95
00690855 Best of Collective Soul $19.95
00141704 Jesse Cook – Works Vol. 1 $19.99
00691091 The Best of Alice Cooper $22.99
00694940 Counting Crows – August & Everything After $19.95
00127184 Best of Robert Cray $19.99
00694840 Cream – Disraeli Gears $19.95
00690819 Best of Creedence Clearwater Revival $22.95
00690648 The Very Best of Jim Croce $19.95
00690572 Steve Cropper – Soul Man $19.95
00690613 Best of Crosby, Stills & Nash $22.95
00699521 The Cure – Greatest Hits $24.95
00690637 Best of Dick Dale $19.95
00690822 Best of Alex De Grassi $19.95
00690967 Death Cab for Cutie – Narrow Stairs $22.99
00690289 Best of Deep Purple $19.99
00690288 Deep Purple – Machine Head $17.99
00690784 Best of Def Leppard $22.99
00694831 Derek and the Dominos – Layla & Other Assorted Love Songs $22.95
00692240 Bo Diddley – Guitar Solos by Fred Sokolow $19.99
00690384 Best of Ani DiFranco $19.95
00690979 Best of Dinosaur Jr. $19.99
00690833 Private Investigations – Best of Dire Straits and Mark Knopfler $24.95
00695382 Very Best of Dire Straits – Sultans of Swing $22.95
00122443 Dream Theater $24.99
00160579 Dream Theater – Selections from The Astonishing $24.99
00690250 Best of Duane Eddy $17.99
00690909 Best of Tommy Emmanuel $22.99
00690555 Best of Melissa Etheridge $19.95
00690515 Extreme II – Pornograffitti $19.95
00150257 John Fahey – Guitar Anthology $19.99
00691009 Five Finger Death Punch $19.99
00690664 Best of Fleetwood Mac $19.95
00690870 Flyleaf $19.95
00691115 Foo Fighters – Wasting Light $22.99
00690805 Best of Robben Ford $22.99
00120220 Robben Ford – Guitar Anthology $24.99
00690842 Best of Peter Frampton $19.95
00694920 Best of Free $19.99
00694807 Danny Gatton – 88 Elmira St. $19.95
00690438 Genesis Guitar Anthology $19.95
00690753 Best of Godsmack $19.95
00120167 Godsmack $19.95
00690338 Goo Goo Dolls – Dizzy Up the Girl $19.95
00212480 Green Day – Revolution Radio* $19.99
00113073 Green Day – Uno $21.99
00116846 Green Day – ¡Dos! $21.99
00118259 Green Day – ¡Tré! $21.99
00691190 Best of Peter Green $19.99
00690927 Patty Griffin – Children Running Through $19.95
00690591 Patty Griffin – Guitar Collection $19.95
00690978 Guns N' Roses – Chinese Democracy $24.99
00691027 Buddy Guy Anthology $24.99
00694854 Buddy Guy – Damn Right, I've Got the Blues $19.95
00690697 Best of Jim Hall $19.95
00690840 Ben Harper – Both Sides of the Gun $19.95
00691018 Ben Harper – Fight for Your Mind $22.99
00694798 George Harrison Anthology $19.95
00690841 Scott Henderson – Blues Guitar Collection $19.95
00692930 Jimi Hendrix – Are You Experienced? $24.95
00692931 Jimi Hendrix – Axis: Bold As Love $22.95
00690304 Jimi Hendrix – Band of Gypsys $24.99
00690608 Jimi Hendrix – Blue Wild Angel $24.95
00694944 Jimi Hendrix – Blues $24.95
00692932 Jimi Hendrix – Electric Ladyland $24.95
00119619 Jimi Hendrix – People, Hell and Angels $22.99
00690602 Jimi Hendrix – Smash Hits $24.99
00691152 West Coast Seattle Boy: The Jimi Hendrix Anthology $29.99
00691332 Jimi Hendrix – Winterland (Highlights) $22.99
00690017 Jimi Hendrix – Woodstock $27.50
00690843 H.I.M. – Dark Light $19.95
00690869 Hinder – Extreme Behavior $19.95
00660029 Buddy Holly $22.99
00690793 John Lee Hooker Anthology $24.99
00660169 John Lee Hooker – A Blues Legend $19.95
00694905 Howlin' Wolf $19.95
00690692 Very Best of Billy Idol $19.95
00121961 Imagine Dragons – Night Visions $22.99
00690688 Incubus – A Crow Left of the Murder $19.95
00690136 Indigo Girls – 1200 Curfews $22.95
00690790 Iron Maiden Anthology $24.99
00691058 Iron Maiden – The Final Frontier $22.99
00200446 Iron Maiden – Guitar Tab $29.99
00690887 Iron Maiden – A Matter of Life and Death $24.95
00690730 Alan Jackson – Guitar Collection $19.95
00694938 Elmore James – Master Electric Slide Guitar $19.99
00690652 Best of Jane's Addiction $19.95
00690684 Jethro Tull – Aqualung $19.95
00690693 Jethro Tull Guitar Anthology $22.99
00691182 Jethro Tull – Stand Up $22.99
00690898 John 5 – The Devil Knows My Name $22.95

No.	Title	Price
00690814	John 5 – Songs for Sanity	$19.95
00690751	John 5 – Vertigo	$19.95
00694912	Eric Johnson – Ah Via Musicom	$22.99
00690660	Best of Eric Johnson	$22.99
00691076	Eric Johnson – Up Close	$22.99
00690169	Eric Johnson – Venus Isle	$22.95
00122439	Jack Johnson – From Here to Now to You	$22.99
00690846	Jack Johnson and Friends – Sing-A-Longs and Lullabies for the Film Curious George	$19.95
00690271	Robert Johnson – The New Transcriptions	$24.99
00699131	Best of Janis Joplin	$19.95
00690427	Best of Judas Priest	$22.99
00690277	Best of Kansas	$19.95
00690911	Best of Phil Keaggy	$24.99
00690727	Toby Keith Guitar Collection	$19.99
00120814	Killswitch Engage – Disarm the Descent	$22.99
00690504	Very Best of Albert King	$19.95
00124869	Albert King with Stevie Ray Vaughan – In Session	$22.99
00130447	B.B. King – Live at the Regal	$17.99
00690444	B.B. King & Eric Clapton – Riding with the King	$22.99
00690134	Freddie King Collection	$19.95
00691062	Kings of Leon – Come Around Sundown	$22.99
00690157	Kiss – Alive!	$19.95
00690356	Kiss – Alive II	$22.99
00694903	Best of Kiss for Guitar	$24.95
00690355	Kiss – Destroyer	$16.95
00690164	Mark Knopfler Guitar – Vol. 1	$22.99
00690163	Mark Knopfler/Chet Atkins – Neck and Neck	$19.95
00690780	Korn – Greatest Hits, Volume 1	$22.95
00690377	Kris Kristofferson Collection	$19.99
00690834	Lamb of God – Ashes of the Wake	$19.95
00690875	Lamb of God – Sacrament	$19.95
00690977	Ray LaMontagne – Gossip in the Grain	$19.99
00691057	Ray LaMontagne and the Pariah Dogs – God Willin' & The Creek Don't Rise	$22.99
00690922	Linkin Park – Minutes to Midnight	$19.95
00699623	The Best of Chuck Loeb	$19.95
00114563	The Lumineers	$22.99
00690525	Best of George Lynch	$24.99
00690955	Lynyrd Skynyrd – All-Time Greatest Hits	$22.99
00694954	New Best of Lynyrd Skynyrd	$19.95
00690577	Yngwie Malmsteen – Anthology	$24.95
00209846	Mammoth Metal Guitar Tab Anthology	$29.99
00690754	Marilyn Manson – Lest We Forget	$19.95
00694956	Bob Marley – Legend	$19.95
00690548	Very Best of Bob Marley & The Wailers – One Love	$22.99
00694945	Bob Marley – Songs of Freedom	$24.95
00690914	Maroon 5 – It Won't Be Soon Before Long	$19.95
00690657	Maroon 5 – Songs About Jane	$19.95
00690748	Maroon 5 – 1.22.03 Acoustic	$19.95
00690989	Mastodon – Crack the Skye	$24.99
00236690	Mastodon – Emperor of Sand	$22.99
00119220	Brent Mason – Hot Wired	$19.99
00691176	Mastodon – The Hunter	$22.99
00137718	Mastodon – Once More 'Round the Sun	$22.99
00690616	Matchbox Twenty – More Than You Think You Are	$19.95
00691942	Andy McKee – Art of Motion	$22.99
00691034	Andy McKee – Joyland	$19.99
00120080	The Don McLean Songbook	$19.95
00694952	Megadeth – Countdown to Extinction	$22.95
00690244	Megadeth – Cryptic Writings	$19.95
00694951	Megadeth – Rust in Peace	$22.95
00690011	Megadeth – Youthanasia	$22.99
00690505	John Mellencamp Guitar Collection	$19.95
00209876	Metallica – Hardwired... To Self-Destruct	$22.99
00690562	Pat Metheny – Bright Size Life	$19.95
00691073	Pat Metheny with Christian McBride & Antonion Sanchez – Day Trip/Tokyo Day Trip Live	$22.99
00690646	Pat Metheny – One Quiet Night	$19.95
00690559	Pat Metheny – Question & Answer	$19.95
00118836	Pat Metheny – Unity Band	$22.99
00102590	Pat Metheny – What's It All About	$22.99
00690040	Steve Miller Band Greatest Hits	$19.99
00119338	Ministry Guitar Tab Collection	$24.99
00102591	Wes Montgomery Guitar Anthology	$24.99
00694802	Gary Moore – Still Got the Blues	$22.99
00691005	Best of Motion City Soundtrack	$19.99
00129884	Jason Mraz – Yes!	$22.99
00690787	Mudvayne – L.D. 50	$22.95
00691070	Mumford & Sons – Sigh No More	$22.99
00118196	Muse – The 2nd Law	$19.99
00690996	My Morning Jacket Collection	$19.99
00690984	Matt Nathanson – Some Mad Hope	$22.99
00690611	Nirvana	$22.95
00694895	Nirvana – Bleach	$19.95
00694913	Nirvana – In Utero	$19.99
00694883	Nirvana – Nevermind	$19.95
00690026	Nirvana – Unplugged in New York	$19.95
00690226	Oasis – The Other Side of Oasis	$19.95
00307163	Oasis – Time Flies... 1994-2009	$24.99
00690818	The Best of Opeth	$22.95
00691052	Roy Orbison – Black & White Night	$22.99
00694847	Best of Ozzy Osbourne	$22.95
00690933	Best of Brad Paisley	$22.95
00690995	Brad Paisley – Play: The Guitar Album	$24.99
00690939	Christopher Parkening – Solo Pieces	$19.99
00690594	Best of Les Paul	$19.95
00694855	Pearl Jam – Ten	$22.99
00690439	A Perfect Circle – Mer De Noms	$19.95
00690725	Best of Carl Perkins	$19.99
00690499	Tom Petty – Definitive Guitar Collection	$19.99
00690868	Tom Petty – Highway Companion	$19.95
00690176	Phish – Billy Breathes	$22.95
00121933	Pink Floyd – Acoustic Guitar Collection	$22.99
00690428	Pink Floyd – Dark Side of the Moon	$19.95
00239799	Pink Floyd – The Wall	$24.99
00690789	Best of Poison	$19.99
00690299	Best of Elvis: The King of Rock 'n' Roll	$19.95
00692535	Elvis Presley	$19.95
00690925	The Very Best of Prince	$22.99
00690003	Classic Queen	$24.95
00694975	Queen – Greatest Hits	$24.95
00690670	Very Best of Queensryche	$22.99
00690878	The Raconteurs – Broken Boy Soldiers	$19.95
00109303	Radiohead Guitar Anthology	$24.99
00694910	Rage Against the Machine	$19.95
00119834	Rage Against the Machine – Guitar Anthology	$22.99
00690179	Rancid – And Out Come the Wolves	$22.95
00690426	Best of Ratt	$19.95
00690055	Red Hot Chili Peppers – Blood Sugar Sex Magik	$19.95
00690584	Red Hot Chili Peppers – By the Way	$19.95
00690379	Red Hot Chili Peppers – Californication	$19.99
00182634	Red Hot Chili Peppers – The Getaway	$24.99
00690673	Red Hot Chili Peppers – Greatest Hits	$19.99
00690090	Red Hot Chili Peppers – One Hot Minute	$22.95
00691166	Red Hot Chili Peppers – I'm with You	$22.99
00690852	Red Hot Chili Peppers – Stadium Arcadium	$24.95
00690511	Django Reinhardt – The Definitive Collection	$22.99
00690779	Relient K – MMHMM	$19.95
00690643	Relient K – Two Lefts Don't Make a Right ... But Three Do	$19.95
00690260	Jimmie Rodgers Guitar Collection	$19.95
14041901	Rodrigo Y Gabriela and C.U.B.A. – Area 52	$24.99
00690014	Rolling Stones – Exile on Main Street	$24.95
00690631	Rolling Stones – Guitar Anthology	$27.95
00690685	David Lee Roth – Eat 'Em and Smile	$19.95
00174797	Santana – IV*	$22.99
00173534	Santana Guitar Anthology	$24.99
00690031	Santana's Greatest Hits	$19.95
00690796	Very Best of Michael Schenker	$19.95
00128870	Matt Schofield Guitar Tab Collection	$22.99
00690566	Best of Scorpions	$22.95
00690604	Bob Seger – Guitar Anthology	$22.99
00234543	Ed Sheeran – Divide	$19.99
00138870	Ed Sheeran – X	$19.99
00690803	Best of Kenny Wayne Shepherd Band	$19.95
00690750	Kenny Wayne Shepherd – The Place You're In	$19.95
00122218	Skillet – Rise	$22.99
00691114	Slash – Guitar Anthology	$24.99
00690872	Slayer – Christ Illusion	$19.95
00690813	Slayer – Guitar Collection	$19.99
00690419	Slipknot	$19.95
00690973	Slipknot – All Hope Is Gone	$22.99
00690330	Social Distortion – Live at the Roxy	$19.95
00120004	Best of Steely Dan	$24.95
00694921	Best of Steppenwolf	$22.95
00690655	Best of Mike Stern	$24.99
14041588	Cat Stevens – Tea for the Tillerman	$19.99
00690949	Rod Stewart Guitar Anthology	$19.99
00690021	Sting – Fields of Gold	$19.95
00690520	Styx Guitar Collection	$19.95
00120081	Sublime	$19.99
00690992	Sublime – Robbin' the Hood	$19.99
00690519	SUM 41 – All Killer No Filler	$19.95

AUTHENTIC TRANSCRIPTIONS WITH NOTES AND TABLATURE

No.	Title	Price
00691072	Best of Supertramp	$22.99
00142151	Taylor Swift – 1989	$22.99
00115957	Taylor Swift – Red	$21.99
00691063	Taylor Swift – Speak Now	$22.99
00690767	Switchfoot – The Beautiful Letdown	$19.95
00690531	System of a Down – Toxicity	$19.95
00694824	Best of James Taylor	$19.99
00694887	Best of Thin Lizzy	$19.95
00690891	30 Seconds to Mars – A Beautiful Lie	$19.95
00690233	The Merle Travis Collection	$19.99
00690683	Robin Trower – Bridge of Sighs	$19.95
00699191	U2 – Best of: 1980-1990	$19.95
00690732	U2 – Best of: 1990-2000	$19.95
00690894	U2 – 18 Singles	$19.95
00124461	Keith Urban – Guitar Anthology	$19.99
00690039	Steve Vai – Alien Love Secrets	$24.95
00690172	Steve Vai – Fire Garden	$24.95
00660137	Steve Vai – Passion & Warfare	$24.95
00690881	Steve Vai – Real Illusions: Reflections	$24.95
00694904	Steve Vai – Sex and Religion	$24.95
00110385	Steve Vai – The Story of Light	$22.99
00690392	Steve Vai – The Ultra Zone	$19.95
00700555	Van Halen – Van Halen	$19.99
00690024	Stevie Ray Vaughan – Couldn't Stand the Weather	$19.95
00690116	Stevie Ray Vaughan – Guitar Collection	$24.95
00660136	Stevie Ray Vaughan – In Step	$19.95
00694879	Stevie Ray Vaughan – In the Beginning	$19.95
00660058	Stevie Ray Vaughan – Lightnin' Blues '83-'87	$27.99
00694835	Stevie Ray Vaughan – The Sky Is Crying	$22.95
00690025	Stevie Ray Vaughan – Soul to Soul	$19.95
00690015	Stevie Ray Vaughan – Texas Flood	$19.99
00109770	Volbeat Guitar Collection	$22.99
00121808	Volbeat – Outlaw Gentlemen & Shady Ladies	$22.99
00183213	Volbeat – Seal the Deal & Let's Boogie*	$19.99
00690132	The T-Bone Walker Collection	$19.95
00150209	Trans-Siberian Orchestra Guitar Anthology	$19.99
00694789	Muddy Waters – Deep Blues	$24.99
00152161	Doc Watson – Guitar Anthology	$22.99
00690071	Weezer (The Blue Album)	$19.95
00690286	Weezer – Pinkerton	$22.99
00691046	Weezer – Rarities Edition	$22.99
00172118	Weezer (The White Album)*	$19.99
00117511	Whitesnake Guitar Collection	$19.99
00690447	Best of the Who	$24.95
00691941	The Who – Acoustic Guitar Collection	$22.99
00691006	Wilco Guitar Collection	$22.99
00690672	Best of Dar Williams	$19.95
00691017	Wolfmother – Cosmic Egg	$22.99
00690319	Stevie Wonder – Hits	$19.99
00690596	Best of the Yardbirds	$19.95
00690844	Yellowcard – Lights and Sounds	$19.95
00690916	The Best of Dwight Yoakam	$19.95
00691020	Neil Young – After the Goldrush	$22.99
00691019	Neil Young – Everybody Knows This Is Nowhere	$19.99
00690904	Neil Young – Harvest	$29.99
00691021	Neil Young – Harvest Moon	$22.99
00690905	Neil Young – Rust Never Sleeps	$19.99
00690443	Frank Zappa – Hot Rats	$19.95
00690624	Frank Zappa and the Mothers of Invention – One Size Fits All	$22.99
00690623	Frank Zappa – Over-Nite Sensation	$22.99
00121684	ZZ Top – Early Classics	$24.99
00690589	ZZ Top – Guitar Anthology	$24.95
00690960	ZZ Top Guitar Classics	$19.99

*Tab transcriptions only.

Complete songlists and more at **www.halleonard.com**

Prices, contents, and availability subject to change without notice.

0318

85. THE POLICE
00700269 $16.99

86. BOSTON
00700465 $16.99

87. ACOUSTIC WOMEN
00700763 $14.99

88. GRUNGE
00700467 $16.99

89. REGGAE
00700468 $15.99

90. CLASSICAL POP
00700469 $14.99

91. BLUES INSTRUMENTALS
00700505 $15.99

92. EARLY ROCK INSTRUMENTALS
00700506 $15.99

93. ROCK INSTRUMENTALS
00700507 $16.99

94. SLOW BLUES
00700508 $16.99

95. BLUES CLASSICS
00700509 $15.99

96. BEST COUNTRY HITS
00211615 $16.99

97. CHRISTMAS CLASSICS
00236542 $14.99

98. ROCK BAND
00700704 $14.95

99. ZZ TOP
00700762 $16.99

100. B.B. KING
00700466 $16.99

101. SONGS FOR BEGINNERS
00701917 $14.99

102. CLASSIC PUNK
00700769 $14.99

103. SWITCHFOOT
00700773 $16.99

104. DUANE ALLMAN
00700846 $16.99

105. LATIN
00700939 $16.99

106. WEEZER
00700958 $14.99

107. CREAM
00701069 $16.99

108. THE WHO
00701053 $16.99

109. STEVE MILLER
00701054 $17.99

110. SLIDE GUITAR HITS
00701055 $16.99

111. JOHN MELLENCAMP
00701056 $14.99

112. QUEEN
00701052 $16.99

113. JIM CROCE
00701058 $16.99

114. BON JOVI
00701060 $16.99

115. JOHNNY CASH
00701070 $16.99

116. THE VENTURES
00701124 $16.99

117. BRAD PAISLEY
00701224 $16.99

118. ERIC JOHNSON
00701353 $16.99

119. AC/DC CLASSICS
00701356 $17.99

120. PROGRESSIVE ROCK
00701457 $14.99

121. U2
00701508 $16.99

122. CROSBY, STILLS & NASH
00701610 $16.99

123. LENNON & MCCARTNEY ACOUSTIC
00701614 $16.99

125. JEFF BECK
00701687 $16.99

126. BOB MARLEY
00701701 $16.99

127. 1970S ROCK
00701739 $16.99

128. 1960S ROCK
00701740 $14.99

129. MEGADETH
00701741 $16.99

130. IRON MAIDEN
00701742 $17.99

131. 1990S ROCK
00701743 $14.99

132. COUNTRY ROCK
00701757 $15.99

133. TAYLOR SWIFT
00701894 $16.99

134. AVENGED SEVENFOLD
00701906 $16.99

135. MINOR BLUES
00151350 $17.99

136. GUITAR THEMES
00701922 $14.99

137. IRISH TUNES
00701966 $15.99

138. BLUEGRASS CLASSICS
00701967 $16.99

139. GARY MOORE
00702370 $16.99

140. MORE STEVIE RAY VAUGHAN
00702396 $17.99

141. ACOUSTIC HITS
00702401 $16.99

143. SLASH
00702425 $19.99

144. DJANGO REINHARDT
00702531 $16.99

145. DEF LEPPARD
00702532 $17.99

146. ROBERT JOHNSON
00702533 $16.99

147. SIMON & GARFUNKEL
14041591 $16.99

148. BOB DYLAN
14041592 $16.99

149. AC/DC HITS
14041593 $17.99

150. ZAKK WYLDE
02501717 $16.99

151. J.S. BACH
02501730 $16.99

152. JOE BONAMASSA
02501751 $19.99

153. RED HOT CHILI PEPPERS
00702990 $19.99

155. ERIC CLAPTON – FROM THE ALBUM UNPLUGGED
00703085 $16.99

156. SLAYER
00703770 $17.99

157. FLEETWOOD MAC
00101382 $16.99

158. ULTIMATE CHRISTMAS
00101889 $14.99

159. WES MONTGOMERY
00102593 $19.99

160. T-BONE WALKER
00102641 $16.99

161. THE EAGLES – ACOUSTIC
00102659 $17.99

162. THE EAGLES HITS
00102667 $17.99

163. PANTERA
00103036 $17.99

164. VAN HALEN 1986-1995
00110270 $17.99

165. GREEN DAY
00210343 $17.99

166. MODERN BLUES
00700764 $16.99

167. DREAM THEATER
00111938 $24.99

168. KISS
00113421 $16.99

169. TAYLOR SWIFT
00115982 $16.99

170. THREE DAYS GRACE
00117337 $16.99

171. JAMES BROWN
00117420 $16.99

173. TRANS-SIBERIAN ORCHESTRA
00119907 $19.99

174. SCORPIONS
00122119 $16.99

175. MICHAEL SCHENKER
00122127 $16.99

176. BLUES BREAKERS WITH JOHN MAYALL & ERIC CLAPTON
00122132 $19.99

177. ALBERT KING
00123271 $16.99

178. JASON MRAZ
00124165 $17.99

179. RAMONES
00127073 $16.99

180. BRUNO MARS
00129706 $16.99

181. JACK JOHNSON
00129854 $16.99

182. SOUNDGARDEN
00138161 $17.99

183. BUDDY GUY
00138240 $17.99

184. KENNY WAYNE SHEPHERD
00138258 $17.99

185. JOE SATRIANI
00139457 $17.99

186. GRATEFUL DEAD
00139459 $17.99

187. JOHN DENVER
00140839 $17.99

188. MÖTLEY CRUE
00141145 $17.99

189. JOHN MAYER
00144350 $17.99

191. PINK FLOYD CLASSICS
00146164 $17.99

192. JUDAS PRIEST
00151352 $17.99

195. METALLICA: 1983-1988
00234291 $19.99

HAL•LEONARD®

For complete songlists, visit Hal Leonard online at www.halleonard.com

Prices, contents, and availability subject to change without notice.

0418